Francis Lieber

FRANCIS LIEBER

An engraving used as the frontispiece of his collected
writings

Francis Lieber

NINETEENTH-CENTURY LIBERAL

BY

FRANK FREIDEL

LOUISIANA STATE UNIVERSITY PRESS

BATON ROUGE

To

Elisabeth Margo
Freidel

Preface

In the 1820's, Francis Lieber, a dynamic young intellectual, fled from Prussian persecution to the United States. He possessed a romantic background, having fought in the Battle of Waterloo, participated in the *Turner* movement, sailed to Greece to fight for liberty, lived in Rome as a protégé of the great historian Barthold G. Niebuhr, and having suffered repeated imprisonment for his political activities.

Lieber brought to America a kaleidescopic array of European ideas. With remarkable energy and enthusiasm he advocated nationalism, free trade, prison reform, international copyright, the codification of international law, and a host of other matters. He coined for himself the appellation "publicist," but he was much more: an immigrant adjusting to a new land, a professor matching wits against unruly college boys, a foe of slavery unhappily enduring the deep South, an ardent Republican advising the Lincoln administration, and an elderly umpire deciding Mexican claims. His career was interwoven with the great intellectual, social, and political issues in America from the presidency of John Quincy Adams to that of Ulysses S. Grant.

In this biography German proper names appear in Anglicized form except in a few instances where the German form is more familiar to American readers.

For aid and encouragement in my task of unraveling the tangled threads of Lieber's manifold activities, I am indebted to a number of persons. I began the study at the suggestion of the late E. M. Eriksson of the University of Southern California, and executed it under the stimulating supervision of William B. Hesseltine of the University of Wisconsin. John D. Hicks of the University of California gave wise counsel during the early stages. K. M. Stampp of the University of California patiently read and criticized the manuscript as it developed into its final form. Richard Hofstadter of Columbia University offered valuable suggestions concerning Lieber's role in the social and intellectual movements of his time. With great generosity, the late Veit Valentin, and Edith Lenel of the Library of Congress, criticized the chapters on the German phase of Lieber's life. A. E. Zucker of the University of Maryland read both these and chapters dealing with Lieber as a German-American, and W. M. Gewehr of the University of Maryland gave advice on many sections.

Miss Mary Lieber supplied helpful information about her family and encouraged me without trying to influence in the slightest the direction of my writing. Professor H. W. L. Dana not only extended to me the gracious hospitality of the Longfellow House, but guided me past the pitfalls surrounding Lieber's relationship with Longfellow. Professor Laura White of the University of Wyoming helped clarify problems concerning Charles Sumner.

For their perceptive editing, I am grateful to Marcus M. Wilkerson and T. Harry Williams of Louisiana State University. In the footnotes I have acknowledged the specific aid of other persons.

The staffs of the libraries cited in the bibliographical essay have without exception been most generous in helping me to utilize their resources. This has been especially true of L. E. Bliss, Librarian, and the staff of the Henry E. Huntington Library, all of whom gave me friendly aid well beyond the point of duty. Miss Norma Cuthbert, Chief Cataloguer in the Manuscripts Division of this library, with great kindness helped me thread my way through the Lieber papers. The Huntington Library, the Harvard University Library, and the Longfellow heirs have granted me permission to quote from their manuscript collections.

A few sections of the biography have appeared in substantially similar form in scholarly journals. They are: "Henry Clay's Efforts, in 1834, to Obtain Francis Lieber, as President of the Transylvania University," *Filson Club History Quarterly*, XVII (1943), 28–38; "Francis Lieber, Charles Sumner, and Slavery," *Journal of Southern History*, IX (1943), 75–93; "Lieber's Contribution to the International Copyright Movement," *Huntington Library Quarterly*, VIII (1945), 200–208; and "General Orders 100 and Military Government," *Mississippi Valley Historical Re-*

view, XXXII (1946), 541–56. I am grateful to the editors for permission to republish parts of these articles.

The Oxford University Press has kindly granted permission to publish copyrighted material from George Wilson Pierson, *Tocqueville and Beaumont in America*, and the Vanderbilt University Press, to quote from R. C. Beatty (ed.), Giles J. Patterson, *Journal of a Southern Student. 1846–48.*

My wife has shouldered a large part of the drudgery in preparing the book.

Frank Freidel

State College, Pennsylvania
March, 1947

Contents

Illustrations

I

The Young Idealist

OCTOBER, 1806. At a window overlooking Breite Strasse in Berlin, a boy sat weeping with eight-year-old fury as he watched a sight heartbreaking to even the smallest Prussian: Napoleon's warriors parading in triumph through the streets of the conquered city. Less than a fortnight after Prussian lines had crumbled before the irresistible attack of French troops at Jena and Auerstedt, hateful Gallic boots were clattering along the cobblestones where the lad had played with his brothers.

Like a tidal wave the armies of the French dictator had rolled on, almost annihilating the fleeing fragments of Prussia's army and threatening to capture fugitive Frederick William III. Meeting very little resistance, the invaders had driven two hundred miles across Germany to the outskirts of Berlin, the undefended capital of a thoroughly defeated Prussia. While Napoleon prepared to move into Frederick the Great's summer palace at Potsdam, Marshal Louis Nicolas Davout, commanding a large part of the French army, marched his corps into the city. Only a miserably armed citizens' militia preserved order; the crack French companies brushed them aside like a schoolboys' drill team as they entered the gates.[1]

Staring with hatred from his window, feeling the humiliation of Prussia as a personal affront, young Francis Lieber sobbed loudly and without restraint. His agitated father feared the soldiers would hear him, and warned him to hush. But the crying did not stop. At last the older Lieber struck his son and pulled him forcibly away. Francis stopped sobbing, but he never forgot that day. He

[1] C. T. Atkinson, *A History of Germany, 1715–1815* (London, 1908), 505–12.

1

recalled it often in his old age and liked to reflect how in the intervening years he had served his fatherland, and, to a far greater extent, his adopted country, America. American or Prussian, he never lost the intense emotional nationalism that led him to make public issues his personal concern.[2]

This fervent nationalism was an abiding heritage from a stanchly loyal father and grandfather. As a child, Francis frequently heard his grandfather tell how he had suffered after the defeat of Frederick the Great in the Battle of Kunersdorf of 1769. The Russians, pillaging Berlin, had captured him, stripped him of his belongings, and subjected him to many indignities. Nevertheless, Francis remembered, the old man inevitably ended his stories by remarking: "But that was nothing; my greatest grief was about Frederick."

Francis' father likewise thought "there was no greater man in all the pages of history." Frederick William Lieber had been a young man in the days when Frederick the Great raised Prussia to the rank of a major power. His patriotic pride stemmed from youthful hero worship, and he loved to entertain his growing boys with admiring anecdotes about "his great king." [3]

Frederick's day passed, and the momentum of his thrust for power dissipated itself. Prussian expansionism cost the elder Lieber heavily, for, in the fighting over the partitioning of Poland, he lost most of his property. Faith in Prussia remained almost the only family possession.

During the period of French domination, the Liebers eluded outright poverty only by the strictest economy and attention to the ironware business conducted at 19 Breite Strasse. The house was already crowded with nine children when Francis arrived on March 18, 1798. Two more followed. Frederick William struggled to feed his brood, educate nine sons, and keep a precarious hold

[2] Lieber to [Matilda Oppenheimer?], 1828, copy, Lieber to Martin Russell Thayer, October 26, 1869, Lieber papers, Henry E. Huntington Library. All manuscripts referred to in this chapter, unless otherwise identified, are from this collection. Lieber to Hamilton Fish, October 26, 1870, Fish papers, Library of Congress. For a discussion of the incident as a starting point of Lieber's intense nationalism see Merle Curti, "Francis Lieber and Nationalism," *Huntington Library Quarterly*, IV (1941), 263–92.

[3] Lieber, "A Reminiscence . . . ," *Southern Literary Messenger*, II (1836), 536–37.

on the family's middle-class social standing. Despite the times, Francis had a happy childhood. He was an attractive, curly-headed boy, lively as quicksilver and a favorite along Breite Strasse despite a reputation as a prankster and daredevil. Generally he was kind and affectionate to his brothers and sisters, but sometimes he teased them mercilessly. His mother could always stop him by calling him a "regular Napoleon." So vile did he consider this epithet that it shocked him to hear her use it.[4]

Talk of war intermingled with his childhood games, and his inability to understand the causes of his country's humiliation did not in the least mitigate his intense feeling of shame. The wretched years after Jena, when every scrap of Frederick's glory had disappeared and Prussia groveled before Napoleon, left an indelible impression upon the lad. More than a half century later, when Bismarck was casting the iron dice to win national glory, Professor Lieber analyzed for his students the causes of the debacle of 1806.

King Frederick William III had lacked every spark of the martial genius of Frederick the Great. Weak as he was virtuous, he had failed to remodel the Prussian army and governmental institutions to meet the challenge of Napoleon. Except for one half-hearted campaign against Revolutionary France, both rested in the senescent torpor which had lulled the land for the two decades since the death of Frederick.

Inefficiency bred apathy which hung like a cloak of gloom over

---

[4] Lieber to [Matilda Oppenheimer?], 1828; autobiographical sketches in Lieber papers, and in Duyckinck papers, New York Public Library; Thomas Sergeant Perry (ed.), *The Life and Letters of Francis Lieber* (Boston, 1882), 82; Edward Dürre, "Errinerungen an Dr. Franz Lieber . . . ," Leipzig *Turn Zeitung*, November 29, 1872, pp. 286–88, 293–94, also manuscript translation edited by Matilda Lieber; Lewis R. Harley, *Francis Lieber: His Life and Political Philosophy* (New York, 1899), 3. Dr. Edith Lenel, who has in preparation a comprehensive study of Lieber's early years, has kindly shown the present writer incontrovertible proof that the actual date of Lieber's birth was 1798. Lieber while in America always claimed 1800, which is the date cited in all American biographical material. Dr. Lenel possesses a photostatic copy of Lieber's baptismal record from the *Geburts-und Taufregister* in the *Kirchenbuchstelle Alt-Berlin*, which shows unmistakably that he was baptized April 15, 1798. The birthdate was given as the eighth not the eighteenth of March, but this well may be in error. As further substantiation, Dr. Lenel has copies of Lieber's educational and police records, all of which indicate that his date of birth was 1798. See also Thayer to Matilda Lieber, July 30, 1874.

the nation, stifling the militancy of previous decades. Patriotic pride continued unabated in only a few families like that of the Liebers. Most Prussian leaders looked with relative indifference upon the growing gallicization of western Germany and were unwilling to make a determined effort to halt Napoleon's aggrandizements.

Germany outside of Prussia had never shared in the fervent military dynamism of the Junker domains. The people cared very little under what particular government they lived. Many along the Rhine favored the Napoleonic version of the French Revolution, but most Germans spent their enthusiasm not upon the conquerors of the soil, but upon the conquerors of the mind. They honored their giants of philosophy, music, and poetry, and gloried in Voltaire's quip that, while France ruled the land and England ruled the sea, Germany ruled the clouds. This was a Germany turning its vital energies not into world enslavement but into world enlightenment through the metaphysics of Kant, the verse of Goethe, and the symphonies of Beethoven.[5]

From the clouds Goethe looked down with little interest upon mundane military affairs; he felt honored when he met Napoleon. Most civil leaders could not for long maintain this Olympian detachment. Prussia, in return for specious promises, allowed the dictator to the west to gobble up lands along the Rhine. Too late, Frederick William III realized that he had been tricked. In the fall of 1806 he declared war, and within three weeks the country collapsed.

Prussia fell into the hands of a ruthless vandal. Napoleon scrawled obscene remarks about Queen Louise on the walls of the royal palace, *Sans Souci;* he sent back to Paris the figures representing "Victory" which had stood over Berlin's Brandenburg Gate. Less spectacular but more far-reaching was the way he drained the country's economic resources through enormous levies and the stoppage of foreign commerce. At Berlin he signed the

---

[5] "Germany and the Prussian Spirit," *Round Table,* September, 1914, pp. 8, 9, quoted in J. A. R. Marriott and C. G. Robertson, *The Evolution of Prussia: The Making of an Empire* (Oxford, 1915), 230. For conditions in Germany at this time, see also C. H. Herford (ed.), *Germany in the Nineteenth Century, A Series of Lectures* (Manchester, 1915).

decrees formally inaugurating the Continental System. These added economic strangulation to the newly aroused patriotic shame of the Prussian people.[6]

Young Francis shared that shame. From the time that Davout's corps entered Berlin he "conceived the greatest hatred toward the French." In the debacle following Jena, the country's strongest fortresses surrendered one after another, hardly firing a shot. The only exception was Colberg on the Baltic coast, which held out month after month against the invader. Its reinforced garrison fought courageously under the leadership of a trio of brave commanders, the most spectacular of whom was the intrepid Ferdinand Baptista von Schill. The Prussian upper and middle classes, awakened from their torpor and galling under the grinding oppression of the French, thrilled at the thought that one spot remained where "the sweeping eagles of Napoleon" had not been able to perch. Schill's audacious raids upon the besiegers won him the admiration of the seven-year-old Francis, who prayed nightly: "That God might cure my Grandmother's cough, bless our beloved King, and let Schill be victorious." [7]

Schill and his associates did indeed remain victorious until the conclusion of peace at the Treaty of Tilsit, July 9, 1807. Napoleon treated Frederick William III harshly at Tilsit—pared the population by half and the army by four fifths, and subsequently set an impossibly high indemnity. By dumping the Prussians into a mudhole of degradation, he scorned them into the path of "regeneration." In a manner as ruthless as Napoleon's, they started down a road paved with blood and iron.[8]

In the place of conservative incompetents came more enlightened reformers, men who realized that only through a sternly renovated government, educational system, and army could Prussia meet the challenge of the dictator's legions. In 1807 Francis Lieber was too young to be molded by these men, but when he became a mature thinker, he owed much to H. F. K., Baron vom und zum Stein, Johann Gottlieb Fichte, and the Humboldt brothers.

[6] Marriott and Robertson, *Evolution of Prussia,* 217–18.
[7] Lieber, "A Reminiscence . . . ," *loc. cit.;* Lieber to [Matilda Oppenheimer?], 1828.
[8] Marriott and Robertson, *Evolution of Prussia,* 221–22, 225.

Stein worked tirelessly to create a modern, united Germany—a nation strong enough to expel the invader and withstand future incursions. His ideal was a self-governing nation under a constitutional monarch, and within Prussia he did build the nucleus of a strong, centralized Germany. He instituted widespread financial reforms, elevated the peasants from serfdom to citizenship, and established an efficient state. At the same time, skilled younger generals remodeled the army from an obsolescent professional body into an active force including all able-bodied males. At no time did it number more than 42,000, the limit set by Napoleon. But the government called up levy after levy of that number, until Prussia was prepared to turn overnight into a nation of citizen warriors.[9]

To sustain the morale of the forces, the intellectuals began to disseminate strongly nationalistic views. Fichte, not Goethe, became spokesman for the German leaders. In the winter of 1806 he delivered in Berlin a series of lectures in which he announced the hypothesis, startling at that time, that a state seeking to increase its internal strength "must desire the gradual abolition of all privileges and the establishment of equal rights for all men." The individual should seek equality and freedom but should be content to enjoy it within the framework of the powerful state, since "true freedom can be obtained only by means of the highest obedience to the law." [10]

In keeping with Fichte's plea that Germany invigorate her national culture, a group of leaders erected a new educational system from the elementary level through the university. It meshed in with the growing military machine by indoctrinating pupils with the high duty of every Prussian to obey the will of his fatherland. As one of its founders wrote in 1808, it functioned to "rouse and nourish every noble principle of life . . . [and] nurse those in-

[9] Guy Stanton Ford, *Stein and the Era of Reform in Prussia, 1807–1815* (Princeton, 1922), 102 *et passim;* J. R. Seeley, *Life and Times of Stein* . . . , 3 vols. (Cambridge, 1878) ; Marriott and Robertson, *Evolution of Prussia,* 225–39.

[10] M. E. Sadler, "The History of Education," in Herford (ed.), *Germany in the Nineteenth Century,* 104–105. Georges Gurvitch, "Fichte," *Encyclopaedia of the Social Sciences,* 13 vols. (New York, 1930–34), VI, 223–25, interprets Fichte's thought as being directly opposed to Pan-Germanism, tending rather toward socialism. Fichte's lectures had only a limited public. Rudolph Meinecke, *Johann Gottlieb Fichte. Zum hundertjährigen jubiläum seiner Reden an die deutsche nation* (Hamburg, 1908).

stincts on which rest the force and dignity of man—love to God, to king and to fatherland." [11]

At the top of the new system was the University of Berlin, which was founded, despite the straitened budget of the Prussian government, in the winter of 1809. Under the direction of William von Humboldt, talented younger brother of Alexander, the geographer, a remarkable faculty began teaching for little more recompense than their patriotic satisfaction. Fichte was professor of philosophy; Frederick E. D. Schleiermacher, theology; Frederick C. von Savigny, jurisprudence; Barthold G. Niebuhr, history; and Frederick A. Wolf, archeology. Every one of them was to exercise an influence upon Lieber.[12]

Their sacrifices to stimulate the fatherland were a reflection of a resurgence of popular faith in Prussia. By the time the French finally evacuated Berlin in the spring of 1808, the Berliners were wildly enthusiastic about the lone regiment of military heroes. They received with a tumultuous welcome the first Prussian troops to enter the city: the Colberger regiment led by the handsome and impetuous Colonel Schill. Francis went with his father to see the procession and, small lad that he was, became lost in the impenetrable crowd. When his hero went by, he could see only the "patches of blue sky which now and then appeared above the heads of my taller equals." But he by no means counted the day a disappointment, for after the parade his father, like countless other excited Berliners, persuaded three or four of the soldiers to take quarters in the Lieber home. Francis remembered: "We made them tell us of Colberg the whole live-long day, and pestered them with a thousand questions."

Soon after Schill returned to Berlin, Francis began a collection of the heraldic seals that were attached to documents and used for the closing of envelopes. He decided to head the collection with the seal of his idol and one day, instead of going to school, went to Schill's quarters. The military hero asked the boy why he wanted a seal. "Because," answered Francis, "I love you, and wish to begin my collection with your coat of arms." "Does your

<hr>

[11] Herford (ed.), *Germany in the Nineteenth Century*, 108–109; Marriott and Robertson, *Evolution of Prussia*, 228–32, 236–37.

[12] Marriott and Robertson, *Evolution of Prussia*, 238.

father love me too?" the colonel asked. "Yes," was the reply, "all the Berlin people do." Schill treated the youth kindly, gave him a number of the coveted seals, and invited him to luncheon. Handing Francis a glass of wine, he urged, "Boy, be ever true to your country; here, let's touch our glasses on its welfare." The next year, Schill gained even greater stature in Francis' eyes when he died in an abortive uprising against the French.[13]

Francis' elder brothers Edward and Adolf, like thousands of other striving, idealistic young men, took part in plots to free their country from the incessant, nagging misery of the French imperial yoke. They chafed under the burdens Napoleon heaped upon their nation: opportunities were circumscribed, and the Continental System led to a dearth of manufactured products and an absence of coffee. Longing for a war of liberation, the elder Lieber brothers belonged to General Gerhard J. D. von Scharnhorst's undercover military system and also to secret societies which met often in the house on Breite Strasse to scheme the downfall of the invaders. Frederick William Lieber, as enthusiastic as the young men, encouraged them in their plotting. Too old to go to war himself, he became a district inspector in the Landsturm, organized for home defense.[14]

In imitation of his elder brothers, the ten-year-old Francis and some of his playmates established a fraternity of perpetual friendship and secrecy. They were to do good works, aid the poor, be loyal to one another, and above all be true to their vow of secrecy.[15]

Like Karl Sand, Frederick Lewis Jahn, and most of his nationalistic contemporaries, Francis was as fervent in his piety as in his devotion to his fatherland. From 1811 to 1813 the Reverend G. F. A. Pauli, an Evangelical minister, prepared him for confirmation. Each week the boy submitted a religious paper to the pastor for correction and discussion. The Reverend Pauli liked the compositions. He found Francis "animated by a lively zeal for everything he recognized as good and right, especially so, however, for the Holy Truth." Francis dearly loved the "excellent

---

[13] Lieber, "A Reminiscence . . . ," *loc. cit.*

[14] Dürre, "Errinerungen an Dr. Franz Lieber . . . ," *loc. cit.*, with translation by Matilda Lieber.

[15] Lieber to [Matilda Oppenheimer?], 1828.

clergyman," but "he did not seem to the unbalanced boy, sufficiently devout, and I went on for myself in my religious excitement." Lieber composed psalms and prayers for his private devotionals, read the Bible, and gave religious instruction to a younger brother. Sometimes he prayed as often as five times an hour, and not a few of the prayers were for a war to liberate the fatherland.[16]

In 1813 came the exciting summons for which Francis and his family had hoped: the King of Prussia called upon his subjects "to rise and flock to his standards for the salvation of the country." Edward and Adolf answered the call immediately, and prepared to leave for Breslau. The streets filled with young soldiers ready to march. The Lieber family, saying farewell to their young warriors, "all wept most bitterly, yet glowed with self-denying patriotic enthusiasm." When his two elder brothers were gone, Francis rushed to his room, knelt before a small press in which he had his herbarium—at that time his most sacred possession—and took a solemn oath that he would "study French, enter the French army, come near Napoleon's person, and rid the earth of that son of crime and sin." The idea of sacrificing two armies when the sacrifice of one life might stop the misery seemed to him preposterous.

Many years later, looking back on his overemotional adolescence, Lieber was able to see in it the formula of assassins, such as Sand, the murderer of August von Kotzebue, and Felice Orsini, who attempted to kill Napoleon III. "See, how nearly patriotic fervour, religious devotion, and boiling hatred of conquerors and assassination can form a ring . . . only the long continued war soon placed a rifle into my hand, and sound education wrung the dagger from my mind." [17]

The War of Liberation of 1813 and 1814 seemed to eliminate the need for Francis to take up either dagger or sword. Napoleon's forces, debilitated by the Russian campaign of 1812, were no equals for the well-drilled and vigorous Allies. The reforms within

---

[16] G. T. A. Pauli . . . , Ein Zeugnis über das Betragen . . . Franz Lieber's . . . im Konfirmandenunterricht 1811–13, February 7, 1820, with accompanying note by Lieber; Lieber to Matilda Lieber, 1828; Lieber to George Stillman Hillard, April 19, 1858.

[17] Lieber to Hillard, April 19, 1858; Lieber to [Matilda Oppenheimer?], 1828.

the Prussian government and army bore fruit in victories. Though the fighting dragged on another summer, the Battle of Leipzig on October 16 to 19, 1813, reversed Jena and assured the ultimate downfall of the French emperor.[18]

During the campaigns the Lieber home in Berlin virtually became a hospital. Edward and Adolf returned home wounded, bringing with them some of their comrades who were likewise recuperating from the war. Francis' sisters and aunts cared for the wounded in hospitals, and his mother took a seriously injured soldier into the home to nurse him back to health. When his brothers and their friends sang camp songs and traded tall stories around the fire, Francis crept into their circle and listened with envy, wishing he too might go to battle. But the might of the French Empire was smashed, and Bonaparte exiled to Elba.[19]

Young Lieber's schooling did not keep pace with his martial and religious enthusiasms. Burning with an overweening ambition to become famous, he tried to cast his career into the mold first of Schill, then Linnaeus. For a long while the study of plants lured him. He acquired a collecting box and press, and dreamed of becoming a great botanist. Frederick William Lieber did not object to Francis' ambition, since he believed in letting his sons choose their own careers. He apprenticed Francis to a botanical garden in Schöneberg near Berlin. Francis soon found that the position was far from being the pastoral idyll he had imagined. He had to blacken boots and perform menial chores for the director, and his love of botany soon turned into an extreme distaste. He persuaded his parents that the apprenticeship was quite unsuitable, and they allowed him to leave.

Francis next desired greatly to prepare himself for the university, but his father's means were insufficient. After that, impressed by the care given his wounded brothers upon their return from battle, he decided upon medicine as the ideal career. Preparing himself through private instruction, by about 1815 he entered the royal Pépinière, an institution at Berlin for military surgeons. Lieber became an academist—that is, one of the pupils

---

[18] For a lengthy account of the campaigns, see Atkinson, *History of Germany, 1715–1815*, pp. 571–643.
[19] Dürre, "Errinerungen an Dr. Franz Lieber . . . ," *loc. cit.*

who did not reside in the school—and attended first-year lectures on anatomy, physiology, and similar subjects.[20]

Scarcely had Lieber entered the peaceful academic halls when his serenity was shattered by the drums of approaching war. In March, 1815, came a violent interruption to his studies:

" 'Boys, clean your rifles,' said my old and venerable father, entering my room, where I was just studying Loder's Anatomical Tables. 'He is loose again.'—'Napoleon?'—'He has returned from Elba.' My heart beat high; it was glorious news for a boy of sixteen, who had often heard with silent envy the account of the campaigns of 1813 and '14 from his two brothers." [21]

Tearfully his mother said "Yes," to her youngest warrior, and the delighted lad sought immediately to enlist as a volunteer rifleman. But Francis had been studying to be a military surgeon, and he could not thus quickly slough off his intended vocation. Though he was only a first-year student, who knew nothing of surgery or sickness, the director of the Pépinière urged him to accept appointment as a surgeon of a company of dragoons! With difficulty the frightened boy escaped the position, and instead stood in line for three hours to enlist in the famous Colberg regiment. The Colbergers were mostly natives of Pomerania—short, sturdy veterans of Colberg's siege of 1806–1807—and had fought in about twenty engagements during the recent War of Liberation. Francis reasoned that since they were stationed nearest the French frontier they were the surest to see action in forthcoming battles. Two of Lieber's brothers also joined the regiment, and a third, Adolf, received a lieutenant's commission.[22]

At the beginning of May the recruits left Berlin to march to their regiments, already stationed across the Rhine. Crowds ac-

---

[20] *Ibid.;* Lieber to [Matilda Oppenheimer?], 1828; Lieber to his parents, October 17, 1828; Perry (ed.), *Lieber,* 82.

[21] Francis Lieber, *Letters to a Gentleman in Germany on a Trip to Niagara* (Philadelphia, 1834), 99 *et seq.* The English edition appeared in two volumes under the title *The Stranger in America: Comprising Sketches of the Manners, Society, and National Peculiarities of the United States, In a Series of Letters to a Friend in Europe* (London, 1835). This section is reprinted in Francis Lieber, *Miscellaneous Writings . . .* (Philadelphia, 1881), I, 151–75; and in Perry (ed.), *Lieber,* 7–24. In his own copy of *The Stranger in America* in the Lieber papers, he changed the age to "fifteen."

[22] Lieber, *Letters to a Gentleman in Germany,* 99 *et seq.;* Lieber to [Matilda Oppenheimer?], 1828.

companied the young soldiers to the edge of the city, shouting their farewells. "The beautiful Brandenburg gate was soon behind us; we began to sing. I looked but forward, happy that it was yet my lot to carry arms in defence of my country." [23]

As the boy marched westward with his column the unfamiliar panorama of the German countryside rolled before him. Into a little pocket diary went notations of factories, mines, cathedrals, churches; and the inscription from over a peasant's door:

> "Where peace is, there is joy,
> Where joy is, there is God,
> Where God is, there is never misery." [24]

As the lad tramped away from peace toward war, he thought of himself, not as a Prussian, but as a German on his way to fight for a united fatherland where personal freedom would flourish. He crossed the Rhine with a feeling of veneration mixed with a "glowing of patriotism," and on May 17 reached Cologne. That night he noted, "This day I bade farewell to my country; the column did the same with cheers." [25]

Amidst ominous rumors the soldiers entered the low country, and marched through Aachen and other pretty little French-speaking towns to Prince Gebhard Leberecht von Blücher's headquarters at Namur. Napoleon too was massing troops and moving them forward. The days of battle could not be far distant. The recruits received back the muskets they had turned in at Berlin and marched before Prince Blücher with their new weapons. The levies now disintegrated into detachments; each unit joined its proper regiment, and drilling and training began in earnest. Thrilled with the military life, young Lieber longed to be tried in battle.

[23] Lieber, *Letters to a Gentleman in Germany,* 100–101; Dürre, "Errinerungen an Dr. Franz Lieber . . . ," *loc. cit.*

[24]   "Wo Friede ist, da ist Freude,
                 Wo Freude ist, da ist Gott,
                 Wo Gott ist, da ist nimmer Noth."
Francis Lieber, "Tagebuch wahrend des feldzugs," May 13, 1815. The original of the diary, extending from May, 1815, to June 18, 1816, is in the Columbia University Library. There are translations both at Columbia University and the Huntington Library. Lieber followed the diary in writing his account of the campaign, in 1834. Lieber, *Letters to a Gentleman in Germany,* 97.

[25] Lieber, "Tagebuch," May 17–18, 1815, Columbia University; Lieber, *Letters to a Gentleman in Germany,* 101.

On June 2, the Colbergers paraded for the first time before their beloved major, F. von Schmidt. The new men were sworn in and on June 9 received powder and shot. Since the volunteers had supplied their own rifles, these were of different calibers, and each man melted down his ration of lead into balls of the proper size.[26]

"It is one of the most peculiar situations a man of reflecting mind can be in, when he casts his balls for battles near at hand," Lieber remembered. That evening he lay in a hayloft with two comrades, and, as they gazed through the rickety roof at the brilliant stars, each pondered on whether or not he would see home again. The next day they engaged in target practice for the first time—only six days before the fighting began.[27]

On the morning of June 11 they halted not far from the battlefield, at the village of Ligny or Fleury. "Before us was a rising ground, on which we saw innumerable troops ascending the plain with flying colors, and music playing. It was a sight a soldier loves to look at." The company, made up almost entirely of lads like Lieber, received orders to advance. Only with difficulty could the old, seasoned sergeant major restrain the impatient boys. Finally, at two o'clock came the order to throw the enemy left wing out of Ligny. The signal came to attack—"and the dull, half-suffocated drum, from within the deep column, was heard beating such delicious music. Now, at last, was all to be realized for which we had left our homes, had suffered so many fatigues, had so ardently longed." Francis' company ran forward madly, disregarding the urgent shouts of its old sergeant and not even firing its guns. The French Grenadiers retreated quickly behind hedges and houses as the boys swept onward. Forgetting to fire in his excitement, Lieber tore the red plume from a grenadier's bear cap and swung it triumphantly over his head.

In the center of the town, the sergeant regained control of his company and deployed them against a group of French. Lieber, stepping suddenly around the corner of a house, confronted a grenadier about fifteen paces away. The Frenchman's bullet grazed his hair; Francis fired and saw his adversary fall dying.

[26] Lieber, "Tagebuch," May 19–June 9, 1815, Columbia University; Lieber, *Letters to a Gentleman in Germany*, 101–102.

[27] Lieber, "Tagebuch," June 10, 1815, Columbia University; Lieber, *Letters to a Gentleman in Germany*, 102.

This was the first shot he had ever fired in battle and with it he had killed a man.

The fighting was long and bloody. Four times the village was taken and retaken. Francis fired again and again until all his ammunition was exhausted except one ball which he saved in case any cavalry soldier should attempt to saber him. He did not wish to leave the field lest he be thought a coward; so for more than an hour he remained amidst the carnage, rummaging for ammunition among the cartridge boxes of dead Frenchmen.

Near nightfall the Colbergers made one more heroic effort to hold Ligny. They fought back through the center, where the battle had been hottest all afternoon. "Three or four layers of dead and living, men and horses, impeded the progress of the soldiers, who were obliged to wade in the blood of their comrades, or to trample upon wounded enemies, imploring them to give some assistance. . . . This last attempt to regain the village, when I was called upon to assist in getting a cannon over the mangled bodies of comrades or enemies, leaping in agony when the heavy wheel crossed over them, has impressed itself with indelible horror upon my mind."

Finally, near evening, the French cavalry pressed too hard for the Prussian riflemen to resist, and orderly retreat began. The troops were too thinned to form the regulation hollow squares to meet each successive wave of cavalry, and clustered in mere "heaps" instead. Still, they obeyed the Prussian army rule: "No firing until you see the whites of their eyes," and repulsed the horsemen.[28]

All that night they marched—a company reduced in numbers from 150 to only 20 or 30. The retreat continued the following day and part of the night. The soldiers plodded, soaked and hungry, through a torrential rain. Their foraging produced so little food that when they encountered a hog, they ate it raw. Early on the morning of June 18, they rejoined part of their regiment from which they had been separated and joyfully cheered Marshal Blücher, whom they passed wrapped in his cloak, leaning against a hummock.

[28] Lieber, *Letters to a Gentleman in Germany*, 105–106.

Blücher decided to battle again, and that afternoon the Colberg regiment stood in reserve near the conflict. As young Lieber watched, fresh troops streamed by into the slaughter, and numerous wounded passed on their way to the rear. He saw "some brilliant charges of our cavalry putting to rout French squares," but did not realize that he was witnessing one of the most famous battles in history—Waterloo.[29]

Suffering overwhelmingly from the cravings of hunger, Francis and a comrade foraged for something to eat after the battle was over. They found a peasant in the cellar of a house and threatened to shoot him instantly unless he gave them bread. Finally the terrified man gave them a small loaf. After eating, the boy prepared to spend the night on the field of Waterloo. By the flickering light of fires built that the wounded might creep to them, the exhausted lad found a henhouse and crawled inside to sleep. Suddenly he heard the signal to march, and found he could not get out. He shouted desperately, and ultimately received assistance and hearty laughter at his expense.

Again the regiment marched an entire night and a day, this time in pursuit of Vandamme's corps, which had seized Namur. Francis suffered excruciatingly from thirst and fatigue, but when he heard the noise of fighting at Namur he suddenly regained his strength. His company charged headlong down a hillside toward the town. Near the foot of the hill was a precipice. The lad peered over it and discovered seven Frenchmen. " 'They will hit me,' I thought, and turning round to call to our soldiers, I suddenly experienced a sensation as if my whole body were compressed in my head, and this, like a ball, were quivering in the air. I could feel the existence of nothing else; it was a most painful sensation. After some time I was able to open my eyes, or to see again with them; I found myself on the ground; over me stood a soldier firing at the enemy. I strained every nerve to ask . . . where I was wounded. 'You are shot through the neck.' "

Francis begged the soldier to shoot him and end his agony, but

29 Lieber, *Letters to a Gentleman in Germany*, 107–108. On the day of Waterloo, Lieber's sole notation in his diary was: "Joined Major Schmidt and Lückewitz. In the evening at . . . [indecipherable] we embraced each other for joy." Lieber, "Tagebuch," June 18, 1815, translation at Huntington Library.

the soldier refused and soon himself fell. "My thirst was beyond description; it was a feverish burning. I thought I should die, and prayed forgiveness of my sins . . . and . . . a speedy end of my sufferings. . . . I received a second ball, which entering my chest, gave me a more local pain than the first; I thought God had granted my fervent prayer."

After a while Lieber fell into a delirious swoon, from which he was revived by a soldier giving him water out of a canteen. He fainted again, and awoke in the evening to find peasants searching for his watch and money and stripping him of clothes. Their rough handling increased his agony, and renewed the bleeding of his wounds. Seeing Francis' predicament, a wounded Westphalian militiaman fired at the vandals to drive them away and hallooed at a near-by surgeon to come and dress the boy's injuries. "At this hour work is left off," the surgeon replied, and proceeded on his way. The Westphalian would have shot at the surgeon also but could not reload quickly enough. Francis' protector then went for aid. He returned about nine o'clock with some peasants who dressed the boy in clothes taken from the dead, treated his wounds, and carried him to a farmhouse.[30]

Fearing that the French would find him there, Francis pleaded to be moved farther away from the battlefield. The Westphalian loaded him into a wheelbarrow and bumped along to another farmhouse, some distance from the main road, where he left him.

Carts came the next day and bore away most of the wounded, but left Francis and several others not sufficiently strong to attract attention. For several days the boy tried vainly to get someone to take him to a hospital. Finally, on the third day after the Battle of Namur, he dragged himself to the road, where two soldiers of his company caught sight of him. "They could not recognize me by my features, because my face was incrusted with blood and earth, but [identified me] by my boots, which the plundering peasants had not succeeded in pulling off." The bottoms of these Francis kept distinctively plated with nails. His comrades, Treuherz and Goldschmidt, tore the door off a stable and used it as a stretcher to carry Lieber to Namur. There the medical authorities

[30] Lieber, *Letters to a Gentleman in Germany*, 108–13. The surgeon's words were: "Es ist jetzt Feierabend."

placed him on one of two boats heavily laden with wounded bound
for a hospital at Liége.

The hospital was an old convent, so overcrowded that at first
the boy lay with many others on straw in the courtyard. A cart
entered and the driver walked along, pulling up fresh cadavers
and throwing them into the cart. "The living were very quick to
show by their motions, that they were not yet ready for the cart."

"At length, I succeeded in getting a place in the same bed with
another. Close to my bed lay a dragoon, whose left arm, shoulder,
and part of the chest had been carried away by a shell shot, so
that part of the interior could be seen; it was the most cruel wound
I have ever beheld."

Weak as he was, Francis left his bed and dragged himself
through the streets of Liége to find a merchant, to whom he had a
letter of introduction and credit. At first his memory failed him
completely, probably because of the neck wound, but gradually it
returned. After three or four days of vain searching, he found the
house. The merchant, Herr Harlez, came out, greeted Francis
cordially by name, and took him into his home.

Lieber rapidly recovered his strength. A fortnight after being
wounded, he was well enough to ride horseback, and in the ensuing months enjoyed a carefree convalescence. He visited the fine
buildings and art masterpieces of Liége, and took several excursions into the country where he saw factories and foundries. All
these he noted in the diary, which he planned to take home to
his parents. But gradually, in late August, the accounts of cathedrals and bridges began to be crowded out by references to a
"Miss Julie."

Each day, Francis walked through the city to a station where
doctors dressed his wounds. There one day he met a wounded
friend who was staying at the home of a wealthy wine merchant.
The friend told Francis of the great kindness with which the
family treated him, especially the sixteen-year-old daughter of the
house. However, the friend was bashful and did not find it easy
to converse with her. When Francis met Julie, he had no such difficulty. He thought she had the face and bearing of an angel; she
looked upon him as a wounded hero. All too soon the idyll came to
an end. In late September, Lieber returned to his regiment at

Namur. He noted wistfully in his diary, "Homesick for Liege." [31]

The boy's health was not strong enough for the incessant long marches and haphazard bivouacking of army life. No longer was there the thrill of battle and the joy of being a hero against huge odds to inure him to hardships. Instead he had the ignoble status of being part of an army of occupation: trouble with the peasants, quarreling among the officers, sickness, and cold. Military discipline no longer thrilled him.[32]

The Medal of the War of 1815 was small compensation for this unpleasant life, and when the discharge came in mid-November, it was no more than a scrap of paper. Francis wrote at the end of the month: "Always going from village to village, always quartered. During this time got a sick leave. Last order of Major Schmidt was terrible—'Not to give all the pay to the riflemen, because there are among them some who do not know how to make use of it.' Obliged to borrow money of the quartermaster." [33]

Finally, in early December, the volunteers left the regiment and began their long homeward march—to Mesier, Charleville, Rocroi, Marienburg, Dinant, Namur, Liége—and each day Francis grew sicker. Finally, at Aachen, he went to the hospital, dangerously ill with typhus, and delirious. The boy returned to consciousness in a fever ward. He asked an old man sitting beside his bed what day it was. The old man answered, "Christmas morning." All the thousand nostalgic associations of a German Christmas crowded in upon him. Remembering other Christmases, his military shell crumpled and left him again a schoolboy, crying bitterly for home and family.

Francis was ill for many weeks, and not until long after peace had been concluded was he well enough to travel home. Letters had miscarried, and his family had given him up. They were overjoyed to see their son—but how different he was from the lad who

[31] Lieber, *Letters to a Gentleman in Germany,* 114–19; Lieber, "Tagebuch," June 21–September 26, 1815, Columbia University.

[32] Lieber, "Tagebuch," November 4, 1815, *et passim,* Columbia University; translation, Huntington Library.

[33] Lieber, "Tagebuch," November 30, 1815, Columbia University; translation, Huntington Library. "F. Schmidt, Obristlieutenant und Commandeur des Colbergschen Inf. Regiments, Dem freiwilliger jäger Franz Lieber . . . wird hiemit das Zeugniss ertheilt: die Denkmunze des Krieges Jahres 1815 tragen zu dürfen, October 8, 1815"; Major F. von Schmidt . . . [to] Franz Lieber . . . [discharge], November 16, 1815.

had marched gaily out of the Brandenburg Gate. As he himself acknowledged, "In one year I had grown older many years." [34]

With determination, the eighteen-year-old war veteran returned to his books. To prepare himself for the university, he enrolled in the Gray Cloister gymnasium at Berlin, where he attended classes primarily in Latin, Greek, and the antiquities, with some instruction in history, mathematics, and modern languages. The wounds he had received at Namur were not yet completely healed and repeatedly caused so much pain that he absented himself often from the classroom. Furthermore, the schoolroom could not compete in appeal with the open field where the *Turners* under Frederick Lewis Jahn held their patriotic exercises.

Francis was only thirteen when "Turnvater" Jahn—the founder of modern gymnastics—opened the first *Turnplatz* in Berlin. Jahn, a powerful and inspiring figure, had spent a turbulent youth studying theology and philosophy at Halle, Göttingen, and Greifswald. Almost singlehandedly he had combated the powerful student dueling corps at Halle, seeking to replace them with nationalistic organizations, the *Burschenschaften*. When Prussia reached her nadir after the defeat at Jena, he began advocating group physical exercises "to strengthen the frames which the effeminacy of modern manners had enervated, and to form a body of men able to expel the French from Germany." [35]

During the War of Liberation, the *Turnvater* commanded the free corps of Lützow, made up of recruits from many German principalities. Upon his return to Berlin in 1816, Jahn became the state teacher of gymnastics and devoted himself to building strong bodies for the Prussian army and ardently nationalistic minds to support the reformers of the Prussian governmental system. As the youthful veterans of the Napoleonic campaigns flocked in great numbers to the classes in the *Hasenheide,* the membership jumped

[34] Lieber, *The Stranger in America*, I, 121–26; Lieber, "Tagebuch," December 3, 1815–March 4, 1816, Columbia University; translation, Huntington Library.

[35] Perry (ed.), *Lieber*, 25–27; Poultney Bigelow, *History of the German Struggle for Liberty*, 3 vols. (New York, 1896–1903), II, 178 *et passim;* [Francis Lieber], "[Review of] *A Treatise on Gymnastics* . . . ," *American Quarterly Review*, III (1828), 136–37; [Francis Lieber], "Gymnastics," *Encyclopaedia Americana*, 13 vols. (Philadelphia, 1829–32), VI, 122; Fred E. Leonard, *Pioneers of Modern Physical Training* (New York, 1915), 13–16; F. L. Jahn, *Deutsches Volksthum* (Lübeck, 1810); Michael Antonowytsch, *Friedrich Ludwig Jahn Ein Beitrag zur Geschichte der anfänge des deutschen Nationalismus* (Berlin, 1933).

to more than a thousand. Glorying in a newborn spirit of freedom, these ex-soldiers made the gymnasia nurseries of nationalism.

During his eight months in the army, Francis had maintained an interest in the *Turners* and their nationalistic ideals. Upon his return home, he joined both Jahn's gymnasium and a military swimming school conducted by General von Pfuel. He became an expert swimmer and, while less proficient as a gymnast, he was one of the most zealous and persevering in the difficult exercises.

Under the *Turnvater*'s tutelage, Lieber grew in strength and recovered from a war-incurred lameness of his left arm. He grew also in nationalistic zeal. Avidly he endorsed Jahn's political credo: "God bless the King, preserve the house of Hohenzollern, protect our country, strengthen the German sentiment, purify our national life from Latin influences and the aping of foreign fashions, make Prussia a brilliant example to the German Union, and knit this union together into the new empire. May God grant, graciously and speedily, the one thing needful and pressing—a wise Constitution." [36]

So apt a pupil was Lieber that he soon became one of Jahn's lieutenants, and a leader in the movement. He was, in the *Turnvater*'s estimation, "beloved by the younger scholars, esteemed by those of the same or more advanced age." As early as 1817, Jahn recommended him as instructor for the gymnasium at Aachen.[37]

In subsequent years Lieber vividly recalled his participation in the thrice-yearly gymnastic festivals on the anniversaries of Waterloo, Leipzig, and Gross-Beeren. Gross-Beeren was a village about eight miles from Berlin, where Prussians had fended off Napoleon's forces on August 23, 1813. On each August 22, in the afternoon, six or seven hundred *Turners* would congregate in Berlin and march, singing as they went, to the village. There they made a supper of potatoes and bread and butter and lodged noisily for the night on the straw in peasants' barns.

[36] Bigelow, *History of the German Struggle for Liberty,* II, 74; Perry (ed.), *Lieber,* 25–29; Eliza C. Follen, *The Works of Charles Follen with a Memoir of His Life,* 5 vols. (Boston, 1841), I, 14–17.

[37] Dürre, "Errinerungen an Dr. Franz Lieber . . . ," *loc. cit.;* F. L. Jahn, "Zeugnis für Franz Lieber . . . ," August 1, 1826.

In the morning, singers awakened the sleepers by loudly chanting verses deriding the French. After breakfast, the entire band congregated on a near-by hill, where Jahn explained to them the battle and held religious services. In the afternoon, the *Turners* demonstrated their gymnastic prowess before friends and relatives who had walked out from Berlin. Before a large concourse of spectators, they began their games with a general foot race, engaged in leaping, tumbling, pole vaulting, and concluded with large and boisterous tugs of war. Then, with the beginning of twilight, all strolled homeward in small groups, singing and joking, or deep in serious discussion.[38]

On the warm Saturday evenings of the summer season, the *Turners* would assemble in great numbers in the *Hasenheide* and exercise together until late in the night. Then they would sleep around a great fire. On the Sabbath mornings their patriotic fervor led to an equally strong religious zeal, and they would re-enter Berlin to attend the services of Schleiermacher or one of the other ardently Prussian theologians. Often Francis would attend the prayer meetings of the eccentric Captain von Plehwe, who with his entire army company would march onto the parade ground and hold religious services.[39]

Of these associates, Schleiermacher most lastingly influenced the mind of the earnest young man. Schleiermacher as pastor of the Trinity Church and professor at the University of Berlin had been indefatigable in arousing nationalistic enthusiasm. He placed great stress upon the importance of the individual in human society, in terms of both moral behavior and political philosophy.

38 [Lieber], "[Review of] *A Treatise on Gymnastics* . . . ," *loc. cit.*, 146–47.

39 *Ibid.;* Perry (ed.), *Lieber*, 28. Two entries in Lieber's diary a few months after he returned from war indicate the nature of these meetings: "June 17 [1816]. A meeting of the Turners at Charlottenburg.

"O, raubt mir nicht mein Ideal,
Mein einsiges der Kindheit noch,
O, Unschuld, du bist schon entflohn,
Lasst mir Ziel, mein Ideal,
Lasst mir mein kindlich Thun.

"June 18. Great exercises with singing—'Schon ist's unter freien Himmel.' 'Was blasen die Trompeten, Husaren heraus.' A powerful speech by Jahn." Lieber, "Tagebuch," Columbia University; translation, Huntington Library. Charlottenburg was then three miles from Berlin. The first of the two songs mentioned in the June 18 entry was by F. K. Hiemer; the second, by Arndt, is printed in *Deutsche Lieder für Jung und Alt* (Berlin, 1818), 85.

Stating that the individual was the most significant standard of evaluation of all spiritual and intellectual life, Schleiermacher emphasized the indissoluble relationship of the individual and the community.[40]

The German theologian lashed out at the superficiality and illogicity of both supernaturalism and rationalism. From the point of view of both philosophy and religion he looked upon the ultimate aim of man as being the achievement of the "highest good." Man could strive toward this, he explained in the *Christian Ethics*, through diligence in four main classes of duties: those to the community or society, to one's vocation, to one's conscience (of which the individual was the sole judge), and to one's personal associates.[41]

The religio-political ideas of Schleiermacher and Jahn largely filled the mind of Lieber, who felt that the order of things advocated by the pastor could come into being at least in part through the patriotic physical exercises taught by the *Turnvater*. With Jahn he journeyed to Neu-Strelitz, Rügen, and through Silesia, arousing interest in the *Turner* movement. However, the zealous youth was not willing to stop at the limits set by the highly loyal but relatively conservative Jahn.

As had his brothers in 1813, now Francis began to turn toward secret meetings. He brought close friends to his home for *Turnrath* committee sessions. They resented the failure of Frederick William III to grant promised constitutional liberties, deplored the lack of unity among the petty German states, and chafed under the odious repression resulting from Prince Clemens W. N. L. Metternich's notorious ascendency. To what extremes they went in their secret plotting is uncertain, but probably their meetings were no more than a means of airing their idealism in vague and romantic terms.[42]

---

[40] Rudolf Odebrecht, "Friedrich Ernst Daniel Schleiermacher," *Encyclopaedia of the Social Sciences*, XIII, 772–73; "Schleiermacher," *Allgemeine Deutsche Biographie*, XXXI, 422–57; R. B. Brandt, *The Philosophy of Schleiermacher. The Development of His Theory of Scientific and Religious Knowledge* (New York, 1941). For an especially valuable discussion of the Germanic origins of Lieber's thought, see C. B. Robson, "Francis Lieber's Theories of Society, Government, and Liberty," *Journal of Politics*, IV (1942), 227–49.

[41] The University of California library possesses Lieber's own copy of Frederick E. D. Schleiermacher, *Ueber die Religion Reden an die Gebildeten unter ihren Verächtern* (Berlin, 1821). Lieber signed and dated the copy, "20/6 XXIV."

[42] Dürre, "Errinerungen an Dr. Franz Lieber . . . ," *loc. cit.*

Francis gave vent to these yearnings for a free and united Germany in great quantities of verse and numerous plays—more noteworthy for their youthful fervor than for their literary merit. Also, he took a leading part in the preparation of a book of songs for the *Turners*. Some years earlier, he and a few friends had collected and printed a few of these; now they prepared an extensive compilation. Frightened by the radical tendencies of the youthful compilers, Father Jahn would have no part in the enterprise.

The result, the official songbook of the *Turners,* appearing in 1818, clearly was an adolescent product. Like most German collections of the nineteenth century it was a remarkable hodgepodge of "Children's, People's, Love, Wine, Fatherland, and Church Songs." Ranging from the great verses of Goethe and Luther to boyish doggerel, the compilation well illustrated the state of mind of the chief editor—yet wavering from seriousness to playfulness to audaciousness.[43]

[43] *Ibid.; Deutsche Lieder für Jung und Alt.* Among the authors of the songs were Luther, Schlegel, Arndt, Goethe, Körner, Klopstock, Novalis, Follen, and Uhland. Many songs were unsigned. Lieber's copy, which includes many manuscript additions and emendations, has this note in the front: "I had this copy with me in France, Greece, Italy &C. . . . For many long years I have not looked at it, but searched for it again this day in order to copy the tune of Ännchen von Tharau for Longfellow who has translated this poem of Dach's. Whoever may get this book after my death, may he keep it well.

"Francis Lieber, Columbia, S. Carolina, 29 January, 1850." Lieber papers.

II

Flight from Reaction

AUGUST VON KOTZEBUE was not only the most clever and urbane writer of comedies in the German Confederation; he was also the most reactionary. To the patriotic youth his reaction seemed nothing short of treason. In 1819 he was living at Mannheim, receiving 15,000 roubles a year from Czar Alexander I of Russia to ply his pen against the student liberals who advocated a unified, constitutional government for Germany. His witty venom stung them to rage and hatred. Into this turbulent atmosphere came a youthful theology student from Jena, Karl Sand. His zeal, as pious and patriotic as Lieber's, was streaked with fanaticism. He felt that he was the instrument designed by Heaven to punish the traitor.[1]

One March day in 1819 Sand by appointment came quietly to Kotzebue's house and handed him a letter. While the dramatist was reading it, Sand thrice plunged a dagger deep into him, crying, "Here, thou traitor to thy country." Sand then turned the dagger on himself. He recovered sufficiently to suffer a year of grilling by the police before they beheaded him.[2]

The assassination of Kotzebue at once thrilled and shocked Lieber, who could understand the motives but could not condone the crime. Sand's "feelings were stronger than his reason," and his irrational deed left the student liberals to reap the whirlwind. The reactionaries had been waiting for just such an act. "They

---

[1] Follen, *Works of Charles Follen,* I, 70–71; Lieber to Hillard, April 19, 1858, Lieber papers, Henry E. Huntington Library. All manuscripts referred to in this chapter, unless otherwise identified, are from this collection.

[2] "Sand," *Encyclopaedia Americana,* XI, 192. This article, explaining Sand's motives, undoubtedly was by Lieber.

24

rejoiced at the opportunity the murder . . . afforded them to prove that there was a conspiracy, and to inflame the mind of the King against those young men who, only four years before, had saved him from his enemies." [3]

Sand's act, coming after the university students' Wartburg festival, climaxed a series of missteps by the liberals. It gave Metternich the opportunity to institute widespread reactionary measures. The agents of reaction set police to spying upon Stein and August W. A., Count Neithardt von Gneisenau, suppressed newspapers, and imprisoned students and liberals by the scores. The *Turners* came under the ban when Metternich branded Jahn's gymnasium a training ground for university rowdyism and demanded that King Frederick William close its doors.

Jahn and his followers not only had to foreswear their exercises at the *Hasenheide* but also to proclaim openly their loyalty to the Prussian government. The police tried to magnify Sand's crime into a widespread revolutionary plot. For months they cross-examined the assassin, hunted through his papers, and rounded up his former associates. At Jena, where he had studied, they arrested his friend Charles Follen, a lecturer in the university and leader of the *Burschenschaften.*

From Follen and Jena the trail soon led back to Berlin and Lieber. Sand had visited *Turnvater* Jahn and Lieber the previous year. In July the police arrested both as dangerous enemies of the state. They charged Lieber with entertaining unpatriotic sentiments, and tried to find in his papers some link with the assassination plot. But they found nothing more incriminating than quantities of flowery adolescent verse and essays in praise of liberty. As proof of Lieber's dangerously subversive tendencies they published some of his stormiest poems. As the liberal Johann J. von Görres later indicated, this blundering attempt to expose Lieber's radical ideas only had the effect of further disseminating them. [4]

The minute search through Lieber's journal ended with ap-

[3] *Ibid.;* Lieber to Hillard, April 19, 1858; Lieber, "account of his political persecutions," manuscript copy.

[4] Follen, *Works of Charles Follen,* I, 71–75; Lieber, "account of his political persecutions," manuscript copy; Lieber, autobiographical sketch [*circa* August, 1854], New York Public Library.

parent success when the police triumphantly pounced upon the entry "all day murder lazy [*mordsfaul*]." Unfamiliar with student slang, they emphasized it with a red pencil, and the court of investigations plied Lieber with question after question to establish his guilt. Did not the phrase really signify "idle in plotting the death of his superiors, lazy in murderous thoughts"? [5]

This slang remark was all the police could find, and after torturing all possible meanings out of it, even they had to grant it was insufficient evidence upon which to base a trial. Their cross-examination also failed to force a confession from Lieber. He swore upon oath that he had never been a member of any secret society; so after four months they released him from prison, still rebellious and unrepentant. The suspicious authorities continued to keep him under close surveillance, open his letters, pursue inquiries, and interfere constantly with his coming and going.[6]

Despite the nuisance of the police at his heels, Lieber resumed his studies for the university. By the fall of 1819, after dropping formal classes and working with a tutor, he took the three-day written examinations covering history, Latin and Greek, and mathematics. In addition, he prepared essays in German and one other modern language, and underwent a full day of oral quizzing. On the whole examination Lieber made a rating entitling him to university entrance. In mathematics he excelled.

Mathematics was a safe subject which would not involve his radical ideology; so it was as a prospective three-year mathematics student that Lieber applied for admission to the University of Berlin. To support his application he presented abundant credentials and testimonials. Nevertheless, the rector, following police orders, refused him admission.

Francis protested indignantly to the Minister of Education, Karl, Freiherr von Stein zum Altenstein. The minister was adamant. He not only refused Lieber permission to attend the University of Berlin, but told him he could not study at any other Prussian university. Altenstein warned the young radical that unless his future conduct was entirely irreproachable he was open to new accusations. His release from prison was due only to in-

---

[5] Perry (ed.), *Lieber*, 29–30.
[6] Lieber, "account of his political persecutions."

sufficient evidence and by no means acquitted him of having fostered disloyal and dangerous opinions.[7]

Lieber then left his native country and traversed Germany to Heidelberg in the comparatively liberal state of Baden. Word from the Prussian police had preceded him, and even Heidelberg refused him permission to matriculate. Bitter and resentful, the young liberal went on to Coblenz where he became acquainted with some revolutionary-minded young men. Enthusiastically he discussed with them the revolt of Spanish troops about to be sent to suppress Bolivar in the New World. In the heat of the conversation he used many "indiscreet" words which he was later to regret.[8]

After relieving his feelings with talk, Lieber went on to Tübingen in Württemberg, but there, too, Prussian reaction dominated. He also applied unsuccessfully at Marburg and Giessen. At last he found an institution that would accept him. In defiance of the Prussian government he matriculated as a theology student at Jena, which was under the patronage of the progressive Grand Duke of Saxe-Weimar. Jena had been a center of student agitation. Because Sand had studied there, Prussia and other German governments had punished it by forbidding their subjects to attend Jena. This was a staggering blow, at once lowering enrollment and standing. Lieber ignored the ban and late in April, 1820, began his studies.

Shortly after his entrance Lieber switched from theology to the liberal arts and specialized in mathematics which he hoped ultimately to teach in a Prussian gymnasium or university. He had, his professor reported, "a great talent in mathematics and an unusual aptitude for instruction." [9]

[7] *Ibid.;* Lieber to Minister der Geistlichen-Unterrichts-und-Medizinal-Angelegenheiten [Karl, Freiherr von Stein zum Altenstein], [October 27, 1823], December, 1819, January 15, 1820, drafts. Altenstein to Lieber, January 1 [or 31?], 1820. Dürre, "Errinerungen an Dr. Franz Lieber . . . ," *loc. cit.,* 286–88, 293–94, with manuscript translation edited by Matilda Lieber. "Gymnasium," *Encyclopaedia Americana,* VI, 118–19.

[8] Lieber to Altenstein, October 27<, 1823; Lieber to [Minister des Innern und der Polizei, Kaspar Friedrich von Schuckmann], March 17<, 1824, drafts; manuscript in Thomas Sergeant Perry's hand, Lieber papers.

[9] Lieber to Altenstein, October 27<, 1823; "Jena," *Encyclopaedia Americana,* VII, 188–89; Lieber, "account of his political persecutions"; matriculation papers, Jena University, April 21, 1820.

Jena was an excellent place for Lieber to begin his studies. With a fine faculty and a library of one hundred thousand volumes, it was one of the most inexpensive yet best of the German universities. But the Prussian officials considered it an unsafe place to allow the young liberal to study, and soon interfered. Lieber tried to forestall their intervention by taking the Doctor of Philosophy degree, just a few months after his matriculation, "in order to acquire the privileges of 'an academic citizen of that institution.' " [10]

Although Lieber received the degree in August, it came too late to protect him. Already the Ministry of Education had instructed his father to withdraw him from Jena. It did rescind its earlier refusal to allow Lieber to attend any Prussian university, and ordered him to matriculate at Halle where he would be under the eye of the police. However, he must cease preparing to be a teacher, since the Ministry would never allow him to be an instructor in Prussia.[11]

Dr. Lieber did not go directly to Halle, but went to Dresden to see the hundreds of famous paintings of the great masters which the Saxon kings had assembled there. "I saw some pictures," Lieber reported, "but irresistibly I was drawn on until I stood before the Madonna di Sisto. I stood surprized—over-

---

[10] "Universities," *Encyclopaedia Americana*, XII, 470–71; Lieber, autobiographical sketch, New York Public Library. Cf. M[aximilian] LaBorde, *History of the South Carolina College* (Columbia, S.C., 1859), 395. Lieber told LaBorde he took the degree to acquire the right of academic citizenship and protect himself from Prussian interference. The phenomenon of Lieber's receiving a Ph.D. after only four months' attendance at a university has led to doubts on the part of recent scholars. Ernest Bruncken, "Francis Lieber, a Study of a Man and an Ideal," *Deutsch-Amerikanische Geschichtsblätter Jahrbuch der Deutsch-Amerikanischen Historischen Gesellschaft von Illinois* (Chicago, 1915), XV, 26, 35–37, questions the degree. M. H. Thomas, Curator of Columbiana, Columbia University, sent a letter to the University of Jena on April 4, 1938, seeking to verify the degree, but in an interview with the present writer, November, 1940, declared he had received no reply. The authenticity of the degree cannot be questioned, however, since there are two copies of the diploma, dated August 4, 1820, in the Lieber papers, togther with a letter from Altenstein, October 22, 1823, mentioning the degree as one of Lieber's offenses. Dr. Edith Lenel possesses copies of the correspondence between the university officials which preceded the awarding of the degree. After 1820, Lieber customarily was addressed as "doctor" in letters from governmental and university officials. Whatever its lack of value as a milestone of academic progress, the Ph.D. was of inestimable aid to Lieber when he came to America.

[11] Ministerium der Geistlichen-Unterrichts-und-Medizinal-Angelegenheiten to Friedrich Wilhelm Lieber, July 24, 1820 (contemporary copy).

come—and wept, and looked again, amazed and touched—and so I stood from nine to one, when the gallery was closed and I walked down those stairs another being—I felt at once, [that] my soul was wider." [12]

With the opening of the fall term, he enrolled at Halle and once more began matching his wits with the police. He refused to change his field as the Ministry of Education had specified, and continued his study of mathematics under the learned Professor Johann F. P. Pfaff. The secret agents kept a close watch upon him; the permission to enter a Prussian university was no act of generosity but the means of putting the dangerous young man where his every move could be checked. Lieber rankled under incessant police intervention. Some of his professors suggested that he go to Dresden, where he would be beyond Prussian reach. Lieber pondered the advice. The curator of the university, Witzleben, advised him to remain at Halle, but since Witzleben only advised and did not order, at the end of the 1821 spring term he transferred to Dresden. There, specializing in military mathematics, he studied applied mathematics under Professor Fischer of the Legmann Scientific School, and topographical problems under Major Becker. [13]

To such an incurable romantic as Lieber, even military mathematics could not have seemed much more than a "safe" subject. During the spring and summer of 1821 theorems and equations fought a losing battle for his attention against the superior attractions of the Greek Revolution. He read with growing fascination reports of the stratagems and proclamations of Alexander Ypsilanti, whose revolt the Turks quickly and ruthlessly smashed. Though the attempt had been a disastrous failure, it stirred to rebellion the half-wild inhabitants of Morea, the southern penin-

---

[12] "Dresden," *Encyclopaedia Americana*, IV, 304; Lieber, autobiographical sketch, New York Public Library; Lieber to George Stillman Hillard, November 11, 1844; *Journal of the Proceedings of a Convention of Literary and Scientific Gentlemen, held in the Common Council Chamber of the City of New-York, October, 1830* (New-York, 1830), 58.

[13] Lieber to Altenstein, October 27<, 1823; Witzleben to Lieber, March 3, 1821; Schuckmann to F. W. Lieber, May 5, 1821; Karl C. A. H. von Kamptz for the Minister des Innern . . . to Lieber, July 3, 1821. Some of Lieber's mathematical notes of this period, including a paper on surveying written while at Dresden, are in the Lieber papers.

sula of Greece, who overthrew the Turks in June, and began a protracted struggle for independence.

Confusing the savage Moreans with the noble and cultured Athenians, romantics everywhere saw in the struggle a modern rebirth of the Golden Age of ancient Greece. Lord Byron and Samuel Gridley Howe were only two of the many hundreds who felt called upon to adventure in the cause of freedom. Lieber found study impossible at a time "when strong men might strike a decisive blow." He could not resist a "youthful ardour to assist the oppressed and struggling descendants of that people whom all civilized nations love and admire," and in the fall of 1821 he decided to offer his services to the Greek revolutionists. Using a mutilated passport, he left on foot for a French port of embarkation.[14]

Lieber found an earlier opportunity to strike a blow than he had anticipated. At Lyons, French *Charbonnieres* revealed plans for an uprising against Louis XVIII, and urged him to prepare for a simultaneous upheaval in Germany. In compliance, Lieber recrossed the Rhine and at Erfurt conferred several times with Major von Fehrentheil, a trusted aide of Gneisenau and commander of a fortress in the vicinity. He also discussed plans with some leading malcontents. He then returned to France and continued on toward Marseilles. The subsequent uprising, confined to France alone, was abortive. Generally called the Strasburg affair, it ended with the shooting of a few officers and sergeants.[15]

At Marseilles Lieber found young Philhellenes assembled from all over Europe—Danes, Poles, Frenchmen, and Italians—ranging in military rank from majors to privates. While they awaited passage to the new Hellas, they held a meeting and organized themselves into a military company. Francis was elected one of a

[14] Kamptz to Lieber, July 3, 1821; Prussia, Königliche Preussiche Gesandischaft [in Dresden], der Königliche Geschäftstrager to Lieber, signed by von Küster. Enclosure: July 11, 1821, . . . Legitimation (copy in Lieber's hand). Francis Lieber, *Reminiscences of an Intercourse with Mr. Niebuhr the Historian, During a Residence with Him in Rome, in the Years 1822 and 1823* (Philadelphia, 1835), 17–18; (London, 1835). A translation by Karl Thibaut appeared under the title, *Erinnerungen aus meinem Zusammenleben mit Georg Barthold Niebuhr* [sic], *dem Geschichtschreiber Roms.* (Heidelberg, 1837). The English version is reprinted in Lieber, *Miscellaneous Writings*, I, 45–148.

[15] Manuscript note in Lieber's hand, with clipping, whole titled, "Lieber and Niebuhr."

committee of five to draw up regulations for the maintenance of order, and to assume command of the entire group. Impatiently they waited week after week as incessant delays prevented their sailing and with dismay watched the launching of a frigate being outfitted for the Turks.[16]

Finally they prevailed upon the French merchants and the German societies of Marseilles to give them a small one-masted brigantine, the *Little Mary,* in which they sailed for Greece. Thirty-four young men, mostly Germans but including six Frenchmen and three Poles, made up the company. Expecting mountain warfare, the band had armed itself with belts, daggers, pistols, swords, and guns; but, because their funds were so small, many had neglected to purchase powder and shot. For their general use they had maps, compasses, spyglasses, and other equipment purchased for them in Paris by an engineering officer. They were poor and had to carry all their possessions, so they took along very few books. Lieber clung proudly to his collection of the *Turners'* songs, but the group owned no military manuals, and their only guide to the Greece of 1822 was the classic *Voyage of Anacharsis.*[17]

When the vessel landed at Navarino officers from British war vessels came aboard and gave disheartening accounts of the Greeks, whom they scorned as worthless rogues. However, since the Greeks sent messages of welcome and hospitable offers, the Philhellenes danced and hugged each other for joy. About three o'clock the news was spread that in two days they were to attack Modon. All shouted gleefully, and with singing and firing of muskets, the eager idealists landed at Navarino. In common with dozens of other groups that preceded or followed, as Napier commented: "All came expecting to find the Peloponnesus filled with Plutarch's men, and all returned thinking the inhabitants of Newgate [prison] more moral." [18]

[16] Lieber to his parents, December 10, 16, 1821, Columbia University Library, partly translated in Perry (ed.), *Lieber,* 31–33.

[17] Francis Lieber, *Tagebuch meines Aufenhaltes in Griechenland während der Monate Januar, Februar und März im Jahr 1822* (Leipzig, 1823), 1–2. The Huntington Library copy contains copious additions and marginalia in Lieber's hand. Cf. partial translation in Perry (ed.), *Lieber,* 34–41. The manuscript diary upon which the printed account is based, "Journal, 1822," is in the Columbia University Library. The paragraphs above closely follow the printed account.

[18] Lieber, *Tagebuch,* 2–7; Perry (ed.), *Lieber,* 34.

31

The high hopes and anticipations of the day on shipboard quickly dissolved in the narrow, dirty streets of Navarino. Lieber found his comrades awaiting him, "and one of them had already been received in the true Grecian style—he had been robbed." The Greeks gave the company an empty Turkish house in which to lodge, but did not furnish any food as they had promised. Bitterly, the Philhellene noted, "but I shall not mention in the future similar falsehoods, for they occurred daily during our sojourn in Greece." [19]

After about a week of such conditions, Lieber and twelve others left the city to join Ypsilanti's forces. The governor warned them that they would fare much worse, but they did not think this could be possible, "for the laziness, cowardice, and untruthfulness which we had witnessed and suffered here, could not be exceeded anywhere else." They set out on horses, for which members of the party had to pay, and traveled in the midst of a violent rainstorm, crossing torrents and at times wading through water up to their waists. Sometimes they induced Greek peasants to carry them. Several days later they reached Kalamatia, where they had to stay in a filthy abode whose former inhabitants had died of a contagious fever. No one could tell them anything concerning the whereabouts of the Greek Senate or troops.

Selling clothing, watches, and whatever else they could spare, the disillusioned young soldiers continued their journey toward Tripolis. In a deep defile in the road they were set upon by one of their drivers who had deserted them and returned with sixty armed peasants to rob them of their horses. Lieber and his friends returned to Kalamatia to complain, and received only facile promises.

By now the Philhellene leader, the cavalry officer, was completely discouraged and boarded a ship bound for Malta. Those who remained were forced to sell their arms to obtain money for food. Though weaponless and no longer in a position to fight, Lieber and a physician friend decided they would see Athens before returning home.[20]

Throughout the month of February the two companions journeyed onward, walking from Kalamatia to Tripolis, Argos, and

---

[19] Lieber, *Tagebuch*, 6–7.   [20] *Ibid.*, 13–53.

Corinth. Everywhere they encountered the same squalor, cheating, and lying. The food was execrable, the accommodations worse, and their small remaining sum of money speedily evaporated. Though Lieber realized that the lawlessness of the people was the inevitable result of hundreds of years of suppression, he was amazed to find that the liberated Greeks thought their new freedom meant complete release from taxation and governmental ties. He witnessed the quarreling between the *capitani* of rival bands over the possession of cattle, and saw that "All that enabled the Greeks to continue their struggle was the wretchedly undisciplined character of their Turkish enemies." [21]

Word reached Lieber that General Karl F. L., Count von Normann, formerly of the Württemberg army, with a corps of about three hundred Philhellenes had landed at Navarino. With his weapons, health, and enthusiasm for the Greeks all gone, he had no stomach to return to Navarino and join the corps. Instead, by mid-March he and his friend decided to leave Greece.[22]

Young Lieber was half-starved and almost penniless by the time he reached the miasmic port of Missolonghi. Surrounded by pestilential marshes and lagoons, it was to be a deathtrap for Lord Byron only two years later. The German might well have died of hunger had he remained there, but fortunately he found a ship bound for Ancona in the Italian Papal Domain. The little tartan was already crowded with forty Greek passengers, and Lieber had to pay double the ordinary fare to buy his passage. He went on board with only a scudo and a half left in his purse.[23]

On the slow and stormy voyage across the Adriatic, Lieber pondered upon the lessons he had learned in Greece. Deeply disenchanted and discouraged, he concluded that "the cowardice and incapacity of the Greeks made them unfit to defend or free their country." [24]

[21] *Ibid., passim;* [Francis Lieber], "Revolution of Modern Greece," *Encyclopaedia Americana,* VI, 23. Less than a decade later, Lieber related some of his experiences to a polite Boston audience, and gave them a realistic picture of Capitani Nikitas' brawling. Lieber, "A Lecture delivered before the Boston Society for the Diffusion of Useful Knowledge, . . . Dec. 11, 1829," manuscript.

[22] Lieber, *Tagebuch,* 69–70; Perry (ed.), *Lieber,* 39–40. Most of Normann's corps subsequently perished.

[23] Lieber, *Tagebuch,* 179–81; Lieber, *Reminiscences of Niebuhr,* 18.

[24] Lieber, *Tagebuch,* 182–83; Perry (ed.), *Lieber,* 41.

Because of his penniless condition Lieber had no food except a scanty supply of bread. During the nine days' passage the Greeks tantalized him with the smell of cooking meals, but not a morsel would they offer him. On Easter Eve the ship entered the port of Ancona, but shortly after arrival a woman died on board, and the passengers had to stay on the vessel in quarantine for a full forty days. Without money, Lieber faced the possibility of having to work for some time as a sailor to meet the expenses of his provisions during the quarantine. He wrote to a friend who was studying art in Rome. The friend immediately sent money to Lieber, and as soon as the time was up he was able to go ashore.[25]

Young Lieber determined that rather than return to Prussian oppression he would visit the Rome about which he had so long studied and dreamed. As soon as he gained his freedom from quarantine, he went to the police office to obtain the necessary signature to his passport. The officer in charge informed him that he had received an order from Rome not to sign the passport of any person coming from Greece, except for a direct journey home. Lieber was thunderstruck. The officer told him that he would direct his passport to any place in Tuscany that Francis wished, as Tuscany lay between Ancona and Prussia.

After some pondering, Lieber had the passport signed to Orbitello, Tuscany, which was not far from Rome. With a Danish comrade, he hired a coachman. Once on the road, they paid the coachman a trifle extra and told him that instead of going to Orbitello they wished to go to Rome. With a thrill Lieber entered the Porta del Populo. "My heart beat as we approached the tame-looking sentinel of the Papal troops, more than it ever had beaten at the approach of an grenadier of the enemy; and the delight I experienced when I had safely passed him, and felt and saw I was in Rome, is indescribable." [26]

Lieber found his artist friend and moved into his lodgings with him. After a rapid glance at the wonders of the city, he realized that he could not long remain there without police permission. After some hesitation, he decided to state his difficult position frankly to Barthold George Niebuhr, the Prussian minister at

[25] Lieber, *Tagebuch,* 181; Lieber, *Reminiscences of Niebuhr,* 18–19.
[26] Lieber, *Reminiscences of Niebuhr,* 22–24.

Rome, hoping that a scholar who had written a history of Rome would not be so cruel as to drive him away from that city before he had time to see and study it. In a condition far from prepossessing, Lieber went to the Prussian Legation in the Palazzo Orsini, or Teatro di Marcello. The young man did not see the minister; but C. K. T. Bunsen, the secretary of the Legation, received him with genuine humanity. He procured for Lieber not only the desired paper to show the papal police, but also a loan from a fund which Prince Henry had placed at Niebuhr's disposal for the assistance of young men returning from Greece.

Lieber, overjoyed, had yet one more request. He asked permission to borrow a copy of Niebuhr's *History of Rome*. His audacious frankness was disconcerting to the secretary, who pointed out that the minister knew nothing of Lieber. Bunsen advised him to ask Niebuhr himself, and made an appointment for the following day.

At the designated hour, the refugee met the famous historian coming downstairs. Niebuhr was small in stature, thin, and near-sighted. When he spoke, his voice was surprisingly high in pitch. But he made up for these minor deficiencies by force of intellect and exceeding kindness of heart. He returned to his room with the excited young man, and for several hours questioned him about Greece. Lieber described his unpleasant wanderings in detail to the distinguished listener, "mourning as an enthusiastic youth is apt to mourn when his fondest hopes are first nipped by cold reality."

At the end of the interview, Niebuhr invited the youth to return for dinner, but, embarrassed by the state of his clothing, Lieber replied: "Really, sir, I am not in a state to dine with an excellency." Niebuhr "stamped his foot, and said with some animation, 'Are diplomatists always believed to be so cold-hearted! I am the same that I was in Berlin when I delivered my lectures.' " Before his insistence the young man's reluctance melted.

After his hardships in Greece, the dinner seemed like a dream to Lieber: the rich and learned table conversation, the charming woman and beautiful children, the delicious foods and beverages, above him the high-vaulted, frescoed ceiling, and the murmuring of a fountain beyond the flowers and shrubbery of a luxuriant garden. Only one unfortunate reality marred his enjoyment of all this splendor: "My dress consisted as yet of nothing better than a pair of unblacked shoes . . . ; a pair of socks of coarse Greek wool; the brownish pantaloons frequently worn by sea-captains in the Mediterranean; and a blue frock-coat, through which two balls had passed. . . . The socks were exceedingly short, hardly covering my ankles, and so indeed were the pantaloons; so that, when I was in a sitting position, they refused me the charity of meeting." The young man's embarrassment was extreme, especially in the presence of ladies. Noticing this, Niebuhr redoubled his kindness, and sent Lieber home laden with books.[27]

The young idealist deeply impressed the historian, who wrote to his sister-in-law about the youth and his misadventures: "The horror which his narrations inspire is not to be described. All this has plunged him into deep melancholy; for he has a very noble heart. He has deeply moved and interested us, and we are trying to cheer his spirits by friendly treatment, and to banish from his thoughts the infernal scenes which he has witnessed. He is one of the youths of the noble period of 1813 . . . who lost themselves in visions, the elements of which they drew from their own hearts; and this terrible contrast between his experience and all that he had imagined—all that impelled him into distant lands, has broken his heart." [28]

Niebuhr decided to rescue Lieber from his melancholy and destitution. He invited the young man to accompany him and his secretary, Bunsen, to Tivoli, where they spent a few happy days. Upon their return, he asked Lieber to come and live with him as his literary assistant. Niebuhr also entrusted his beloved curly-headed son Marcus to the young romantic's tutelage. In return for the assistance and tutoring Niebuhr tried to supplant Lieber's disillusionment with his own moderate philosophy:

"I hope . . . to convince him that just as his experience in Greece taught him the visionary nature of his wishes and expectations, so he would have made the same discovery in any other nation where the masses are liberated from all forms [of govern-

[27] *Ibid.*, 14, 24–31, 45.

[28] Barthold Georg Niebuhr to Mme. Dora Hensler, June 7, 22, 1822, in C. K. T. Bunsen and others, *The Life and Letters of Barthold George Niebuhr . . .* , 2 vols. (London, 1852), II, 220–21.

ment]; but that the Noble and Beautiful are not a dream, and will never be wholly wanting in the world, however terrible may be its condition." The historian wanted to impress upon the student that "the evil which prevails so widely, could not be found among the rulers unless it existed in the multitude; that change of form [of government] can bring no deliverance unless the individual can be first improved." [29]

Niebuhr impressed these lessons upon Lieber during the happy months that followed. The Grecian misadventure had destroyed many of his cherished preconceptions; the brilliant and patient teacher skillfully replaced them with new attitudes and techniques. These ultimately were to transform the revolutionary-minded man into a cautious, moderate social scientist.

In many fundamentals Lieber was to take over Niebuhr's ideology as his own. He jotted down notes on his conversations and recorded them equally indelibly in his mind.

Niebuhr, saturated in the doctrines of Edmund Burke, deeply distrusted the French Revolution, yet equally despised the old regime and the émigrés. "His ideal was orderly development by process of law," and his model, Great Britain, Lieber noted. During the period of French domination over Germany, he had published a study of Great Britain "to show what liberty in reality is"—constitutional liberty within the bounds of the law.

Niebuhr had served the Prussian government primarily in the field of finance, but his avocation was classical studies. He became one of the first professors in the new University of Berlin, and before enraptured students lectured on the ancient world as though Greece were Prussia and Alexander were Napoleon. He extolled the orderly legal system of the Roman Republic, and its substantial mainstay, the hard-working, productive free peasant.

In the year after Waterloo, Niebuhr became ambassador to Rome where he spent much of his time with his historical studies. Critically examining the sources, utilizing the new tool of philology, and sifting legend from historical fact, he reconstructed the Roman Republic. With penetrating hypotheses he filled gaps between the fragments to recreate minutely a state with plausible institutions.

[29] *Ibid.*

While the historian recognized the significance of the individual, he omitted from his writings the vivid descriptions of personalities which were so notable in his lectures and conversation. His style was tedious, and his text so loaded with proofs, details, and digressions that it was most difficult to read. Nevertheless, Niebuhr's researches analyzed the Roman political system as never before and made the history of Rome a living study. His scientific method and his emphasis upon the state profoundly affected nineteenth-century historical writing.

Lieber worshiped his erudite mentor and uncritically absorbed both his strength and weakness. Niebuhr gradually colored the young man's mind a more conservative hue. He stimulated in him a great interest in gathering source materials and in the study of governmental institutions. Unfortunately the historian also planted, or accentuated, a prolixity of writing style, a distrust of the common man, and a decided Francophobia. Niebuhr told Lieber that the French were utterly incapable of maintaining free institutions and a republican form of government; in his mature years Lieber blew upon that note like the ceaseless, mournful skirl of a bagpipe.[30]

On the positive side, Niebuhr as strongly fed Lieber's hatred of despotism. "The history of Joseph, as given in the forty-seventh chapter of Genesis," he pointed out, "is a most dangerous precedent for an artful premier: 'Give me thy land and liberty, and I give thee bread.' "[31]

Upon Niebuhr's insistence and with his aid, Lieber wrote an account of his Greek misadventure. The historian sent the manuscript to his friend Frederick A. B. Brockhaus, the great Leipzig publisher, who issued it the following year. A Dutch edition under the title, *The German Anacharsis,* soon followed. The Amsterdam publisher sent Lieber no royalties, but acknowledged his indebtedness with a case of fine old Hock.[32]

While living with Niebuhr, Lieber reveled in the great sculp-

[30] G. P. Gooch, *History and Historians in the Nineteenth Century* (2d ed.; London, 1913), 14–24; Lieber, *Reminiscences of Niebuhr,* 57, 61–62, 81; J. W. Thompson and B. J. Holm, *A History of Historical Writing,* 2 vols. (New York, 1942), II, 153–56; Dietrich Gerhard, "Niebuhr," *Encyclopaedia of the Social Sciences,* II, 372–73.

[31] Lieber, *Reminiscences of Niebuhr,* 84, 106.

[32] *Ibid.,* 32, 55–56; Lieber, *Tagebuch,* 73–79; manuscript journal, "Rom"; autobiographical essay.

tures, paintings, and architecture of Rome. Wandering among the ruins, he profited greatly by the profound knowledge of Bunsen, who was writing a lengthy work on Roman antiquities. The erudite Niebuhr was also a helpful companion. "To walk with him over the ancient forum was like passing along with a guide from classic times, so clear was the whole scene before his eyes." [33]

During the winter months, a distinguished array of visitors came to the Teatro di Marcello, and the young radical found himself hobnobbing with the most brilliant of the conservatives. One day in November Lieber encountered a fine-looking man standing in the salon of the Legation. The visitor addressed him in Italian. To Lieber's ear the accent seemed French; so he obligingly replied in that tongue. Thus they continued a halting multilingual conversation until Niebuhr entered and addressed the visitor in German. He was Baron Alexander von Humboldt, the great geographer and favorite of King Frederick William. The King had come to Verona in October, 1822, along with other representatives of the Quadruple Alliance to devise ways and means of punishing Spain and Piedmont for their recent revolutions. After the Congress convened, King Frederick William III and his entourage visited Rome before returning to Prussia.

While Niebuhr showed King Frederick William the sights of Rome, the ambassador pleaded the case of his protégé, now fast sloughing his radicalism, yet still under police proscription in Prussia. The King was in a generous mood, and promised Niebuhr that the young man could return to Prussia and resume his studies unmolested.[34]

The welcome sight of his King recalled strongly to Niebuhr's mind the memory of his homeland and strengthened an old resolve that, in order to provide adequately for his children's education, he must leave Italy. With the Concordat he had arranged

---

[33] Perry (ed.), *Lieber,* 44–50, contains extended excerpts from the Rome journal; Lieber, *Reminiscences of Niebuhr,* 118. In addition to his journals, Lieber kept a record of principal events as reported in the *Journal des Debats, Diario Romano,* and other publications. These, together with pamphlets and several copies of the *Diario,* are in the Lieber papers.

[34] Perry (ed.), *Lieber,* 45 *et seq.;* Lieber, *Reminiscences of Niebuhr,* 71–72; Bunsen, *Niebuhr,* II, 211. Lieber reminded the Minister of Police that Frederick William had promised him immunity, in a draft letter, March 17<, 1824. See also manuscript note and clipping, "Lieber and Niebuhr."

signed, the Prussian government granted him a furlough. In May, 1823, with his family and the tutor he started the northward journey.

Lieber regretfully took leave of Rome, "so beautiful in the morning light." As the party reached the north of Italy, Niebuhr rejoiced to see Gothic architecture, but it struck Lieber unpleasantly after the "grand symmetrical lines of the basilicas." At Innsbruck, he sadly said good-by to the Niebuhr family and traveled slowly northward alone. In August, 1823, he arrived in Berlin, ready to put into execution a well-formulated plan of action.[35]

Lieber took as his motto the words of Leonardo: "If thou canst not do that which thou wilt, do that which thou canst." Perhaps he had not cast off entirely the political opinions which he had aired so fervently in his *Turner* days; but he did realize that the government of Prussia was too powerful for him, and that only through conformity could he hope for a career in Germany.

Lieber would rather have patterned his career after that of his idol, Niebuhr, and concentrated upon literary studies of government and history. But such subjects were dangerous—Lieber could not easily hold his tongue. So in conformity with his motto he turned his mind once more toward mathematics. Although Lieber had maintained a tenuous interest in the field through attending some lectures at the Sapienza in Rome, even there he had concerned himself less with equations than with noting the papal system of censorship over the writings of the professors.[36]

Backed by as powerful a sponsor as Niebuhr, the young man soon gained the good will of the Prussian officials. Kaspar F. von Schuckmann, Minister of the Interior and of Police, assured him that he should meet with no difficulties from the police. Encouraged, Lieber began petitioning for governmental aid to help him with his studies. After long negotiations he received the sum of two hundred thalers for two years' study, beginning Easter of 1824.[37]

[35] Perry (ed.), *Lieber,* 45–52.

[36] Lieber to Schuckmann, >August 20, 1823, draft; Lieber to Altenstein, [October 27<, 1823], draft. See also Lieber's notes on the Sapienza lectures.

[37] Lieber to Altenstein, August 20<, 1823, draft; Kamptz to Lieber, August 21, October 13, 31; Altenstein to Lieber, October 22; Lieber to Altenstein, October 27<, 1823, February 5, 1824, drafts. Kamptz's title was "Oberregierungsrath," a position

Francis spent a quiet winter in Berlin, taking private lessons from Martin O. Ohm, and in turn tutoring pupils scattered around the city. Thanks to his friendship with Niebuhr, his interesting experiences, and his excellent conversation, he established himself in the highest intellectual circles. He met Leopold von Ranke, a promising young history professor at the University of Berlin, and maintained his acquaintance with Alexander von Humboldt, who was a Germanic counterpart of Mirabeau. Soon he added the acquaintance of Alexander's brother William, a renowned philologist. The brothers Humboldt frequented the salon of Hofrätin Henrietta Herz, the charming daughter of a Jewish financier, who through sheer intellectual power had become the warm friend of many of Germany's leading figures. Lieber and his new companions spent many evenings in her home.

More often Lieber revolved in the orbit of Julius Eduard Hitzig, one of the leading legal minds of his day, and later an important figure in the Prussian cabinet. Hitzig interested the young man in criminology, but was more concerned with criticizing his poetic and dramatic attempts. At Hitzig's he passed stimulating evenings with E. T. A. Hoffmann, poet and musician, and with Adelbert von Chamisso, Prussia's best botanist, who was also an excellent poet. Chamisso was most famous for his prose narrative about Peter Schlemihl, the man who sold his shadow. It was also at Hitzig's home that young Lieber became intimate with Frederick H. C. Fouqué, Baron de la Motte, a prolific romantic writer past the peak of his achievement, mainly known as the author of *Undine*.[38]

But the Ministry of Police did not keep its word and Lieber felt himself under the shadow of constant watchfulness. This irritated and upset him so that, despite his eminent and entertaining friends, he longed for the quiet of the University of Bonn, where Niebuhr had taken a professorship. In February, giving as his pretext ill health resulting from the severe winter, he applied to the Minister of Education for permission to matriculate at Bonn.[39]

---

he filled in the Ministry of Police in 1823, and in the Ministry of Education the following year.

[38] Perry (ed.), *Lieber*, 54. Various references to these people appear in the Lieber correspondence and journals.

[39] Lieber to Altenstein, February 5, 1824, draft.

Before he could return to the sheltering household of Niebuhr, the police demanded that he appear immediately before the investigating commission at Köpenick. Blazing with righteous indignation, Francis hurried to Minister Karl C. A. H. von Kamptz, who told him kindly that the police wanted him merely as a witness. Lieber allowed them to take him to Köpenick, about eight miles from Berlin, and appeared protestingly before the court of inquiry. Within a month the police ordered him back to Köpenick, where they questioned him again about the operations of the secret societies and the details of his conversations upon the 1819 visit to the Rhineland. Lieber declared repeatedly, upon oath and in writing, that he had never belonged to any political society and had never been in connection with any. He reiterated his desire to be "a loyal and useful citizen," and complained about the repeated accusations and disturbance of his peace of mind.[40]

These vehement statements temporarily placated the police. Though von Kamptz refused Lieber permission to leave Prussia, a month later the councilor allowed him to depart for Halle. Once more Halle was distasteful, and Lieber renewed his request for permission to transfer to Bonn.[41]

No sooner had the Ministry of Police granted the permission than it demanded that Lieber return to the capital at once for questioning. Berlin was in a state of great excitement. The police had discovered what they thought were certain proofs of a plot between German and French secret societies for the overthrow of their respective governments, and Lieber was suspected of connection with it. He was once more taken to Köpenick, the ancient fortress on the banks of the Spree. There he spent many melancholy days:[42]

[40] [F. W. Lieber] to Schuckmann, [February 14,] 1824, draft; Lieber to [Königliche Ministerial Untersuchungs Commission in Köpenick, Berlin, February<, 1824], draft; Königliche Ministerial Untersuchungs. . . . Commission to Lieber, March 12, 1824; Lieber to [Schuckmann], [March 17<], 1824, draft. In stating under oath that he had not belonged to any political society, Lieber, being pious, quite possibly told the truth. The *Turners* had been technically nonpolitical; Lieber's association with Sand, Follen, and others had been in their capacity as individuals, not as members of organizations, and he had not entered Jena until after the dissolution of the *Burschenschaften*. His relations with the *Charbonnerie* were probably similarly informal, but most certainly he acted as their agent when he returned to Germany to confer with Fehrentheil and other conspirators.

[41] Perry (ed.), *Lieber*, 56; Lieber to [Kamptz, August 9, 1824], draft; Kamptz to Lieber, August 24, 1824; autobiographical sketch.

[42] Perry (ed.), *Lieber*, 56; Lieber note with clipping, "Niebuhr and Lieber."

"September 2,[1824], I am permitted to read my Boccacio which I had taken with me—to laugh when I feel like weeping. Oh! the misery of a prisoner's life; how one longs for the pure sweet meadow beyond these narrow walls! Be happy, my dear ones. In spirit I am with you. To be a prisoner is to be blind: we see nothing; deaf—we hear nothing.—Köpenick." [43]

During this period wild rumors electrified Berlin. The police continued to make large numbers of arrests; the most important people in Germany were suspect—the King of Württemberg, Gneisenau, Humboldt, Savigny, and Niebuhr. Lieber's friend Charles Follen, who had fled to Switzerland in 1820, left for America just ahead of Prussian demands for his extradition. Day after day, Lieber's inquisitors tried to wrest from him information about Fehrentheil and two others who had also been arrested. Doggedly he refused to tell what he knew. Once more he insisted upon the royal pledge of immunity. The King acknowledged it, but the officials told Lieber that although he should not be held responsible for the past he was bound now, especially in gratitude, to tell everything he knew about his fellow prisoners. To try to force the information out of him, they alternated periods of questioning with long, solitary periods of waiting in his cell. They took away his books, pen and paper, and his many journals and diaries. Carefully they pored over these, marking in red those passages where Lieber recorded a conversation with Countess De Serre about Karl Sand; where he had recorded from the newspapers the official disclosure of the *Charbonnerie* plot; and where he had noted efforts to prove the existence of the secret order in Germany. All their seeking disclosed nothing positively incriminating.[44]

In later life, Lieber remembered not the gloom but the high spirits—days when he sat in prison munching oysters and reading Boccacio. Casting away the guiding ideals of his childhood and youth—sacrifice for others, resignation, and service to God and Freedom—he plunged unreservedly into intellectual hedonism through a mental life as wide as his physical existence was re-

[43] Lieber diary, September 2, 1824, translated copy. This is one of only two entries for the period when Lieber was imprisoned—probably the police took the diary away from Lieber along with books and writing materials.

[44] Perry (ed.), *Lieber*, 56–57; autobiographical sketch, New York Public Library; Lieber note with clipping, "Lieber and Niebuhr," journals and diaries, "Rom." The notes on the *Charbonnerie*, marked in red by the police, were from the *Journal des Debats*, August 22, 29, 1822.

stricted. Shortly after his release, Lieber published from among his many manuscripts *Fourteen Wine and Love Songs,* a hilariously convivial array, under the pen name "Arnold Franz." [45]

After some months the police told Lieber that Fehrentheil and his two companions had confessed and implicated Lieber. The student was shocked and incredulous, but the police showed him their confessions. Still he remained firm. The officials told him they would keep him in prison until he confessed, even though he were to remain incarcerated for the rest of his life. The young man's spirits were not high enough to vault this crushing blow. He wrote Niebuhr a despairing letter which touched the historian deeply. For a long time Niebuhr had been trying to gain Lieber's freedom, even though he himself was under suspicion. Cautiously he had noted: "Such carelessness in leaving a good man to languish in fetters makes me indignant, though no cruelty is intended." Upon receiving Lieber's note the historian renewed his efforts, and early in April he made a trip to comfort his protégé. His last intercession with Schuckmann proved successful, and Lieber was freed on condition that he remain in Berlin until the investigations ended.[46]

Lieber soon revisited Hitzig's and Hofrätin Herz's, but did not resume his mathematical studies. To continue his university career when he could not possibly expect the Prussian government to allow him to practice his vocation was manifestly futile. Instead, Lieber tried his hand at literature. He sent some of his wine songs to Jean Paul Richter, aged romantic literary giant, asking frankly for his opinion. Lieber received no reply, and, taking the silence for disapproval, gave up his literary aspirations. Not until twenty

[45] Copy of note by Lieber, September 12, 1857, on flyleaf of the poems; Perry (ed.), *Lieber,* 59; autobiographical sketch, New York Public Library. Lieber's own copy of the poems is not in the Lieber papers, nor has the present writer been able to locate a printed copy in the United States. Manuscript copies exist in the Huntington Library and the University of Illinois Library. The Illinois copy is appended to a manuscript compilation by H. A. Rattermann, "Deutsche-amerikanische gedichte des 18. jahrhunderts." Perry gives as bibliographical data: Arnold Franz, *Vierzehn Wein- und Wonnelieder,* Berlin: T. H. Riemann, 1826. 12 mo. 32 pp. Lieber dedicated the poems to Karl Maria von Weber, composer, and C. F. Zelter, friend of Goethe.

[46] Bunsen, *Niebuhr,* II, 316; Lieber note with clipping, "Lieber and Niebuhr." Perry (ed.), *Lieber,* 60, misleadingly quotes Niebuhr in such a manner as to make it appear that he was writing for the fourth time to the King concerning Lieber. The letter to the King was a plea on Niebuhr's part not to be sent again as Minister to Rome.

years later did Lieber find that Jean Paul had written encouragingly, but the letter had been missent.[47]

In July the young man received through Niebuhr a position as tutor in the family of Christian G., Count von Bernstorff, Minister of Foreign Affairs. The police gave him permission to take the position, and he spent a happy, pastoral summer. Though the absolute power the count exercised over the peasants disturbed Lieber, he enjoyed merry excursions to seaside and lakes with the gay young ladies. He returned to Berlin in October. A relative who had not seen him since before he went to Greece found him quieter, an aesthete and literateur. "He knew a great many ladies, and had become very different from what he was in the old *Turner* days. To be sure, even then he used to write poetry, but his patriotic, gymnastic, semi-religious ideas had been succeeded by more serious intellectual interests." [48]

In the winter of 1825–26 Lieber found himself, at the age of twenty-seven, without future or vocation. That November the court of investigations again ordered him to appear, and he felt himself to be upon the brink of new persecutions. By now he was "fearfully weary of the repetition of these affairs." Though Niebuhr continued to work tirelessly in his behalf, the young man realized that for him Germany held no future. Keeping his plans secret for fear the police should reincarcerate him, he prepared for escape to England and political freedom.[49]

[47] Autobiographical sketch, New York Public Library; Perry (ed.), *Lieber,* 60–61; Lieber journals.

[48] Perry (ed.), *Lieber,* 60–61. The cousin, Bauer, was a theologian and also went to England. Dürre wrote that Lieber's character was "more absorbed and thoughtful." Dürre, "Errinerungen an Dr. Franz Lieber . . . ," *loc. cit.,* 286–88.

[49] Niebuhr wrote at Lieber's request a letter of recommendation to Christian G. Count von Bernstorff, Minister of Foreign Affairs, February 22, 1826. Probably Lieber had intended to apply for a consular position, but he did not deliver the letter. Perry (ed.), *Lieber,* 62–64, and manuscript journals.

III

Land of Liberty

I N THE late evening of May 17, 1826, a carriage clattered out of Berlin carrying Francis Lieber to a new world and a new life. Yet far from thrilling with anticipation, the young man was sunk in black melancholy. Breaking ties with his beloved parents was not easy. He had spared their feelings by not telling them of his departure, but once on his way the full realization that he might never see them again burst upon him, and he wept bitterly.

The uprooting was complete and irrevocable. Fifteen years were to elapse before his return—years which carried away his parents and molded the romantic young German into a solid American professor. As he left Berlin, Lieber had not yet made up his mind whether he would remain at his immediate destination, England, or sail on to the New World. Ten days later, caught up in the swirling kaleidoscope of London, he was too busy orienting himself to worry about painful leave-takings or uncertain future.

Putting up at the George and Vulture, where accommodations were both bad and expensive, Lieber busied himself carrying letters of introduction to Germans in London. One of them was to his idol, Karl Maria von Weber. He had been so captivated with Weber's stirring melodies for Karl Theodor Körner's patriotic lyrics that he had dedicated to the composer the *Fourteen Wine and Love Songs*. Lieber, with his usual uncanny knack for being at the right place at the most dramatic time, called on Sunday, June 4. The tubercular composer, exhausted from the task of completing and conducting his opera "Oberon," received his visitor while lying weak in his bed. Lieber enjoyed a unique

46

privilege in so doing him homage, for the next day Weber died.[1] With his funds dwindling, Lieber could spend very little time visiting idols. Instead he had to scurry around hunting a livelihood. Most Britons were not eager to employ an earnest young immigrant with a very slim grasp of the English language. A few hired him to teach them German, but none offered him steady work. For months Lieber struggled unhappily to win a bare subsistence. Once, after he had been ill, an anonymous friend saved him with a gift of £10. Other small sums came from articles on England for German publications and from itinerant instruction in German and Italian. Gradually the number of pupils increased—among them was a niece of the Rothschilds—and he posted from Regent Park to Islington, from Islington to Finsberry Square, and thence to Clapham, dispensing knowledge at six shillings a lesson.[2]

In November the line of duty brought him into the home of a well-to-do German, George Oppenheimer, who was a Bond Street merchant and a communicant of the Church of England. There he was hired to teach Italian to a beautiful, vivacious, and talented nineteen-year-old girl, the daughter Matilda. Lieber was a dashing and romantic figure, with a striking profile, steel-blue eyes, and black curly hair. His adventurous past, glib tongue, and sentimental technique had long since made him an incorrigible heartbreaker. But in Matilda he more than met his match. Together they read the romantic epic poetry of Tasso, and before long Lieber was pouring out verses of his own to the lovely young lady. By spring she had consented to become his wife.[3]

A man who wishes to marry must find permanent occupation. Lieber redoubled his search for stable employment. He even held some slight hope of a chair of Germanic languages in the proposed University of London. Through letters of introduction he had made the acquaintance of the dynamic group of English intel-

[1] Perry (ed.), *Lieber,* 64–68, contains a translation of Lieber's diary for the period. Lieber's uncertainty as to his plans when he left Prussia is shown by the fact that he carried a letter of introduction from Henrietta Herz to Edward Everett in America, dated May, 1826. Everett to Lieber, May 5, 1852, Lieber papers, Henry E. Huntington Library. All manuscripts referred to in this chapter, unless otherwise identified, are from this collection.

[2] Perry (ed.), *Lieber,* 64, 68; Lieber to Hillard, February 6, 1851.

[3] Perry (ed.), *Lieber,* 68. Several dozen poems to Matilda, written during this period, are in the Lieber papers. Letter to the writer from Mary Lieber, August 12, 1945.

lectuals who were planning the institution. These included the banker, George Grote, already gathering material for a great history of Greece; Henry Brougham, a prominent Whig advocate, later to be one of the authors of the Reform Act of 1832; and twenty-two-year-old John Stuart Mill, destined to higher fame than the others as one of the greatest *laissez-faire* philosophers.

These men encouraged Lieber; so he wrote to Germany for recommendations. From Niebuhr came an excellent one, accompanied by a warning that competition would be stiff. But delay was to be the greatest obstacle; long before the University of London took form, Lieber was established in America.[4]

While the young German did not find his niche in the institution planned by the Whigs and utilitarians, he did enrich his thinking with many of their political, economic, and educational ideas. Education translated into utilitarian terms especially intrigued him, and he assiduously studied the Lancastrian monitorial schools.

During these years the same "pedagogical fever" which, after the Jena defeat, had swept over Germany was racking England. Lieber heard Johann H. Pestalozzi's name there as often as at home, and marveled at the almost weekly appearance of new books on education, "sometimes good and frequently bad." Most of them sought to apply practical and profitable methods to scholarly enterprises, and usually failed because of their tendency to require inhuman speed.

Of the many novel systems, only the Lancastrian seemed to have much merit. Lieber's sharp eyes took in every detail of the instruction techniques involved. The oldest and most trusted pupils took lessons from the master and in turn taught the lower departments. By observing the strictest discipline and order, the master and monitors ran the organization "like a great piece of clock-work," at very low cost.

Cheapness was important. Lieber believed that it offset the requisite rote learning which educational theorists viewed with

[4] Niebuhr to Lieber, March 23, 1827, accompanied by a recommendation in English. A translation of this letter, containing Niebuhr's interesting views on English politics, appears in Lieber, *Reminiscences of Niebuhr*, 35–38, and in Lieber, *Miscellaneous Writings*, I, 67–69. Names omitted in the translation are: Mill and Cowell.

such repugnance. He believed all primary education functioned through memorization, and by the Lancastrian method vast numbers could learn who otherwise would find the cost prohibitive. Every individual should be able to read and write. Else "in the present state of the world, he is excluded from half the benefits of existence. Where a large population is imperfectly supplied with the means of instruction, schools of this character will be of great benefit." [5]

One of the young intellectuals who shared Lieber's enthusiasm for turning out educated citizens on the assembly line was Mrs. Sarah Austin, beautiful and clever wife of John Austin, who developed the famous Austinian theory of jurisprudence. While her husband was training some of England's most brilliant legal minds, Mrs. Austin was translating into English many of the German classics.

From Lancastrianism, Lieber's discussions with Mrs. Austin turned to utilitarianism in general. Soon the young Englishwoman introduced him to the aging Jeremy Bentham. Lieber agreed heartily with his aim to "maximize" human happiness. But whether through difficulties with English or a too-thorough grounding in German political principles, Lieber stayed out of the utilitarian orbit. In subsequent years he borrowed from Bentham for his own system, but also delivered the utilitarians some raps on the knuckles.

Although Lieber did not become a utilitarian, he found employment in America through the Benthamites. Mrs. Austin introduced him to one of the active exponents of utilitarian ideas, John Neal of Portland, Maine. Neal, though still in his early thirties, had produced at top speed a series of adventure novels second only to James Fenimore Cooper's in popularity. With the same headlong intensity, he had thrown himself into a dual advocacy of Bentham and of his native America in the British reviews. Gymnasiums also interested him. Was it not necessary to preserve a healthy body as a fit housing for an enlightened mind? And who was bet-

---

[5] Francis Lieber, *Ueber die Lancasterische Lehrweise* (Aus No. 122 und 123 der *literarischen Blätter der Börsen-Halle*) (Hamburg, 1826). A summary appears in [Francis Lieber], "Mutual Instruction," *Encyclopaedia Americana*, IX, 114–16. Lieber wrote the article September 14, 1826. Perry (ed.), *Lieber*, 67.

ter qualified than Lieber to administer physical training? Neal filled the German's head with fine schemes for a profitable career as a gymnasium director in America.[6]

Years had elapsed since Lieber had assisted *Turnvater* Jahn, but vigorously he returned to physical education and began giving free gymnastic instructions at the London Refuge of the Destitute. Soon his hopes for a lucrative position received a sharp boost. George Bond, a New Englander, was in London looking for a permanent instructor for the newly founded Boston gymnasium.

Physical education was an innovation in America—one of the revolutionary concepts which the handful of New England intellectuals who had studied in Germany brought back with them. The education of children, they expounded, should be physical as well as mental; in the same fashion that pedagogues systematically stuffed their minds with Greek, Latin, theology, and mathematical tables, physical instructors in a systematic and mechanical manner should develop their bodies to house their minds. Children should spend a certain number of hours weekly in the gymnasium —neither for pleasure nor military training, but to make them better able to earn a lucrative living.

A year earlier, in 1825, Charles Beck, who had been a fellow pupil with Lieber under *Turnvater* Jahn, founded the first American gymnasium. It was at Round Hill School, where George Bancroft and Joseph Cogswell were trying to transplant to America some of the educational concepts they had learned in German universities. At Cambridge, Charles Follen likewise was promulgating Jahn's ideas. In addition to his German classes at Harvard and his lectures on jurisprudence before Boston attorneys, he gave informal physical instruction to Harvard students. The enthusiasm spread to Boston, where a group of notables formed a gymnasium association and persuaded the busy Follen to act as temporary instructor. In the fall of 1826, at the same time that Bond was in London, he began his classes.[7]

Wishing nothing less than the best, the Bostonians had aspired to obtain *Turnvater* Jahn himself. Failing in that, their agent con-

[6] Perry (ed.), *Lieber*, 67.

[7] [Lieber], "Gymnastics," *Encyclopaedia Americana*, VI, 122; Perry (ed.), *Lieber*, 67–68; Follen, *Works of Charles Follen*, I, 152 *et seq.;* [Lieber] "[Review of] *A Treatise on Gymnastics* . . . ," *loc. cit.*, 126, 240.

sidered a Mr. Buck. Anxiously, Lieber pressed his credentials upon Bond. They could hardly have been more excellent. Jahn, in a notarized recommendation, highly lauded the applicant's morals, ability, and patriotism. Major General Ernst H. A. von Pfuel likewise commended his ability as a swimmer and instructor in a military swimming school.[8]

Why not establish a swimming school in addition to the gymnasium, proposed Lieber. He offered to come if the gymnasium association would provide him with apparatus and ground, free passage to America, and a guarantee of eight hundred dollars for the first year. In addition he would like an advance of funds to establish the swimming school, which he would operate as his own private enterprise. He gave Bond a copy of the proposals and recommendations to forward to Boston, and the New Englander assured Lieber that if the association could not obtain Mr. Buck, he should have the position.[9]

For months Lieber waited while the Bostonians deliberated. In the late winter Charles Follen persuaded the directors to hire Lieber, and wrote offering him the position. Jubilantly, Lieber accepted.[10]

In his enthusiasm Lieber envisaged himself already an American. Toward the new shores he directed the ardent nationalistic emotion with which he had regarded Germany. America would fulfill all the aspirations which his fatherland had so thoroughly crushed. There he would pursue his soaring ambitions unhampered by bureaucratic ministries and police spies. Never again would his unorthodox ideas stand in the way of advancement or lead to a dark cell at Köpenick. He looked forward rather than backward and thought of himself not as an exile, but as a prospective citizen of the United States.[11]

Niebuhr thought Lieber's decision wise and wished him as

[8] Lieber to George Bond, September 21, 1826, enclosing copies and translations of recommendations by Jahn and de Phael [von Pfuel], also a list of six proposals, Boston Public Library. These were printed in the *American Journal of Education,* I (1826), 699–701. Jahn's original recommendation, dated August 1, 1826, is in the Lieber papers.

[9] Lieber to Bond, September 21, 1826, Boston Public Library.

[10] Lieber to Bond, January [1827], Boston Public Library; Follen to Lieber, February 21, 22, 1827, Lieber papers; Lieber to Dr. John G. Warren, April 3, 1827, Massachusetts Historical Society.

[11] Lieber to Warren, April 3, 1827, Massachusetts Historical Society.

much happiness as possible "in a foreign and not inspiring country." The historian counseled Lieber against falling "into an idolatry of the country and that state of things which is so dazzling because it shows the material world in a favorable light. . . . Remain a German, and without counting hour and day, yet say to yourself that the hour and day will come when you will be able to return." [12]

But Lieber, reading avidly everything he could find about America, dreamed of a permanent career in the land of personal freedom. He would make the trip alone, and, when he had established himself, send for his beloved Matilda. From Manchester, where he paid a farewell visit to his fiancée, he wrote his family: "Believe me that I do not expect a paradise, but I look forward eagerly to the prospect of a more settled and active life, and an honorable and useful position in a young republic, which, however imperfect it may still be, yet gives a field for the practice and application of talent and ability." While he would miss the intellectual life of Europe, he would prefer being "in a land of progress, where civilization is building her home, while in Europe we can scarcely tell whether there is progression or retrogression." [13]

Lieber glowed with the warmest expectations during the voyage. Transformed into a thoroughgoing republican, he felt he was leaving a Europe "too petrified and ossified" in the customs of the Middle Ages to accept the new and greater ideas which were finding their soil, and taking root, in the United States. "There never has existed, to my knowledge, a government that has been formed so entirely for the good of the people." [14]

Lieber landed in New York on June 20, 1827—twelve years, almost to the hour, after he had fallen wounded in the Battle of Namur. Fascinated by the new city, amazed at its cleanliness and prosperity, he wrote to Dr. John G. Warren, president of the gymnasium association, that he would sail for Boston in a few days, as soon as he had "seen some schools, hospitals and other

[12] Niebuhr to Lieber, September 13, 1827, Lieber papers, translated in Lieber, *Reminiscences of Niebuhr*, 38–44, and Lieber, *Miscellaneous Writings*, I, 70–73.
[13] Perry (ed.), *Lieber*, 69–70. Lieber to his parents, May 12, June 10, 1827.
[14] Perry (ed.), *Lieber*, 70–71.

MATILDA LIEBER

A portrait probably painted in London prior to 1821,
now in the possession of Mrs. Charles F. Stearns

monuments of national civilization and . . . done some businesses." [15]

Boston was a prosperous commercial city of about sixty thousand, built on a narrow peninsula stretching out into Boston Harbor. Its crooked and narrow streets were well paved and drained; almost all of them had sidewalks of large, square flags. The market-house, courthouse, and other fine public buildings, granite-façaded in the Doric style, pleased Lieber, who felt them especially suited to a republic. Even the piers were sometimes made of granite. Thousands of feet of them ran into the sea on the eastern half-circle of the town. Too, an obelisk of granite was being erected at Bunker Hill. Lieber told the Bostonians: "Your granite and marble are as great a blessing as the most bountiful cornfields."

"Everything—houses, gardens, streets, and men and women—wears the appearance of prosperity," the stranger remarked, and nowhere did he see a beggar. The Statehouse, standing on a hill overlooking the green Common; the lovely country houses with their luxuriant gardens, stretching out as far as Commercial Point, and the water view beyond, all delighted Lieber.

Along the busy wharves and in the crowded markets he could see the material basis for this prosperity, for wealth still came to Boston more through her ships than through her factories. She was the second commercial city in America, and her warehouses were overflowing with exotic goods: bales of lambs' wool, barrels of whale oil from New Bedford, chests of Souchong tea, puncheons of St. Croix rum, cases of Bengal indigo, tierces of rice, bags of crude saltpeter, tongs of Santo Domingo logwood, boxes of soap and mold candles, and barrels of Danish hard tallow and of fresh Genesee flour. Even two beautiful antelopes from Smyrna were offered for sale.

Concerning the people of Boston, Lieber commented a fortnight after his arrival: "It is more difficult to judge of men than

---

[15] Lieber to Warren, June 20, 1827, Massachusetts Historical Society. This, like all Lieber's letters to Americans, was in English. For six or seven years, Lieber continued to feel more at home when writing German than English, and used it customarily in his journals and letters to his wife. However, he studied English assiduously and within a year was writing articles which after editing could hardly be detected as the work of a foreigner.

of granite, and I have not been here long enough to form an opinion." Not until later did the German come to see close similarity between most Bostonians and their native rock, for Boston of 1827 was disposed to receive the learned foreigner with the utmost cordiality. Self-conscious and introspective, opulent enough to enjoy leisure in which to cultivate the arts and sciences, the leading citizens of the metropolis were trying almost as assiduously to make it the Athens, as to maintain it as the market place, of the United States.

For the erudite or would-be patron of letters, Messrs. Hilliard and Grey sold Latin and Greek classics, scientific works, belles-lettres, and, on subscription, John Lingard's many-volumed *History of England*. Professor P. Bachi gave lessons in Italian and Spanish to the daughters of the elite. Elders met to gossip at the Athenaeum or displayed themselves at the hall over the New Market, where for twenty-five cents one could see Louis David's "Coronation of Napoleon"—a great painting in the eyes of Boston because its figure-crowded canvas was thirty-six feet long and twenty-six feet high. Heatedly the music lovers were arguing in the columns of a newspaper the merits of the "Handel and Haydn Society"—Lieber thought they sang wretchedly. Anti-Sabbatarians pointed out the innocence of Sunday excursioning to Nahant, but a reactionary, failing to recognize the new intellectual enlightenment of the American Athens, thundered back in Puritanical wrath: "Abolish the Sabbath, or even observe it but thrice a month . . . and our country will see robbery and oppression and bloodshed and the blackest of the black catalogue of crimes legalized by the very power that should protect it, and the world will see once more a republic in ruins." [16]

Polite Boston tried to suppress such rude outbursts of its dour past. Shoving Puritan ancestors into the closet and turning the key, it dressed its fine-looking daughters in Parisian fashions and engaged in easy and gay social life. Like a *nouveau riche*, it displayed an insatiable craving for intellectual prestige. Thus the tremendous acquisition of books for the Athenaeum—soon to include Jared Sparks's masterly coup of a large part of George Wash-

[16] Perry (ed.), *Lieber*, 71–76; Boston *Daily Advertiser*, July 6, 1827; Boston *Columbian Centinel*, June 30, July 7, September 22, 1827.

ington's library. Thus the shaking of Harvard out of its moribund torpor by the infusion of new scholarly zeal, brought back from the universities of Germany by George Ticknor, the modern language student, and Edward Everett, the polished classicist. Through them, New England had discovered the pre-eminent superiority of German scholarship and had shown a great willingness to welcome Charles Beck and Charles Follen. Scant wonder that those who combined mammon worship with the deification of the intellect bowed to Dr. Francis Lieber of Prussia, so highly lauded by the great Niebuhr, as a new and satisfactory idol.

The German liberal had arrived in Boston at the most exciting time of the year—just as the country was preparing to celebrate Independence Day. Doctor Warren sent Lieber an invitation to attend, and on the Fourth of July they went together to the Statehouse. The German arrayed himself, for the first time in his life, in full dress "—tights and all that,—a regular, newly imported London fashionable."

The celebration was entirely typical, but to Lieber, a subject of the despotic King of Prussia, every minute was thrilling. The senate chamber of the Statehouse was filled with dignitaries. Warren introduced his guest to the governor, splendid in uniform. Then in a long procession the band, the Independent Cadets, officials, guests, and the faculty and students of Harvard College marched slowly through the streets to the Old South Church. There the Reverend George Ripley offered a fervent prayer, and a leading attorney delivered the conventional oration. Others—even newspaper correspondents—might have dozed, but the serious young immigrant followed the speech very carefully and approved every word, later saying: "He spoke of the dangers to which a republic is exposed, such as false ambition, party spirit, and sectional prejudice, and reminded his hearers of the great deeds accomplished and of the prosperity of the entire country."

The party then returned to a collation at the Statehouse, at which elegant toasts beyond number were washed down with draught after draught of suitable beverages. At length the governor turned to Lieber for a toast. The pleased German meant to give, "Liberty to all the civilized world," but it came out in English, "May all nations soon enjoy liberty who deserve it." Never again would Lieber's linguistic inadequacies lead to such a simple utterance. His companion, Dr. Follen, in three years had learned American ways, and proposed magnificently: "The Ark of human liberty, floating upon the deluge which covered the West and the East, and bearing in its bowels the seeds of the regeneration of Mankind." [17]

Quickly Lieber established himself in a circle of Germans and Germanophiles. Although his only close friends from Germany were his fellow refugee, Follen, and the Prussian consul, Gossler, he found a surprisingly large number of New Englanders who either had studied in Germany or had learned its language and literature. To Edward Everett, austere young classicist who had abandoned his Harvard chair for a seat in Congress, Lieber brought a letter of introduction from Henrietta Herz. Everett had been a favorite of the *Höfratin*'s during his years of study at Berlin. By receiving a Ph.D. from Göttingen in 1817 he had earned the distinction of being the first American to gain a German degree. Niebuhr had advised his protégé to cultivate Everett as his closest American friend, but the cold, highly polished New Englander was to prove none too congenial a friend, though a pleasant enough acquaintance.[18]

Inland, at Northampton's Round Hill School, were Cogswell and Bancroft, who had studied together at Göttingen. Bancroft was only a few months younger than Lieber, and like him had obtained the Ph.D. degree at a remarkably early age—only a month after Lieber. Afterwards he too had attended Schleiermacher's lectures in Berlin and had become a friend of the Humboldt brothers. Cogswell had reveled in the three hundred thousand books at Göttingen, a full eight times as many as in sedate Harvard's proud collection. He had returned with dreams of immense American collections. By putting them into effect he became one of America's first great librarians.

Other New Englanders who had not visited in Europe also were interested in Germany and sought Lieber's conversation. John Pickering, son of the arch-Federalist Timothy Pickering, had recently moved his law practice from Salem to Boston. In his spare

[17] Perry (ed.), *Lieber*, 71–76; Boston *Columbian Centinel*, July 7, 1827.
[18] Everett to Lieber, May 5, 1852; Niebuhr to Lieber, September 13, 1827.

time he mastered all the principal European and Semitic tongues, was even familiar with several of the Chinese group, and became a leading authority on the languages of the North American Indians. To Lieber, who had acquired a love for philology through Niebuhr and William von Humboldt, here indeed was a stimulating friend.

Amidst these fascinating acquaintances Lieber basked in his honored position as instructor of gymnastics and swimming. He opened a summer quarter at the gymnasium, which children and their parents could attend for from three to six dollars. The gymnastics, advertised the trustees, would make weak and unhealthy individuals into athletes, endow children with fine constitutions in which to house their literary acquirements, and enable busy men of sedentary occupations to gain "the exercise required to preserve health in a shorter time than they could obtain it in any other way." [19]

With his gymnastic program launched, Lieber devoted himself to founding the swimming school, an unknown enterprise in America. Though the season was already well advanced, the swimming teacher obtained a site, lumber, and carpenters, and supervised construction of dressing rooms and a large semicircular enclosure on the bay, near the milldam. Lieber had copied both the plans and the method of construction from Major General von Pfuel.

Lieber was not able to begin sessions until July 23—a day which ushered in a cold, rainy week—because of delay in construction. Not until the beginning of August could the school open in earnest. Lieber had planned to charge ten dollars per person, but, because of the lost time, reduced his fees to seven dollars. The school failed to flourish. Few thrifty Bostonians wished to waste money upon such foolishness. [20]

Recognizing that training in swimming often saved lives, the Massachusetts Humane Society hailed the advent of the school, and arranged with Dr. Lieber to take four pupils from each of the

[19] Perry (ed.), *Lieber*, 71–76; Boston *Daily Advertiser*, June 30, 1827, *et seq.*; Boston *Columbian Centinel*, June 30, 1827.

[20] The plans for the swimming school are in the Lieber papers; Boston *Daily Advertiser*, July 12–August 6, 1827; Boston *Columbian Centinel*, July 16–28 *et seq.*, 1827; M. A. de Wolfe Howe, *The Humane Society of the Commonwealth of Massachusetts* . . . (Boston, 1918), 113–14.

Boston public schools and teach them swimming at four special hours daily. The German would instruct a total of thirty-six pupils for one hundred dollars. But only eight appeared for the free training, and Lieber received sixty dollars instead. Despite this discouraging lack of patronage, Lieber continued his instructions assiduously.[21]

One morning in early September, President John Quincy Adams, himself a remarkable swimmer, visited the school.

"After I had explained my plan to him," Lieber recounted, "1 asked him if he would do me the honour to swim with me, and if he preferred, we would go outside the enclosure, in order to avoid the frolicking boys. . . . The old man looked at the boys, and said: 'No, I prefer to stay here, if they will not laugh at me. . . .' We prepared ourselves . . . and this man of sixty-one sprang headlong into the water from a spring-board six feet high. . . . He praised the school, and expressed the wish that there were many establishments of the kind in the country, which would greatly tend to promote the public health." [22]

With the coming of cool weather, the swimming school closed and Lieber turned his full attention to the management of the

[21] Boston *Columbian Centinel,* July 28, 1827. In the Lieber papers, Library of Congress, is an admission slip issued to J. P. Bradlee, for the season 1828, in return for a payment of $10.75. On the reverse side, Lieber published the regulations:

"1. The School will be opened every day, (Sundays excepted) from half past five in the morning, until one o'clock—and from four o'clock, until eight in the evening.

"2. No person will be permitted to swim without swimming drawers.

"3. Every pupil will put himself under the direction of the assistant to whom the Instructor refers him.

"4. No pupil will be allowed to swim without the particular superintendence of a teacher, until he has proved himself able to swim half an hour at least, uninterruptedly—and those who have attained this, will put a red cord round their swimming drawers.

"5. Upon the word being given, *'Leave the water,'* by the Instructor, or one of his assistants, every person will be required to obey the call immediately.

"6. Boys will not be allowed to enter any other apartments than those assigned to them.

"7. As a conformity to the above Regulations is indispensable, and a proper regard to good order, decorum and safety are deemed essential to the Institution, the Instructor feels obliged to consider a violation of either in a pupil, as dissolving his connection with the establishment and its privileges for the season. FRANCIS LIEBER."

Lieber owned two treatises on swimming, now in the University of California library: *Ueber das Schwimmen* (Berlin, 1817), and *The Art of Swimming . . .* (Baltimore, *circa* 1821).

[22] Lieber to his parents, September 6, 1827; Perry (ed.), *Lieber,* 77–78.

Boston gymnasium. But Lieber's pupils were few. At the opening term, a year earlier, about four hundred had enrolled, but the fad soon wore off as caricatures of the gymnasts appeared in print shops. The monotony of the regimented exercises drove off those unaffected by ridicule. After about a year only four pupils remained and the gymnasium closed.[23]

Long before it failed, Lieber accurately diagnosed its ills and outlined an American plan for physical education, which he introduced at least in part at the Boston gymnasium. His insuperable difficulty was that, to be popular with the students, the gymnasium had to offer recreation; to be popular with the parents that paid the bills, it had to offer tangible proof of its economic worth.[24]

Hence Lieber, through the Boston press, emphasized the profit motive for body building.[25] Likewise, the gymnasium should play an important role in national defense. It might well replace the corrupt training day when every able-bodied man came to carouse and drill halfheartedly in the town square. Every village should have its gymnasium—a stanch bulwark of the republic. Through the monitorial system, one or two instructors might easily direct a thousand pupils. As for the boys, they would develop strong bodies and easily learn to become obedient to military discipline.

To make these exercises more alluring to Americans, Lieber advocated that they take the form of sports. Regimented calisthenics were easy to direct, but individualistic New England boys felt no joy or power through acting in unison. Nor did the equally individualistic Lieber encourage it. Instead he recommended enterprise, competition, and participation in sports. Even in Berlin he had noticed a tendency toward a loss of interest in calisthenics when youths became more mature. For Americans he advocated a comprehensive physical education program fitted to age, sex, and individual requirements.[26]

---

[23] Directors of the Boston gymnasium to Lieber, September 22, 1827; Leonard, *Pioneers of Modern Physical Training*, 41.

[24] See especially [Lieber], "[Review of] *A Treatise on Gymnastics . . . ,*" *loc. cit.*, 126–50.

[25] "Hegeia [*sic*]," Boston *Columbian Centinel*, September 29, 1827.

[26] [Lieber], "[Review of] *A Treatise on Gymnastics . . . ,*" *loc. cit.*, 141–46; [Lieber], "Gymnastics," *Encyclopaedia Americana*, VI, 122; [Lieber], "[Review of] *A Treatise on Calisthenic Exercises, arranged for the Private Tuition of Ladies.* By

The young physical instructor criticized all existing programs for women as being mere modifications of those for men and aimed at the male objective of strength. Instead, he wished to build a program for women based upon "two great ends . . . *health* and *grace.*" Dancing taught grace, but soon became too enervating; horseback riding was available to but few; calisthenics or drill overdeveloped muscles and bored participants. As a solution Lieber proposed exercises not unlike eurythmics—graceful, rapid walking, "a variety of movements of the legs . . . , balancing, . . . [and] gymnastical plays."

Lieber glowingly predicted that by following this program Americans could become "a race endowed with bodily powers equal to those of the ancient Spartans, and minds like those of the accomplished Athenians." [27]

Bostonians yearning for the brains of Athenians and the brawn of Spartans were too scarce to enable an enterprising but poor young immigrant to bring his bride-elect to the New World; so Lieber soon turned his attention to other, more lucrative fields. Nevertheless, he remained a lifelong advocate of physical training. When, in 1834, he drew up a comprehensive plan of elementary and secondary education for the proposed Girard College for Orphans, he stressed the need for a well-rounded system of instruction which would include hygiene and sex education as well as swimming and personal education.[28]

Although Lieber's writings on physical education were one of his minor contributions, they did point the way toward a system not to be adopted until the twentieth century. Not until physical education experts had tried and discarded several formal systems did they turn to competitive and recreative sports, without know-

Signor Voarino . . . [and] *The Elements of Gymnastics, for Boys, and of Calisthenics, for Young Ladies* . . . by Gustavus Hamilton . . . ," *American Journal of Education,* II (1827), 487–91. This last was probably Lieber's first article in an American magazine; it contains his fullest discussion of physical education for women.

27 "Hegeia [*sic*]," Boston *Columbian Centinel,* September 29, 1827; [Lieber] "[Review of] *A Treatise on Gymnastics* . . . ," *loc. cit.,* 141; [Lieber], "[Review of] *A Treatise on Calisthenic Exercises* . . . ," *loc. cit.,* 487–91.

28 Francis Lieber, *A Constitution and Plan of Education for Girard College for Orphans, With an Introductory Report, Laid Before the Board of Trustees* (Philadelphia, 1834), 112–20. At the age of fifty-four, Lieber spent a week instructing and swimming with ten girls. Lieber to Samuel B. Ruggles, August 24, 1852, Lieber papers, Library of Congress.

ing that Lieber had recommended them nearly seventy-five years before.

When, in the fall of 1827, Lieber realized that the gymnasium was a passing fad, he cast about for other means of adding to his income. Through the aid of Niebuhr, he became Western Hemisphere correspondent for the seven periodicals published by Johann F. C. Cotta, the German newspaper magnate. To each he sent suitable material concerning not only the United States but also neighboring British provinces and Latin America. Political affairs went to the *Allgemeine Zeitung,* single anecdotes to the *Morgenblatt,* extensive statistical and ethnographical accounts to the *Politische Annalen,* and so on.

Niebuhr advised Lieber sagely on his new duties: he should be as conscientious and letter-perfect as though he were an ambassador sending home reports to the foreign office. Above all, he should send "no political dissertations and generalities, but facts simply and concisely related." In a day when newspapers crammed their columns with violently partisan editorials, it was a large order but an exceedingly valuable one. It sent Lieber to newspapers, periodicals, pamphlets, and to notable personages. He familiarized himself with every phase of American life which he thought might be of interest to readers. Thus he gathered quantities of valuable information for himself, and at the same time was one of the first interpreters of America for the Germans.[29]

Lieber continued his correspondence to German newspapers for the better part of a decade. He sent Baron Cotta long descriptions of the American countryside, interviews with famous Americans he met, accounts of strange customs, and interesting anecdotes. He clipped and translated large quantities of the material, but in addition prepared some long, serious essays. One of these, on American banks, Cotta praised warmly.[30]

---

[29] Niebuhr to Lieber, September 13, 1827, Lieber papers, translated in Lieber, *Reminiscences of Niebuhr,* 38–44, and Lieber, *Miscellaneous Writings,* I, 70–73. Lieber showed the letter to Follen who was impressed with Niebuhr's excellent advice upon the duties of a newspaper correspondent. Follen, *Works of Charles Follen,* I, 213.

[30] Perry (ed.), *Lieber,* 87 *et passim.* Much of this material and opinion found its way into Lieber, *Letters to a Gentleman in Germany.* Beginning with American newspapers of May, 1827, Lieber accumulated vast quantities of clippings and notes, now in the Lieber papers, Huntington Library.

Lieber's accounts were rambling, discursive, and tended toward the first person, but they were seldom dull. Throughout they became tinctured with the prejudices of the prominent Americans with whom Lieber associated and the newspapers that he read. The young German was thoroughly enthusiastic about America: Here the middle class had already won every issue for which he had fought in Prussia. Here the *bourgeoisie* were free to amass wealth in any way they saw fit, untrammeled by the government. On the busy wharves and in the fine parlors one could see the unparalleled benefits of this excellent system. Even the laborers were far better off than those in Europe, though they tended to get out of hand and tamper with the government. But like his friends and his newspapers, Lieber in a few years came to feel that by ousting President Jackson one could eliminate the remaining evils and protect the banker and merchant. The unobservant might easily think that the revolutionary had turned reactionary when he reached the land of promise, but the same middle-class liberalism that had plunged Lieber into Prussian prisons made him a "safe" companion of the Kents, Biddles, and Storys.

IV

Francis Lieber: Encyclopedist

I E B E R lay on his bed one afternoon daydreaming of schemes which might make him well-to-do and famous. He longed to marry Matilda but could not possibly afford to do so on his uncertain income as a swimming and gymnastics instructor and a correspondent for Cotta's newspapers.

Jared Sparks had created a furore in Boston by bringing eight trunkloads of Washington's letters from Mt. Vernon to edit and publish. Perhaps Lieber could translate some of the more interesting ones into German, but Sparks's editing was still in a beginning stage.[1]

As he lay staring at the ceiling, the young man conceived a much better plan—one that might even pay well enough to bring Matilda to the New World. He might translate into English the excellent German encyclopedia by Brockhaus—the twelve-volume *Conversations-Lexikon.* It had been a tremendous success in Germany and should sell well in America too. Since its original publication in 1812, Brockhaus had sold eighty thousand sets, not counting two pirated editions in German and translations into Danish, Swedish, Dutch, and French.[2]

---

[1] Lieber to Sparks, September 7, 1827, Sparks papers, Harvard University. H. B. Adams, *The Life and Writings of Jared Sparks* . . . , 2 vols. (Boston, 1893), I, 311–12. Later, Professor Frederick von Raumer of Berlin supervised a condensed German translation.

[2] The account of how Lieber conceived the idea is in LaBorde, *History of South Carolina College,* 397. Lieber endorsed this as correct in a memorandum to Norman Lieber, 1859, Lieber papers, Henry E. Huntington Library. All manuscripts referred to in this chapter, unless otherwise identified, are from this collection. Lieber based his translation upon the seventh edition, *Allgemeine deutsche Real—Encyklopaedie für die gebildeten stände.* (*Conversations-Lexikon*) (Leipzig, 1827–29), and *Allgemeine Encyclopadie der Wissenschaften und Kunste in alphabetischer Folge* . . . (Leipzig, 1818). For details concerning the work, see Francis Lieber (ed.), *Encyclopaedia Americana,* I, lv–v. It remains the standard German encyclopedia; *Der Grosse Brockhaus; handbuch des wissens* . . . , 20 vols. (Leipzig, 1928–35).

It was an audacious idea for one who had taken his first English lesson less than two years before, but Lieber lacked neither self-assurance nor persuasiveness. Quickly he drafted a prospectus and circulated it among his German-reading New England friends. Ticknor, Bancroft, Everett, and others familiar with the merits of the *Conversations-Lexikon* wrote letters heartily endorsing his scheme.[3]

Fortunately, too, Americans needed a good, cheap encyclopedia containing articles on their native land. Encyclopedias aplenty were on sale, but without exception they were massive, almost prohibitively expensive publications. Clearly the field was open for a work occupying a middle ground between newspapers and libraries, inexpensive and understandable, and suitable for widespread American sale.[4]

Nevertheless, Lieber could find no Boston publisher willing to risk so extensive and costly an enterprise. Only one firm in America was likely to undertake its promotion. That was the Philadelphia house of Messrs. Carey, Lea & Carey, which since its foundation in the 1790's by Mathew Carey, an Irish immigrant, had grown to be the pre-eminent American publisher. Through low-priced mass-production methods and a host of glib-tongued itinerant book agents, headed by Parson Weems of the cherry tree legend, it had extended its markets as far west as the Mississippi.[5]

To Carey's, Lieber carried his scheme in mid-January of 1828. He obtained a three months' leave of absence from his few gymnasium charges easily enough and started southward. He offered the publishers a wide array of suggestions—not only would he edit an encyclopedia, but if they did not like that he would prepare a Latin dictionary, or even one of the foolish but fashionable souvenir albums.[6]

[3] George Ticknor to Lieber, November 25, 1827; Charles Follen to Lieber, November 23, 1827; Everett to Lieber, November 17, 1827; George Bancroft to Lieber, December 22, 1827, originals in Lieber papers; published with a prospectus in an advertisement, *North American Review*, XXVII (1828).

[4] [John Neal], "Encyclopaedia Americana," *North American Review*, XXXIV, (1832), 265; [Robert Walsh], "Encyclopaedia Americana," *American Quarterly Review*, VI (1829), 347–49.

[5] Adams, *Life and Writings of Jared Sparks*, I, 48–49; *Niles' Weekly Register*, February 21, 1829; Lea & Febiger, *One Hundred and Fifty Years of Publishing, 1785–1935* (Philadelphia, 1935), 20–23.

[6] Lieber to Matilda Oppenheimer, January 18, 1828, copy, Lieber papers. The letter, badly mutilated, appears in part in Perry (ed.), *Lieber*, 81.

The cautious Careys wished time to ponder the encyclopedia scheme. While they did so, Lieber enlarged his circle of acquaintances and continued his travels. He took a letter of introduction to Peter Duponceau, "one of the most learned men in America," who had come with Frederick W. L. G., Baron von Steuben, a half century earlier to serve in the Continental Army. In the intervening years he had pleaded scores of cases before the Supreme Court and in his spare time had written eruditely on the Indian language.

Lieber tried to interest the philologist in a proposed association for the study of the languages of the North American Indians and the Sandwich Islanders. The society would preserve the findings of missionaries, and, with the aid of the American government and some European governments, collect and publish the investigations in a journal, called, perhaps, the *Indian Library,* with Lieber as editor. Neither society nor magazine materialized, but Duponceau was friendly and promised to contribute to the encyclopedia.[7]

Lieber was even more impressed when he visited Joseph Bonaparte, brother of Napoleon and former King of Spain and Naples. The exiled Joseph maintained a mansion in Philadelphia and a country-seat at near-by Bordentown, New Jersey. Both were filled with paintings which delighted the art-starved Lieber.

On a subsequent visit he was in ecstasy over Joseph's friendliness. He was the "kindliest, worthiest, mildest, and most modest old man" the former Prussian infantryman had ever met. Lieber recalled: "His short stature and his bearing reminded me of Napoleon as I had seen him in the midst of his bodyguard in front of the castle in Berlin." Joseph discoursed on a multitude of interesting things about his family, his career, the Revolution, and Robespierre, until Lieber felt that he saw Napoleon himself before him and for a time forgot his lifelong Francophobia. In a detailed correspondence, Joseph supplied the young editor with material for the many encyclopedia articles on the Bonaparte family and the Empire.[8]

---

[7] Lieber to Matilda Oppenheimer, January 18, 1828, copy; the plan for an association is in a manuscript, Lieber, "The Indian Languages of America . . . ," January 21, 1828. Lieber, "Comment on Duponceau," copy, *circa* August 5, 1833; Lieber to Duponceau, November 5, 1829, Historical Society of Pennsylvania.

[8] Lieber to Matilda Oppenheimer, January 18, 1828, copy; Lieber to A. D. White,

From visiting the former king, Lieber went to the dirty, scraggly city of Washington to meet the present leaders of the United States. They were already preoccupied with the fierce presidential campaign of 1828. The inquiring young German went everywhere and met everyone. He even broke away from the Adams men with whom he had associated almost exclusively in Boston and met some of the prominent Jackson supporters. Senator Edward Livingston of Louisiana presented him with a copy of the penal code he was pressing upon Congress. Vice-President Calhoun, who hoped by climbing upon the Jackson bandwagon to become President himself four years later, was so cordial to Lieber at a ball that the young German afterwards went around to his home to call.

Congress, the National House where he stayed, drawing rooms and street corners all rocked with political discussion. The barrage of partisan talk inspired him to indite:

> Now Jonathan let's talk a little on election,
> It is a relish such a chit chat chit
> But one condition, whilst we so converse
> Give up to chew and spit.[9]

Lieber was to have little time for political chitchat in the months ahead. Upon his return to Philadelphia he found that the Careys had decided to go ahead with the encyclopedia. He would be editor and entrepreneur with full authority to enlist whatever aid he could find to translate and remold the *Conversations-Lexikon* into an American publication. His recompense would be a substantial flat fee rather than a royalty. To Lieber, launching an uncertain project, this seemed a splendid arrangement; in later years when sales mounted incredibly he thought it little short of fraud.[10]

August 17, 1871; Perry (ed.), *Lieber*, 84. Some 29 letters from Joseph Bonaparte, together with 15 documents, are at Johns Hopkins University. Included is a draft article on "Lucian Bonaparte," which illustrates how Lieber wrote and revised manuscript.

[9] Lieber, notebook entitled "London, Boston, Poetry." Lieber to Livingston, March 1, 1828, Boston Public Library.

[10] Lieber to Matilda Oppenheimer, January 18, 1828, copy; Lieber to Ticknor, April 23, 1828, translation. Neither the Lieber papers nor the records of Carey, Lea & Carey at the Historical Society of Pennsylvania and the American Antiquarian Society contain any details of financial arrangements. The publishing house records

In April, 1828, Lieber returned to Boston, glowing with enthusiasm and overflowing with plans. Immediately he plunged into his gargantuan task, and prepared a flamboyant eight-page prospectus for the *North American Review*. The readers of the *Review* had never before seen such a huge advertisement for a single work, and that the opulent Philadelphia publishers would unhesitatingly spend forty dollars in one burst of fanfare was an earnest of the magnificence of their forthcoming production.[11]

To bring forth a work in keeping with so ambitious a prospectus was a difficult undertaking, as Lieber soon began to discover. He needed an assistant badly; so he hired twenty-four-year-old Edward Wigglesworth, scion of a long line of Puritan divines and theology professors, who had recently finished reading law with Judge William Prescott. Lieber and Wigglesworth set up their office at the corner of State and Exchange Streets and hired a dozen persons to translate at fifty cents per German page and numerous others to write original articles for a dollar a page—the same rate of pay as the *North American Review*.

Lieber especially began to emphasize the writing of original articles, as he found that to suit his readers the encyclopedia would have to be far more than a mere translation of the *Conversations-Lexikon*. He must delete hundreds of articles and at the same time rewrite or add hundreds of others. Lieber and Wigglesworth undertook much of this themselves, but also scoured the young republic for its most distinguished authorities as writers of the main articles.[12]

Facile Robert Walsh, editor of the *American Quarterly Review*, supplied a number of lengthy American biographies, in keeping with a fad for lives of colonial and Revolutionary heroes. Adams,

for these years could not be located. Lieber told Beaumont in 1831 that the publishers were giving him "the bagatelle of 100,000 francs"—about $20,000. This is probably a correct approximation, since Lieber, not the publishers, paid translators, writers, and editorial assistants. G. W. Pierson, *Tocqueville and Beaumont in America* (New York, 1938), 377. Lieber said he had only a few hundred dollars left upon completion of the work, and years later expressed his sense of outrage in a letter to Hillard, November 4, 1856.

[11] *North American Review*, XXVII (1828).

[12] *Ibid.*, and details in the Lieber papers. Jared Sparks met Lieber in Washington in February, 1828, and "suggested to him the expediency of enlisting several gentlemen as contributors to supply the deficiency of American articles." Sparks promised to contribute articles on history and biography to the first volume. Adams, *Life and Writings of Jared Sparks*, II, 48–49.

Allen, Arnold, Barlow—all the Revolutionary great—paraded in full panoply and alphabetical order through the pages of the *Americana*. The parade stretched to such an alarming length that the warriors all but crowded out philosophers, physicians, and theologians. Benedict Arnold occupied a disproportionate nine pages—twice as much as Franklin and nearly the same as a de-Weemsed Washington.[13]

Like American patriots, American fauna received marked attention. Dr. John D. Godman, anatomy professor at Rutgers Medical College, rewrote for the encyclopedia large segments of his three-volume *Natural History of the American Quadrupeds*. His articles contained not only detailed technical information, but interesting personal observations on the birds and animals familiar to American readers. There was the alligator (the males roar alarmingly during the mating season), the bat (which Dr. Godman suspected carried bedbugs into houses), and the bison (whose large herds were sure to become nonexistent because of great slaughter with European weapons).[14]

Here was the beginning of a panel of writers for a truly American encyclopedia. Armed with these mainstays whom Carey's had obtained, Lieber began to call upon a host of American specialists for articles in their given fields. Caleb Cushing, an able young lawyer-politician, promised to supply articles on Latin America. Moses Stuart, indefatigable professor at Andover Theological Seminary, agreed to translate or write many of those upon religion.[15]

Edward Everett promised to prepare articles on the classics, and George Ticknor, on modern languages and literature—especially a succinct critique of Spanish letters. To Benjamin Silliman, Yale professor, founder of the *American Journal of Science* and great American popularizer of science, Lieber wrote asking if he would correct translated articles on mineralogy and allied subjects and add "what is most important for this country." [16]

[13] [Walsh], "Encyclopaedia Americana," *loc. cit.*, 349–50.

[14] "Godman," *Encyclopaedia Americana*, V, 538–39, *et passim*. When Godman died, Dr. R. E. Griffith supplied articles to the letter "S"; Charles Pickering agreed to supply all the rest, "bating however, the *Sea Serpent*, which I must unequivocally decline." Pickering to Edward Wigglesworth, April 14, 1832.

[15] Cushing to Lieber, December 9, 1830, Lieber papers.

[16] Lieber to Silliman, November 17, 1828, Boston Public Library. Lieber offered

The encyclopedist's greatest catch was Judge Joseph Story, who agreed to write the law articles. Judge Story, though not yet fifty, had been an associate justice in the United States Supreme Court for seventeen years. There his growing conservatism had led him to ally himself with John Marshall, and he turned his scholarship to providing precedents for Marshall's decisions.

Story carried out the arduous duties of the Washington court sessions and of a circuit covering most of New England. In addition, after 1829 he served as Dane Professor in the Harvard Law School and began a voluminous series of *Commentaries*.

As though this were not enough, the Justice promised Lieber, whom he befriended, that he would write all the important law articles for the *Americana*. Story himself prepared the list of about a score of them, which he invariably turned in before the deadline. Erudite but understandable, these articles on both American and Roman law made the encyclopedia a worth-while acquisition for any young lawyer and gave the publication a prestige it otherwise could not have enjoyed.[17]

Lieber and his assistant worked hard through the summer months, making arrangements with numerous other writers and trying to pile up sufficient materials for the first few volumes. The German translated, revised, wrote original articles, and made extensive use of scissors and paste pot. He borrowed bodily from encyclopedias, books, and periodicals. Carey's was generous in loaning copies of many books. At the suggestion of Judge Story, he followed many articles with bibliographical citations.[18]

Despite his editorial work, Lieber continued as gymnasiarch and director of the swimming school. He found time to maintain a number of pleasant friendships. Gossler, the Prussian consul, Follen, and many others helped divert him. He spent much of his

---

the prevailing rate of pay for the translations, corrections, and original articles. The present writer found no evidence that Silliman contributed to the *Americana*, but it was well provided with lengthy, up-to-date geological articles.

[17] Lieber-Story correspondence, May 21, 1828, *et seq.*, Lieber papers. Lieber acknowledged his gratitude to Judge Story, who had insisted that the articles remain anonymous, both in the preface of the *Encyclopaedia Americana*, XIII, 4, and more fully in *On Civil Liberty and Self-Government* (3d ed.; Philadelphia, 1874), 213. Story's son listed the articles which he said "comprise more than 120 pages, closely printed in double columns." W. W. Story, *Life and Letters of Joseph Story*, 2 vols. (Boston, 1851), II, 27.

[18] Story to Lieber, April 17, 1829.

time in a stimulating intellectual relationship with John Pickering, "the first savant of Boston," who was one of his contributors. Often the conservative, studious Pickering visited Lieber at his cluttered office, bringing unasked-for armloads of books for him to peruse. Together they ruminated over the need for a universal orthography for the aborigines of North America and the South Seas, and every Saturday evening they instructed each other in English and German. They read, wrote, and translated, using as a text *Hamlet* in English and in Schlegel's German translation.[19]

Lieber labored on into the fall and through the long winter. By April he was reading proof on Volume I and already was deeply engrossed in Volume III. In September, Volume I of the *Encyclopaedia Americana* was published, and Lieber basked in a gratifying but meaningless outburst of acclaim from the newspapers. Poe had yet to pour acid on the critic's pen and inaugurate standards of genuine evaluation. Proclaimed the press: "a work without which no library worthy of the name can hereafter be made up"— *Yankee;* "A compendious library and book of reference"—New York *American;* "the most convenient and satisfactory *Encyclopaedia* we have ever seen"—*National Journal,* and so on.[20]

Not all words fell so musically upon Lieber's ears. Misprints, errors, and omissions appeared; he had been none too critical of the sources of his material. Henry Carey ferreted out some of these errors and corrected them. This displeased the proud editor, and Carey had to placate him by pointing out that the publishers would not have made the changes had there been time to consult him.[21]

This was gentle criticism. Inadvertently, poor Lieber stepped into a veritable wasps' nest when he followed David Hume's pro-British account of the Irish insurrection of 1649. Venerable, cantankerous old Mathew Carey proved in his letter to the unwary

---

[19] Lieber to [Matilda Oppenheimer?], September, 1828, translated copy. John Pickering prepared an article on "Agrarian Laws of Rome," and another, more than 20 pages long on "Indian Languages." The latter was translated into German. M. O. Pickering, *Life of John Pickering* (Boston, 1887), 364, 381–82, 409. Pickering to Lieber, August 20, 1833, February 19, 1834.

[20] Lieber to his parents, March 28, 1828, April 24, 1829, translated copies. See the highly laudatory excerpts from these reviews in an advertisement in the rear of Lieber, *Reminiscences of Niebuhr.*

[21] Henry C. Carey to Lieber, December 15, [1829], February 10, 1830.

editor that he had not lost his skill in invective in the years since he had left his native Erin.[22]

Such annoyances could cast no shadow upon Lieber's happiness, for that fall, along with Volume I, Matilda had arrived. As early as the previous spring, Lieber had begun to plan for her passage. His ardor for her had increased rather than waned, and he by no means enjoyed bachelor living. He tried to become orderly in his personal affairs—paying out for translations and articles made exact accounts a necessity—but he had less success with his room. "The chairs are often covered with linen that has been brought in by my washerwoman," he admitted. "The other day an old gentleman called on me, and there was not one unoccupied chair to offer him. He said dryly: 'Shall I sit on these newspapers or take them in my lap?'—and looking around the room, said, 'I should advise you to marry.' " [23]

No advice could have been more in keeping with Lieber's desires, but Matilda could not take passage until late in the summer when a brother could accompany her. "Oh, Mrs. Lieber, how much courage it must have taken in those days to cross the ocean to a strange country to be married," Alice Longfellow exclaimed to the aged Mrs. Lieber, more than a half century later. Matilda looked at her with surprise and quietly replied: "It took no courage to cross the ocean to join Lieber." [24]

But the day of the scheduled arrival passed and still the ship did not appear. Worried and impatient, the tormented Lieber fidgeted at New York Harbor: "I have been waiting ten days. Ships have arrived from every direction, even from Liverpool, and yet the Caledonia with its precious treasure, is not in yet. I am almost worn out; I can neither sleep at night nor occupy myself during the day. . . .

"My love with its ten thousand horsepower, and my pale face, and this terrible headache make me feel like a poor Tyrolese eagle shut up in a cage with its wings clipped. Not one of Columbus' sailors looked with such longing eyes toward the land as I now gaze out on the sea." [25]

22 Mathew Carey to Lieber, February 10, 1830.   23 Perry (ed.), *Lieber*, 32.
24 Lieber to his parents, April 24, 1829, translated copy, Lieber papers. Alice Longfellow to Mary Lieber, January 25, 1919, Longfellow House.
25 Lieber to his parents, September 5, 1829, translated copy.

Finally, after another fortnight, the *Caledonia* arrived; the Liebers were married and went to Philadelphia on a gay honeymoon. The Careys were most affable, and Joseph Bonaparte entertained them at his country estate. Soon Lieber was back at Boston where, following an American custom, he established his bride in a boardinghouse. He continued to spend his mornings in editorial work and gymnastics. Afternoons he returned to Matilda, who, since her knowledge of English far exceeded his, assisted in the translation and copying. Evenings they enjoyed gay times in a lighthearted Boston circle.[26]

Lovely Matilda whirled along zestfully with or without Francis. When her husband was away she filled in the vacant moments with long, chatty, amorous letters to him in which she switched rapidly from German to Italian to French to Spanish to English, as best suited her whim.[27]

Scant wonder that Lieber was happy. In addition to enjoying his gay home life, he basked in the prestige coming to him as editor of the encyclopedia. The *Americana* sold exceedingly well. In October Henry Carey reported fifty subscriptions within the past five days; by the following February five thousand had come in. The number constantly mounted—not only during the period of publication but for two or three decades later. Lieber, through having his name in large black letters on the title page and through his correspondence with dozens of personages, was well on his way toward becoming a renowned American. In November of 1830 came the palm of intellectual Boston—election to membership in the American Academy of Arts and Sciences.[28]

All this Lieber savored to the utmost; he found the incessant, geometrically increasing drudgery less to his liking. He bogged down and fell far behind his schedule of a volume every three months. Carey incessantly prodded him to get back onto schedule. Finally, with the assistance of Thomas Gamaliel Bradford, an-

---

[26] Lieber to his parents, September 29, 1829, translated copy; Matilda Lieber to Lieber's parents, October 17, 1829, copies; Perry (ed.), *Lieber,* 84–86.

[27] For example, Matilda Lieber to Francis Lieber, June 3, 1830, and innumerable letters in the Lieber papers.

[28] Perry (ed.), *Lieber,* 87; membership certificate, American Academy of Arts and Sciences, November 10, 1830.

other New Englander of distinguished ancestry and a geographer of some ability, he broke the editorial log jam. By December, 1830, the fifth volume was on the press, and Lieber assured the subscribers that henceforth they would appear at the promised three-month intervals.[29]

Perhaps the belated volumes of the *Americana* would have reached the printer more speedily had not the resourceful Lieber and his able young wife been wracking their brains for additional sources of income. They were eager to establish themselves in a home of their own. A young Lieber was on the way; boarding-houses with their noise, clatter, crowded tables, and lack of privacy were far from pleasant. Henry Carey continued to be the recipient of schemes for new and more magnificent works, until in desperation he assured Lieber that he was "almost principled against undertaking anything new." [30]

Nevertheless Lieber did produce one extra book: a by-product of his ebullient enthusiasm for the Revolution of 1830. Early in September, the ship *Hibernia* appeared off Sandy Hook and signaled in the news that France was once more revolting against tyranny, that Charles X had fled his throne. When the news reached the table of the Boston boardinghouse, the savant, himself so recently a zealous European revolutionist, was at first incredulous. When newspapers confirmed the tidings he became loquaciously jubilant, yet regretful that the news was from France, not Germany: "If nightcaps and the cap of liberty were one, how free would Germany be!"

Amidst the excitement, Matilda gave birth to a fine boy, Oscar Montgomery—no subject of Prussian tyranny, but a free citizen of the United States. In his lusty baby son, born during the new revolution, Lieber saw the symbol of a new era. Monarchy was succumbing to democracy; the struggle for deliverance might be long, much blood might be shed, cruel wars would ensue, but the result was inevitable. "Italy is full of combustible matter. Hungary will want to recover her lost privileges. Poland would strive to be

---

[29] H. C. Carey to Lieber, December 15, [1829]; preface, *Encyclopaedia Americana,* V, 3.
[30] H. C. Carey to Lieber, February 10, 1830.

free, and Germany will reawaken through blood and war to her struggle for unity and civil liberty." In this fine period, Oscar would grow to manhood.[31]

Here was a "noble subject for the pen." With a high-spirited introduction Lieber gathered together the *Americana* articles on France and sent them forth under the aegis of Carey as a separate publication. At the same time, with Matilda's assistance, he rapidly translated a collection of French eyewitness accounts of the "glorious days" of the July Revolution, to which he added "stirring revolutionary songs." The compilation appeared at the same time as the *Americana* production, but through a Boston publishing house and without any mention of Lieber's name. It was a showy little book, bound in the tricolor, with the very pages divided into three sections—red, white, and blue.[32]

Small enterprises of this nature appealed to Lieber, but the *Americana* pressed, and he spent most of his time trying to stay ahead of his six compositors. "Ah, I assure you," he complained, "The Euminides following Orestes were a bagatelle in comparison to my haunting six printer's d——s." And in his turn Euminides Lieber tracked down many an unwary celebrity who in an unguarded moment had promised to contribute. Senator Edward Livingston agreed to write on Louisiana, the penal code, and so on. He wriggled out finally by the double plea of illness and his unexpected elevation to the position of Secretary of State. Lewis Cass, Governor of Michigan, delegated to another the preparation of an article on Michigan Territory. Senator William L. Marcy of New York met Lieber at Boston and prepared a remarkably nonpartisan account of the Antimasonic repercussions of the Morgan affair.[33]

---

[31] Perry (ed.), *Lieber*, 89–90.

[32] [Francis Lieber], *France: A Series of Articles Reprinted from the Encyclopaedia Americana* (Philadelphia, 1831), 79 pp.; [Francis Lieber, editor and translator], *Events in Paris, During the 26, 27, 28 and 29 of July, 1830, by Several Eye Witnesses . . . Translated from the Fourth Paris Edition* (Boston, 1830), 197 pp. Lieber's name has never before been connected with this little book. Probably he produced it *sub rosa* for fear it would interfere with his similar production published by Carey & Lea. He referred to the work on various occasions in later years: "While in Boston he also published a translation of a French work on the July Revolution in 1830," autobiographical sketch, *circa* August, 1854. He included it by name in "A list of my literary works . . . ," *circa* 1850.

[33] Lieber to Dr. James M. Mathews, March 9, 1831, Historical Society of Penn-

General Henry A. S. Dearborn, head of the Massachusetts Horticultural Society, wrote an article on horticulture, and Frederick Rapp dictated a lengthy account of his communist communities at New Harmony, Indiana, and Economy, Pennsylvania. Nathan Appleton, wealthy congressman and cotton merchant, earlier had written on cotton manufacturing. "Pigeons return to their peas," Lieber reminded him, and persuaded him to write on the new mill town of Lowell.[34]

While Lieber worked endlessly at his uninspiring task, he gave vent to his feelings of exasperation in a bludgeoning satire which appeared in the *New-England Magazine*. As "Timothy Quicksand," he proposed to edit an *Encyclopaedia Epistolographica* from the contents of the dead-letter office. One of these letters, from Lord Bookseller to his serf author, proposed an encyclopedia. It ought, in keeping with the times, to be "twenty-four-mocyclopaediac"—small in size, light in language, and superficial in contents: "dilute history into romance, and it will be great for the age."

Sarcastically the young publicist held forth on a theme he endlessly sounded for the next forty years—a denunciation of the fickle, shallow, ungrateful American public:

"What does the reader wish to find if he turns to an Encyclopaedia? Detailed, accurate facts? By no means! General impressions, wholesale assertions, condensed in the easiest form, and swallowable shape; gilt pills are wanted, and a few curious facts, which at the proper time, may be thrown out like flowers accidentally falling from a tree in blossom. Much is to be learned, no time to be lost. The book must teach quickly or it is useless." [35]

Nevertheless, Lieber's life was on the whole very enjoyable, especially in the idyllic summer of 1832. In retrospect it seemed to both Francis and Matilda to have been among the happiest of

sylvania; Livingston to Lieber, May 22, June 19, 1831; Cass to Lieber, July 26, 1831; Lieber to Matilda Lieber, August 26, 1831; Marcy to Lieber, September 22, November 16, 1831.

34 Lieber to Dearborn, March 9, 1831, Massachusetts Historical Society; Rapp to Lieber, September 20, 1831, Lieber papers; Lieber to Appleton, 1831, Massachusetts Historical Society.

35 [Francis Lieber], "Dead Letters, Opened and Burned by the Postmaster-General, Revived and Published by Timothy Quicksand. Livraison I. *Gaudeamus Igitur*," *New-England Magazine*, I (1831), 505–11.

their lives. They moved to Newton, taking with them the thirteen-year-old Fanny Appleton, the interesting and promising daughter of Nathan Appleton.

Fanny had long since attracted Lieber's eye, when from his office he used to see her with her staglike walk returning from school to the Appleton mansion on Beacon Street. He had soon become fast friends with Fanny and her more comely but less keen-minded sister Mary. To Fanny he had given a pair of ear-drops accompanied by a clumsy but goodhearted little poem; Fanny became a warm friend of Matilda's and a favorite with baby Oscar.

Lieber, with Matilda and Fanny, went to see Audubon's original drawings of birds at the Athenaeum, which he thought were magnificent. He excitedly talked to the ornithologist while they were swimming together at the swimming school. Audubon had just returned from Florida and was planning a trip to the Bay of Fundy. He told Lieber that the following year he would go to Labrador; instantly the young scholar offered to accompany him.[36]

While Lieber preoccupied himself with daydreaming not only of explorations but also of definitive writings and lucrative university chairs, he continued grinding away at the encyclopedia month after month. Finally, with great relief, on February 1, 1833, he put his name to the preface of the final volume. In a little less than five years he had completed the task of editing an encyclopedia which was to remain standard in America until the time of the Civil War.

"I am contented with my occupation because it has enabled me to marry," Lieber wrote near the beginning of his undertaking, "but if I were a man of means I should occupy myself quite differently, and devote my time to working out thoughts which have been in my mind many years. It is not pleasant to feel I am giving several years of my life to a book which must eventually be supplanted. It will certainly be of some value in disseminating information, and I shall thus have contributed my mite, even though

[36] Fanny Appleton journal, and undated note from Fanny Appleton to the Liebers, accompanying flowers, Longfellow House; Lieber to Fanny Appleton, undated, giving her a pair of eardrops, Lieber papers; Perry (ed.), *Lieber*, 95–96.

it is but a little drop, to the stream of knowledge. I am ambitious to leave a work behind me, be it ever so small, which will live in spite of the changes of time." [37]

True enough, the *Americana*, like every other encyclopedia, was ephemeral, but through it the young German patriot made one of his most lasting contributions to American cultural development and nationalism. Here was pabulum for the self-education of many an ambitious young man; here were descriptions and explanations of American achievements and institutions which might well add to the pride of the self-conscious young republic; and here, thanks to Joseph Story, was a strongly nationalistic interpretation of the Federal government.

Lieber had in truth edited an American encyclopedia. The German *Conversations-Lexikon* was no more than a basis. Almost all the significant articles were new or rewritten—and from the American point of view. Dozens of the most qualified persons had written about those phases of American culture that they knew best. The sum total was probably the broadest and most elaborate of contemporary appraisals of America in the Jacksonian period. [38]

The articles on science, religion, and government, despite minor inaccuracies, well presented the advance of knowledge to the 1830's. Indeed, Lieber had striven almost to the point of error to make the *Americana* timely. He wrote lengthy accounts of the Greek Revolution, the July Revolution, the English Reform Act of 1832, and the establishment of the new Kingdom of Belgium.

Nevertheless, much that caused the *Americana* to become dated was due less to disproportion than to the rapid growth of the United States. By the time of the Civil War, when the encyclopedia was still in use, young readers must have snickered to read that a broad, uninhabitable desert spread from the Rockies to the Missouri River, that the United States was quite interested in the Mexican province of Texas, or that another Mexican province, California, was populated only by a handful of Spaniards and Indians.

[37] *Ibid.*, 83.
[38] For a list of contributors to the later volumes, see *Encyclopaedia Americana*, XIII, 3–4.

In addition, the *Americana* suffered from unevenness of style and contradiction of fact. The *Chinese Repository,* published in Canton, complained of the article "Canton" that "almost every sentence . . . is more or less erroneous." Statements in the article on New York City, by a Mr. Delafulo, contradicted those by Dr. T. Romeyn Beck and B. F. Butler in their article on New York State. Scissors and lozenges (bits of sealing wax for affixing clippings to paper) too often filled gaps in Lieber's knowledge. When a reviewer criticized an article for containing Germanisms, Lieber triumphantly countered that he had clipped it from *Nicholson's Encyclopedia.* Many who had prepared articles for Lieber similarly borrowed either from the writings of others or from their own previous productions.[39]

A wide range in writing style likewise marred the encyclopedia. The translations were dry and Germanic; the legal articles precise and technical; most of Lieber's contributions discursive and speculative, but penetrating. In discussing some subjects connected with his past he could not keep out autobiographical remarks. Conversations with King Joseph were too heady a wine for the ex-rifleman, and he discussed the Bonapartes *ad nauseam.* To a considerable extent Joseph had succeeded through his lengthy correspondence with Lieber in getting into the *Americana,* and thus before the American public, lengthy and sympathetic portraits of all his family. At least the young editor did not swallow the thesis that Napoleon was really democratic and had been forced into his despotism by the British. Some years later he pointedly refuted it, but in the *Americana,* through sheer weight of detail, he had unwittingly helped build the Napoleonic legend.[40]

Lieber had written varyingly on a wide array of topics. His

[39] *Chinese Repository,* I (1832), 161–70. Cf. Lieber, *The Stranger in America,* I, 243; Lieber to Thayer, January 22, 1868; Butler to Lieber, April 7, 1832; Lieber to Charles Sumner, September 15, 1841. The articles on the Mississippi Valley in the *Encyclopaedia Americana,* VII, 539, and in the *Quarterly Register of the American Education Society,* III (1830), 119, were a rather typical example of close similarity. William Channing Woodbridge, the editor of the *Register,* was an important contributor to the *Americana.*

[40] See "Napoleon," *Encyclopaedia Americana,* X, 569–93, and articles on Joseph, Lucien, Louis, Jerome, Murat, Maria Louisa, Bacciochi, and Borghese. Typically, in the article "Bonaparte," *Encyclopaedia Americana,* II, 181, Lieber declared: "The members of the family of Napoleon live retired and much respected, manifesting great taste for all the fine arts and the sciences." [Francis Lieber], "Was Napoleon a Dictator?" *Putnam's Monthly,* V (1853), 12–21.

essays on Goethe and Kant were able; that on Hegel worthless. His witty essay on cookery typified his informality: "It is not great things, but trifles, which principally make up the sum of human happiness. Who would not think a dull razor, which draws tears from the eyes every morning, or a creaking tavern sign, which disturbs us every night, a much greater evil than the single sharp pang occasioned by the drawing of a tooth? An act, therefore, like eating, which is repeated several times each day by the millions who inhabit the globe, is a subject worthy of serious investigation."

From his own observation, Lieber commented that Americans ate too much meat, thus became dyspeptic. They should include more fruits in their diet. Similarly, he thought proper investigation of the culinary art would reveal many valuable facts. Medical men should study "the intimate connexion of different diseases, in various countries, with the common dishes."[41]

These flaws were minor compared with the total significance of the work as a highly usable compilation of knowledge of interest to Americans. It was small compared with present-day encyclopedias and was unillustrated; nevertheless, it crowded nearly seven million words into almost eight thousand pages. It contained about twenty thousand articles—"abridged treatises upon every subject of inquiry to which the well-informed or the ill-informed can possibly have occasion to refer." The contents equaled in quantity thirty-six to forty-eight English octavo volumes, which in the United States would have cost about $150. The price of the *Americana* was only $32.50.

Cheap in price, the *Americana* came at precisely the correct time and sold phenomenally. Thousands of Americans were ready to buy an encyclopedia as a means of self-improvement. The era was one when the common man was struggling for hegemony, and he was sure his greatest weapon in the battle was education. Not only did he fight for free schools for his children, but he sought knowledge for himself—and an encyclopedia was a favorite device for self-education.

The *American Journal of Education* urged: "Those who can, by any honest mode of economy reserve the sum of two dollars and

41 [Lieber], "Cookery," *Encyclopaedia Americana*, III, 511–14.

fifty cents quarterly, from their family expenses, may pay for this work as fast as it is published; and we confidently believe that they will find at the end that they never purchased so much general, practical, useful information at so cheap a rate." [42]

In this favorable atmosphere the *Americana* flourished. Carey's sold a large number of copies until the depression of the late 1830's. Then they turned from trade books to medical works. But the *Americana* sales continued to rise, as it was issued from a host of publishing houses scattered over the United States and Canada, which purchased or rented Carey's stereotype plates. Ruefully Lieber watched the mounting sales—which he himself later estimated reached one hundred thousand sets—for after he had completed his editorial tasks he received not one extra cent. Indeed, in the later forties when a supplementary volume appeared, Carey's did not even invite him to be the editor.[43]

Sets of the *Americana* were to be found everywhere, from the British Museum to the Canton quays. Almost every well-to-do American home possessed one. When Lieber called on President Jackson he found the latest volume on a White House table. Many of the sets passed into young hands which one day would be influential. As late as 1915, Professor John J. Halsey recalled that from the *Americana* "I got a large part of my early education—reading a large portion of it topically before I went to college." In the 1830's a recent Harvard Law School graduate, Charles

---

[42] *American Journal of Education,* IV (1829), 432–36. See also [Neal], "Encyclopaedia Americana," *loc. cit.,* 268.

[43] Lea & Febiger, *One Hundred and Fifty Years of Publishing,* 25; Henry Vethake (ed.), *Encyclopaedia Americana Supplementary Volume . . .* (Philadelphia, 1847). Some of the *Americana* editions were: Philadelphia: Carey, Lea & Carey, 1829–32, 1830–32; DeSilver, Thomas & Co., 1835, 1836; Thomas, Cowperthwait & Co., 1840; Lea & Blanchard, 1845, 1846, 1847, 1848, 1849, 1850. Boston: B. B. Mussey & Co., 1854; Sanborn, Carter & Bazin, 1855, 1858. Brockville, Upper Canada: Horace Billings & Co., 1835. Lieber reported in 1837: "Whiley, the publisher, tells me that without a question the Americana is now by far the best American large book. It has sold better dur[in]g the last year than ever before, and will have an astonishing run. It is the only book now selling &c. &c." Lieber to Matilda Lieber, September 1, 1837. He wrote Sumner, September 15, 1841: "A few days ago Carvill told me that their house alone made from $7000 to 8000 clear by my Americana." Lieber even claimed that there was a British piracy. Cf. Gustave de Beaumont and Alexis de Tocqueville, *On the Penitentiary System in the United States, and Its Application in France; with an Appendix on Penal Colonies, and also, Statistical Notes . . . ,* translated from the French, with an Introduction, Notes and Additions by Francis Lieber (Philadelphia, 1833), xxxiv–xxxv.

Sumner, received it as a prize in an essay competition. Charles Eliot Norton, Harvard's great professor of aesthetics, as a child browsed through it so repeatedly that twenty years later he could still recite the volume titles, "A-Bat, Bat-Cat, Cat-Cha," and so on. By the 1850's, the encyclopedia was even among the scanty store of books of a rather obscure Illinois lawyer-politician, Abraham Lincoln.[44]

[44] Lieber to Matilda Lieber, October 11, 1831; Albion Small, "Fifty Years of Sociology in the United States," *American Journal of Sociology*, XXI (1916), 728. Lieber to Sumner, August [16], 1870. Norton to Lieber, April 13, 1868. Robert Lincoln told Butler an 1851 edition of the *Americana* was among his father's possessions. Nicholas Murray Butler, *Across the Busy Years* . . . , 2 vols. (New York, 1940), II, 389–90. George Ticknor Curtis cited the *Americana* as the source for a biographical sketch of James Wilson in his *History of the Origin, Formation, and Adoption of the Constitution of the United States* . . . , 2 vols. (New York, 1854), I, 462.

V

Americanization

FRANCIS LIEBER, on February 17, 1832, stood before the bar of the United States District Court of Massachusetts. Solemnly, and with a profound feeling of the significance of his act, he renounced allegiance to the King of Prussia and became a citizen of the United States. He was proud of his new citizenship and felt that now he was a full-fledged American in every sense of the word. He did not realize that he had been undergoing a steady process of Americanization ever since coming to the New World, and that the process, far from being complete, was not to culminate for many years.[1]

Already Lieber was building a solid position for himself as an American scholar, but he was only gradually coming to understand New World institutions. Above all, he failed to grasp that one most baffling to foreigners, politics. His other great difficulty was his seeming inability to sink substantial economic roots in the new soil.

Progressively as the *Americana* project approached an end, the ambitious young German, now laden with family obligations, worried more and more about his future. Though his intellect had won him a sound reputation, he found it almost impossible to transmute it into even a few dollars. During the early 1830's countless schemes for writing and teaching spun around in his resourceful mind, but in the end almost every one was fruitless.

Especially the young man hoped he might earn a living as an editor. He planned a number of journals, none of which ma-

[1] Lieber, certificate of naturalization, February 17, 1832, signed by Francis Bassett, Clerk of the U.S. District Court for . . . Massachusetts, Lieber papers, Henry E. Huntington Library. All manuscripts referred to in this chapter, unless otherwise identified, are from this collection.

82

terialized. They would have been of a profundity and degree of specialization not feasible until the end of the century, when America possessed sufficient scholars to support them.

One of the most intriguing of these would-be periodicals was a geographical, statistical, and ethnographical magazine for which Lieber drew up a prospectus in 1830. He proposed a bimonthly periodical which would print reviews and extracts of the newest publications on geography, journeys, voyages, and other expeditions; translations from French, German, and Italian magazines; digests of all American and most foreign statistical reports; ethnographic descriptions of customs, religion, and morals of both civilized and savage nations; biographical notices; and news of expeditions.

The plan was sufficiently intriguing to win commendation from both the eloquent Unitarian, William Ellery Channing, and the paragon of navigators, Nathaniel Bowditch. The flaw was a publishing commonplace: Americans did not patronize serious quarterlies. Even *Silliman's Journal*, which covered geography along with all the other sciences, struggled to maintain a meager existence after more than a decade of publication.[2]

Three years later, Lieber ran into the same difficulties when he projected a review which was to be an "archive" of the best American writings and materials on history, politics, jurisprudence, etc. Lieber's friends once more wrote letters of endorsement and encouragement. Jared Sparks was especially enthusiastic. John Pickering, wary conservative lawyer that he was, could see clearly that like most other schemes for periodicals it was foredoomed to failure. "You ask about using my name," he commented, "—& you know my old objections. There can be no doubt, that in this country of businessmen the pursuit of *literature* is injurious to a professional man."[3]

When he planned a more practical periodical, Lieber came closer to success, but even this scheme was stillborn. He actually per-

[2] Lieber, "Geography is a science . . . ," February 11, 1830, with endorsements by Nath[anie]ll Bowditch, March 15, 1830, and W[illia]m E. Channing.

[3] Lieber to Sparks, July 13, 1833; Sparks to Lieber, July 20, 1833, Harvard University; Pickering to Lieber, July 22, 1833; Story to Lieber, July 30, 1833; Levi Woodbury to Lieber, March 12, 1833; Lieber to C. J. A. Mittermaier, April 24, 1833, copy, Lieber papers. Lieber hoped to have as contributors: Jared Sparks, Joseph Story, Washington Irving, Albert Gallatin, John Pickering, and James Kent.

suaded a Boston publishing firm to send out a printed prospectus for an American Catalogue, similar to one published in Germany, containing the authors and titles of all works published within the United States and Canada during the past year. Even here, Lieber was a full thirty years too early.[4]

While his ambitions to become a magazine editor were to prove futile, the young man did begin a lengthy, intermittent career as a public speaker. In the fall of 1829 he was able to augment his income and widen his circle of acquaintances through a series of lectures before the Boston Society of Useful Knowledge. He hesitated to speak before a large public gathering in a tongue in which he was not yet completely at home. Nevertheless, the series was quite successful—as talks by a handsome and intense foreigner always were.

Lieber delivered a lucid survey of the Ottoman Empire, its decline, its dominion in the Balkans, and the Greek Revolution. To make the lectures graphic and convincing he drew a tale or two from his own experiences. The ladies complimented him, and Channing, he of the measured phrase, delighted the earnest German by remarking surprise that he could speak so fluently in an alien language.[5]

Out of the lectures grew an invitation to prepare two articles for that sanctum of the New England intellect, the *North American Review*. One of these, a reworking of the talks, was a competent historical analysis of the Ottoman Empire. It was an intelligible picture, and added measurably to his stature as an American scholar.[6]

Activities like these helped spread the reputation of the encyclo-

---

[4] *American Catalogue*, printed prospectus, in Lieber papers. Carter & Hendee were to publish the first number in October, 1830, but so far as can be ascertained it did not materialize. Lieber planned to model the catalogue after the *Allgemeines Bücher-Verzeichniss* published semiannually in Leipzig.

[5] Perry (ed.), *Lieber*, 89; Lieber, "A Lecture delivered before the Boston Society for Diffusion of Useful Knowledge . . . Dec. 11, 1829." This is a complete manuscript of his series of lectures and comprises several hundred pages.

[6] [Francis Lieber], "German Association of Naturalists and Physicians," *North American Review*, XXI (1830), 85–93. Portions of the manuscript are in the Lieber papers. [Francis Lieber], "Turkey," *ibid.*, 291–308. Lieber based the latter article on Leopold von Ranke, *Fuersten und Voelker von Sud Europa im Sechszehnten und Siebzehnten Jahrhundert,* . . . ; Joseph von Hammer, *Geschichte des Osmanischen Reiches aus den Quellen;* and Hammer, *Des Osmanischen Reiches Staatsverfassung und Staatsverwaltung.*

pedist beyond New England. When in 1830 a group of New York notables sent out a call for a literary convention to discuss plans for the proposed University of the City of New York, Lieber was among the fifty-two heads of colleges, professors, scientists, and men of distinction who received invitations.[7]

Daniel Webster, Judge Story, and some others could not be there, but the job-hungry young German, smelling possible appointment in the new institution, arrived in New York that October with a well-considered speech. An impressive group of savants were present: Sparks, Livingston, the aged, retired Albert Gallatin, long Secretary of the Treasury, Professors Silliman and Henry Dwight of Yale, and Theodore Dwight Woolsey, later to be president of Yale. But in the main, New York clergymen, under the leadership of Drs. James Macfarlane Mathews and Jonathan Mayhew Wainwright, dominated the convention.[8]

With enthusiasm the scholars outlined proposals for a type of academic institution far superior to any then known in America. Henry Vethake of Princeton, one of the nation's most distinguished academic leaders, burst a veritable iconoclastic bombshell by denouncing in scathing terms almost every one of the established landmarks of the collegiate system.[9]

Lieber's remarks, based on his personal experience in German universities, contained equally exotic proposals, but his first concern was to prevent a European innovation. New York newspapers had suggested that the new institution emulate the German system of stimulating professors by making them dependent upon student fees for their support. Lieber vehemently fought this on the grounds that it would make the students the judges of the faculty. Some of the most significant fields would draw relatively few students, and professors seeking large recompense would try to be popular rather than profound.

Neither did Lieber condone the prevalent Scottish utilitarian feeling that the university should offer only useful or professional courses. Above all else, the university should instruct in those

[7] *Journal of the Proceedings of a Convention of Literary and Scientific Gentlemen, Held in the Common Council Chambers of the City of New-York October, 1830* (New-York, 1830); *American Quarterly Review*, IX (1831), 283–314; T. F. Jones (ed.), *New York University, 1832: 1932* (New York, 1933), 22–23.
[8] Jones (ed.), *New York University*, 22–23.   [9] *Ibid.*, 24–25.

areas not immediately useful which lead to the intellectual growth of the student. Especially it should establish chairs in history, astronomy, German literature, gymnastics and swimming. All but one of these were fields with which the young German was thoroughly conversant.[10]

After the prepared speeches, Lieber undertook boldly despite his poor English to answer questions from the floor. To Lieber's delight, Gallatin two days later "spoke at length & supported every thing I have said in the written communication—" the university should confine its first attention to the faculties of science and letters, rather than to law, medicine, theology, and the classics.

Though the German's earnest plea for a liberal-arts university awoke sympathetic interest in Gallatin, it made not the slightest impression upon the Reverend Dr. Mathews, pastor of the South Dutch Reformed Church of New York. To Lieber's misfortune, Mathews was elected chancellor a few months later. He and his coterie of dominies were to turn the new university into a typical classico-theological college noteworthy primarily for religious conservatism and faculty wrangling.[11]

Nevertheless Lieber's trip was a decided success. Everyone treated him with "great distinction" and Gallatin invited him to dine with a small group at his home. There he met Chancellor James Kent, whose mind, sound as it was conservative, was at the height of its powers. Kent had just finished writing the commentaries which gave him foremost rank among American jurists. During his own lifetime they were to go through six editions; eight more were to follow in less than a century after his death.[12] Kent was most cordial and presented Lieber with a set of the *Commentaries*. When Lieber commented upon his erudition he replied, "Nothing like you, nothing like you." [13]

The young scholar proudly brought home to Matilda tales of these triumphs and of his innocent flirtations with the belles of New York. Then he settled down to a campaign to obtain a chair at New York University, when it should begin instruction. For many months he carried on a correspondence with Chancellor

[10] *Ibid.;* Perry (ed.), *Lieber,* 94.
[11] Jones (ed.), *New York University,* 25–28; Lieber to Matilda Lieber, October 23, 1830, August 26, 1831.
[12] Lieber to Matilda Lieber, October 23, 25, 27, 1830.   [13] *Ibid.*

Mathews concerning a set of lectures he had been invited to deliver. "Sir, I would lecture with all the delight and zeal, which ever inspired a Knight for his queen's banner," he had assured the Chancellor. But when he found out the lectures were to be delivered gratis, the "delight and zeal" evaporated into protests that his "arduous labors" held him in Boston.[14]

Still, the mirage of a professorship floated before Lieber's eyes, and he did agree to lecture twice a week toward the end of March, 1832. Negotiations had reached this stage in November, 1831, when the orthodox Chancellor got wind that Lieber might be a religious heretic and hinted for a confession of faith. Heatedly the young German-American shot back a confession of faith, not in theology, but in American freedom of conscience: "If I detest and hate secret police in politics, I abhor it in religious affairs . . . both [are] a cancer of humankind. . . . I have left Germany because the police tormented me; I have no idea to find it here like there. Let people assail me publicly; I am ready for any attack but I will not answer to back-biters." [15]

Negotiations dragged on for another year, but Lieber never delivered the lectures, and he never received an invitation to a chair at New York University.[16]

Lieber was genuinely, if not conventionally, religious, and had he wished might have written Mathews to that effect. With zest he was helping introduce iconoclastic German theological concepts into the Calvinistic clime still chilling parts of New England. He delighted in arguing German theology and discussing the problems raised by Schleiermacher's abstruse religio-philosophy with Professor Moses Stuart of Andover.[17]

[14] Lieber to Mathews, March 9, 28, September 25, 1831, Historical Society of Pennsylvania; Lieber to Matilda Lieber, March 12, 1831, Lieber papers.

[15] Lieber to Mathews, November 14, 1831, Historical Society of Pennsylvania. Lieber expressed himself more fully to John Delafield, November 15, 1831: "I have heard here that some person has been busy to spread an unfavorable report respecting my creed, which may—as slander always travels quick—also reach you. I never speak on religion except with those, of whom I know that words convey more than words, i.e. with my friends; well, knowing that true religion nourishes the heart like an etherial [sic] dew from above, but which vanishes under the rough handling of controversy. Thus friends alone could know my heart, & as no friend, probably has set such slander agoing, I think I conclude not very unmathematically, that the back-biter knew nothing of me." Historical Society of Pennsylvania.

[16] Lieber to Mathews, June 20, August 7, 1832, Historical Society of Pennsylvania.

[17] Stuart to Lieber, June 22, 1830.

However, that was mere conversational avocation. Might not one as a life work apply the new European concepts of history and political theory to a study of America? Might not one apply the calipers of the German social scientist to the unique young republic, and from a study of the antecedents and growth of the United States bring forth a monumental history of representative government? The idea appealed greatly to Lieber. Veering more and more toward the twin stars of scientific history and political science, he wrote exuberantly to Professor Leopold von Ranke, who above all others was setting the new standards for the social sciences:

"As it is said of the great Copernicus that to the fact that he happened to live in Italy is due the sublime idea of his planetary system, so it is important for the historian to live in a politically active country, such as England or the United States. . . . In Germany the student of history can study it only in the libraries; In Italy, in retrospection; but in England and America, in its actual existence. And for the present time, of which the key is the democratic principle . . . the United States and France seem to me to be the high-schools of history." [18]

With the progress of the human race daily more rapid and the circle of civilization enlarging with every year as the world moved from monarchy to democracy, how could one better employ oneself than as an observer and interpreter of the whirl of events? Where could one better carry on this noble occupation than in America?

By chance, Lieber picked up some of the poetry of *Turnvater* Jahn, the chauvinistic type of verse which he himself had once tried so hard to match, and was shocked: "That an enthusiasm so hollow, so unhealthy and unnatural, could exist to such an extent amongst those who seemed to be the most ready to do something for the people, is painful." With a feeling of sadness he looked back upon the rabid violence of his youth. Indeed, he could think of no period of Germany's past which refreshed, elevated, or cheered him. "Only here in America," he exclaimed to himself, "have I learned the true value of liberty; and here is the turning-point of my life." [19]

While Lieber was looking forward to the period when he could

[18] Perry (ed.), *Lieber*, 89. [19] *Ibid.*, 89–91.

win fame as an expositor of the government of the United States, two young Frenchmen crossed his path, one of whom was to eclipse him thoroughly as an interpreter of American democracy. Alexis de Tocqueville and Gustave de Beaumont, two aristocratic youths of strongly Bourbonist families, had found themselves in an intolerable position after the Orleanist July Revolution. Far from sharing Lieber's enthusiasm for the "Glorious Days," they were in a quandary. They had taken an oath of allegiance to the new monarch, Louis Philippe, which degraded them among their families and friends. At the same time, as members of a defeated party they were unlikely to receive preferment from the government.

To resolve their dilemma, Tocqueville and Beaumont obtained permission to visit the United States to study the prison reforms in which America led the world. Arriving in April, 1831, they had plunged into their study with vigor and journeyed as far west as the frontier trading post of Green Bay. Toward the end of the summer they returned to the East and arrived in Boston in September. At first Brahmin society was haughty, since they had no letters of introduction, but their interest in penitentiaries ultimately proved an *open sesame.*[20]

At the home of gay, garrulous old Mrs. Harrison Gray Otis, Lieber met these two serious, well-informed young men. He was as delighted with the inquiring Frenchmen as they were with him. In the next few days they saw a great deal of each other, and Lieber discoursed authoritatively to them upon the American social and economic system—a subject in which they also were intensely interested. Though their avowed object in visiting America was to study prison reform, both had dreams of other and greater works. Beaumont was to produce a not-too-significant novelized account of slavery, and Tocqueville, the *Democracy in America,* a work which would achieve immortality and indeed lead to Lieber's proudest boast in future years—that the most prominent three of a certain class of politico-philosophers were Montesquieu, Tocqueville, and Lieber.[21]

[20] Pierson, *Tocqueville and Beaumont in America,* is a brilliantly analytical and encyclopedic account of their journey and its fruits.
[21] *Ibid.,* 377; Perry (ed.), *Lieber,* 91; Lieber to his parents, September 18, 1831, Lieber papers; Lieber to Ruggles, October 23, 1856, Lieber papers, Library of Congress.

The German-American had left his fatherland because of dangerous political ideals, the Frenchmen learned. But now his years in the United States had taught him the impossibility of transplanting American democracy to Europe. Tocqueville carefully jotted Lieber's observations in his diary: "We Europeans, we think to create republics by organizing a great political assembly. The Republic, on the contrary, is of all the governments the one that depends most on every part of society. Look at this country! The Republic is everywhere, in the streets as in Congress. If an obstacle embarrasses the public way, the neighbours will at once constitute themselves a deliberative body; they will name a commission and will remedy the evil by their collective force, wisely directed. Does a public ceremony, a banquet, take place, you will likewise see a gathering, a deliberation, and an executive authority arising therefrom. The concept of an authority preceding that of the parties interested does not exist in any one's head. The people has the Republic to the marrow of the bones.

"Another time he said to us: How can a man who has seen America believe that it is possible to transplant its political laws to Europe, and especially at one fell swoop? Since seeing this country I can't believe M. de Lafayette in good faith in his theories; one can't deceive oneself so grossly. For my part, I feel myself inclined to believe every day more strongly that constitutions and political laws are nothing in themselves. They are dead creations to which the morals and the social position of the people alone can give life." [22]

Lieber also discoursed to the French observers on the purity of American morals—the double standard of conduct—which made it possible for a good woman to be far more coquettish than in Europe, since everyone knew she would not overstep certain bounds. And he explained to the surprised aristocrats how, because of the American respect for the law, the hangman himself could ply his trade without the slightest loss in social standing. To fortify his remarks, he gave Tocqueville the seven volumes of the *Americana* which had been published up until then.[23]

[22] Pierson, *Tocqueville and Beaumont in America*, 377–78.
[23] *Ibid.*, 378–80, contains Tocqueville's account of the conversations upon morals and the sheriff. Lieber gave a rather highly colored version of the latter conversation in *Letters to a Gentleman in Germany*, 34–35.

Tocqueville took the *Americana* to France with him, and ultimately used it as one of the reference works in preparation of *De la Democratie*. Perhaps from it rather than from the *Commentaries* came the many ideas of Joseph Story which the disgruntled Justice, in a later complaint to Lieber, claimed Tocqueville had woven into his work.[24]

Fired by Beaumont's and Tocqueville's interest in American institutions, Lieber determined to put into execution his long-contemplated plan for a history of representative government. He innocently assumed that scholars could receive subsidies from the state, and since he would need a sinecure in order to undertake the task, he determined to seek aid from leading government officials.

Leaving Boston in early October, 1831, he traveled overland to Albany to see Judge William L. Marcy, who was to remark in the Senate the following January that he could see "nothing wrong in the rule that to the victors belong the spoils of the enemy." Lieber, fresh from the anti-Jackson stronghold, asked Marcy if he would not obtain government support for the project. Marcy was remarkably cordial. He approved the idea and praised Lieber, but frankly told the young German-American that "in a popular government like ours, everything depends upon patronage, and those who have worked for a party in power are sure to be the favored ones in all appointments." [25]

Nevertheless, Marcy told Lieber that if he would write a letter the following January outlining his plans, he would show it to the President and the Jacksonian senators. In addition, he gave Lieber a strong letter of recommendation to the new Secretary of War, Lewis Cass. Considering that Lieber had unequivocally allied himself with the enemies of the Jackson party and suffered the further handicap of foreign birth, Marcy showed him exceptional favor.

From Albany, Lieber hastened to Washington to press his case in person. He called upon his only two acquaintances among the cabinet members, Secretary of State Edward Livingston, and Secretary of the Navy Levi Woodbury. Both encouraged him in his scheme, and Woodbury introduced him to President Jackson.

24 Pierson, *Tocqueville and Beaumont in America*, 377, 730–31.
25 Lieber to Matilda Lieber, October 9, 1831; Perry (ed.), *Lieber*, 93.

Lieber, to his surprise, found that Jackson had "a noble and expressive countenance." He "has the appearance of a venerable old man, his features by no means plain; on the contrary, he made the best impression upon me. We conversed on the state of Europe, on the Poles, &c." Jackson in his turn liked the voluble foreigner, and invited him to dine with the cabinet.[26]

At the dinner, Lieber listened politely to expositions of Jacksonian democracy but saw no reason why he should not cling to his own more conservative views. Even Marcy's blunt words on spoils had failed to change his misconception that his erudition and scholarly aims should entitle him to a lucrative government position. That was the system even in autocratic Prussia; why should it not hold good in democratic America? Had not both his Whig friends in New England and his Jacksonian friends in New York and Washington bestowed praise? That he should not receive financial aid was unthinkable. Quite possibly at the very moment that Senator Marcy thundered his defense of the spoils system he may have had before him on his desk in the Senate a letter from Lieber asking not only monetary assistance in writing the "History of Representative Government," but also appointment as minister to the new Kingdom of Belgium! [27]

No answer to the letter came. The politically naïve Lieber continued to press his proposals, and received soft-worded, evasive answers from which only an inexperienced optimist could extract hope. One versed in American political ways would have sooner expected blood from a stone. Not for a quarter of a century did the political philosopher's practical education advance to the point where he grasped the intimate connection between controlling votes and holding office.[28]

Lieber was not to share the awards of the Jackson supporters, but he did hold in common with them one firm belief—a growing faith in the American nation. He demonstrated this clearly in the fall of 1832 when the state-rights forces challenged the principle

[26] Lieber to Matilda Lieber, October 11, 1831; Perry (ed.), Lieber, 92–93.
[27] Lieber to Marcy, January 3, 1832, Historical Society of Pennsylvania.
[28] Lieber to Marcy, January 30, April 5, 1832, Historical Society of Pennsylvania; Lieber to Marcy, July 16, 1833, State Historical Society of Wisconsin; Marcy to Lieber, February 4, March 31, 1832; Butler to Lieber, April 7, 1832; Livingston to Lieber, April 12, 1832, Lieber papers.

of Federal supremacy. South Carolina put to test nullification, which Calhoun had formulated four years previously, and solemnly proclaimed that after February 1 the tariff laws of the United States would be null and void and of no effect within the state.

President Jackson immediately issued a ringing proclamation threatening to use force of arms to maintain the law, and property-minded New England, forgetting its dislike of Western democracy, rallied quickly to his support. Lieber attended a large meeting at Faneuil Hall where Daniel Webster, Harrison Gray Otis and Thomas H. Perkins all spoke for Jackson. Excitedly he wrote Secretary of State Livingston, who he was sure had written the proclamation, congratulating him upon it and assuring him it was within the bounds of the Constitution. Livingston cordially replied that he wished to communicate the letter to the President. "Your constitutional views of the great questions that now agitate the public are in my opinion perfectly correct and show a profound study of the principles of our government—and a correct knowledge of its practical operation." [29]

Lieber's patriotism was not coldly legalistic but warmly enthusiastic, as he showed the following summer when he accompanied Secretary of the Navy Woodbury aboard the frigate *Delaware,* about to take Livingston to France. All the ship's yards were manned and at the masthead flew the American flag. "It was a noble sight!" Lieber burst forth, "Ye nullifiers, can you look at our flag and persist in your narrow wretched politics? What men you must be, to sell all the Alps for a mole-hill!" [30]

With equal vigor Lieber defended his beloved America from the attacks of a British traveler who called upon him at his Boston study. The Reverend Mr. Isaac Fidler found the learned Doctor poring over a work on hieroglyphics, and was not impressed. Neither was Lieber, when the clergyman ventured to criticize American ways in a stupid, supercilious manner. If Beaumont and Tocqueville had thought that Lieber did not believe in American democracy they were mistaken; he viewed it through Justice

[29] Livingston to Lieber, December 24, 1832.
[30] Perry (ed.), *Lieber,* 96–97; Lieber to Marcy, July 16, 1833, State Historical Society of Wisconsin.

Story's conservative spectacles, but left no doubt in Fidler's mind that he was a thoroughgoing, alarmingly violent partisan of his adopted land.

The German-American, who could understand English class-divided politics much more easily than he could the hodgepodge American party system, knew very well that the flood of English travelers arriving in the early 1830's had descended upon democratic America largely to gather material to support the opponents of parliamentary reform. By ridiculing American democracy they might be able to block a wider extension of the British suffrage, the issue then rocking England almost to the brink of revolution. The Reverend Fidler was a mediocre lesser light; Mrs. Frances Trollope and Captain Basil Hall had made Americans writhe and fulminate.

Lieber "had passed . . . some time in London," the outraged cleric reported, "and had witnessed the mal-administrations of the higher orders there, and the slavery and degradation of the lower. 'The professions,' he went on, 'are depressed for want of encouragement, and literature and science are humbled in the dust. In America, any native may become President; and multitudes might be mentioned, who have risen to be members of the national legislation [sic] from the humblest parentage and birth. In England, it is impossible for talents to be rewarded or to meet with encouragement.'"

In reply to this, the forthright Tory sputtered a strong defense of his beloved British system. He discoursed on the excellence of the aristocracy and bragged of his native isle: "A third rate talent in the professions there, is certainly equal to the highest in the States. I am greatly mistaken if any first rate professional man exists in all America." And thus airing his indignation, he left Lieber's study abruptly.

Later, when Fidler held forth on the superiority of Albion at Pickering's house, it was the turn of American literary gentlemen to take rudely precipitous departure.

Following these heated exchanges, the blunt Briton penned his views on Lieber: "I perceive, that a foreigner, to gain the favour of the American public, must vilify his own nation, and condemn all hereditary rule. The native Americans sit wrapped up in self-complacency, and inhale the grateful fragrance of slavish adulation. The swindler, the profligate, the idle, the disaffected,—they who have deprived others of their property, or who have squandered their own, find that the price of American patronage is cheaply paid: they flatter and falsify. A person of higher principles, who is able by his talents and industry to maintain himself in Europe, will never stoop to this sort of baseness." [31]

Poor, dull Fidler wrote a book on his experiences, filled with ridiculous statements, garbled words, and pseudo erudition that would have made even Mrs. Malaprop blush. When it appeared in print, Pickering and his Cambridge friends joyously rushed to tear it to shreds.[32] Cold, scholarly Alexander Everett, editor of the *North American Review*, former minister to Spain, himself took lance in hand and charged the Fidler straw man. It was a shaky, flimsy thing which toppled at the first thrust, but the outraged Bostonian trampled back and forth upon it for a full forty-one pages.

In making the demolition complete, Everett paid warm tribute to the "German scholar": "As Dr. Lieber has, we understand, succeeded very well here, he has not of course had the same motive for reforming his political creed, which prevailed with our author, and we cannot consider it as fair or reasonable in the latter to be angry with him for not having done so. The intimation that because Dr. Lieber has succeeded where Mr. Fidler did not, the former must necessarily be a 'profligate, idle, disaffected swindler, who has deprived other people of their property, or squandered his own' . . . is as incorrect as it is unhandsome." [33]

From the ruins of Fidler's structure arose a tall, imposing Lieber, who had achieved a signal triumph—the august Brahmins had claimed him as one of their own and had defended him nobly in the pages of their sacred *North American Review*. Indeed, Lieber had become an American.

[31] Isaac Fidler, *Observations on Professions, Literature, Manners, and Emigration in the United States and Canada* (London, 1833), 61–65, 72–73. Lieber's words are given as reported by Fidler.
[32] Pickering to Lieber, July 22, 1833.
[33] [Alexander Everett], "Fidler's Observations on the United States," *North American Review*, XXXVII, (1833), 273–314.

VI

The Temperate and Reasonable Reformer

ALMOST every American of the Jackson period was
something of a reformer, and Lieber, thoroughly in the
spirit of the time, had his choice of a wide variety of
causes. He might have followed his old associate Charles Follen
into abolitionism, or he could have thrown in his lot with some
utopian colony; but the bombastic, fanatic professional reformers,
the women's-rights advocates, the abolitionists, and the utopians
were pariahs in the eyes of decent conservatives.

Lieber's every inclination carried him in an opposite direction. If he were to seek a living as a reformer, it was logical for
him to ally himself with the well-to-do patrons of the unfortunate,
who advocated thrift, temperance, and schooling in the trades as
a panacea for pauperism and crime.[1]

Unerringly, the ambitious intellectual joined the most prominent of the wealthy and respectable reformers, those Philadelphians who for decades had labored to improve conditions in prisons and penitentiaries. By becoming a widely known exponent of
their world-renowned "silent system," he augmented rather than
marred his prestige. Even Chancellor Kent, who had fought against
removal of the property qualifications for voting in New York and
was suspicious of almost every reform, granted as much. After
carefully perusing Lieber's notes on American penitentiaries, he
avowed: "I canot say I disagree with you on any point. You are
such a temperate & reasonable reformer, & so free from all ultra
Reform & fanaticism." [2]

[1] Merle Curti, *The Growth of American Thought* (New York, 1943), 368–96, contains a brilliant analysis of the bases of American reform movements of the middle
period.
[2] Kent to Lieber, September 2, 1833, in interleaved copy of Beaumont and
Tocqueville, *On the Penitentiary System in the United States,* Lieber papers, Johns

Lieber's enthusiasm for prison reform stemmed from his friendship with Beaumont and Tocqueville. During a visit to Boston, the zealous Frenchmen had fired him with their enthusiasms. To do so was easy, since Lieber as a political prisoner had spent many long months in Prussian dungeons. In democratic America his record of incarceration was a mark of honor, not a stigma, and as a one-time political prisoner interested in reform he joined the august company of John Howard, the father of modern prison reform, and even the Marquis de Lafayette. Lieber never tired of prison reform, nor of recounting his own experiences as a prisoner. Even before he became acquainted with Beaumont and Tocqueville, Lieber had corresponded with German experts on criminal law; an intensive study of penology was a logical progression. As ever, Lieber was alert for lucrative literary opportunities, and before the French experts left Boston he obtained their promise to send advance sheets so that he could translate their forthcoming report on American penitentiaries.[3]

By the time the advance sheets arrived, at the beginning of 1833, the energetic Lieber was fast becoming a prison authority in his own right. In preparing the article "Prison Discipline" for the *Americana,* he had leaned heavily upon the researches and prejudices of the pious Louis Dwight, secretary and guiding force of the Boston Prison Discipline Society, who was the passionate exponent of the Auburn system of separate confinement by night and communal but silent labor by day. Lieber later discarded these views to espouse the rival Pennsylvania system of solitary confinement during both day and night. While passing through Philadelphia in October, 1831, he visited the new Eastern Pennsylvania Penitentiary, "the best in existence, according to DeTocqueville and DeBeaumont," and struck up a warm friendship with the genial Quaker warden, Samuel Wood. Subsequent visits and a

Hopkins University. For a general account of the prison reform movement, see Blake McKelvey, *American Prisons, A Study in American Social History Prior to 1915* (Chicago, 1936), and for special treatments of the Pennsylvania system, Harry Elmer Barnes, *The Evolution of Penology in Pennsylvania, A Study in American Social History* (Indianapolis, 1927), and Negley K. Teeters, *They Were in Prison, A History of the Pennsylvania Prison Society, 1787–1937* (Chicago, 1937).

[3] Pierson, *Tocqueville and Beaumont in America*, 439; Gustave de Beaumont to Lieber, November 9, 1832, Lieber papers, Henry E. Huntington Library. All manuscripts referred to in this chapter, unless otherwise identified, are from this collection.

growing rapprochement with Philadelphia, as he prepared to move
from Boston, led him to disavow sharply his earlier views and prepare for the appendix of the last volume of the *Americana* an
article on the Pennsylvania system in which he stoutly argued the
merits of solitary over silent confinement.[4]

During subsequent months Lieber studied with a scientific thoroughness all the important penitentiaries in the eastern United
States, and though demonstrating at once a marked preference for
the Pennsylvania system, spent much time visiting rival institutions, debating penological problems with wardens, and gathering
prison reports, statistics, and information with which to improve
the French work. He studied the treatises of, and corresponded
with, the leading German penologists, Nicolaus Heinrich Julius,
and C. J. A. Mittermaier, professor of criminal law at Heidelberg.
He mulled over problems with Roberts Vaux, the Quaker philanthropist who was one of the prime movers of the Philadelphia
Society for Alleviating the Miseries of Public Prisons, and from
Dwight learned the necessity of taking full psychological advantage of the solemn moment when the convict doffed civilian
dress for prison garb. He visited ominous Sing Sing, and conversed
with the martinet Elam Lynds, its warden, who authorized an
average of six whippings daily. With remarkable thoroughness
he investigated corporal punishment, even trying the whip in
order to experience "the effects . . . in as great a degree as the
refractory convict does." The pain, he reported, was acute.[5]

In consequence of his thorough preparation, by the time Beaumont and Tocqueville's report arrived Lieber was in no mood to
subordinate himself to the anonymity of a mere translator. Rather
he preferred to function as editor, critic, and commentator. In
addition, he shaped the report into a formidable piece of ammunition for the Pennsylvania war against the Auburnites. From the

[4] Perry (ed.), *Lieber*, 92.

[5] Beaumont and Tocqueville, *On the Penitentiary System*, x; Lieber to Vaux,
February 5, 1833, Historical Society of Pennsylvania. Lieber's notes and clippings
on crime which he accumulated through a lifetime, and his correspondence with
Mittermaier and Julius are in the Lieber papers, Huntington Library. Pamphlets he
gathered comprise the better part of a seven-volume collection in the University of
California library. He recorded many of his opinions and experiences in the interleaved copy of *On the Penitentiary System*, Johns Hopkins University.

first ten advance sheets he accurately sensed the leanings of his French friends and commented: "They seem to me, to judge from the beginning, to give the decided preference to the Pennsyl. System, though, as a matter of expediency, considering the costs, they, perhaps advise the adoption of the Auburn system in France." Beaumont and Tocqueville could be equivocal, but Lieber was avowedly "a warm supporter of uninterrupted solitary confinement with Labor" and shaped his comments and additions accordingly. In so doing he added much to the already elaborate report.

In addition he tacked on a thirty-page introduction sketching his own views upon prison reform. He supplanted the material in some of the appendices with new data of his own, lengthened the section on temperance societies in order to gratify Mathew Carey, and at the end republished his defense of the Pennsylvania system from the *Encyclopaedia Americana*. At every juncture he added so many notes that the reader must have felt as though he were wading through a symposium between two sets of authorities.[6]

The aggressive young man carried his partisanship even into the dedication: to Edward Livingston, a worker for the solitary system; C. J. A. Mittermaier, a German adherent to the cause; and Roberts Vaux. Vaux wholeheartedly approved Lieber's course: "The [French] Commrs. have manifested great zeal, & industry in their duty, but they seem to want resolution to determine & proclaim regarding the *best* system, viz., the Pennsylvanian. . . . Thy notes have invariably shed light upon their text & in many instances corrected gross errors. . . . Thy annotations happily have always aided the reader to juster conclusions."[7]

As expected, when the prison report appeared in Philadelphia in the summer of 1833, it served as one of the chief explosives in the battle between the two groups of reformers. Carrying over into their avocations the same passionate and vituperative partisan-

[6] Lieber to Vaux, January 11, 1833; Lieber to Mathew Carey, May 13, 1833, Historical Society of Pennsylvania.
[7] Vaux to Lieber, May 5, 1833, Huntington Library; Vaux to Lieber, September 22, 1833, Johns Hopkins University.

ship with which they engaged in political and theological disputes, they expended at least as much energy upon disputation as they did upon improving American prisons.[8]

Although at the time partisan zeal tended to obscure the sound merit of the treatise, later scholars with justice regarded it as a classic in the science of punishment. The French writers had contributed an excellent study of the rise of American prison reform.

Out of the general revulsion against the overcrowding and foul physical and moral conditions of American jails, two rival reform programs had developed by the 1830's. One was the Auburn system which Lynds, a retired army captain, developed in New York. He locked the prisoners into separate cells at night and in the daytime imposed silence while they labored in common shops. Infringement led to merciless lashing. Lynds, a stern disciplinarian, even succeeded in forcing a gang of prisoners to build their own penitentiary at Sing Sing. Though cruel, the Auburn system was economical and comparatively efficient. Due to its economy and to the zealous campaigning of Louis Dwight, many states in the North founded prisons along its general pattern.

The mild-mannered Philadelphians were not looking for an economical mode of punishment. Rather they wanted a "penitentiary" system which, as the name denoted, would cause the prisoner to become penitent and reformed. To carry out their ideal, they built the Eastern Penitentiary of Pennsylvania, a model, fireproof prison with separate cells for each prisoner. Inmates received material for labor and books—usually of a religious nature —but throughout the period of confinement remained in solitude.

This system, thought the Pennsylvanians, prevented the prisoners from contaminating each other, eliminated the stigma of being seen in prison, led to the contemplation necessary for true penitence, and caused the prisoner to be truly reformed upon his re-entrance into the outside world. Opponents felt that solitary confinement because of its psychological effect upon the human mind was far too cruel a punishment. To thrifty Americans, there was the unanswerable argument that it was too expensive.

[8] Thus the Philadelphia-published *American Quarterly Review*, XIV (1833), 228–54, proclaimed: "A happy selection was made in Dr. Lieber as translator, the whole of whose labour bears testimony of close investigation of the subject . . . and serves as an antidote to any poisonous influence it may contain."

In this sober fashion, the Frenchmen reported upon American prisons. Lieber showed no such moderation in his comments. He himself had spent eight months in solitude, surrounded by books and papers and visited by friends. It had been a period of deep contemplation, of reordering his life. Why should it not work the same way for every dull-minded thief, forger, or prostitute? Likewise, what was better than solitude to cure a man of "a vitiated love of excitement, (such as is found in robbers, pirates, burglars &c.)"?

As for the cost, Lieber tellingly remarked: "But the problem of expense can only be truly solved by showing the cheapest method of keeping prisoners to be that which is most likely to reform them." [9]

Despite such comments, Lieber's introduction and notes were more than merely another polemic in an arid dispute. Both in the published book and in subsequent notations and correspondence, Lieber's inquiring mind encompassed the entire field of penology. In fact, the word "penology" itself was of his subsequent coinage. He adopted for his maxim, "Mild laws, sure judges, wise punishments," and sought to devise means to carry it into effect.[10]

The key, he felt, was the shift from physical force to moral power, a prime step in the rehabilitation of convicts. The Auburn plan, which when well administered entailed a minimum use of the whip, shared with the Pennsylvania system in the "new victory of mind over matter." "There is . . . a very great difference in punishments which consist of privations, and those which are composed of actual inflictions," Lieber emphasized. "The latter irritate our feelings much more, and lead to hatred and vengeance, whilst the former curb with more calmness." Under kindly, nonviolent treatment, prisoners ceased to feel at war with society.

In addition to the penitentiaries, the entire system of correction

[9] Beaumont and Tocqueville, *On the Penitentiary System, passim,* especially 298–99. Lieber wrote similarly to Mittermaier, February 24, 1833.
[10] Most writers have credited Lieber with invention of the word "penology." F. H. Wines, *Punishment and Reformation, An Historical Sketch of the Rise of the Penitentiary System* (New York, 1895), 2, and L. N. Robinson, *Penology in the United States* (Philadelphia, 1923), 1. Lieber first used the word in *A Popular Essay on Subjects of Penal Law and on Uninterrupted Solitary Confinement at Night and Joint Labour by Day, in a Letter to John Bacon, Esquire, President of the Philadelphia Society for Alleviating the Miseries of Public Prisons* (Philadelphia, 1838).

needed refashioning in the same spirit: houses of refuge for juvenile delinquents, separate incarceration of suspects awaiting trial, and separate prisons for women, which were then unknown. Above all, those merely under suspicion, children, and minor offenders must be kept separate from hardened criminals. "If it is noble to reclaim fallen virtue, it is much better still to prevent the fall."

Lieber emphasized the need to treat the convict neither as saint nor fiend. In justice, he should be punished, not brutalized; should lose his liberty, but not be subjected to filth and corruption. Prison should rehabilitate the criminal so that he would not again prey upon society.

Society could benefit even more from crime prevention. Certainty of punishment was one great deterrent of crime. Juries would not convict if laws were too rigorous; governors were far too prone to pardon. Hence Lieber later recommended to the Pennsylvania legislators that they abolish the death penalty and at the same time take the pardoning power out of the hands of a single man and hedge it around with restrictions. He cited Cesare Beccaria's statement that as punishments become more mild, clemency and pardon are less necessary. Certainty of punishment should extend to all classes and both sexes. Lieber abhorred leniency for the well born and exclaimed: "A well educated man, who commits a common crime, such as theft &c, ought to be punished at least with equal severity as a poor man." As for females, "There is no greater degradation of woman than . . . to relax the severity of law in trying & punishing her, as if she . . . [were] an unaccountable being, a being without moral worth." [11]

Lieber made one further contribution in his translation. He peppered the text with words new to the English language: "bureaucracy," "criminalist," and others. He delighted in filling in the inadequacies of the new idiom with mouthy words of his own making, and occasionally he turned or translated one that stuck in the language.[12]

[11] Interleaved Beaumont and Tocqueville, *On the Penitentiary System,* Johns Hopkins University. Lieber to Feating (draft), January 2, 1834.

[12] Kent to Lieber, September 2, 1833, in interleaved Beaumont and Tocqueville, *On the Penitentiary System,* Johns Hopkins University, comments upon the new words. For a definitive discussion of both the Report and Lieber's emendations, see Pierson, *Tocqueville and Beaumont in America,* 705–13.

Altogether, Lieber's work was far more than a conventional translation. Jared Sparks and other Americans wrote Tocqueville that the book had made a great reputation in the United States, but the surprised Frenchman complained that Lieber "feels himself obliged to contradict the smallest truths we utter about America." [13]

At the same time that Lieber translated the *Penitentiary System* into English, the learned Dr. Julius prepared a German version, also with comments, but more satisfactory to the French authors than Lieber's. From the two translations, they gathered Lieber's less obnoxious footnotes and some of Julius' additions to prepare a second edition in answer to their critics at home. Finally, by the forties, Tocqueville's hand was forced in the Chamber of Deputies, and he came out openly as a wholehearted defender of the Pennsylvania system.[14]

Whether or not the report as edited by Lieber made the French authorities *personae non gratae* with the Auburn group in the United States, it most certainly made the German-American one of the leading figures in the prison reform movement, and for more than a decade the main apologist for the Philadelphia society. When in the winter of 1835 his beloved system was under investigation by the Pennsylvania legislature for alleged irregularities of the warden and his assistants, Lieber came stanchly to the defense of both Samuel Wood and his techniques. The report of the majority of the investigators exonerated Wood completely. Again in 1843, when Charles Dickens launched a sentimental attack upon the Eastern Penitentiary in his *American Notes,* the prison society turned to Lieber to refute the libel.[15]

Though Lieber continued to sound the praises of the solitary system, he rapidly broadened the base of his penological studies.

[13] Pierson, *Tocqueville and Beaumont in America,* 708.
[14] *Ibid.,* 710–13; N. H. Julius, *Amerika's Besserungs-System, und dessen Anwendung auf Europa* . . . (Berlin, 1833); Beaumont and Tocqueville, *Système Pénitentiare . . . seconde édition entièrement refondue et augmentée d'une introduction, etc.,* 2 vols. (Paris, 1836); Beaumont and Tocqueville, *Système Pénitentiare . . . Troisieme Édition . . .* (Paris, 1845).
[15] "Eastern Penitentiary. Report of the Joint Committee of the Legislature of Pennsylvania Relative to the Eastern Penitentiary at Philadelphia . . . ," *Hazard's Register of Pennsylvania,* Philadelphia, April 25, May 2, 1835; [T. B. McElwee], *A Concise History of the Eastern Penitentiary . . .* (Philadelphia, 1835), 60–70; Teeters, *They Were in Prison,* 503–505.

Planning to write a comprehensive treatise on criminology, he continued to pay frequent visits to penitentiaries and to gather quantities of materials on both American and European crime and punishment. He never prepared the treatise, but he did write lesser works. In 1838 he developed a theory of punishment that fitted into his political philosophy—*A Popular Essay on Subjects of Penal Law*—and in 1835 he produced a pamphlet on the relation between education and crime.[16]

Through the use of criminal statistics, Lieber attempted to show that education, especially in the trades, was one of the surest deterrents of crime. Especially he sought to refute the charge made in Parliament that education, far from reducing crime in the United States, had the opposite effect. A government which introduced schools, Lieber noted, was likely to be vigorous in its policing; hence the number of convictions might increase without the real amount of crime rising.

Of greater significance as civilization became more complex was the gulf between the untrained and the educated. "There are no individuals more exposed to crime than the ignorant, in a civilized community," Lieber warned. They were less firmly linked to society, less able to earn a living, and lower in their own esteem and in that of the community.

He admitted education was no panacea for crime—some well-educated persons would always be found in prisons—but it did inculcate some moral lessons, provide discipline to tie the individual to society and the nation, train him to be temperate, and prepare him to earn a better living. Education would help eliminate the poverty-stricken class; poverty bred crime.

Both in his pamphlet on *Education and Crime* and in his translation of Beaumont's and Tocqueville's report Lieber's realistic recommendations bore striking resemblance to those of Jeremy Bentham, but the utilitarian impress upon him was indirect. Utilitarianism was the philosophical mainstay of all but the most evangelistic supporters of American prison reform, and in joining the movement, Lieber swallowed its rationale. Nevertheless, Lieber subsequently developed a formal theory of penology at vari-

[16] Francis Lieber, *Remarks on the Relation between Education and Crime, in a Letter to the Right Rev. William White* . . . (Philadelphia, 1835).

ance with utilitarian thought and enjoyed high standing as an authority in his own right both in Germany and in England. Julius looked to him as the leading American expert, and upon visiting the United States went to him for a letter of introduction to Warden Wood. Joseph Adshead gave Lieber's ideas currency in England.[17]

The young German-American, believing in his own originality, acknowledged no debt to Bentham. He scorned utilitarianism, if taken in a materialistic sense, as "the barbarism of our times," but his obligation was inescapable, not only in penology but also in the field of education.

While in England, Lieber had developed a knowledge of the Lancastrian schools through the charming Sarah Austin. These impressed him, but it was hard to determine when he drew upon his English observation and when upon the German fountain-head to which the utilitarians too turned for many of their educational concepts. It was Mrs. Austin who translated into English the report on German education by Victor Cousin which so deeply influenced the French and American school systems.[18]

Through playing a vigorous role at the New York educational convention, the scholar had convinced many Americans that he was a sound expert on pedagogy. Hence, when the Directors of the Girard Trust in Philadelphia, dominated by Roberts Vaux and Nicholas Biddle, wished plans for a training school for orphans, they turned to him.[19]

---

[17] Lieber's utilitarian penological ideas came through Livingston. See W. B. Hatcher, *Edward Livingston, Jeffersonian Republican and Jacksonian Democrat* (University, La., 1940), 267, 286; Edward Livingston, *A System of Penal Law for the United States* . . . (Washington, 1828); Joseph Adshead, *Prisons and Prisoners* (London, 1845), 75–76, 115–17; and the identical [Adshead], *The Fallacies of the Times* [London, 1845], 75–76; N. H. Julius, *Nordamerikas sittliche Zustande. Nach eigenen Anschauungen in den Jahren 1834, 1835 und 1836*, 2 vols. (Leipzig, 1839). A fragment of Lieber's letter introducing Julius to Sam Wood and, interestingly, the Marquis de Lafayette's letter introducing Beaumont and Tocqueville to Wood, March 28, 1831, are in the collection of Marion R. Silver, who has kindly made them available to the present writer.

[18] Lieber, *A Popular Essay on Subjects of Penal Law*, 93; Lieber, *Ueber die Lancasterische Lehrweise.*

[19] The Directors first commissioned Lieber in 1832, then decided upon a public competition for a $400 premium. When the Directors gave way to a board of trustees, it withdrew the competition and renewed the offer to Lieber. C. A. Herrick, *History of Girard College* (Philadelphia, 1927), 6–7; *United States Gazette*, December 11, 1832; Lieber to Vaux, November 20, 26, December 2 [14], 1832, Historical

Lieber enthusiastically prepared a plan of education in keeping with the spectacular five-million-dollar Girard bequest. He wished it to be the means of "carrying over some of the fruits of long and toilsome experience in Europe . . . and planting them [in] the fresh and rich soil of this new world." Consequently, he liberally interpreted the will to embrace no mere orphan school but a comprehensive polytechnic and teacher-training institution. It would offer a wide range of courses and encompass shops, laboratories, an observatory, and a press. He proposed the discussion technique for teaching some courses, and wished to bar corporal punishment on the upper levels.[20]

Lastly, Lieber proposed sending "a proper and well-prepared person" to Europe to inspect orphan asylums and polytechnic institutes and to acquire books and scientific apparatus. By no accident, the qualifications for this person, as well as those for the president, corresponded closely to those of Francis Lieber. Privately he confessed: "To be sure, it is no lofty idea, to beat orphan-bottoms all one's life along but—I would be perhaps not quite useless." Hopefully he submitted his report to Nicholas Biddle and the directors. They ordered it printed, paid him a premium of five hundred dollars, and even considered the European mission.[21]

From his New England friends Lieber received laudatory comments. Joseph Story considered the plan "invaluable for the materials it affords, the principles which it develops, & the sound doctrines which it inculcates." John Pickering hoped that Lieber would become "the *soul* of the new body in that Institution." Utilitarians welcomed the proposals with equal warmth. Mrs. Austin reported Lord Brougham's approval, and wrote that Lady Byron, who had started a school near London, was trying some of the suggestions.[22]

Society of Pennsylvania; Lieber to Biddle, September 1, 1833, Huntington Library. Frank Freidel, "A Plan for Modern Education in Early Philadelphia," *Pennsylvania History*, XIV (1947), 175–84.

[20] Lieber, *Girard College*. See the interleaved copy with appended letters, Johns Hopkins University, and MS., "My views on some points connected with the Organization of Girard College," May, 1834, Huntington Library. The introduction to the plan is reprinted in Lieber, *Miscellaneous Writings*, II, 497–523; Lieber to Biddle, September 1, 1833.

[21] Lieber, *Girard College*, 145–48; Lieber to Sparks, February 20, 1832, Harvard University; Perry (ed.), *Lieber*, 98; Herrick, *Girard College*, 8.

[22] Story to Lieber, February 15, July 24, 1834; Pickering to Lieber, February 19,

As Joseph Story had forewarned, the report augmented the German-American's reputation more than his purse. Though Carey, Lea & Blanchard printed the plan, Lieber owned the edition, and found few buyers. At the end of the year he despairingly pressed the New York legislature to buy a quantity for fifty cents a copy or less. A decade later, Girard College still had fifty copies on hand.[23]

The plan, which so delighted intellectuals, made no impress upon the practical Philadelphia politicians who were to control the Girard legacy. Even when sponsored by native-born Americans, German educational ideas were slow to win acceptance among the nationalistic American public, which saw a taint in anything introduced from abroad. Had Lieber been another Horace Mann, his task would have been difficult; laboring under a thick accent and a turgid, Germanic writing style, he found it impossible.

Probably lack of public interest prevented Lieber from ever publishing his later mature views upon the role of education in America: Truly popular democracy and the growing demands of industry for technical knowledge necessitated general training. The state should furnish all that was essential or that could not or would not be provided by private enterprise: common schooling, higher education, and special research. The immediate utility was of no significance, for "all knowledge elevates, tempers, and civilizes. Education alone is freedom and civilization. . . . Security and safety depend greatly upon diffusion of knowledge." [24]

Glowing from the sympathetic letters of the intelligentsia, Lieber did not realize his failure for many months. Early in 1834 he even planned to utilize the quantities of German materials he had gathered to prepare a two-volume work he would entitle "Letters on Education." Practical-minded Jared Sparks pointed out that this would be of undoubted value but problematical success.

1834; Mrs. Sarah Austin to Lieber, March 15, 1835, Huntington Library. Lieber to Story, April 23, 1834, Story papers, Library of Congress. See also, *Magazin für die Literatur des Auslandes*, October 8, 1834, pp. 483–84 and A. P. Stanley, *The Life and Correspondence of Thomas Arnold, D.D.* (New York, 1846), 269, 302–303.

[23] Lieber to Marcy, December 22, 1834, Historical Society of Pennsylvania; Herrick, *Girard College*, 8.

[24] Lieber, *Girard College*, 21–25; Lieber, note in interleaved J. B. Say, *A Treatise on Political Economy* . . . , opposite 436, Johns Hopkins University.

Lieber must think not in terms of Europe with its cheap labor, but in terms of the United States, "where the young men crowd in throngs into active life, and fill up spheres in which intellectual attainment or culture is not necessary to success. When do you think the time will come, that the University of Berlin, with its brilliant array of professors, would flourish in Philadelphia? Not till the forests shall all be felled to the foot of the Rocky Mountains, and 'every rood of ground maintains its man.' " [25]

Lieber could not afford to wait for a more populous America to bring a suitable living his way. Rather he scrabbled around for odds and ends to keep his family fed. In Washington he visited the Congressional Library, and was shocked to discover its poverty and paucity. Richard Peters, recorder of the Supreme Court, urged him to draw up a report for Congress urging a larger appropriation. Thus he might become librarian. He should also submit to Congress a plan for a great national statistical bureau, and through that obtain a fat commission. The New York Mercantile Library Association, which conducted excellent evening lecture series for apprentices, employed him to deliver three talks on commercial topics. In addition to these bagatelles were the usual schemes for books and periodicals.

Lieber even toyed with plans to enter business to make enough money to retire in ten years and devote himself to scholarship. He offered to work for Nathan Appleton in his cotton wholesaling establishment, but Appleton was not interested. He drew up an elaborate scheme for an exclusive private school and obtained the endorsements of leading Philadelphians. For many months he canvassed his acquaintances from New England to Washington, but received only empty promises. [26]

While on a visit to Washington he did become acquainted with

[25] Sparks to Lieber, February 4, 1834; Lieber to Sparks, January 25, 1834, Harvard University.

[26] Lieber to Story, January 20, 1834, Story papers, Library of Congress; Lieber to J. M. Wayne, March 27, 1834, New York Public Library; P. C. Fuller to Lieber, July 15, 1834; J. W. Stebbins to Lieber, November 15, 1833; T. G. Bradford to Lieber, January 10, 1834, Huntington Library; Lieber to Appleton, January 31, 1834, Massachusetts Historical Society; printed circular, "Dr. Lieber proposes . . . ," Philadelphia, February 11, 1834. Endorsees were John Sergeant, J. R. Ingersoll, Peter S. DuPonceau, N. Biddle, T. K. Mitchell, M.D., Robert Walsh, Wm. White, N. Chaperan, M.D., Wm. Drayton, and W. E. Horner, M.D.; Perry (ed.), *Lieber*, 98.

many of the nation's leading political figures. In the Senate chamber the learned German-American encountered debonair, flattering Henry Clay. "I did not think you were so young a man," Clay remarked. "Your reputation is far in advance of your years." [27]

Every morning Lieber sat in the Senate gallery, drinking in the debate. "There was probably never more oratorical talent collected within an assembly of forty-eight men than at present in the Senate," he noted. Eagerly he pursued his new acquaintances—but did not even mention in his journal the one who was to be his closest friend. That was a gifted young protégé of Judge Story's, a recent Harvard Law School graduate named Charles Sumner. "He was then a great, tall, lank creature, quite heedless of the form and fashion of his garb," a daughter of Richard Peters remembered years later, " 'unsophisticated', everybody said, . . . but the fastidiousness of fashionable ladies was utterly routed by the wonderful charm of his conversation."

Francis Lieber, with his slow, precise, but unceasing flow of anecdotes and ideas, covering two hemispheres and every conceivable topic from Kantian pacifism to the Parisian styles in ladies' bonnets, was an alluring mentor for the knowledge-hungry youth. And what could prove more gratifying to the discursive savant than an eager, uncritical, enthusiastic admirer? They met through a note of introduction from Peters and quickly formed a strong liaison. Sumner found himself reading the able treatise on Girard College, and henceforth was under Lieber's spell.[28]

Upon his return home the scholar, delighted with Sumner's admiration, asked Judge Story for the address and Christian name of the young lawyer. The Justice obliged and an incredibly voluminous correspondence began, which—save for a decade's interruption—continued until Lieber's death. Sumner, who was editor of the *American Jurist,* gladly opened its columns to the erudite publicist, who responded by submitting contributions at a bewildering rate. Likewise the eager and loyal admirer served without complaint for more than a decade as press agent, research assist-

[27] Perry (ed.), *Lieber,* 99; Lieber to Appleton, March 31, 1834, Massachusetts Historical Society. Appleton had given Lieber a letter of introduction to Clay.

[28] Perry (ed.), *Lieber,* 99; Edward L. Pierce (ed.), *Memoir and Letters of Charles Sumner,* 4 vols. (Boston, 1877–93), I, 125–27, 140.

THE LIFE OF FRANCIS LIEBER

ant, and errand boy for Lieber, who never hesitated to press yet a new and more exacting task upon him. In his turn, Sumner drank so deeply at Lieber's fountain of knowledge that in 1841 Lieber gayly confided to his wife: "The rogue plumes himself with my sayings. Well, he has a right, for he gives me always some good and substantial thing or other for my writings." [29]

While in Washington in the late winter of 1834, Lieber was less interested in Sumner than he was in getting the opinion of jurists on whether or not he might undertake a law career. Criminal law fascinated him and already he had promised Mittermaier he would prepare a treatise on the subject. However, John Sergeant was cool, Clay advised him to move West, and Justice Story told him that with his halting English and scholarly turn of mind he would fit better into "some Academical Professorship in a literary city."

Harvard University was to receive a legacy to found a history professorship, and Story thought few men so well qualified as Lieber for the position. Indeed, if Jared Sparks did not want the position, the Justice thought the German stood an excellent opportunity. Happily Lieber mulled over the new possibility. History was his "favorite science"; he would feel honored to be "the first professor of history perhaps in all America," and he could devote himself to scholarly researches. It was a lovely dream, that hope of a Harvard professorship; for more than two decades it never entirely evaporated from his mind.[30]

Amidst these evanescent hopes, Lieber departed from Philadelphia in June on a trip to Niagara to gather material for a book on America. Most English travelers who had taken quick jaunts through the States had turned out exasperating, authoritative volumes, superciliously denouncing the scenery and governmental system, the manners and mores of their American cousins. The Americans frothed violently against these "libels," but just as

[29] Lieber to Story, March 27, April 23, 1834, Story papers, Library of Congress; Story to Lieber, April 28, 1834, Lieber to Matilda Lieber, August 15, 1841, Huntington Library. The bulk of the Lieber letters to Sumner, numbering in all over seven hundred, are in the Huntington Library. Sumner's replies are in the main in the Sumner papers, Harvard University. Lieber's letters outnumber Sumner's replies by about three to one, but the actual disparity was not this great, since many of the Sumner letters are missing. Probably Lieber wrote Sumner about a thousand letters and notes. During the Civil War their correspondence was at times almost daily.

[30] Lieber to Story, March 27, April 23, 1834, Story papers, Library of Congress; Story to Lieber, April 5, July 24, Huntington Library.

110

strenuously hastened to buy them. Lieber hoped to capitalize upon the fad by writing a book of light chatter in which he praised his adopted land.

He recorded in vivid language the details of his trip. From New York he embarked on a river steamer for Albany, where he transferred to the new railroad, "the least *exciting* of all travelling." While one bowled along at the rate of a mile every four minutes, pent up in a narrow compartment with little of interest outside, and that little dashing by too fast to be observed, "you find nothing to entertain or divert you, except now and then a spark flying into the window of the car and burning a hole in a lady's veil." Passage along the Grand (Erie) Canal running through the Mohawk Valley was far more interesting.

As for Niagara, it thrilled and awed Lieber as had nothing else in America. Its terror reminded him of the time when he had stood on the brink of Vesuvius; its beauty, of the view from the castle of Acocorinth. "Niagara is like a powerful ode, a rhapsody in which nature herself has seized the mighty harp and plays a rapturous tune." [31]

Using his Niagara experiences as a framework, Lieber threw about them all kinds of anecdotes, tidbits, and discourses: the American women, American place names, his Waterloo adventures, the question of abolition, and numberless other topics. Many were frivolously entertaining; others foreshadowed his serious work. Throughout the summer he rapidly composed the book, though Nicholas Biddle warned him that, with all business at a standstill, he could not possibly find a publisher. But when, in November, he finished the manuscript, it was far too delightful a potpourri for Carey, Lea & Blanchard to refuse. [32]

This excursion into belles-lettres appeared under the ungainly title, *Letters to a Gentleman in Germany, Written after a Trip from Philadelphia to Niagara.* To the author's disgust, the English publisher, Richard Bentley, without permission dropped this

[31] Francis and Matilda Lieber to Fanny Appleton, May 5, 1833; Lieber, *The Stranger in America*, I, 259–62, II, 1–32, 310 *et passim.* Lieber poured forth his feelings concerning Niagara in an effusive German poem in manuscript at the Huntington Library.

[32] Lieber, *The Stranger in America*, I, 12, 98; Perry (ed.), *Lieber*, 100; Lieber, manuscript, "My Window in Manhattanville," 1833.

monstrosity for *The Stranger in America*. Whatever the title, it delighted reviewers. Charles Sumner exclaimed: "I think the Peace Society could do nothing better than to reprint yr Chapter on Waterloo as a tract. . . . It gives the most vivid sketch I have ever read of the horrors of war." Mainly, reviewers took the occasion to pay back English detractors. The *American Quarterly Review* screamed like the American eagle that "His views . . . are not the callow production of a brain which has expended its first efforts upon a subject grand enough for the most matured intellect, but emanate from a mind . . . liberal and unprejudiced . . . candid and intelligent." [33]

Loud as was Lieber's praise of American customs, he continued to dream wistfully of delicious air castles in Europe. In the fall, the Girard trustees would meet to decide whether or not to send him on an educational mission, and he hoped for the day when they might make his wishes realities.

But he wished to return as a visiting American, not as a Prussian going back to his fatherland. "I cannot say I have homesickness for Germany," he explained, "—but for Europe, for science and art." He emphatically deplored the speculativeness of German science, the absurd worship of Frederick the Great which colored German politics, and the misfortune that Prussia's superior school system caused her to ridicule democracy.

"The idea of a Constitutional Government, and of liberty founded on firm laws, has never been understood by Prussia," the young German-American lamented. "Hegel has done infinite harm to the cause of science. Instead of earnest, thoughtful investigation, and a discreet acknowledgment of previous experience, he is full of arrogance and presumption." [34]

For all its undemocratic pomposity, Prussia would provide music, art, and intellectual stimulus, in sharp contrast to the best America could offer. Nicholas Biddle favored sending Lieber immediately, and called a meeting of the committee on scholastic affairs for the first of October. Lieber impatiently awaited that day, pivotal in his life. But the dreams were vain, for a majority

[33] Sumner to Lieber, April 7, 1835, Harvard University. Bentley added an analytical table of contents to the work.
[34] Lieber to Mittermaier, September 13, 1834 (copy); Perry (ed.), *Lieber*, 101.

of the committee felt that the mission was outside the scope of the Girard will and voted "no." Crushed, Lieber later confided to his journal: "I have suffered much these days. I cannot yet write without a bleeding heart." [35]

Since the young scholar could not return to Europe, perhaps he would be forced to find his fortune in the West. The Harvard history professorship would not materialize for another six years, and that left as his primary hope the vacant presidency of Transylvania University in Kentucky. Since reactionary religious factions had forced the resignation of President Horace Holley early in 1827, the Kentucky institution had floundered in a trough of theological dispute. It was a college in little more than name.[36]

Impressed by Lieber's academic achievements, Henry Clay as early as the previous spring had urged him to apply for the vacant post. The thought of moving away from even the few books and sparse learning of the East Coast dismayed him. When in the summer Clay again suggested he apply, he replied that he could not make up his mind without knowing the particulars.[37]

The persuasive Senator answered with a lengthy, glowing picture of both Lexington and Transylvania University. The presidency would pay $1,200 and provide a residence. Finally, when the European bubble burst, Lieber belatedly applied. Clay received the application too late. The trustees appointed instead a Reverend Thomas W. Coit, whose administration was to be as unsuccessful as those of his predecessors.[38]

Certainly Lieber's hesitation had saved him from a most unpleasant ordeal, but at the end of 1834 he was where he had been at the beginning: still overflowing with publication projects and

[35] Lieber to Story, October 11, 1834, Story papers, Library of Congress; Biddle to Lieber, October 2, 1834, in interleaved Lieber, *Girard College,* Johns Hopkins University. Perry (ed.), *Lieber,* 101. Ironically, the trustees elected Alexander D. Bache president of the College and sent him on a similar mission to Europe less than two years later. H. W. Arey, *The Girard College and Its Founder* . . . (Philadelphia, 1852), 34.

[36] Niels Henry Sonne, *Liberal Kentucky,* 1789–1828 (New York, 1939); Robert and Johanna Peter, *Transylvania University, Its Origin, Rise, Decline and Fall* (The Filson Club Publications No. 11, Louisville, 1896), 158–61.

[37] Frank Freidel, "Henry Clay's Efforts, in 1834, to Obtain Francis Lieber, as President of Transylvania University," *Filson Club History Quarterly,* XVII (1943), 28–38. Clay to Lieber, July 1, 1834.

[38] Clay to Lieber, September 15, 1834. Lieber to Story, October 11, 1834, Story papers, Library of Congress; Clay to Lieber, December 3, 1834.

governmental schemes, barely keeping his head above water, and wondering if he ever could become established.

The worried young man pressed Little & Brown of Boston to publish his Latin Dictionary, even though it would compete with one by his old friend Follen; he urged Pickering to get him a contract for a volume of Greek and Roman antiquities; he tried to sell New York newspapermen on an advertising paper or shopping news, the "Alphabetical Advertiser"; and he proposed to Harper's a life of Prince Blücher. He pressed Levi Woodbury, the Secretary of the Navy, for appointment as envoy to Greece and Turkey, and urged upon congressmen his plans for a statistical bureau. He asked Story to suggest a school or college text which would yield profits. But above all came the repeated refrain, "God grant that I find at last a fixed spot." [39]

This he was to find where he least expected it, and in a setting almost as tempestuous as Transylvania University—South Carolina College.

[39] Lieber to Sumner, July 2, 1834; Pickering to Lieber, November 25, 1834, Huntington Library; Sumner to Lieber, July 17, 1834, Harvard University; Lieber to Story, November 8, 1834, Story papers, Library of Congress; Lieber to [Little and Brown?], December 17, 1834, Lieber papers, Library of Congress; Perry (ed.), *Lieber*, 101–102.

VII

Exile to South Carolina

THE chair at South Carolina College was created for Dr.
Lieber after a thoroughgoing faculty shake-up. The
rebuilding came several years after the storm of nullification nearly wrecked the institution. During the height of the state-
rights controversy, nullifiers and unionists with their bitter antagonism, and militant churchmen with their shouts of heresy
buffeted the college unmercifully. Even when the excitement died
down, they continued to press old animosities until President
Cooper resigned and the enrollment fell to a handful of students.
The trustees soon saw that only drastic measures could save the
institution; so at the end of 1834 they jettisoned the staff and re-
furbished the college with a less vulnerable set of scholars.

One man—the brilliant, irascible Thomas Cooper—brought
fame to the college, and through his extreme contentiousness led
it to this sorry impasse. Until Dr. Cooper's arrival in 1820, South
Carolina College had followed the sleepy, uneventful classical
path of almost every small institution of higher learning of its
time. During the first fifteen years of its existence, a pious and
conservative faculty led students through the conventional collegiate labyrinths from "Xenophon's Cyropedia" to "Locke's
Essay." Planters and merchants sent their sons, and, even as the
founding legislators had hoped, the college provided the lads with
Latin and Greek phrases and sent them on to pulpit, bar, and
hustings. South Carolina College quickly became the training
school for political leaders of the Palmetto State.[1]

[1] LaBorde, *History of South Carolina College,* 1–31; E. L. Green, *History of the
University of South Carolina* (Columbia, S.C., 1916). For an able discussion of the
classical curriculum, see George P. Schmidt, "Intellectual Cross-currents in American
Colleges, 1825–1855," *American Historical Review,* LII (1936), 46–67.

115

Then came the "sad year" of 1820—sad for lovers of the theologico-classical curriculum. Down from the North came the famous Dr. Cooper to become professor of chemistry, and soon president. He had been long in the public eye as a lawyer, unofficial physician, judge, chemist, agitator, and clergy baiter, and his past was as spectacular as his list of vocations was varied. Everywhere he had demonstrated a rare genius for stirring up virulent partisan controversy.[2]

At South Carolina College he showed no less talent for arousing the strongest emotions in his friends and foes. He was sixty, and built like a tub, but with the fire of a young man he trumpeted the glories of science and utilitarianism, and drastically remodeled the college courses to meet the practical needs of future lawyers, doctors, and clergymen.[3]

Above all, Dr. Cooper never missed an opportunity to shout his denunciations of the clergy. To him, all were hated foes, but none so much as the Presbyterians. Although they were few in number, they occupied a dominant position in the social structure. The denomination had come into South Carolina along with the Scotch-Irish frontiersmen, but its rigid system of control had ill fitted the democratic frontier. Poorer settlers tended to follow the lure of Baptist and Methodist camp meetings, and seceded from the old faith. Those aggressive Scotch-Irish who shouldered their way upward to form a prosperous second-generation planter aristocracy remained Presbyterians. They found in the Calvinistic doctrines a powerful buckler with which to shield their economic system and a keen-edged sword with which to challenge the hegemony of the Episcopalian aristocrats of the coastal area.[4]

The poorer sects had at first scorned education as a luxury, and

[2] Dumas Malone, *The Public Life of Thomas Cooper, 1783–1839* (New Haven, 1926) ; LaBorde, *History of South Carolina College,* 171.

[3] Thomas Cooper, *Lectures on the Elements of Political Economy* (Columbia, S.C., 1826) ; [Review], "Lectures on the Constitution of the United States," *American Quarterly Review,* I (1827), 501–502.

[4] George Howe, *History of the Presbyterian Church in South Carolina,* 2 vols. (Columbia, 1870–83) ; H. J. Ford, *The Scotch-Irish in America* (Princeton, 1915), 365–412 *et seq.;* W. W. Sweet, *The Presbyterians, 1783–1840* . . . (*Religion of the American Frontier,* II, New York, 1936) ; W. M. Gewehr, *The Great Awakening in Virginia, 1740–1790* (Durham, 1930), 187–219, discusses the essentially democratic nature of the Great Awakening to 1790; by that time the evangelical churches were already changing in character. H. R. Niebuhr, *The Social Sources of Denominationalism* (New York, 1929), 155.

a baneful impediment to divine inspiration, but the Presbyterians saw in the early nineteenth century that by controlling the colleges they could train and mold the minds not only of their own clergy but of the entire leadership of the South. Consequently, in 1818 they maneuvered their way into control of the University of Georgia, and thereafter sought to gain control of other institutions. Cooper, who, as one of them admitted, was "brilliant in conversation; terrible in controversy," had been an irritating thorn in their side.[5]

As an aggressive minority, the Presbyterians labored ceaselessly to rid South Carolina College of this dangerous iconoclast. Finally, in 1831, the state legislature ordered his religious views investigated. Cooper defended himself brilliantly with an able plea for religious liberty and was exonerated. Doubtless his success came in part because his views on many important issues were popular: he was an agitator for nullification, a supporter of slavery, and a foe of the protective tariff. After his vindication, since he was by now an old man, he decided to relinquish his stormy post.[6]

As soon as President Cooper resigned, the pious folk of South Carolina demanded a thoroughgoing purge of the college. Cooper, they claimed, had contaminated the institution with his dangerous ideas; frightened parents were keeping their sons at home or sending them north for their education. The enrollment fell to about fifty, then to twenty. Clearly the college must remove Cooper's taint, or it would fall to pieces. The trustees, yielding to the pressure, at the close of 1834 demanded the resignation of the entire faculty and began a search for suitable replacements.

They offered the presidency to a Northerner, Benjamin Silliman, Yale's great popularizer of science, who combined profound scientific training with undoubted piety. Silliman declined. Likewise, Thomas R. Dew of the University of Virginia, leading exponent of the proslavery argument, refused the chair of political

[5] E. M. Coulter, *College Life in the Old South* (New York, 1928), 193–214; Sonne, *Liberal Kentucky;* Gewehr, *The Great Awakening in Virginia,* 218–34.

[6] Malone, *The Public Life of Thomas Cooper,* 252–401; LaBorde, *History of South Carolina College,* 127–80; Colyer Meriwether, *History of Higher Education in South Carolina* (U.S. Bureau of Education, *Circular of Information* No. 3, 1888, Washington, 1889), 147–59; Leon Yakeley, "The Development of Higher Education in the Jacksonian Period, 1825–1840," (Unpublished Doctoral Dissertation, University of Southern California, 1936).

economy. Francis Lieber, though little more enthusiastic, was far more impecunious and could not reject the offer Dew spurned when it came his way.

The South Carolina agent to sound out Northern candidates was Colonel William Drayton, powerful Unionist leader in the nullification controversy, who had just moved to Philadelphia. There Nicholas Biddle and Joseph Ingersoll brought Lieber to his attention. Toward the end of January, 1835, he called upon the young German-American and was impressed with the scholar's broad range of knowledge. Here was no ordinary catch: a man trained in the finest continental universities, tutored by the historian Niebuhr, associate of the leading intellects of the North, editor of an excellent encyclopedia, and an authority upon prison reform, political economy, and education. Only his religious concepts and his attitude toward Southern institutions remained open to question. Any doubts in Drayton's mind were dispelled by Lieber's evident personal piety and his ardent defense of free trade. The presence in the scholar's household of a black "servant," George, lent him by a Puerto Rican brother-in-law, probably clinched the matter.

Lieber's "various accomplishments and attainments, both in private life and as a public instructor," reported Drayton to the governor of South Carolina, "in the opinion of the most distinguished literary and scientific gentlemen in the United States, eminently qualify him for the presidency of a college." Negotiations began.[7]

Lieber was little better pleased at the prospect of teaching in South Carolina than he had been over the thought of becoming president of Transylvania, but times were hard and soon another baby would arrive. James Kent, Joseph Story, John Sergeant, Joseph Ingersoll, Nicholas Biddle, and Edward Livingston all

[7] LaBorde, *History of South Carolina College*, 175, 189–90; Robert Y. Hayne, Henry W. DeSaussure, David Johnson, William Harper, and Patrick Noble, *Appeal in Behalf of the South-Carolina College* (Charleston, 1835), 6, 14; G. P. Fisher, *Life of Benjamin Silliman . . .*, 2 vols. (New York, 1866), I, 295–97; Lieber, journal, January 27, 1835, copy in Lieber papers, Henry E. Huntington Library. All manuscripts referred to in this chapter, unless otherwise identified are from this collection. Drayton to Lieber, Philadelphia, [1835], University of South Carolina Library.

wrote strong recommendations; the South Carolinians invited him to Charleston for an interview.[8]

Charleston was lovely when Lieber visited it at the end of March. The city was filled with stately mansions and semitropical trees and shrubs; but already many of the houses needed fresh paint, for, like the state, it was passing its prime. The rapid westward sweep of the cotton kingdom had brought prosperity in the early 1800's as the Scotch-Irish yeoman farmers of the Piedmont underwent metamorphosis into slaveowning planter aristocrats. Then, to the detriment of South Carolina, the sweep continued into the newer, richer lands of western Georgia, Alabama, Mississippi, and out toward the Texas frontier. Charleston tended to become a backwater while the more accessible ports of Savannah, Mobile, and New Orleans boomed; upland planters found prices declining sharply as cotton from richer Western lands flooded the market. Numerous Carolinians sought a way out of the impasse by moving westward; a very few urged crop diversification and improved methods of agriculture; and the great majority had looked for the solution through nullification of the tariff.[9]

The tariff was a tangible evil—for a large part of South Carolina's cotton went to England, and returning imports paid a half-million dollars a year in duties at the Charleston customhouse. Aggrieved Carolinians saw here the crux of their troubles: they contributed far more than their fair share of governmental expenses to subsidize Northern factory owners. With more fervor than accuracy, George McDuffie told planters that in effect the government was seizing forty out of every hundred bales of cotton they produced. Since attempts to obtain redress through Congress had failed, the only solution was separate action by the state.

[8] Perry (ed.), *Lieber*, 104.

[9] Avery Craven, *The Coming of the Civil War* (New York, 1942), 60–66, emphasizes the economic interpretation of nullification. In 1811, South Carolina grew about 50 per cent of an 80 million pound cotton crop; in 1834, less than 15 per cent of a 457 million pound crop, F. J. Turner, *Rise of the New West* (New York, 1906), 47. Prices had been exceedingly low from 1826 through 1832, L. C. Gray and E. K. Thompson, *History of Agriculture in the Southern United States to 1860* (Washington, 1933), II, 698–99. D. F. Houston, *A Critical Study of Nullification in South Carolina* (Harvard Historical Studies, Vol. III, Cambridge, 1896), 44; J. G. Van Deusen, *Economic Bases of Disunion in South Carolina* (New York, 1928), 17–58, grants this, but emphasizes the injustices of the tariff.

Through a logical formula called nullification, they could declare the tariff null and void within their state borders.

This doctrine found wide support among distressed cotton planters, but by no means won universal endorsement. Many prosperous rice planters suffering no Western competition, large numbers of conservative Charleston merchants fearing nullification would unsettle business, numerous old-line former Federalists sensing the inadequacies of the doctrine, and a fringe of Piedmont farmers suspicious of any planter proposal—all these formed a militant unionist minority. They had polled a substantial 17,000 votes against the 23,000 for nullification in the fall election in 1832. The majority at a special convention had voted to nullify the tariff in a few months, and the threat had worked. Congress rushed through a compromise tariff, but it was far less significant in bringing about recovery than a cycle of high cotton prices. The basic destructive economic forces worked on undiminished.[10]

The nullification controversy was fresh in the minds of Carolinians who conversed with Lieber. Robert Y. Hayne, who had debated in the Senate with Webster and returned home to lead the nullification convention, showed the rather shocked scholar the well-equipped state arsenal, which was costing the taxpayers a full ten thousand dollars a year. By now Hayne had plunged into the promotion of railroads, the main means by which Charlestonians hoped to tap the Western markets. Lieber made a friend of General James Hamilton, another former governor, who, though not too strong a nullificationist, had commanded the South Carolina state troops during the crisis.

While Lieber liked the nullification leaders, he felt far more sympathetic toward James L. Petigru, "the greatest private citi-

[10] Van Deusen, *Economic Bases of Disunion*, 30, 331–32. The ideas expressed in the paragraph are not Van Deusen's. Most writers have failed to see much economic significance in the nullification vote: "A plot of the vote shows clearly that there was no marked sectionalism in the vote. The supporters of each party were distributed nearly equally in both the interior and the coastal sections." C. S. Boucher, *The Nullification Controversy in South Carolina* (Chicago, 1916), 207. A replot along crop lines by the present writer would indicate that the upland cotton areas, where cotton production was heaviest, were about three-fourths in favor of nullification; the Piedmont fringe was well over 60 per cent opposed; the sea-island cotton and rice districts of Beaufort, Colleton, and Charleston were about 60 per cent in favor; the heaviest rice-growing area (Clarendon, Williamsburg, and Georgetown) was approximately 53 per cent opposed; and Charleston was a little over 52 per cent in favor.

zen that South Carolina has ever produced." Petigru, though a former law partner of Hamilton's, had been a stancher Unionist than Hamilton was a nullifier. At a dinner party Hayne gave in honor of Lieber, both Hamilton and Petigru shocked the young man by telling him how closely the factions had approached bloodshed. Two groups had met each other angrily on a dark street one night, and one of the nullifiers knocked Petrigru into the gutter. Riot was imminent, but quickly the nimble-witted Unionist called out to Hamilton, "I slipped and fell," then whispered in his ear, "For God's sake move on." [11]

The trip likewise gave Lieber his first view of the slave-plantation system of the deep South. General Hamilton invited him to a rice plantation on Pennyworth Island. There barefoot Negro servants brought a sumptuous repast, including four different meats, and afterwards Lieber rode with Hamilton along the embankments to visit neighboring plantations.[12]

After a fortnight the young German-American returned home, taking with him the expectation that he would receive a professorship of the college but not the coveted presidency. His erudition impressed the South Carolinians, but General Hamilton wisely noted that two obstacles would bar him from the presidency: he was a full ten years too young to be acceptable and his fluent English carried a strong German accent. Hamilton felt that Lieber spoke better English than any foreigner he had met, but the German-American had not, and subsequently did not, master the difficult "th" sound. He continued to say "dings" for "things." The president must speak English without a flaw, since "the power of the President in the discipline of the college is most effectually exerted in eloquent and impressive exhortations to the students." Nevertheless, Lieber could admirably fill the professorship of history and political economy. For either office, Hamilton promised his most friendly and zealous support, "as I have never in a short acquaintance formed a higher estimate of any individual or cherished for a comparative stranger a more lively esteem." [13]

[11] Lieber journal, March 21, 25, 26, 1835, copy in Lieber papers. Lieber to Everett, October 27, 1863, University of South Carolina.
[12] Perry (ed.), *Lieber*, 104–105.
[13] Hamilton to ?, April 1, 1835 (contemporary copy in Lieber's hand). Hamilton supported Lieber at the trustees' meeting, C. A. Heckscher to Lieber, June 6, 1835.

On June 5, 1835, the Board of Trustees of South Carolina College elected Lieber to the chair of history and political economy at a salary of two thousand dollars a year and a house. Lieber at once accepted, but with a heavy heart. "Oh! my poor life!" he exclaimed. Yet even before his trip to Charleston he had accurately appraised the situation: "I must bid farewell to all that is most precious and dear to me, and shall be compelled to live in a Slave State; yet I shall . . . have a settled sphere of activity, and shall be able to exert my influence in the right direction. It will give me the means of supporting my family, and the time to write on subjects which have long occupied my mind."

"Remember how my heart clings to European culture and science," Lieber beseeched his Heidelberg friend Mittermaier, whom he urged to send books, pamphlets, letters, criticisms, anything to lessen the burden of exile. From South Carolina College, he requested a catalogue of the library so he would know what works he must bring to augment it.

Lieber feared too that he might be forgotten in the North. He urged Sumner to act as a "standing committee of vigilance" to republish in Boston papers whatever comments about him appeared in English newspapers and reviews.

Yet the scholar recognized the kindness and friendliness of the South Carolinians, and felt that besides gaining economic security he would obtain recognition as a leader. He still hoped for election to the college presidency in the fall. In any event, he confidently expected to gain prominence as a reformer. He had visited Charleston's poorhouse and jail and had discovered how extremely backward South Carolina was in penal law and prison discipline. He was sure leading citizens would back him in a movement to remedy the situation. In addition, he would write the long-contemplated books on criminal law and American constitutional liberty. The exile might be discouraging, but Lieber intended it to be fruitful.[14]

Governor George McDuffie also favored Lieber, McDuffie to James L. Petigru, March 24, 1835 (contemporary copy in Lieber's hand). Concerning Lieber's accent, see Meriwether, *Higher Education in South Carolina*, 176.

[14] Lieber to Edward W. Johnston, secretary of the trustees of South Carolina College, June 13, 1835, trustees' papers, University of South Carolina; Lieber to Sumner, April 13, June 6, 1835; Matilda and Francis Lieber to Fanny Appleton, April 20, 1835; Lieber to Mittermaier, June, 1835, translated copy; Perry (ed.), *Lieber*, 105; LaBorde, *History of South Carolina College*, 191. Sumner obligingly acted as literary and press agent for Lieber. He ran scores of minor errands without

As a farewell to the culture he loved, and as an act of almost filial devotion, Lieber prepared a short book of reminiscences of Barthold George Niebuhr. While rearranging his papers he had come upon the diaries, notes, and commonplace books he had kept during the halcyon months in Rome. The journals brought back poignant memories of the great scholar— "he dead and I an exile! —I felt as if I walked through an Italian garden, charming indeed, with perfuming flowers, and lovely alleys and fountains . . . but I felt, too, as if I walked alone in it . . . every spot reminded me of him, and what I owe to him." [15]

From among his notes Lieber quickly assembled a collection of his patron's table talk to which he prefaced a delightful autobiographical introduction. With charming candor, Lieber recounted Niebuhr's kindly reception of the ragged, penniless, and discouraged youth, and the boy's acute embarrassment over dining in ill-fitting clothes among the assemblage of fine ladies. His description was so amusing that newspapers and reviews copied it widely. Indeed, a year later when he met the Governor of Puerto Rico that worthy inquired if he were the Lieber whose pantaloons would not meet his sock tops. [16]

Unfortunately the quality of the book was far below that of the lively introduction. It was a long hodgepodge of not-too-acute sayings with frequent interpolations by Lieber. The London *Quarterly Review* protested with some justice that the author had not sounded the depths of understanding of the great man, and young Henry Longfellow commented in his diary, "here and there the writer's vanity peeps out too conspicuously. He cannot help strutting out from the background—from behind the scenes—to say to the audience 'Ladies and Gentleman [*sic*]!—if I had only a part in the play, I should say so and so.' " [17]

Most readers and reviewers were less critical. Edgar Allan Poe, whose pen could be scathing, pronounced the style of the intro-

---

complaint, solicited publishers, and published puffs in the *Atlas* and other Boston journals. See Sumner to Lieber, June 8, December 2, 1835, Sumner papers, Harvard University, and the ample correspondence for these years.

[15] Perry (ed.), *Lieber*, 105. Lieber finished the manuscript in time to send it to England with George Ticknor. Earlier he had asked Henry Wadsworth Longfellow to speak to Bentley about it. Lieber to Ticknor, May 2, 1835, copy.

[16] Woodstock, "The Scholar's Breeches," *The Literary World*, VII (1850), 265.

[17] "Reminiscences of . . . Niebuhr . . . ," *Quarterly Review*, LV (1835), 234–50; Longfellow journal, March 29, [1836], Longfellow House.

duction one of "irresistibly captivating *bonhommie* and *naïveté*." Sumner loyally vowed that Niebuhr's character stood out "like a king's head on a piece of coin," and attributed any deficiency of brilliance in the quotations to a lack of depth on the part of the subject. On the whole the *Spectator*, the *Literary Gazette*, and the American reviews were favorable; the little book was a success. In addition to Bentley's publication in England, Carey, Lea & Blanchard issued it in the United States, and a German edition appeared at Heidelberg.[18]

Lieber turned immediately from the reminiscences of Niebuhr to the compilation of data for his projected work on American politics, but in the summer of 1835, before he had even arrived in the South, the stridency of South Carolina political realities rudely broke into his theorizings. He was thoroughly steeped in the German tradition that a scholar is a servant of the state and largely above parties, and, since he had gained his new post through the support of both unionists and nullifiers, he thought he had no reason to expect personal difficulties. He had overlooked the militant Presbyterian party, which had failed in its plans to fill the faculty with its own clergy or communicants. Shortly after the trustees announced their appointments, the Presbyterians began stirring up resentments. Similar tactics at the University of Virginia years before had led Jefferson to brand them "the most intolerant of all sects, the most tyrannical and ambitious, ready at the word of the law-giver, if such a word could now be obtained, to put the torch to the pile, and to rekindle in this virgin hemisphere, the flames in which their oracle Calvin consumed poor Servetus. . . ."[19]

Now they were ready to burn Lieber academically, and for fuel they possessed his more than ample writings. Delving into the *Encyclopaedia Americana*, they brought forth excerpts to damn him as a tariff man, an abolitionist, and a foe of state sovereignty. Worst of all, they claimed that his Girard Report had proved him an atheist.

[18] "Reminiscences of . . . Niebuhr . . . ," *Southern Literary Messenger*, II (1836), 125–27; Sumner to Lieber, December 2, 1835, January 9, 1836, Harvard University; Boston *Daily Atlas*, January 6, 1836; [C. C. Felton], "Reminiscences of . . . Niebuhr," *North American Review*, XLIII (1836), 120–32.

[19] Clement Eaton, *Freedom of Thought in the Old South* (Durham, 1940), 285.

Lieber danced in a lively manner as the flames of accusation licked around his feet. From the Girard Report he brought forth long excerpts to prove his piety, and he protested that he could not stand responsible for every word in the *Americana*—the burden of Atlas would have been slight compared with his, had he himself written every article. He had asked a South Carolinian to prepare an article, but the gentleman had been too busy to comply. He made no direct defense of state rights, but could with candor plump strongly for minority rights: he opposed all forms of absolutism, including democratic absolutism, "where the representative of sovereignty considers himself the actual sovereign, which in republics is the case when the majority believe they are the people themselves, uncontrolled in power."

Lieber side-stepped the horrible charge of abolitionism with equal agility. Only a few days earlier he had spiked the rumor that he was editor of the *Philanthropist*. Now he wished to put a permanent end to all such pernicious charges; so he pointed to the irony that a writer in the London *Monthly Review* had accused him of lending his pen to "sharpen still more the arguments which have been used against abolition." The theorist studiedly avoided a positive statement of his views on slavery, but cannily defined an abolitionist in such a way as to place himself outside that proscribed circle. "An abolitionist," he declared, "is a person who is desirous of immediate and unconditional emancipation of that part of our population which labors under servitude, and who openly or clandestinely maintains the expediency or right of meddling with this subject, for any one else but each State within her limits. —And, sir, I am not an abolitionist." [20]

As Lieber spread his disavowals through the press of South Carolina, his supporters in the state rushed to quench the Calvinistic fire. One group boldly published an accusation that the Reverend Dr. Benjamin Gildersleeve, editor of a Presbyterian organ, the Charleston *Observer,* and the Reverend Richard S. Gladney, editor of the Columbia *Times and Gazette* and the *Southern Christian Herald,* were directing their tirades against

[20] Lieber to the Columbia *Telescope,* July 16, 1835, together with a favorable editorial on the Girard Report, Columbia *Telescope,* August 1, 1835, clipping in Lieber papers, Huntington Library. Lieber to ?, July 10, 1835, Lieber papers, Library of Congress.

Lieber because their own candidates had been defeated. Since they failed to control the faculty, they were urging churchmen to boycott South Carolina College in favor of the Presbyterian-controlled University of Georgia. Lieber's defenders flatly labeled this "a course of vulgar intrigue and shuffling for office . . . sufficient to disgrace the dirtiest stalls of a horse market." [21]

Hayne and a highly distinguished group of trustees wrote a more dignified reply to the Presbyterians. To vindicate Lieber's character, they published a laudation by Governor George Mc-Duffie and excerpts from the excellent letters recommending the professor-elect. Deriding the charge that South Carolina College and the new professor were anti-Christian, they commented that apparently even Dr. Lieber's open profession of religion, membership in a Christian church, and exemplary conduct did not invest him with sufficient piety. Could only Presbyterian clergy achieve the requisite standard? [22]

Backed by potent political figures, Lieber emerged unscorched, but the embers still remained, and always there would be factions ready to blow them aflame. Even while the charges against him smoldered, he clipped a letter from the Charleston *Courier* in which John England, the distinguished Catholic Bishop of Charleston, carefully denied to the people of South Carolina that he had "received and retained one of the mischievous productions which have been sent hither from New York." Bishop England further claimed that his school for free Negroes was entirely within the law, and that he was entirely willing to acquiesce to the wishes of the people in his conduct of it. Across the top of the clipping Lieber disgustedly scrawled: *"Politics* No Master so absolute as the people! A cringing bishop! How careful he steps &C." [23]

Lieber in Pennsylvania could view Bishop England's disclaimer

[21] John G. Brown, N. Herbemont, Albert Moore Smith, James H. Taylor, Theodore Stark, *The True Motives Exposed for the Attacks Upon the South Carolina College*, [1835]. The writers printed a letter purportedly showing connivance between Gildersleeve and the officials of the University of Georgia.

[22] Hayne and others, *Appeal in Behalf of the South-Carolina College.* Twenty years later, Lieber noted on the outside of his copy of this pamphlet and the one cited above: "Two publications showing that the beginning was pretty much as the end. Found in packing my books previous to leaving Columbia, in December, 1856." Lieber papers.

[23] John [England] to Charleston *Courier*, July 29, 1835; Alexander H. Brown to Charleston *Courier*, July 30, 1835, in clipping with annotation by Lieber.

with contempt, but Lieber in South Carolina was to take lessons from him in the art of cringing. That same autumn, Bishop England sympathetically explained to him the machinations of the party "which under the pretext of religion indulges in that malevolence of disappointed monopoly." It was so powerful in the state, England warned, that Southern society would not forgive him his religion. "My dear bought experience has taught me that I made a most disastrous mistake in imagining that what I deemed liberality was to be found in the land . . . because I thought that there men left each other free in their intercourse with heaven."

Bishop England congratulated Lieber on the success of his faction in the contest over the college faculty, and advised urgently: "Keep free of political & religious parties, preserve discipline & order in the establishment—turn the abilities you have to account for your Students. Answer no attack made upon you & you must succeed." This was hard advice for a man of Lieber's contentious nature to follow, but it was as sound as it was hard, and for many a year the professor found it his salvation.[24]

Lieber would have been still more melancholy when he boarded the steamer for Charleston had he known that what he expected to be a brief interlude would lengthen into a sojourn of twenty-one years. Certainly, upon his arrival with his wife and two sons at the sleepy little capital town of Columbia, he regarded it as little other than a temporary abode. It was a small, unexciting country village of less than four thousand population—a funnel where the Broad and Saluda rivers met to form the Congaree, down which flowed the upland cotton to the coast.

Columbia, like Washington, was a capital by legislative fiat, and also like the national capital was laid out in a flourish with broad, unpaved streets. Many of them were lined with houses of a slipshod, "shotgun" construction—two or three rooms scattered along a narrow hall at one side of the house—but magnolia, oak,

[24] John [England] to Lieber, October 27, 1835, University of South Carolina. Lieber's extreme caution after his arrival is well illustrated by the fact that the only evidence that he struck up a friendship with the proscribed Dr. Cooper is in a letter Cooper wrote H. C. Carey, November 4, 1835, Edward Carey Gardiner collection, Historical Society of Pennsylvania. The present writer is indebted to Dr. George Winston Smith for calling his attention to this letter.

127

THE LIFE OF FRANCIS LIEBER

and mimosa trees, and yards brilliant with roses, azaleas, camellias, and wisteria overcame this ugliness. The South Carolina College campus on Sumter Street was most attractive. It formed a delightful elm-shaded quadrangle, similar in design to that of English universities, faced by a double line of buildings. These, with their gray-painted brick walls of early-Republican-style architecture, reflected accurately the solid, conservative ideal of the institution.[25]

Columbia was normally a drowsy country town, but during the legislative sessions, upcountry yeoman farmers and poverty-stricken sand-hillers intermingled bellicosely in its streets with meticulous Charleston dandies. Indeed, the very appearance of some of these exquisites must have served as a challenge to a brawl. One appeared in Columbia resplendent in "a bottle green cassimere coatee, buff Marseillese vest, loose pantaloons of finest white linen, with a ruffled shirt, a bell-crowned beaver hat, and around his neck a black silk Barcelona handkerchief showing a double bow-knot in front. On his feet white silk stockings and low quartered pumps." [26]

The solid element, led by the Hampton family, greatest planters in the state, Colonel David J. McCord, head of the local branch of the Bank of South Carolina, and the faculty of the college, temporarily under the chairmanship of the genial Henry Junius Nott, a whimsical writer of belles-lettres, whiled away their time with gay soirees, hunting parties, or long conversations which most often centered around the two most engrossing topics: crops and politics. To abstruse intellectual conversations not concerning Southern institutions they lent a polite, but sometimes not too attentive, ear. Yet they were far from backward in asserting the complete intellectual supremacy of the college of which they were so proud, nor could they help looking down a trifle upon the newcomer, who in addition to being from outside South Carolina, had not even been born within the United States.

[25] For descriptions of South Carolina College and Columbia, see W.P.A. Federal Writers' Project, *South Carolina: A Guide to the Palmetto State* (New York, 1941), 212–25; Helen K. Hennig (ed.), *Columbia, Capital City of South Carolina* (Columbia, 1936); J. F. Williams, *Old and New Columbia* (Columbia, 1929); and E. L. Green, *History of the Buildings of the University of South Carolina* (Columbia, 1909).

[26] Hennig (ed.), *Columbia*, 244.

128

Even if the social leaders of Columbia could not take the Liebers entirely within their hearts, they could and did show them most lavish hospitality. Before their arrival, Governor George Mc-Duffie urged them to spend a week at his plantation home, Cherry Hill, and when they reached Columbia in early October, Professor Nott put them up in his own home for a fortnight. Then they moved into a four-room apartment on the campus, and, as their furniture had not yet arrived, the friendly Hamptons loaned them beds. Lieber glowed with pleasure over this generosity and thought the people fine and openhearted, but he abhorred his surroundings. Within a fortnight after his arrival, he sounded an indictment of the South which he would never rescind, "Everything is arid here; arid soil, arid life, arid society; nor a breath of scientific air, nor a spark of intellectual electricity . . . surely, forever I could not live so; I would rather go to Alabama and become a planter, make a competency in five years, and then [write.]" [27]

Lieber based this and endless later denunciations upon dissatisfaction with the immaturity of his restless students, the lack of intensive scholarship among his cultivated Southern friends, and the backwardness of the economic system built around slavery. To an even greater extent his bitterness grew out of thwarted ambition. As time passed, his reputation waned. The many Northern positions for which he aspired danced like so many jeering phantoms just behind his grasp. He could not even obtain the consolation prize: the presidency of his own college. His career, which had resembled a meteor, now threatened to assume the curve of a burned-out skyrocket; and he who had been the intimate—and aspired to be the equal—of great intellectuals and statesmen, bridled at the thought of wasting his days as an indifferent disciplinarian presiding over unappreciative adolescents. The intense young man rapidly began to age and sour.

But Lieber was fundamentally practical. His family was large and their needs many; hence prudence demanded that, distasteful as his new position might be, he should establish himself at South

---

[27] McDuffie to Lieber, September 23, 1835; Lieber to Sumner, October 27, 1835. Perry (ed.), *Lieber*, 108–109. William M. Geer, "Francis Lieber at the South Carolina College," *The Proceedings of the South Carolina Historical Association*, 1943, pp. 3–22. This competent account emphasizes the scholar's chronic discontent, since it is based in considerable part on Lieber's complaints to Ruggles.

Carolina College until some more attractive opportunity came his way. Since he was clever and possessed a winning personality, he did this fairly easily by shaping his conduct outwardly at least in conformity with the prejudices and mores of South Carolina.

He began college instruction with a will. He had never taught before, and, with his accent, maintaining discipline would be a problem. The students had a reputation for turbulence, and had even rebelled against the authority of their beloved Dr. Cooper. The dull, quiet campus in which by day the students monotonously recited back to the professor the Sallust, theorems, and moral principles enunciated by musty textbooks, often re-echoed at night to the boisterousness of pranks, night riding, bonfires, or effigy burning. Perhaps due to the monotony of the curriculum, perhaps because they were several years younger than the average a century later, they were as wild and unruly as all other American collegians of their generation. Lieber knew that, in keeping with custom, he would face a "trial of strength." It was not long coming; by the middle of November he was accepting the congratulations of Robert Y. Hayne upon being the master of his classroom. Disciplinary problems continued to arise, but Lieber was never in serious straits.[28]

With equal success Lieber sold himself to the officials and people of the state through a well-conceived inaugural address. Speaking before the governor and state legislature in early December, he embroidered upon the theme that history and political economy were highly essential studies for the leaders of democratic nations. College should be training for life; there the student should learn to study, contract scientific habits, and store his mind with a nucleus of useful knowledge. It should inspire the student's soul with morals and fortify him with religion. How better could he imbibe the requisite realization of virtue than through history, which in an ethical point of view was "practical morals"?

Lieber realized that the college functioned primarily to train political leaders; so he reminded the legislators that the study of history was nowhere so important as in a republic, where it should govern the conduct of individuals as "makers, executors, and defenders of the laws and institutions of their society." He

[28] Hayne to Lieber, November 16, 1835.

sketched an elaborate philosophy of history as a continuum of institutions and masses of which even the leaders were only a part, but carefully fitted his remarks to the level of his conservative audience: "History is the memory of nations, oh! how many have been lost for want of this memory, and on account of careless, guilty ignorance!"

The new professor sketched more rapidly his views on political economy. After displaying sufficient erudition, he played directly upon the sympathies of Carolinians, and to their delight argued with intense vigor in favor of free trade: "Strange," he remarked, "that man should have seriously to debate about free trade any more than about free breathing, free choice of color of dress, free sleeping, free cooking." [29]

Professor Lieber received universal congratulations; Hayne, Hamilton, Petigru, and many others declared they were delighted. Governor McDuffie told the South Carolina College students that it was "deep philosophy garnished with splendid eloquence." True, Lieber had failed to mention either state rights or the "peculiar institution," but he had ended all questions as to his orthodoxy on religion and free trade, and had demonstrated the lofty erudition that the citizens expected of a faculty member. The trustees ordered 2,500 copies of the address printed, and, upon their distribution, newspapers and journals added to the general laudation. William Gilmore Simms, ablest of the Southern novelists, writing in the *Southern Literary Journal,* admitted Lieber had used English "as an instrument of thought and not for purposes of embellishment," but praised him as "a ripe scholar . . . a profound philosopher." [30]

Lieber's ineptness with English was one of his weakest points. Just as Carolinians expected him to be profound without being

[29] Francis Lieber, *On History and Political Economy, as Necessary Branches of Superior Education in Free States. An Inaugural Address Delivered in South Carolina College. Before His Excellency the Governor and the Legislature of the State, On Commencement Day the 7th of December, 1835* (Columbia, 1836), 26 pp., reprinted in Lieber, *Miscellaneous Writings,* I, 179–203.

[30] William C. Preston to Lieber, March 10, 1836, University of South Carolina; Lieber to Sumner, December 13, 1835. Perry (ed.), *Lieber,* 110. [Review of] "Lieber, On History and Political Economy . . . ," *Southern Literary Journal and Monthly Magazine,* II (1836), 74–76. The Charleston *Courier,* February 5, 1836, stated, "the mode in which both topics are treated evinces a cultivated and discriminating mind, much given to discursive speculation and prompt at ingenious and happy illustration."

critical, so they also felt entitled to an elegance of expression on the part of their professors. Indeed in a region where the spellbinding orator could expect to occupy the pinnacle of success, in the state which sent Robert Y. Hayne and William C. Preston to the United States Senate, Lieber felt pressure upon him to demonstrate his mellifluousness of style, if not orally at least in print.

Before many months he found an outlet for his belles-lettres: Edgar Allan Poe invited him to contribute to the *Southern Literary Messenger*. Lieber sent a fairly-well-written account of his boyhood in Berlin, and the next year, an article on the naming of race horses. The latter was supposed to be humorous, but it was as ponderous in its playfulness as a St. Bernard puppy. It was one of his least successful efforts, but even his best gave him only dubious standing as a stylist.[31]

Lieber was always to feel gnawing doubts about his Southern friendships, but apparently the qualms were mostly on his side. Although he never felt entirely at home with his South Carolina acquaintances, his unquestioned devotion to free trade, *laissez faire*, and the Bank of the United States established him firmly in the esteem of South Carolina's Whig aristocrats. Senator Preston was one of his closest friends, and for years he enjoyed the companionship of Colonel McCord and his talented and spirited wife Louisa. He was an intimate of the great landowning Hampton family and stood high in the confidence of the conservative leader of the bar, James Petigru. Over a period of time, Lieber came to be on friendly terms with almost every leading political and intellectual figure in the state: John C. Calhoun, Thomas Cooper, Joel Poinsett, Richard Manning, James H. Hammond, Langdon Cheves, James W. Miles, and William Gilmore Simms among others. During his first months in South Carolina, the newcomer rode thirty-five miles on a deer hunt with the Hamptons, founded a mock club with McCord, and munched mince pies sent him by H. L. Rhett.[32]

[31] Lieber, "A Reminiscence . . . ," *loc. cit.*, 535–38. The article was in the form of a response to a letter of Poe's; Lieber, "On Hipponomastics, a Letter to Pierce M. Butler, Esq. . . . On the Naming of Race Horses," *Southern Literary Messenger*, III (1837), 297–300.

[32] Lieber to Sumner, January 20, 1836; Lieber journal (copy), April 30, 1836; constitution of club formed with McCord; Rhett to Lieber, January 2, [1836?].

Lieber's relations with his fellow faculty members were, on the whole, less cordial. Occasionally he found a highly congenial friend: one was Preston during his years as president of the college; another was Matthew J. Williams, a Unionist mathematics instructor from West Point. Upon his arrival he established a pleasant relationship with Professor Nott, though he scoffed at the bland dabbler's picaresque short stories. In the fall of 1837 Nott died in a steamship catastrophe, and Lieber felt the full impact of the loss, for the trustees replaced him with a twenty-five-year-old theological firebrand, the Reverend James Henley Thornwell. The young preacher, a nineteenth-century Jonathan Edwards, who had once been a favorite pupil of Cooper's, had turned Presbyterian clergyman and led the vigorous fight against the iconoclastic college president. The fundamentalists exulted: "Who could have dreamed, when this ribald infidelity was in the zenith of its power, that it was even then nourishing in its bosom a champion for the truth, who would soon enter the lists, and take up the gage of battle." [33]

Already Lieber had recorded his opinion of such champions: "This morning Professor Jones of the Theological Seminary preached in the college chapel," he noted in 1837. ". . . hell, eternal damnation, 'God looks in despair upon the damned.' Such positive blasphemies were uttered that I felt excessively sorry for having taken Oscar with me. The idea of eternal damnation, even of the very worst, is so abhorrent and unphilosophical that it is very difficult to me to imagine any reflecting man that believes sincerely in it." Between the crusader Thornwell and the philosopher Lieber no common sympathy could exist.[34]

Ironically, Lieber felt the strongest antipathy toward the Ellets, the faculty couple who might have been most congenial. Both were from the North. William H. Ellet was one of the nation's most distinguished chemists; his wife Elizabeth was a young, charming, and vivacious poet and writer of remarkable popularity and

[33] Matilda Lieber to Fanny Appleton, October 29, [1837]; Lieber to Mary Appleton, October 29, [1837]. LaBorde, History of South Carolina College, 109–10 et seq. B. M. Palmer, The Life and Letters of James Henley Thornwell . . . (Richmond, 1875), 146–47; P. L. Garber, James Henley Thornwell, Presbyterian Defender of the Old South [Richmond, 1943].
[34] Perry (ed.), Lieber, 115.

prolificity whose contributions flooded the women's magazines. Yet to Lieber she was a "repulsive woman." In 1835 the Ellets occupied the other half of the double house assigned to the Liebers, and in the following years continued to live in close proximity to them on the campus. During a large part of that time, Mrs. Ellet worried the handsome professor with her strange behavior. She professed the greatest friendship and admiration for him, yet through her overlavish praise and sly gossip seemed bent upon undermining his position. In 1842 she and her husband spread rumors that Lieber was to be ousted from the college; three years later while Matilda was abroad, Lieber complained about Mrs. Ellet's embarrassingly profuse kindness.[35]

The feud between the Liebers and Ellets was an exception; on the whole Lieber's relationships were outwardly cordial and correct, but inwardly cold. They lacked the spark of true congeniality and sympathy to fire them into the deep and intimate friendships, the "soul-sharing" which the romantic and warmhearted German-American so deeply cherished. He acquired a permanent feeling that he was a misfit and nonconformist.

"We live extremely retired," Matilda commented in 1840, "are vexed when our neighbors ask us to tea, and are getting [to be] downright misanthropists." Lieber complained, "here I am shriveling and withering like a plant torn out by [a] mischievous hand and thrown by the roadside," and to his wife he remarked, "one half year will as completely separate us from S.C. as if we had never been there, because no fibre of our soul is connected with the life there—no sympathy, no friend, no love to the place, no deep-rooted or penetrating interest." [36]

[35] Green, *History of the Buildings of the University of South Carolina,* 156. Samuel Gridley Howe to Lieber, August 17, 1842. Lieber in a revealing letter to his wife, June 1, 1845, declared: "Last night Mrs. Izard sent me, with her gratulations a cherry pie—the second I have from her. She is a lady and one is always safe with her, but Mrs. E. has really made several dead sets at me and besides is actually injuring me by her abnormous kindness; for having returned from Savannah and the Low-country she tells in the whole town, and the professors right in the face that the College is dreadfully unpopular, that they think all the professors inefficient, except myself, and that I am a most distinguished man &c &c. Now you know how such things always place one in a false position."

[36] Matilda Lieber to Fanny Appleton, November 1, 1840; Lieber to [Hillard], [March, 1839]; Lieber to Matilda Lieber, July 17, 1838. Many comments like these

One of the major sources of Lieber's ill-feeling toward the South was the slave system and his inability to speak freely of his feelings about it. He had written sincerely when he proclaimed through the South Carolina press that he was no abolitionist. He did indeed feel that states and states alone had the right to handle the problem, and moreover that immediate, unconditional emancipation might create more problems than it would solve. There his defense of the system stopped. His newspaper letter of the summer of 1835 was the only public statement on slavery to appear over his name during the twenty-one years he spent in South Carolina.

While, in strict compliance with Bishop England's advice, he maintained a stout silence, privately he deplored slavery and all its ramifications. He chafed and ultimately became embittered under his self-imposed muzzle, but kept quiet rather than jeopardize his livelihood or perhaps even his life. He could rationalize, too, that it would be out of keeping with his constitutionalism to tamper with the system. As an outlet for his exasperation and loathing, he developed what he had already begun in the North, a broad study of the Negro and slavery.[37]

Lieber's distaste for teaching was almost as great as that for slavery, yet he soon developed into one of the most distinguished American college professors of his time. In many of his techniques he was decades, indeed a generation or more, ahead of the rank and file of his colleagues. He often complained of the futility and obscurity of his position, but he was an important man in the eyes of the state, and, in comparison with most professors, exceedingly well paid. Through its college, South Carolina offered a high level of training for the scions of the upper class, at the same time that it almost ignored schooling for the lower levels;

---

are printed in Perry (ed.), *Lieber*. Eaton, *Freedom of Thought in the Old South*, 57–59, quite correctly disagrees with Lieber's exaggerated statements on the intellectual aridity of South Carolina. However, to a large degree, Lieber was aiming his complaints at those whom he hoped would find him a better position in the North. His dislike for his Southern friends stemmed more out of his frustrated ambition and their lack of like-mindedness with him on slavery and other reform issues than from their lack of culture.

[37] For a full discussion of Lieber's attitude toward slavery, see Chapter XI. Perry (ed.), *Lieber*, 109–10.

135

and Lieber filled an important role as a teacher of politics in an institution which existed primarily for the preparation of Southern political leaders.[38]

As well he might, Lieber assumed a serious attitude toward his public responsibilities, and assured Calhoun: "I am constantly mindful that I am paid by the *State*, and have no right to use my chair for propagandism of specific and personal views, although I am aware that a professor is no abstract being—no empty bottle, and that what he considers sacred truth he may not only, but is bound to teach; so, for instance, Free Trade is with me." [39]

Despite this compliant credo, Lieber's vigorous personality made it impossible for him to trim too closely to the Southern wind. Although he was duly respectful toward the constitutional rights of the states, he developed strong arguments for nationalism in the classroom. His students remained ardent state-righters, and in some instances ultimately became Confederate leaders, but that was no fair gauge of failure. Though some of his doctrine seemed novel and even startling, most of it fitted comfortably into moderate ideologies, whether of South or North. In noncontroversial fields the earnest theorist made a definite impression upon his students.

Giles Patterson, who attended Lieber's classes in 1846–48, left ample proof of this in his journal. Patterson, the son of an up-country planter, was to become a prominent lawyer. Shortly after enrolling he noted that he had been "entertained by an excellent lecture" by Lieber, and a few days later remarked, "The better I get acquainted with this man the more do I admire him." Altogether, the serious-minded young man mentioned Lieber in nearly

[38] J. P. Anderson, "Public Education in Ante-Bellum South Carolina," *Proceedings of the South Carolina Historical Association,* 1933, pp. 3–11. A newspaper clipping in the Lieber papers analyzed the 1,500 graduates of South Carolina College up to 1854 as including 12 governors, 21 judges, 8 United States Senators, 31 Representatives, 194 South Carolina legislators, 382 lawyers, 188 doctors, and 81 ministers. The emphasis upon training political leaders continued. Under the heading "Jewels of Carolina," a 1901 listing included 18 Confederate generals, 16 governors, and so on, but did not enumerate a single intellectual leader. Lieber's former students included one lieutenant general (Wade Hampton), three major generals, five governors, and three United States Senators. *The Centennial Celebration of the Granting of the Charter to the South Carolina College . . .* (Charleston, 1902), 58–59.

[39] Lieber to John C. Calhoun, December 29, 1847, in J. F. Jameson (ed.), "Calhoun Correspondence," *Annual Report of the American Historical Association for the Year 1899* (Washington, 1900), II, 1156.

half the entries. Time and again he recorded long, accurate summaries of lectures. Several times these skirted around state rights and slavery, but generally they contained in germinal form some of Lieber's most important ideas. Though few of the students were as sober as Patterson, many were as intensely interested in Lieber's major field of politics. On the eve of the Civil War one of them wrote his old professor "that he had left behind him a thousand young men who w[ou]ld gladly see him back once more."[40]

Lieber introduced his students to a broad range of the social sciences. In 1835, for example, he lectured to sophomores on the science of history and the development of Greece, then turned aside to dictate "a table of the most important historical facts from the beginning of history to the year 1832." He taught seniors a rapid survey of political economy and lectured to the juniors on current events. In this course, he used newspapers as his texts. He himself had attended similar "newspaper lectures" at Halle, "in which history was caught alive." In subsequent years he broadened his range of courses to include almost the whole of the social sciences. He gathered large quantities of materials on political theory, fused them in the crucible of the class, then poured them into his books.[41]

To the distress of his colleagues and some trustees, the new professor regarded texts only as a stimulus, not as the mainstay of his courses. He liked best to disagree with them; moreover, he subordinated the conventional assignment-recitation method to the lecture technique. Students attended three recitation periods a day, each of which lasted a full two hours. Lieber often stole these periods for lectures; he seldom held recitations more than two thirds of the time. He assembled these lectures from a tremendous range of information and delivered them freely from notes. Frequently he broke his abstruse theoretical discussions with interesting, even sensational, anecdotes and illustrations. These might conceivably be from the local newspapers or from Homer,

[40] J. H. Mellichamp to Lieber, December 8, 1859; Lieber to Sumner, December 6, 1845. Giles J. Patterson, *Journal of a Southern Student 1846–48* . . . (R. C. Beatty, editor, Nashville, Tenn., 1944), 28–29, 31 *et passim*.

[41] Lieber, Report to the Chairman of the Faculty of South Carolina College by the Professor of History and Political Economy, November 24, 1835, University of South Carolina. Lieber to Sumner, April 21, 1868.

and upon current cotton prices at Liverpool or the courtship habits of South Sea Islanders. Often he would read to his history classes, perhaps from Shakespeare's *Julius Caesar* or, after its publication in the early 1840's, from Macaulay's "exquisite" *Lays of Ancient Rome.*

No matter what the course, Lieber invariably pointed out parallels between the past and present. His constant maxim was Niebuhr's admonition that one should interpret the past in terms of the present, and view the present as dispassionately as though it lay a millennium behind. As emotional a man as Lieber could not always hold to this ideal, but the quality of his lectures was remarkably high. They were as fresh as they were original, since he steadfastly refused to divide his classes and deliver the same lecture a second time. He felt it no more possible, he bluntly assured elegant President Jared Sparks of Harvard, than to "eat my dinner twice, as we sometimes see cats do it." [42]

The students considered attendance at lectures a lesser evil. The better ones took careful notes which they often wrote out in full after class, and kept stiff-bound blank books in which to enter titles of books and subjects to study later in life, while the dullards dozed or daydreamed. But poor students could not enter the classroom sure of a pleasant nap, since they could never tell ahead of time when they would face recitations. Around the walls a score of busts of Lieber's heroes—Penn and Kant, Cicero and Demosthenes, Washington and Calhoun—stared down benignly at the students' terror: the rows of blackboards or "wooling boards." In student slang, "wooling" meant a hard quizzing, and woe to him who had not studied the assigned readings and topics.

On recitation days, Professor Lieber called three students to the preparatory bench at the front of the room and sent an additional four to the "wooling boards," appropriately labeled "names," "chronology," "geography," and "battles." Sometimes a student would have to write a string of as many as sixty or seventy

---

[42] Lieber to Sparks, February 15, 1850, Harvard University; Lieber to Bancroft, March 17, 1858, Massachusetts Historical Society; Lieber, statement of his method of instruction; Lieber to Mrs. George Ticknor, February 10, 1855; Lieber to Hillard, December 17, 1842. The Lieber papers at the Huntington Library and Johns Hopkins University contain many of these sets of lectures and interleaved, heavily annotated copies of textbooks.

names, which with their identifying tags paraded down the boards and onto a considerable part of the floor. Meanwhile the professor gave assignments and quizzed the occupants of the "anxious bench." He would call upon one of the better students to give a skeleton of the entire lesson, and have another state the three or four most important truths or inconsistencies of the book studied. At the end of each recitation, Lieber in Socratic fashion pointed out the errors, but generally he gave blackboard assignments and extra recitations to the students in the best third of the class rather than to the poorer ones. These latter faced retribution in the extended oral and written examinations at the end of the term.[43]

While Lieber's instruction bored the inept, it kindled the warmest enthusiasm in those who were brilliant. He instituted a prize system to reward his more able students, and often carried on correspondence with them long after their graduation. "To my apprehension never was instructor more painstaking, luminous, or able," declared one of them years later, even after the bitterness of the Civil War had intervened. "The text-book furnished only a meagre theme for his daily discourses. Treasures of expansion, illustration, and philosophical deduction were evoked from his great storehouse of knowledge and reflection. His classes were always full. He claimed and received the closest attention. The relation between teacher and pupil was maintained at a high standard, and he evinced, on all occasions, a special pleasure in enkindling a desire for exact and liberal knowledge in his department, in satisfying all inquiries suggested by the topics under discussion, and in directing the attention of his scholars to the highest sources of information." [44]

Professor Lieber was no great disciplinarian, yet he had less trouble than many of his colleagues. From the thirties through the fifties, the faculty meetings were one long, gloomy discussion of punishments, expulsions, and dismissals. In 1837 he had to testify in behalf of one student at a murder trial growing out of a town-and-gown riot. Twenty years later, students were still attempting

---

[43] Lieber, statement of his method of instruction. Patterson was not called upon for a year, then underwent a forty-five minute quizzing, which he described in his journal. Patterson, *Journal of a Southern Student*, 50, 53–54.
[44] Col. C. C. Jones to H. B. Adams, cited in Meriwether, *Higher Education in South Carolina*, 177–78.

duels, and after one particularly boisterous outbreak the professors felt constrained to resolve that to explode a bomb on campus was a worse offense than drunkenness. Lieber detested these dragged-out meetings, where he said he felt as though he assembled with a conclave of mummies. During President Preston's regime, he tried to beg out of them; in Thornwell's last year, he found them even more odious because the other professors always unctuously followed the vote of the president.

Lieber detested even more thoroughly his share in maintaining student discipline. On New Year's night, 1847, he had to restrain some sophomores from burning a tar barrel on campus. He grumbled and mourned over his monthly turn at maintaining order in the commons. When he caught one of his students cheating on a final examination he was furious. The student had found a proof sheet of the questions among the printer's wastepaper. To Lieber's disgust the faculty bowed to the student's powerful parent and instead of expelling him, "let him out." [45]

Long before the end of his twenty-year sojourn, Lieber, with his stiff military posture and his unmistakable German accent, had become a campus legend. Many were the tales his colleagues and students told. In his grade book he had marked, "fool, fool, fool" against the name of one boy every time he came up for recitation. "What is Bologna noted for?" he had asked the class one time, then himself replied, "For professors and sausages." The class laughed, and Lieber deftly added, "Oh gentlemen, you need not laugh. Wherever dere are professors and sausages, dere you will find students and hogs." And when, in compliance with college regulations, he had given chase one night to a turkey-stealing student, the lad led him around to a pile of bricks. Lieber came down heavily on all fours, slowly rose, rubbed his shins, and, the student solemnly maintained, *sotto voce* exclaimed, "Mein Gott! All dis for two tousand dollars!" [46]

Yet Lieber enjoyed his students, and loved to laugh and joke

[45] Faculty records, May 12, June 19, 1837, February 27, March 8, 1854, *et passim*, University of South Carolina; Lieber to Mary Appleton, October 29, [1837]; Lieber to Hillard, March 12, 1854; Lieber to Matilda Lieber, August 30, September 1, 1853, June 12 [24?], 1854; Lieber to Dorothea Dix, February 29, December 1, 1852. Patterson, *Journal of a Southern Student*, 44.
[46] Meriwether, *Higher Education in South Carolina*, 175–76.

with them whenever campus custom would permit familiarity. With eleven of them in 1855 he solemnly drew up an "Anti-Weed Pledge," in which the signators all agreed not "to put tobacco of any kind or shape, into our mouths or noses, for the next four years." Anyone who broke the rules must pay a dollar to charity for each violation. There could be only one exception. Those who so signified after their signature might smoke three cigars a day. Lieber's name and that of the students followed. After each was the notation, "Three Segars." [47]

These pleasant adjustments came slowly as the years mellowed Lieber. In his first winter at South Carolina College he was still a young man of thirty-seven, overbrimming with ambition and chafing under the new yoke. He ignored his Southern surroundings as much as possible, and wrote incessantly to his Northern cronies and acquaintances, deploring his position, damning the South, and urging them to find him Northern employment. It was the beginning of a lifelong epistolary orgy, which at times caused even his closest friends to gasp with amazement. Especially he bombarded the adulatory young Sumner—not alone with letters, but with requests and errands of every sort. In 1837, when Sumner was departing for Europe, the scholar requested, "my dear fellow, if it were not asking too much, I would beg you to grant me a pigeon hole in your mind while abroad say, if you could, a memorandum book with this title: 'All sorts of stuff for Lieber.'" Scant wonder that Lieber's patron Joseph Story, himself known as a highly garrulous conversationalist, quipped to the departing Sumner: "What poor Lieber will do without you, I know not. He will die, I fear, for want of a rapid, voluminous, and never-ending correspondence." [48]

Lieber flooded many others with his letters, and upon Sumner's departure turned much of the torrent upon the young lawyer's partner, George Stillman Hillard. Hillard was a gentle, retiring Brahmin, possessed of a brilliant literary style, but hampered by

[47] "Anti-Weed Pledge," January 3, 1853.
[48] Lieber to Sumner, September 23–25, October, 1837; Pierce, *Sumner,* I, 159. Charles B. Robson, "Papers of Francis Lieber," *Huntington Library Bulletin,* February, 1933, No. 3, pp. 135–55, contains an excellent analysis of his correspondence. In the Huntington Library collection alone there are an estimated 743 letters to Sumner and 237 to Hillard. Robson's analysis of the collection lists 46 principal correspondents, and 140 represented by one or more letters.

too many aches and pains and personal sorrows ever fully to realize his potentialities. He was a ready correspondent and as adept as Sumner at running errands. With melancholy prophecy he wrote Lieber: "My life is constantly embittered by disease, pain, and what is worst of all, a dull drowsy languor which makes all exertion frightful. . . . I feel sometimes as if my life would be like a book full of title pages—a succession of abortive efforts, of plans unperformed and hopes unrealized." [49]

Through Hillard, Sumner, and Joseph Story, Lieber felt an occasional breath of Boston in the stultifying Southern air. Sometimes too, a Northern visitor passed his way. Early in 1836, Dr. John G. Palfrey, pastor, professor, and dull historian of New England, who had just become editor of the *North American Review*, stopped by and gave Lieber some delightful hours. "It does one's heart good," the professor exclaimed, "to see a *cant-less* minister; a divine who has not tatooed himself with the vulgar, rude, commonplace figures of sectarian holiness; who knows & shows that he has received from God an individual soul." [50]

Above all else, Lieber won temporary escape from his distasteful surroundings during every summer vacation. Almost invariably he dashed to the North where he could hunt for a job and converse gayly and convivially with old friends and new. Each time the summer solstice drew to a close, Lieber, like Persephone, found himself unwillingly drawn back to the nether regions, but always with the hope that through the magic formula of a new and startlingly erudite book he could gain permanent release.

Through the short winter, the beautiful spring, and into the hot months of 1836, Lieber labored prodigiously gathering materials for the work he was sure would bring him a congenial position and great acclaim. It was to be a detailed study of the relationships of the citizen with his government: the *Manual of Political Ethics*. He worked in a cramped study into which came the strident noises of the nursery, but his ambition drove him on despite fatigue and irritations. By May he had gathered the requisite notes, papers, and abstracts, and the plan of the work in all its details was clear

[49] Hillard to Lieber, September 28, 1835.
[50] Lieber to Sumner, January 20, 1836.

in his mind. "The book," he exulted, "with the exception of writing it, is quite finished." [51]

The writing had to wait until fall while Lieber, not at all to his liking, sailed with his family to Puerto Rico to visit his planter brothers-in-law. The scholar studied Puerto Rico thoroughly, but restlessly; he longed to be at work on the *Political Ethics*. Finally, in mid-October, he headed back toward the United States, aboard a small brig.[52]

Adverse winds blew the vessel off its course, and on the evening of October 30 the passengers could see the light off Cape Hatteras. It was a dark night, and a few minutes later in a heavy squall they smashed into a southbound ship. The collision carried away the jib boom, bowsprit, foretopmast, and figurehead, and crushed the yards and masts. Day after day the crippled ship limped onward, trying to make New York. After the most harrowing experiences, one evening in mid-November they sighted Neversink Light at the entrance to New York Harbor.

The next day the Liebers were lolling in the luxury of the Astor House. "Glorious beds. Byron might have said 'It is sweet' to sit down to a clean plentiful table after the tossing on a crippled vessel, when the waves begrudge one even a cup of tea, without sugar or milk. We revel in fresh butter and warm rolls, and the sight of dear friends whose beaming faces tell us how happy they are to see us safe after all our danger and privations." [53]

[51] Lieber to Mittermaier, [May 10, 1836], translated copy; Lieber to Sumner, June 18, 1836.

[52] Lieber to LeLouef, June 6, 1836, Duke University; Lieber to William Bard, July 11, 1835, Bard College; Lieber journal, 1836, copy; Jose de la Peña to Hilario de Artacho, September 13, [1836], Huntington Library.

[53] Lieber journal, 1836, copy; Lieber to Sumner, November 15, 1836. Story and others sent hearty congratulations upon Lieber's escape. Story wrote December 19, 1836, "I congratulate you & your wife on this affecting deliverance from the very jaws of death by a good providence. . . . Your friends here were deeply affected with the Tale of your sufferings; & Sumner & I especially dwelt on it—as one does on a powerful & agitating Dream." Oddly, this experience is not mentioned in Perry (ed.), *Lieber* or other of the biographies.

VIII
Francis Lieber: Political Philosopher

I A M glad that you are returned to resume your political & moral labours," Justice Story congratulated Lieber after the scholar had returned from Puerto Rico. "How gloriously does the Topic you have chosen, connect itself with History, the Instructor & the Guide of all just speculations. . . . Sure I am that it will contain wisdom, that ought to teach us, & awake reflections, which ought to strengthen us in our political actions & in our political principles." [1]

The topic, a study of the citizen in a democracy and his manifold relationships to his government, was a problem upon which Lieber had pondered ever since his landing in the New World.[2] Lieber's study was needed in America. The United States in 1840 lacked treatises to link political theory with American reality. Her political philosophy lagged far behind social, economic, and governmental development. While Bentham and the Manchester school revised Locke's natural-rights philosophy to meet the needs of nineteenth-century industrial England, the United States still trailed along, trying to interpret a growing commercialism in the North and a highly stratified plantation system in the South in terms of the agrarian liberals and mercantile conservatives of a bygone age.

There were many, of course, to write in defense of various segments of the new state of things: Calhoun was working out a theory of concurrent majorities for the political system of the South while George Fitzhugh would in the fifties enunciate theories to

[1] Story to Lieber, December 19, 1836, Lieber papers, Henry E. Huntington Library. All manuscripts referred to in this chapter, unless otherwise identified, are from this collection.
[2] Lieber, "Memorandum for Norman," October 1, 1859.

144

justify its society. In the North, reform found its philosophical spokesmen in Brownson and the transcendentalists, but the new economic order depended mainly upon the judicial decisions of Marshall, the speeches and pleas of Webster, and the legal treatises of Story and Kent.

No one since the Federalists had developed a systematic political philosophy to meet the needs of the groups that were rapidly achieving control of the nation. The United States in 1841 came for the first time under the control of a monied ruling class operating through the medium of the Whig party. These Whigs continued to pay lip service to the natural-rights philosophy of the eighteenth century, ill-fitting though it was, since they had not as yet evolved a new scholarly rationale to take its place. Lieber was to devote his career to the development of the new ideology, and when it crystallized in the gilded age—a lush period for scholarship as well as for big business—it bore unmistakable signs of his handiwork.[3]

Lieber's treatise on *Political Ethics* grew out of the stresses and strains, the achievements and failures, of the American system. Delving into his European background, Lieber pulled out scraps of ideas from hither and yon which he hammered and trimmed until he had fashioned them into an explanation for the system he so ardently admired. He accepted with hearty approbation the Federalist ideology and conservative doctrines which Story and Kent in their monumental commentaries had set foursquare upon the foundation of positive law, but unlike them, Lieber went far beyond the Constitution, the *Federalist*, Blackstone, and court decisions. He discussed subjects outside the cognizance of positive law, and rested his entire system not merely upon legal precedents but also upon an elaborate ethico-philosophical basis.[4]

With ready scorn, Lieber discarded from consideration the work of his few American predecessors. Treatises on political economy were primarily economic, and the lone political textbook in general

---

[3] Lieber, *Manual of Political Ethics Designed Chiefly for the Use of Colleges and Students at Law,* 2 vols. (Boston, 1838–39). All references hereafter are to the more available second edition, 2 vols. (Philadelphia, 1875). See II, 394. An interleaved, heavily annotated copy of the first edition is in the Lieber papers, Johns Hopkins University.

[4] *Ibid.*

use was in the nebulous field of "moral philosophy." *Moral and Political Philosophy* by William Paley, an English archdeacon, was a typical product of the eighteenth century. It provided a connecting link between Locke and the utilitarians, and was still the most widely used text in the American colleges of Lieber's day. "What an old granny that Paley is!" Lieber snorted while at work on his *Political Ethics*. "Not once have I looked at him to see what he had to say, without finding him drivelling." [5]

Lieber regretted that so few English and American scholars of the nineteenth century were writing exclusively upon political philosophy. Political theory, he lamented, ended with Locke, and political economy began with Adam Smith. Most of his contemporaries, engrossed by the productive results of the new union of science and industry, had turned their attention to the more specifically economic topics and left it to Lieber to emphasize once again the field of politics.[6]

In 1835 Justice Joseph Story encouraged Lieber to undertake the enterprise, helped clarify his ideas, and recommended to him the title, "Political Ethics." Indeed, the Justice even prepared an agenda of the principal topics he should cover. Story, his colleague at Harvard Law School, Simon Greenleaf, and his protégé, Charles Sumner, continued to aid Lieber with suggestions and citations, but the execution and, above all, the techniques for preparing the manuscript were Lieber's own.[7]

[5] Anna Haddow, *Political Science in American Colleges and Universities 1636–1900* (New York, 1939), 94–97. C. E. Merriam, *American Political Theories* (New York, 1928), 305, and R. G. Gettell, *History of American Political Thought* (New York, 1928), 309, label the *Political Ethics* as the first systematic treatise on political science to appear in America, but B. F. Wright, *American Interpretations of Natural Law* (Cambridge, 1931), 261–62, ascribes that distinction to Nathaniel Chipman, *Sketches of the Principles of Government*, which was published in 1793. However, it was, as W. A. Dunning pointed out, "something nearer to systematic political science than America had known before; and the influence of the work, by the mere fact of its monopoly of the field was very great." Dunning, *Essays on the Civil War and Reconstruction and Related Topics* (New York, 1897), 360–61. Lieber to Sumner, October [16?], 1837, April 21, 1839. Paley, *The Principles of Moral and Political Philosophy* (7th ed.; Philadelphia, 1788). Lieber's detailed critical notes are in the Lieber papers.

[6] Lieber, *Political Ethics*, I, 394; interleaved copy, Johns Hopkins University, opposite I, 356.

[7] Lieber's and Story's original outlines are in Story to Lieber, July 30, 1835, and enclosure. See also Lieber to Sumner, August 25, September 1, 1835; June 18, 1836.

Lieber's ambitions and ideals exceeded his ability. He wished to emulate Niebuhr, who had based his history of Rome upon facts rather than upon mere supposition. Lieber would similarly introduce the empirical method to the study of political theory. He would follow what he considered modern techniques by substituting for mere theorizing, as he wrote in a memorial on statistics, "a careful collection of detailed facts, and the endeavor to arrive at general results by a comprehensive and judicious combination of them." Lieber's anthropological approach bore marked similarities to that later employed by William Graham Sumner. A pioneer sociologist, Albion Small, testified in 1916 that he "frequently recurred to [Lieber's writings] as samples of the spirit in which social problems should be studied, rather than as direct sources of social doctrine." [8]

In preparation of the *Political Ethics,* as in his other work, Lieber made extensive use of the South Carolina College library, which, while by no means adequate for his purposes, possessed one of the better collections in the United States. The professor acquired quantities of books for both it and his private library. The latter was already large and was ultimately to number around five thousand volumes. He wrote copious notes in the margins of those he used most, and interlarded his own works and a few others with additional notes, clippings, and correspondence. These were often the basis for new editions.[9]

Despite the cost, Lieber wrote constantly to government officials and scholars to obtain specific information and publications.

[8] Albion Small, "Fifty Years of Sociology in the United States," *American Journal of Sociology,* XXI (1916), 728–29. Robson, "Francis Lieber's Theories of Society, Government, and Liberty," *loc. cit.,* presents a most valuable analysis of Lieber's contributions, and lays stress upon his fact-gathering techniques and proposals for a statistical survey.

[9] There are innumerable examples of these and other Lieber techniques in the Lieber papers at the Huntington Library and Johns Hopkins University. Lieber's library is now on general accession at the University of California, which obtained it shortly after his death. Books are identifiable through a manuscript catalogue, but few found by the present writer contain notable marginalia. An earlier catalogue of the library, made about 1860, is in the Lieber papers.

In 1850, the South Carolina College library had 18,400 volumes. This was as many as the University of Virginia, and more than Columbia or Princeton. The Harvard Library, largest in the country, contained 84,200 volumes. C. C. Jewett, *Notices of Public Libraries in the United States* (Smithsonian Reports. Appendix to Fourth Annual Report . . . Senate Document, Misc. No. 120, 21 Cong., 1 Sess., Washington, 1851), 155.

He saved magazines and newspapers, clipped prodigiously, and jotted his ideas on any available scrap of paper. His pigeonholes, portfolios, pamphlet holders, and commonplace books, appropriately labeled, "e.g. Woman, Negro Race, Language &c.," all overflowed.

"When I have deeply meditated on a subject, . . ." Lieber explained, "I set down the chief points and argument (always adding the date) and put the paper in a portfolio. Perhaps I add from time to time, modify or change. It is thus that I can trace some of my most important arguments through a long series of years." [10]

Through these methods, Lieber gathered tremendous quantities of material for the *Political Ethics* and subsequent works. Much of it was an unwieldy, bewildering, and useless clutter; some of it was fruitful and revealing. Lieber's scholarly methods were inferior to those of his great German contemporaries, but for probably that very reason he retained a universality of interest which they in their scientific precision were sloughing off. His work was to appear best by quantitative measure rather than by an appraisal of its ideas, and no concise summary could capture his innumerable ill-organized ramifications, digressions, and illustrations. These at the same time repelled later scholars and gave the work perhaps its most considerable merit.

The footnotes reflected the encyclopedic nature of the scholar's inquiring mind. Effortlessly he carried his readers through a half-dozen languages and periods. In his first five pages he referred to the Bible, Hippocrates, a Belgian writer, Plato, Aristotle, Quintillian, Seneca, and a dictionary of the Low Saxon dialect (Bremen, 1770). Next he cited a German work on the Kawi language of Java. If no more than a compendium, the work would have been remarkable. Its interesting examples amazed the reader and pro-

[10] Lieber memorandum. Ironically, this note is undated. Examples of Lieber's mode of gathering information through correspondents are the following: Story gave him data on resistance to unlawful acts of authorities, Story to Lieber, April 10, 1836. Secretary of War Lewis Cass sent him similar material on army obedience, Cass to Lieber, April 17, 1836. Calhoun obtained for him a copy of the North Carolina state constitution, Calhoun to Lieber (about 1836). Jared Sparks answered a query about Anthony Wayne, Sparks to Lieber, September 11, 1837, Sparks papers, Harvard University; Sparks to Lieber, October 1, 1837. A rabbi cited the Talmudic law on trying capital crime, Mayer to Lieber (about 1837). Charles Sumner supplied quantities of valuable criticisms and information. Sumner to Lieber, September 17, October 26, 1837, and numerous other letters.

vided irrefutable ammunition for many a young lawyer trying to impress a court. Professor Simon Greenleaf of Harvard Law School remarked: "Your studies lead to all science & all nations, & your books have an interest like Dickens's from the graphic character of your illustrations." [11]

Lieber went too far; he buried his ore under avalanches of examples. He wished also through profuse citations to acquaint Americans with a wide body of writings. In a period when footnotes were customarily extremely brief or nonexistent, his voluminous ones drew sharp criticism. [12]

Historians of political theory have labeled Lieber an eclectic. He gathered seeds from the rich German harvest of his youth and planted them in America. In subsequent years he gathered more— not from Germany but from England. Some of the ideas died in the strange soil of the New World; others flourished, and with subsequent mutations came to appear indigenous and distinctly American.

Lieber was pleased when critics identified the *Political Ethics* as essentially an American work, yet he recognized his debt to his mentors. "No German I know could have analyzed public life as I have done, having had the advantage of a practical citizen's life for many years, in a vast republic," he emphasized. "No American probably could have written other parts without first entering deeply and laboriously into continental knowledge." [13]

Here, then, was Lieber's role: to interpret the political phenomena of the New World in the ideological terms of the old—to explain, identify, and label. It was all old, yet at the same time new, since Lieber could harvest only what would take root in American soil. To trace the origins of his ideas would necessitate unraveling a snarl of interwoven sources; Professor Charles Robson has ably outlined the most important of these. There can be no doubt, for example, that there was much of Edmund Burke in Lieber's writ-

[11] Lieber, *Political Ethics,* I, 17–26. Simon Greenleaf to Lieber, April 11, 1842.
[12] Lieber to Hillard, January 24, 1839; Lieber to Sumner, May 28, 1847. Francis Bowen had called Lieber pedantic. Lieber also favored indices, although his *Political Ethics* lacked one: "Books without indices are 'like chambers without handles.'" Lieber to Hillard, January 6, 1839.
[13] Lieber to J. B. Boyd, March 29, 1840, Lieber papers, Library of Congress.

ings. Yet how much of the influence came directly through reading the English conservative, how much through Niebuhr, Schleiermacher, and the German milieu, how much from Story and Kent, and yet again how much from that main current of Whig thought in the exact center of which Lieber steered his *Political Ethics?* It is significant that Lieber dedicated his *Political Ethics* to the Englishman, Henry Hallam, and the American, Joseph Story.[14]

Lieber was witness to an age of tremendous change. On the continent of Europe he saw an emergent nationalistic, liberal middle class striving to wrest power from the nobles of the old regime. In England, where the aristocrats of the forge had already mastered those of the field, he viewed the burgeoning iron works of Birmingham, the spewing collieries of Newcastle, and the spreading textile mills of Lancastershire, all heralding the new age of industrial supremacy.

Yet Lieber seemed hardly aware of the inseparable ties between the new industrialism and growing middle-class liberalism. To him the significance of the political changes outweighed that of the technical ones, and he concentrated upon the shift from government by court or cabinet to national or popular control. Future generations, he predicted, would regard his as the era "in which broad ideas of substantial civil liberty were more clearly defined and more widely secured for a large number of nations; in which the primary relation of the citizen to the state became a distinct subject of intense political action." This was the age of constitutions.[15]

In this constitutional era, the citizen enjoyed new rights and perplexing responsibilities. These Lieber took as his particular field of investigation. Much as he revered Kent's and Story's applications of the common law to the new age, and deeply as he

[14] For an excellent discussion of Lieber's sources, and especially his debt to Burke, see Robson, "Francis Lieber's Theories of Society, Government, and Liberty," *loc. cit.* The following works, according to Robson, throw light upon Lieber's German background: Friedrich Meinecke, *Weltbürgertum und Nationalstaat* (München und Berlin, 1908); William Metzger, *Gesellschaft, Recht und Staat in der Ethik des deutschen Idealismus* (Heidelberg, 1917); and Carl Schmitt, *Politische Romantik* (2d ed.; München, 1925). Cf. *ante,* Chs. I and II.

[15] Lieber, *Political Ethics,* I, 393. Hereafter, this work is cited as *PE.*

admired the Hamiltonian interpretation of federalism, he felt the positive law inadequate as a guide to the new order. The relationship of the citizen to the state went beyond the cold formality of the law, since law without popular support was a dead letter.[16]

Primarily Lieber wished to lay down sound precepts to guide the citizen in his many activities beyond the province of positive law. To do so required two stout volumes: the first setting forth an ethical and political system; the second developing out of the system maxims to cover every possible responsibility from the conjugal relationship to the chief magistracy.

Lieber consciously constructed his political philosophy by selecting what he considered to be the best parts of previous systems, and in developing his eclectic system he manifested a strong dualism. Before he began to write, he admitted: "I not only venture upon an entirely untrodden path, but upon a most dangerous one, where nothing but the precise middle will do." [17] He approached political theory as a German moralist awake to American practicalities; he based his system upon both historical and philosophical foundations; he envisaged man's life as revolving around the twin poles of individuality and sociality. The individual's relationship to society was reciprocally one of rights and duties; and the most advanced form of government under which he could live was one of checks and balances, of federal dualism. Lieber's writings even seemed to idealize the middle class, combining as it did the industry of the masses and the solid economic foundation of the aristocracy.

First, Lieber set up an ethical system resting upon the freedom of will and essential individuality of man, who at the same time, could fulfill his destiny only in society. Therefore, Lieber accepted as one of his fundamental concepts an idea widely current in the Germany of his youth and highly developed by his teacher Schleiermacher: "Man's individuality and sociality form the two poles round which his whole life revolves." [18]

The historical evolution of individualism marked one of the greatest advances of the modern state over antiquity. From being

---

[16] *Ibid.*, I, 393–98, cf., I, 408–10; Lieber, *Miscellaneous Writings,* I, 365. The latter citation is from Lieber's inaugural at Columbia University in 1858, which contains the most concise and highly developed statement of his main ideas.

[17] Lieber to Sumner, August 25, 1835.   [18] *PE,* I, 20–33, 57–63.

an end in itself the state had become a means to an end. The change had come about through the growth of Christianity, with its emphasis upon the moral worth of the individual; the conquest of the Roman Empire by northern tribes possessing a keen feeling of individual independence; the enlargement of states and development of representative government; and the rise of capitalism and expansion of Europe.[19]

Man's individuality, Lieber told a correspondent, "is an indissoluble, inalienable attribute of his humanity." Applied to ethics, individualism produced moral liberty and responsibility; applied to man's relationship to others, it was justice; applied to government, it meant civil liberty. In their respective fields, it meant freedom of thought and artistic creation. Individualism also sanctioned the indispensable gradation which penetrates all society. Above all, applied to things it meant property, for "property is the realization of man's individuality in the material world." [20]

While Lieber gave great emphasis to individualism, he did not neglect the opposite pole, society, which he discussed mainly in terms of its political manifestation, the state. Society, Lieber decided two decades later, was a continuity. It was not only "a certain number of living individuals bound together by bonds of common laws, interests, sympathies, and organization," but also "these and the successive generations with which they are interlinked." [21]

"Act on individualism alone," Lieber warned in his more mature years, "and you would reduce society to a mere crowd of egotistical units, far below . . . the ant hill; act on socialism alone, and you would reduce society to loathesome despotism, in which individuals would be distinguished by mere number, as the inmates of Sing Sing." Of the two alternatives, that of socialism worried Lieber almost exclusively. Indeed, in the 1850's he admitted having tried and discarded the new term "sociology," which even George Fitzhugh, the ultraconservative slavery apologist, ac-

---

[19] *Ibid.*, 81, 159–62, 172, 370–79; cf. II, 81–82.
[20] Lieber to Sumner, August 27, 1837. Cf. "property . . . is the reflex of man's individuality," interleaved *PE*, Johns Hopkins University, opposite I, 120.
[21] Lieber, *Miscellaneous Writings*, I, 336–37, 363–64. Lieber emphasized that society was a continuity of all man's institutions. Interleaved *PE*, Johns Hopkins University, opposite II, 174.

cepted. Lieber rejected it because he felt it implied that society absorbs almost all individualism.[22]

Man's individualism and his role in society led to the next hypothesis that every man possessed certain rights together with complementary obligations. These were inherent, equal, and an outgrowth of natural law. "A natural right," Lieber used to tell his students, "is a claim which a human being has on society flowing directly from his or her nature as a human being, or from the attributes of humanity." These were by no means inalienable, since that would assume the fallacious contract theory, and indeed despotism often unrighteously denied them. Natural rights included a wide assortment of things: communication, locomotion, appropriation of what belongs to no one, production, justice, protection, education, and those things enumerated in the Declaration of Independence and the Bill of Rights. They did not include the right to vote: that was a political right. Some decades later, Lester Ward was to poke fun at those theorists who, like Lieber, used the word "natural" to cover only those rights of which they personally approved.[23]

Lieber was less interested in enumerating these rights than in stressing the accompanying obligations. "Right and obligation are each other's complements, and cannot be severed without undermining the ethical ground on which we stand." Later in his career, he emphasized: "In this twinship of right and duty lies the

[22] Lieber, *Miscellaneous Writings,* II, 365–66. He declared (p. 363): "The radical error of the communist consists in his exclusive acknowledgement of the principle of socialism, and his endeavors to apply it even to that which has its very origin and being in individualism—property. . . . The radical error of the individualist . . . is, that he wholly disavows the principle of socialism and, generally, reasons on the unstable and shaking ground of expediency alone. He forgets that both, individualism and socialism, are true and ever-active principles, and that the very idea of the state implies both; for, the state is a society, and a society consists of individuals who never lose their individual character." See also Lieber to Sumner, February 2, 1864: "that odious word Sociology."

Lieber also noted (pp. 366–67) that the extreme of anarchism had completed the circle, so that "the most enthusiastic socialists . . . have actually come to the conclusion that there need be and ought to be no government at all among men truly free." Cf. Harvey Wish, *George Fitzhugh, Propagandist of the Old South* (Baton Rouge, 1943).

[23] *PE,* I, 200–204; Lieber, "A Shorthand Sketch of Lectures forming Part of a Course on the Representative System Delivered in the Columbia College Law School . . . 1867," and manuscript note of about the 1860's. Lester Ward, *The Psychic Factors of Civilization* (Boston, 1893), 100, cited in Richard Hofstadter, *Social Darwinism in American Thought, 1860–1915* (Philadelphia, 1944), 63.

embryonic genesis of liberty, and at the same time the distinction between sincere and seasoned civil liberty and the wild and one-sided privilege of one man or a class; or the fantastic equality of all in point of rights without the steadying pendulum of mutual obligation." [24]

Both rights and obligations grew out of natural law, which to Lieber was establishable through the theorem of Spinoza that, "I exist as a human being, *therefore* I have a right to exist as a human being." Lieber based his concept of the natural law upon the proposition that the existing state of man in society was the natural and normal one. "Man was essentially made for progressive civilization, and this, therefore, is *his* natural state." He ridiculed the contract theory and Rousseau's ideas of the noble savage; at the same time he righteously denounced the empiricism of the utilitarians as setting up power and expediency as the only criteria. Nevertheless, Lieber borrowed from both sources. He drew upon the realism of the historical school, but also tried to preserve the idealism of the older philosophers. The compromise retained the familiar sound, yet so satisfied the demands of a rapidly changing order that it met with the full approval of Kent, Story, and Greenleaf. Sadly enough, Lieber was not original even in his eclecticism. His combination of Schleiermacher's theories and Niebuhr's methods had led him to a concept remarkably similar to that of Karl von Rotteck, the German liberal.[25]

[24] Lieber, *Miscellaneous Writings*, I, 264, 357. The slogan "No Right without its Duty; No Duty without its Right," became a fetish with Lieber. He placed it on the frontispiece of his *Notes on Fallacies of American Protectionists* (4th ed.; New York, 1870), and upon his stationery. Sometimes he expressed the same idea in the condensed form, "Droit Oblige." He was furious with the Marxists when they used the slogan upon their banners. Rudolf Gneist developed somewhat the same idea in Germany. J. C. Bluntschli, "Lieber's Service to Political Science and International Law," Lieber, *Miscellaneous Writings*, II, 9–10.

[25] Lieber, *PE*, I, 71–72, 128–33. Lieber was aware of his debt to Rotteck; he considered dedicating the second volume to Rotteck and Ranke or F. P. G. Guizot. Lieber to Hillard, April 6, 1839. This combination of the empirical and speculative methods was also fundamental in Schleiermacher's political philosophy. "Just as he rejected every abstract, normative and formalistic construction in ethics on the ground that it passes over the individual and neglects the actual dynamic force of moral behavior, so he also repudiated any sort of 'metaphysical politics,' in the sense employed by Plato and Fichte, which undertook to regulate all political activity by categorical imperatives." Rudolf Odebrecht, "Schleiermacher," *Encyclopaedia of the Social Sciences*, XIII, 572–73. Cf. Brandt, *Philosophy of Schleiermacher;* Wilhelm Dilthey, *Leben Schleiermachers* (Berlin, 1922). Hegel rather than Schleiermacher gave these ideas their most outstanding development, but Lieber had ardently ad-

The difficulties became apparent when Lieber applied his precepts to the practical functioning of the citizenry. Should one unfailingly obey laws? Natural law did not transcend positive law, but was identical to it wherever positive law was in keeping with nature or the spirit of the times. Where the positive law fell short, the citizen was at liberty to disobey it. An extremely bad state of affairs might even lead to the fearful but at times salutary expedient of revolution. However, Lieber strongly advocated unfailing adherence to wise laws, and abhorred the thought of lynch law or mob rule.[26]

Man's rights and obligations developed through his essential social relationships. His earliest association was in the family unit —and upon the family Lieber laid great stress. The helplessness of infants led to a protracted period of education during which the child developed habits of obedience, respect, love, and a consciousness of mutual dependence.[27]

While the family was evolving, various other institutions developed within the unit. Among these was language, which led to transmission of knowledge, gave continuity, and made man feel he was closely united with a permanent society. Another was division of labor, which grew out of physical differences and social needs. That implied exchange and barter, "another bond of society," which in turn suggested property.[28]

Through the steadily improving institutions of the family, language, and property, man moved toward higher and higher stages of civilization. While polygamy continued to chain Asia to patriarchal despotism, the European family evolved toward monogamy.

---

mired the theologian and disliked the philosopher. Lieber to Mittermaier, September 13, 1834, copy; *The Critic*, II (1882), 351. Niebuhr's influence upon Lieber was, of course, profound. Henrietta Herz may also have indoctrinated Lieber with the views of Burke. For her significance, see Reinhold Aris, *History of Political Thought in Germany from 1789 to 1815* (London, 1936), 251–59. For a discussion of Lieber's view of natural law, see Wright, *American Interpretations of Natural Law*, 265–66. Cf. Chs. I and II.

[26] *PE*, I, 204; II, 152–55, 164–76.

[27] *Ibid.*, I, 98–103. Lieber refuted the theories of Jean Baptiste Say and other followers of Locke and Rousseau who claimed that the family, the state, and other institutions had evolved from the mature reflection of man "as if he knew at the time to what momentous consequences they would lead." Lieber's theory was simple. Men developed institutions like the family "Because they could not help it." *Ibid.*, I, 104–106.

[28] *Ibid.*, I, 106–26.

The monogamous family served as a wellspring of the one institution which could achieve civilization—the modern state. "The State arises every day anew in the family, and . . . the family to the State, like feeders to [a] Canal." Whoever tampered with the family, or the institution of monogamous marriage, menaced the state. Lieber saw a sinister design in that "all societies in which communism had been carried out to any extent, have made light of monogamic wedlock."[29]

Like property and the family, the state was "aboriginal with man." "Man cannot be man without society. Society cannot exist without a jural relation between its members, because no member ought to give up, or can give up, his individuality. Society, considered as to its jural relations, or jural society, is the state. The necessary existence of the state, and that right and power which necessarily or naturally flows from it, is sovereignty."[30]

The state was the instrument which functioned to regulate the relationships between men—to maintain right. "The state is founded on those rights which are essential to all members, and which can be enforced." Its primary role is protection, both of the individual and society as a whole, in intangibles as well as material things.[31]

As the state existed of necessity and was the natural society in which man lived, the individual in accepting its protection reciprocally owed it some duties. But always it should remain a means, not an end in itself swallowing up man's individuality, for "the state does not make right, but is founded upon it," and "the individual stands higher than the state." Aristotle and the ancients were incorrect in their view that the state was paramount and that the individual received his value from it alone.[32]

This limitation loomed large in Lieber's mind—as indeed it did in the minds of all middle-class Americans of his day. Nevertheless, he outlined three large fields in which the state might act: it should provide all those things man could not, should not, or

[29] *Ibid.*, I, 137–45; II, 121–38; interleaved *PE*, Johns Hopkins University, opposite I, 163; Lieber, *Miscellaneous Writings*, I, 361–62; "What I have Done," [1861]. Lieber's views upon women received sympathetic response from Bishop Alonzo Potter. Potter to Lieber, February 24, 1842. Cf. Alice Felt Tyler, *Freedom's Ferment: Phases of American Social History to 1860* (Minneapolis, 1944), 254.
[30] *PE*, I, 217.   [31] *Ibid.*, I, 151; Lieber, *Miscellaneous Writings*, I, 358.
[32] *PE*, I, 159–62, 172.

would not obtain as an individual. Lieber granted "the necessity of public education (the common school for those who are deprived of means or destitute of the desire to be educated; and the university, which lies beyond the capacity of private means); of the support of those who cannot support themselves (the pauper, and the poor orphans, and sick); of intercommunication and intercommunion (the road and the mail); of the promotion of taste and the fine arts, and the public support of religion, or the abstaining from it; and the duty of settling conflicting claims, and of punishing those that infringe the common rules of action." [33]

The state should interfere where the public interest was strongly involved. Despite *laissez faire*, practical circumstances necessitated great modification and regulation of the highly essential right to acquire property. Otherwise, and wherever possible, the state should "leave as much to private exertion as the public weal, comfort and morality allow. Individual industry, private combination, and associations, which are conscious that they depend upon themselves alone, are possessed of a vigor, keenness, and detailed industry" not to be found in enterprises debilitated by government regulation or operation.[34]

The right and power of a state to exist and protect was sovereignty, "the source of all vested power." It was a "power and energy naturally and necessarily inherent in society."

Sovereignty manifested itself also through law and power, both of which derived their force from society. Not only did society through public opinion generate law, but the largest part of the law enjoyed a more continuous existence than government. While revolutions shifted governments, they seldom affected more than a minimum change in the total body of law. Likewise, while society could delegate power to a monarch or government, the sovereignty remained in its hands, and the great bulk of law existed *"always* above the *prince."* [35]

[33] Lieber, *Miscellaneous Writings*, I, 358–59; *PE*, I, 173–74. Lieber emphasized: "Life is absolutely necessary for man, and if he cannot possibly obtain medical assistance, society is bound to furnish it. Public hospitals are not a mere matter of charity, they are a matter of right."
[34] *PE*, I, 176.
[35] *Ibid.*, I, 228–38, 249. "I first make sovereignty an attribute of society . . . separating it from supreme power. I am thus enabled to avoid the error and consequent mischievous reasonings of the contract, without falling into the opposite

Lieber's concept of sovereignty went well beyond the positive law. As far as the law went, he followed Blackstone and Hallam, both of whom had used the contract theory to justify the dethronement of James II in 1688. This implied that sovereignty was vested in society. Lieber went on to emphasize that society exercised its sovereignty through public opinion, or the sense and sentiment of the community which, molded by the leaders, interpreted the laws and at times either forced or stopped their execution. It "is the continued sovereign action of society and also the link between society at large and the state, when a given society is either narrower or wider than a given state." [36]

The power of public opinion to "impel the indolent and restrain the licentious" received tremendous impetus through the press. It could function like a mighty burning glass to collect the scattered rays of public opinion and bring them to focus so powerfully that they would force an issue.

Because it was so gigantic, the power of the press, like other powers, was potentially tyrannical. Lieber chided the party press of his day for its frequent mendacity and scurrility, yet recognized its great capacity for good. His recommendation was that the press should not be hampered with legal restrictions, but encouraged to develop responsibility and a high standard of ethics.[37]

Another force, closely related to public opinion, was patriotism. Since Lieber was fundamentally nationalistic, he looked upon patriotism as highly significant and assigned it a definite role in society as "the transition and link between the state as the jural institution, and the society as the aggregate of living men. . . . It is that sympathy which brings affection into the state." True

---

error of mere might into which all have fallen who disregarded the contract." Lieber to Hillard, December 3, 1838.

[36] *PE*, I, 223–26; II, 220–21, 273–75. Lieber had long been interested in this problem. In a footnote to his translation of Beaumont and Tocqueville, *On the Penitentiary System*, 126, he had declared, "an immense difference exists between a French police officer, the member of a powerful and independent body, extending with its million arms over the whole country, and an American police officer, a harmless and comparatively powerless single individual, under the constant surveillance of public opinion." Simon Greenleaf had helped clarify his views of the effects of public opinion in a long and highly significant letter, the crux of which was that "When public opinion, or the will of the sovereign changes, in a matter not contained in an express statute, the change is shown in the decisions of the judicial tribunals." Greenleaf to Lieber, October 26, 1837.

[37] *PE*, II, 205–22.

patriotism was "that sacred enthusiasm which prompts to great exertions and has the welfare, honor, reputation of the country at large in view." [38]

Patriotism manifested itself toward a nation or state, not merely toward a government. Carefully Lieber distinguished between the state and government. The latter was that institution through which the state, or jural society, ordinarily functioned. It derived its power from the sovereign force of the state.[39]

What, then, was a legitimate government? That which existed according to the fundamental laws and usages of the state, or which the people accepted. If the people were satisfied with the government, no one could doubt its legitimacy since "the government is simply and solely for the benefit of the society." No matter how grievously a government oppressed a people, as long as they acquiesced the government was legal.[40]

The form of a government might vary considerably; its success depended upon how well it fulfilled its stable objectives. As civilization progressed, certain forms such as the principle of representative government came to be accepted as superior. "But who would like to be tried by a jury of Bushmen, or insist upon the introduction of popular representation with two chambers in Turkestan?" The fact that a governmental principle was excellent in theory did not mean that it could be superimposed successfully upon a people not yet ready for it. A government to be successful must grow out of existing institutions.[41]

Recognizing the indigenous limitations upon forms, Lieber nevertheless set up criteria for good government. It should set about attaining the stable ends of the state through steady progress unmarred by sudden and violent change. It should interfere as little as possible with man's individuality; at the same time it should afford to society "the best opportunity for the highest industrial and mental action." It should be a government of security, based not on the personality of those in authority but upon institutions rooted in the history of the nation. It should build a rich culture without sacrificing the essential interests of the ma-

---

[38] *Ibid.*, II, 84–95, interleaved *PE*, Johns Hopkins University, opposite II, 198; Lieber, *Miscellaneous Writings*, I, 357.
[39] *PE*, I, 238–41.   [40] *Ibid.*, I, 275–77.   [41] *Ibid.*, I, 310–18.

jority. Lieber wished to see no more impressive palaces built like that of Louis XIV with taxes wrested from the squalid masses.[42]

Too many people argued that the best government was an absolute monarchy with a truly wise and just king. Just the opposite was true, since this type of government undermined the state by exposing it to an inept successor upon the death of the ruler. It blinded "the people, who, content with their physical welfare, and perhaps the brilliant energy of the government, are ready to abandon all law and all institutions, placing implicit confidence in their rulers, until recovery is too late." A highhanded absolutism might be the best government in a transition period, as indeed was the case when Peter ruled Russia, but this was the exception, not the rule.[43]

Equally fallacious was the ideal of the French Revolution that since the people were the object of all government as well as the source of all power, the best government was that in which the people exercised absolute power. This "democratic absolutism" meant in practice placing the power in the hands of the majority, which arrogated to itself the name of the people and trampled upon minority rights.[44]

Lieber's scorn of the mob knew no bounds. He applied to them an old Roman epithet: they were the bilge water of the ship of state. This simile expressed "their loathesomeness, danger, and fickleness, which together with a gust of wind, may indeed throw the vessel on her beam ends." Their very existence was proof of their excitement and unfitness to judge; their composition was usually from among the lowest part of the populace.[45]

The remedy for mobs was simple: encourage them to acquire property. "The mob disregards property," he explained. By implication, this was because they had none. If the people were to maintain civil liberty they must enjoy "a state of substantial independence"—middle-class status, which they could achieve through education and maintain through legislation protecting property. Otherwise, the state would divide into *"below,* a large abject class of submissive paupers, and *above,* a turbulent or arrogant class of a few powerful proprietors." [46]

[42] *Ibid.,* I, 318–20. [43] *Ibid.,* I, 175–77, 320–22. [44] *Ibid.,* I, 322.
[45] *Ibid.,* II, 140, 177–78. [46] *Ibid.,* I, 456–58; II, 178–79.

Rule of the propertyless masses, or "democratic absolutism" was the very antithesis of liberty. True liberty was embodied in institutions, the main function of which was to protect the rights of the minority. "He who has power, absolute and direct, abuses it; man's frailty is too great; man is not made for absolute power." Therefore, the sovereign people should not themselves exercise supreme authority but devolve it upon agents whom they should surround with checks and balances. It was the protection of liberty, not the fact that the people had become too numerous, which created the necessity for representative government.[47]

Though Lieber strongly approved of American constitutional forms, he considered the fundamental spirit or essence of the government more significant. The ideal state rested not only upon positive law but upon a powerful organic basis. Lieber had expressed this idea in rather elementary form in his conversations with young Tocqueville, he was to elaborate powerfully upon it in his emphasis upon institutions in the *Civil Liberty and Self-Government*, and finally his correspondent Johann K. Bluntschli in the latter half of the century was to carry it to its logical but absurd conclusion.[48]

Lieber divided all states into autarchies and hamarchies (ruled together). An autarchy was a state "in which public power, whole and entire, unmitigated and unmodified, rests somewhere, be this in the hands of a monarch, or the people, or an aristocracy, it matters not for our division.[49] "Hamarchy, on the other hand, is that polity which has an organism, an organic life, if I may say so, in which a thousand distinct parts have their independent action, yet are by the general organism united into one whole, into one living system. Autarchy acts by power and force; hamarchy acts and

---

[47] *Ibid.*, I, 324–50.
[48] Lieber told Tocqueville: "The Republic . . . is of all the governments the one that depends most on every part of society. Look at this country! The Republic is everywhere, in the street as in Congress. If an obstacle embarrasses the public way, the neighbours will at once constitute themselves a deliberative body; they will name a commission and will remedy the evil by their collective force, wisely directed." Pierson, *Tocqueville and Beaumont in America*, 377–78. Cf. F. W. Coker, *Organismic Theories of the State* . . . (Columbia University Studies in History, Economic, and Public Law No. 101, New York, 1910), 104–14 on Bluntschli. Coker apparently did not think Lieber's ideas significant enough to include in his study. J. K. Bluntschli, *Das Moderne Völkerrecht der Civilisirten Staaten* (Nördlingen, 1868).
[49] *PE*, I, 352.

produces as organized life does: in the autarchy laws are made by the power; in the hamarchy rather generated: in the autarchy the law is absolute, after it has been made; in the hamarchy the law modifies itself in its application and operation. The political organism may prevent its action entirely, not by force, but simply because it cannot operate. In the autarchy the law is the positive will of power; in the hamarchy it is much more the expression of the whole after a thousand modifications. . . . A hamarchy [can] be compared . . . only to the living animal body, in which numerous systems act and produce independently in their way, and yet all functions unite in effecting that which is called life. . . . Hamarchy is materially republican. . . . On the other hand . . . bureaucracy is decidedly autarchic in its character." America and England were hamacratic; France and Germany, autarchic.[50]

Into this framework of political philosophy, Lieber with an incredible consistency packed a multitude of concrete applications. His inquiring mind roamed further afield than any of his predecessors and most of his successors to encompass the entirety of society. With his eye primarily upon the America of his day, he laid down a tremendous number of precepts, and, since the fields he explored were new, his material at points possessed a freshness and originality lacking in his formal political philosophy. Much was trite and banal, parts rose little above the typical homilies of the professor of moral philosophy, but here and there he struck sparks that illuminated bits of the political landscape.

With his tremendous, voracious discursiveness, Lieber turned his attention first in one direction, then another. He examined the moral virtues upon which the safety of the state depended: justice, fortitude, perseverance, consistency, moderation, honesty, frugality, continence, and patriotism. Then he turned to specific problems: the relation of education to crime, the role of woman, obedience to laws, limitations upon trade unions, liberty of the press and pulpit, problems of voting and nonvoting, the functioning of the party system, qualifications for public men, state instruction of congressmen, responsibilities of legislators, executives, judges,

[50] *Ibid.*, I, 352–53. Lieber meant his analogy to a living organism only in a metaphoric sense. Lieber, "What I have Done" [1861]. Herbert Spencer developed the same idea, but did not go as far as Bluntschli. Lieber's biological analogy was pre-Darwinian; Spencer's was traceable to a direct biological basis.

juries, and lawyers, abuse of the pardoning power, the justification of righteous war, and the proper conduct of warfare.

Many of these topics through their nebulousness evaded scientific treatment. Yet the pages on voting stimulated him to launch probably the first significant statistical study of election habits, and from his remarks on the ethics of armies he was ultimately to develop the first modern codification of the laws of land warfare. The international law of war followed by most belligerents in the two world wars of the twentieth century are directly traceable to the last chapter of the *Political Ethics*.

Many of Lieber's discussions served as incisive commentaries upon the American political system of his day: "If we are engaged in an arduous endeavor . . . we gradually lose sight of other considerations, and not unfrequently are betrayed even so far as to forget the ultimate object and be ready to sacrifice everything to the means." [51]

With broad strokes, Lieber filled in his canvas with a beautiful American panorama, a little troublesome to Democrats, but glorious indeed to Whigs of both North and South. Not a word on slavery marred its pages. An ardent proslavery reviewer was to read into the opus complete sanction for the "peculiar institution"; a Northern abolitionist was to cite it as justification for open resistance to the Fugitive Slave Act. Lieber opposed overcentralization, and had slapped at state rights with such downy blows that even peppery Beverley Tucker of William and Mary College, who several years earlier in the *Partisan Leader* had predicted bloody war between the sections, quoted Lieber with wholehearted approval. The same pages that drew such unqualified praise from Chancellor Kent, the foe of universal suffrage and all liberal ideas, evoked from Lieber's most caustic critic, the Democratic reformer Orestes Brownson, the admission that "the principles are of the liberal political school." [52]

[51] *PE*, I, 431, 440–41.
[52] Tucker to Lieber, October 22, November 5, 1840; Lieber to Dorothea Dix, September 12, 1852; Lieber to Hillard, September 11, 1852. Beverley Tucker, *A Discourse on the Importance of the Study of Political Science* . . . (Richmond, 1840), 13–14. The article linking the *Political Ethics* to the Southern system was by Lieber's friend, D. J. McCord. McCord. "Lieber's Political Ethics," *Southern Quarterly Review*, XII (1847), 464–504. Even Thornwell approved of it: "The one source-book in social and political theory which he heartily recommended was Francis Lieber's *Political Ethics*." Garber, *James Henley Thornwell*.

By the time Lieber had finished the first volume of the *Political Ethics*, the panic of 1837 had begun, and times were so hard that it took Lieber more than a year to obtain a publisher. Clay, without reading the manuscript, gave him a letter of commendation, and Calhoun, after reading several inconsequential preliminary chapters, wrote cautiously that "With some, not important exceptions, I am disposed to concur in the views that you take." Justice Story studied the section on political theory and gave Lieber a letter to show publishers in which he recorded his high praise. "It constitutes one of the best Theoretical treatises on the true nature & objects of Government, which has been produced in modern times," Story declared. "Such a work is peculiarly important in these Times when so many false Theories are afloat, & so many disturbing Doctrines are promulgated." [53]

The three testimonials lent the manuscript something of the position of a Whig campaign document. In the summer of 1838 a new Boston publishing house, Little and Brown, decided to risk taking the manuscript. They published the first volume immediately, and the second the following year. [54]

Lieber waited confidently for the public verdict upon the *Political Ethics*. The only flaw he could see was its great length. The first volume alone was weighty, and the second half again as long as the first. Hillard had labored long and valiantly to weed out the worst Germanisms, but had no authority to pare the redundancies. Even the author himself was taken aback by the length of volume two: "It is enough to drag a man with cork and bladder to the bottom." Nevertheless, Lieber, who suffered from no false modesty, repeatedly appraised the *Political Ethics* for his friends: "I know that my work belongs to the list which begins with Aris-

---

[53] Lieber to Sumner, September 7, 17, 1837, Lieber papers; Sumner to Lieber, August 15, September 11, 1837, Harvard University. Lieber to Matilda Lieber, July 29, August 1, 2, 4, 17, 1837; Story to Lieber, August 15, 1837; Calhoun to Lieber, September 11, 1837; Clay to Lieber, September 16, 1837.

[54] Lieber contracted to receive a 10 per cent royalty. Lieber to Matilda Lieber, July 4, 1838. The details of publication are in the Lieber-Charles Folsom correspondence, Boston Public Library. Sumner arranged for William Smith to publish an English edition. Smith published five hundred copies of the first volume, but they sold so slowly that rather than publish the second volume he imported a hundred copies. Lieber's sole return from this edition was twenty-five copies, most of which he subsequently exchanged for other books. Sumner to Lieber, November 16, 1838, Harvard University; Smith to Lieber, April 12, 1839, April 16, 1840.

totle, and in which we find the names of Thomas More, Hobbes, Hugo Grotius, Puffendorf." [55]

Many of the scholar's powerful friends seconded his flattering opinion of his own creation. None delighted Lieber more than Chancellor Kent, who lauded it in a footnote to a subsequent edition of the *Commentaries*. Several years later, the aged jurist met Lieber on a ferry. The younger man reported: "He said in his warm-hearted, chopped way: I love your books, I love you; you are so sound, so conservative, you are so very safe. When I go on board your books, I always know that the helm is right; and you are so very instructive. You are a very safe writer." A decade later, Lieber still glowed at the memory of Kent's words. "Now, of all things that have ever been said of me," he mused, "nothing has sunk so deep into my heart." [56]

Reviewers were singularly indifferent to the two big volumes. Not only did the *Democratic Review* ignore them, but few American magazines printed full-length articles. Most of them, like the *New York Review*, the *Southern Literary Journal,* the *Knickerbocker,* and some newspapers, wrote the usual short, commendatory notes, so uncritical as to be meaningless. Perhaps the only able friendly review to appear in the United States was that which Luther Cushing, one of Lieber's lawyer acquaintances, wrote for the *American Jurist.*[57]

[55] Lieber to Hillard, November 30, 1839; Lieber to Sumner, August 13, 1838. Hillard went to an extreme amount of work for Lieber during these years, proofing not only the *Political Ethics* but a number of other books, and running innumerable errands in addition. When Lieber was so ungracious as to complain bitterly over typographical errors in the second volume of the *Political Ethics,* Hillard replied mildly, "I am sorry, but I felt a little hurt that you should have complained of them so energetically, for you know how impossible it is for a manuscript to be correctly printed except under the eye of the author himself, especially such a patch-work, folded, twisted one as yours, that would frighten the ghost of old Faust himself." Lieber apologized sincerely, and earlier had been appreciative enough to send Hillard a fifty-five-volume set of Goethe. Lieber to Hillard, January 6, 16, May 19, 1839, April 8, 1840; Hillard to Lieber, March 30, 1840.

[56] Story to Lieber, November 24, 1838; Lieber to Matilda Lieber, September 6, 1841. The incident with Kent took place in New York, not in Boston in August as reported in Perry, *Lieber,* 155. Lieber to Hillard, January 8, 1852; Kent to Lieber, September 18, 1838. James Kent, *Commentaries on American Law* (12th ed.; edited by O. W. Holmes, Jr., Boston, 1873), I, 3.

[57] [L. S. Cushing], "Lieber's Political Ethics," *American Jurist and Law Magazine,* XXI (1839), 40–55; XXIII (1840), 467–74. The *New York Review,* IV (1839), 245, declared, "it would be far better for the people on our great national anniversary, to listen to a chapter from it, than to idle declamations which are then

America's biggest literary gun from which Lieber had expected the loudest boom, the *North American Review,* remained silent. Palfrey, the ineffectual editor, turned the review copy over to Francis Bowen, a Harvard tutor and writer on philosophy, whom the Brahmin Hillard considered a "literary Ishmaelite." Instead of praising the *Political Ethics,* he ripped it to shreds. Warm-hearted Hillard and Professor Greenleaf persuaded Palfrey to reject the review, and Bowen published it in the *Christian Examiner,* where it attracted less attention. Bowen was not very penetrating. He attacked the obvious flaws in style and structure, but confined his comments almost entirely to Lieber's treatment of ethics—or rather to what Bowen regarded as his lack of a system of morals and politics.[58]

Justice Story had warned Lieber that his *Political Ethics* was "too *anti*-transcendental to please some visionaries," and indeed the one thoroughgoing American review the two volumes received was a lambasting in two numbers of Brownson's *Boston Quarterly Review.* Brownson gibed at Lieber's very subject as being untenable. He declared that ethics could apply only to men or nations, and that the ethics of nations, which Lieber was writing about, could be only international law. Next he pricked the syllogism upon which Lieber based natural rights: "I am a man: therefore I have a right to be a man," by substituting the word "thief" for "man." Above all, he devoted himself to demolishing Lieber's conservative ideas on property. Brownson would make property an attribute of society as well as of the individual.

The Boston reformer was even more critical of the second volume. The "single phrase, obey the laws," he commented, "seems to constitute of itself the whole code of political ethics, as the term is explained by the author . . . if all the irrelevant matter were stricken out, there would in fact be nothing left in the book."[59]

---

poured forth upon our former glory and our prospective greatness." See also, *Southern Literary Journal,* IV (1838), 401.

[58] Hillard to Lieber, November 19, 1838, January 12, 1839; Francis Bowen, "A Review of Lieber's Political Ethics," *Christian Examiner,* XXVI (1839), 32–54, reprinted in Bowen, *Critical Essays* . . . (Boston, 1842), 331–52.

[59] Story to Lieber, May 9, 1840. [Orestes A. Brownson], "Manual of Political Ethics," *Boston Quarterly Review,* II (1839), 113–23; III (1840), 181–93. A. M. Schlesinger, Jr., *Orestes A. Brownson, A Pilgrim's Progress* (Boston, 1939). Cf. Ch. IX and Lieber to Hillard, March 4, 1839.

As a soothing antidote to Brownson's venom, Lieber received a well-considered analysis of the first volume in the mighty *Edinburgh Review*. The great English Whig journal decried Lieber's lack of logic and organization, but praised the sound materials he had presented. The London *Literary Examiner* was even more laudatory.[60]

Almost every reviewer, whether friendly or hostile, noted Lieber's fundamental flaw, his clumsy, discursive style and bad arrangement. With more kindness than veracity, that master stylist, William Hickling Prescott, wrote that his prose was "a wonderful achievement for a foreigner," but even Lieber's friend Luther Cushing commented upon the grievous lack of compactness and scientific order so essential in an elementary work for students. Brownson in one of his less vituperative moments ascribed the lack to a want of maturity: "The materials collected are valuable; the author's reading is really extensive and varied; but in his haste to make a new book out of the stock of information which he has collected, he has not given himself time to digest his facts, or to mature either his thoughts or his style."[61]

The repellent form and style undoubtedly contributed more than any other factor to the relative obscurity of the *Political Ethics*. In the 1890's Professor W. A. Dunning in analyzing Lieber confessed: "It is a serious task to follow his system through the mass of illustrations and digressions in which it is embedded." Professor James Walker of Harvard admitted to Lieber in 1846 that much as he admired the study he had dropped it after using it in three classes, because of its unwieldiness, diffusiveness, and want of method. Samuel Gridley Howe, the reformer, dipped into it after his election to the Massachusetts legislature, and wrote with amazement: "Indeed, Lieber, that book is a mine of wisdom—it might be put into a shape to be one of the most popular & useful books ever written; now, it is not read! There is more *stuff* in that

---

[60] "Manual of Political Ethics," *Edinburgh Review*, LXXIII (1841), 55–76; *Literary Examiner*, April 14, 1839, pp. 228–29.

[61] Prescott to Lieber, September 22, 1838. Prescott said of the second volume: "It is a book so full of suggestion that the reader has done only half his work when he has read a Chapter, for it puts him on a train of thinking for himself which he must carry on after he has closed the volume." Prescott to Lieber, November 26, 1839. Brownson, "Manual of Political Ethics," *loc. cit.*, II, 115.

book than would provide capital for 100 vols of our common school & college books; & tis a shame that the public cannot have the benefit of it." [62]

Many friends and acquaintances urged Lieber to prepare a readable abridgment. For years he gathered materials and toyed with the idea, but never actually undertook it. Apparently he came to realize that he was incapable of crisp, compact writing, for he tried unsuccessfully to persuade Theodore Sedgwick and several others to write the abridgment for him.[63]

The sale of the two volumes trickled on year after year until finally after about a decade the edition of a thousand was exhausted. Despite this small sale, his handiwork came to acquire a high reputation because it was a formidable although cumbersome weapon for champions of the emerging economic and political system. A second edition appeared only after Lieber's death, but already in his lifetime, in the growth to political maturity of the group that took over leadership during the Civil War and Reconstruction, Lieber saw the triumph of many of the principles he had cautiously enunciated in the *Political Ethics*. The embarrassing remainder, he stoutly disavowed.[64]

Many of the leading scholars of the latter nineteenth century drew upon Lieber. His greatest influence was in the field of political science, where he could include among his friends and admirers President Theodore Dwight Woolsey and Professor Noah Porter of Yale; President Andrew Dickson White of Cornell; Judge Thomas M. Cooley of Michigan; Daniel Coit Gilman, later to be

[62] Walker to Lieber, September 7, 1846; Howe to Lieber, January 17, 1843. Dunning, *Essays on the Civil War and Reconstruction*, 360–61.

[63] Lieber to Judge Charles Patrick Daly, April 11, 1857, New York Public Library. Lieber to Samuel Austin Allibone, March 22, 1857; Hillard to Lieber, May 21, June 4, 1859.

[64] The publishers felt that the first volume of the *Political Ethics* sold well during the initial months. By 1843, of the editions of a thousand of each volume, 820 of the first volume and 447 of the second had been sold, though the price was as high as $6.00 or $6.50 at a distance from Boston. By 1847 the first volume was out of print and about 300 of the second volume remained unsold. Little and Brown planned either to import 300 copies of volume one from England, or to reprint that number. They declined to publish a new edition or a condensation. By 1855 both volumes were out of print, and the copyright reverted to Lieber. The steady sale of the book was due to its use as a text. Cushing to Lieber, October 31, 1838; Lieber to Hillard, February 28, 1843; Hillard to Lieber, April 14, 1843; Robert J. Walker to Lieber, September 8, 1847; Cornelius Conway Felton to Lieber, August 14, 1854; Hillard to Lieber, April 2, 1855.

president of Johns Hopkins University; and John W. Burgess, who was to be his successor at Columbia.[65]

Thorstein Veblen, whose perceptiveness in economic thought stood at almost polar extremity from Lieber's, was to develop to a high point the institutional interpretation of American culture in which the political theorist pioneered. This relationship, which Professor Joseph Dorfman has carefully evaluated, was probably not accidental. Veblen was a student of William Graham Sumner's, and Lieber's system had left a marked impress upon the sociologist's thinking.[66]

As Albion Small acknowledged, Lieber's treatises contained much rudimentary sociology. Sumner, the originator of the concepts "folkways" and "mores," studied them while a Yale undergraduate and used them as texts during his early years as an instructor. Professor Lee M. Brooks has demonstrated a striking parallel between many of the ideas and even some of the wording in certain sections of the *Political Ethics* and the *Folkways*. Sumner never credited the German-American scholar, and indeed his disciple and collaborator, A. G. Keller, in the 1940's could not recall ever having heard Lieber's name. But in 1875 young Sumner had written the political theorist's widow: "I was educated on Dr. Lieber's works, & am using them now in my instruction. I was very glad that his works were republished because I did not know of anything else to take their place." [67]

[65] Letters from most of these men are in the Lieber papers, Huntington Library. An English philosopher and political theorist, William Whewell, Master of Trinity College, wrote so parallel to Lieber that some of Lieber's admirers made charges of plagiarism. When Lieber visited Whewell in 1845, the English scholar asked permission to use the word "jural" in Lieber's sense of the word without mentioning the source. Subsequently upon the appearance of Whewell's *The Elements of Morality including Polity*, 2 vols. (London, 1845), which did not mention Lieber, President E. D. MacMaster of Miami University drew up a list of a long series of parallels. MacMaster concluded that, while plagiarism would be too strong a word to use, Whewell had read Lieber's book very closely. After Lieber's death, the story spread in the newspapers that Whewell was guilty of serious plagiarism. Lieber to Matilda Lieber, January 23, 1845; MacMaster to Lieber, December 5, 1845. See clippings in Lieber papers, and McCord, "Lieber's Political Ethics," *loc. cit.*, 503–504.

[66] Joseph Dorfman and Rexford Guy Tugwell, "Francis Lieber: German Scholar in America," *Columbia University Quarterly*, XXX (1938), 189.

[67] W. G. Sumner to Matilda Lieber, October 2, 1875; Lee M. Brooks, "Sociology in the Works of Francis Lieber," *Social Forces*, VIII (1929), 231–41; Anna Haddow, *Political Science in American Colleges and Universities, 1636–1900*, 177. A. G. Keller to the present writer, May 20, 1944.

In ways similar to this, Lieber helped stimulate each of the emerging fields of social science. A number of the ideas he introduced, though not always with his name attached, grew through many channels to become part of the national cultural heritage.

IX
Scholar, Publicist, or Hack?

T H E encyclopedic-minded Lieber outlined his universe in the all-inclusive system of the *Political Ethics*. Bulky as it was, he could not stay within its bounds, and, even before he had finished, his prodigious energy and sweeping curiosity were taking him afield into innumerable sidelines. From all this output of varying quality upon a multitude of topics arose a question he never squarely faced: Was he a scholar, a publicist, or a mere hack?

The prolific and often careless way in which Lieber wrote and his ceaseless efforts to earn money with his pen were marks of the hack; the novelty and genuine merit of many of his ideas earned him high status as a scholar and publicist. Perhaps it was the latter role that he fancied most, for it was as a publicist that he gratified his insatiable thirst for recognition and lent impetus to a variety of significant reform movements.

Among these movements was the demand for an improved census. Beyond doubt, the country badly needed the statistical program which Lieber long advocated. Dr. Adam Seybert had proudly announced in his *Statistical Annals of the United States, 1789–1818* that "no other nation has hitherto furnished an equal body of authentic information," but when Lieber tried to gather facts for the *Encyclopaedia Americana* and the *Political Ethics,* he found this far from being true. Secretary of State Livingston informed the scholar that he had not even been able to collect accurate tax information. As early as 1834, the German-American called attention to America's lag behind Europe, and drew up tangible plans for reform to press upon Congress. Jared Sparks, the New England historian, heartily approved of his proposals, but warned him that party spirit in Washington would make them hard to achieve.[1]

Lieber took a broad view of statistics. "The subjects properly falling within the province of statistics," he observed a few years later, "are all those which belong to human society or affect it, and the observation of whose repetition . . . can be expressed numerically, so that their total gives an accurate statement of the *status* . . . of a given society. . . . We understand by statistics the account of ever changing human society, taken at a fixed period." [2]

In keeping with this concept, Lieber drafted a comprehensive scheme for statistical compilation in a memorial to Congress. He sent it to Calhoun, who introduced it in the Senate with words of high approbation; Webster likewise lauded it and suggested printing twice the usual number of copies.[3]

In the memorial Lieber called attention to the great gaps in American statistical knowledge and proposed that Congress publish a broad analysis of the statistics of the United States. Cold facts, he suggested, would expose many fallacious suppositions and draw attention to evils not previously suspected. Therefore they would serve as a significant basis for legislation. In 1847, when Lieber renewed his recommendations, he remarked with keen prescience that a statistical board would not only be of practical value to the government but also of incalculable benefit to the community through "furnishing information for business operations." [4]

For an individual to prepare a complete statistical compilation

---

[1] Curti, *The Growth of American Thought*, 253. Lieber to Sparks, January 25, 1834; Sparks to Lieber, February 4, 1834, Sparks papers, Harvard University. Cf. Adams, *Life and Writings of Jared Sparks*, I, 186–87. Lieber to Nathan Appleton, January 31, 1834, Massachusetts Historical Society; Lieber to J. M. Wayne, March 27, 1834, New York Public Library.

[2] Lieber to Joseph Henry, October 22, 1847 (letter-book copy), Lieber papers, Henry E. Huntington Library. All manuscripts referred to in this chapter, unless otherwise identified, are from this collection.

[3] *Register of Debates in Congress*, U.S. Senate, 24 Cong., 1 Sess., April 18, 1836, XII, 1198. Webster to Lieber, April 13, 1836; C. C. Cambreleng to Lieber, May 21, 1836; Lieber to Ticknor, February 22, 1837 (copy).

[4] Francis Lieber, *Memorial . . . relative to Proposals for a Work on the Statistics of the United States* (U.S. Senate, 24 Cong., 1 Sess., Senate Document No. 314, Washington, 1836), 17 pp., interleaved copy, Lieber papers, and "Lieber's Memorial," *Southern Literary Messenger,* II (1836), 596–97.

would be almost impossible because of the scattered nature of the material and the necessity for access to the governmental archives. Consequently, Congress should appropriate funds and grant the statistician the franking privilege. Thus financed, he should gather information from a wide variety of sources in broad fields which Lieber outlined in considerable detail: the country, the inhabitants, nature and man in relation to each other, commerce and industry, intercourse and communication, standard of comfort of freemen, moral and intellectual culture, charity, political state, army, navy, pensions, and medical statistics. Under "standard of comfort," for example, statistics should include the price of food as compared with the price of labor, the price of various kinds of meats, grains, and beverages, the quantity of bread consumed, the price of clothing and housing, the amount of goods used by various class groups, how people ordinarily dressed, how much it cost to maintain able-bodied men, old people, women, and children, and how many hours and days people generally worked.

Lieber realized that Congress would not at once put into effect as comprehensive a survey as he had outlined in his memorial. He bided his time, and in 1838, when the census of 1840 was under consideration, proposed enlarging the scope of this census. The 1820 census had collected a set of industrial statistics so poor that in 1830 Congress had returned to the original scheme and ordered population figures alone. Lieber suggested the 1840 census begin collecting additional pertinent information. He pointed out that it could be done at trifling expense, and recommended that a committee of Congress be appointed to consider the next census and outline new schedules. To avoid the errors of too hastily gathered information, Congress should remove the conduct of the census from the inept United States marshals who ran it as an additional bit of political plunder and delegate it to separate commissioners of the census.[5]

Although the exact influence of Lieber's suggestions cannot be determined, President Van Buren in his annual message to Con-

[5] Lieber, "Letter on the Census of 1840, to the Hon. Hugh S. Legare, M.C.," Columbia *Telescope*, April 21, 1838. This letter, dated February 13, 1838, appeared also in the Washington *National Intelligencer* (clipping in Lieber papers). Cf. Ch. VIII.

gress, December 8, 1838, recommended that Congress increase the scope of the census of 1840. The legislators complied, and passed an act providing that the marshals should "collect and return in statistical tables . . . all such information in relation to mines, agriculture, commerce, manufactures, and schools, as will exhibit a full view of the pursuits, industry, education, and resources of the country." Unfortunately, the ill-paid and inefficient marshals presented returns which the American Statistical Association, of which Lieber was a member, tore to pieces as ridiculously inaccurate. As a single instance, in many towns the enumerator found more colored insane than the total number of Negroes.[6]

Nevertheless, the census of 1840 made a start toward a nationwide statistical survey, and in future years Lieber continued to press for improvements. When the 1850 census approached, he renewed his suggestions for a Board of Statistics. He felt it might well be connected with the new Smithsonian Institution, and interested its distinguished secretary, Joseph Henry, in his scheme. He also broached the subject to Senator Thomas Corwin of Ohio and Secretary of the Treasury Robert J. Walker, but Sparks's forebodings still held good. Lieber's statistical researches throughout his lifetime were to remain personal or to have the backing of private organizations only.[7]

Another recommendation Lieber urged as a result of his tribulations in gathering material was the complete reorganization of the post-office department. Lieber complained incessantly of the inefficiency of the postal service and the twenty-five-cent fee he had to pay when he received letters. He advocated taking the

[6] Carroll D. Wright, *The History and Growth of the United States Census* . . . (U.S. Senate, 56 Cong., 1 Sess., Senate Document No. 194, Washington, 1900), 32–39. Lieber's membership certificate in the American Statistical Association, dated March 13, 1840, is in the Lieber papers. Though Lieber was a corresponding member, he took little part in the association. With the exception of its excellent critique of the 1840 census, the association achieved little of national value in the field of contemporary statistics until after the Civil War. *Constitution and By-Laws of the American Statistical Association with a List of Officers, Fellows, and Members and an Address* (Boston, 1840), *ibid.* (Boston, 1862); *Memorial of the American Statistical Association Praying the Adoption of Measures for the Correction of Errors in the Returns of the Sixth Census* (U.S. Senate, 28 Cong., 2 Sess., Senate Document No. 5, Washington, 1844).

[7] Lieber to Ruggles, May 2, October 3, 1847; Lieber to Walker, September 28, 1847, Lieber papers, Library of Congress; Lieber to Henry, October 22, 1847; Lieber to Matilda Lieber, August 22, 1847.

postal establishment out of politics and bringing down the rate to levels comparable with Rowland Hill's penny postal reform in England. He published these proposals and discussed them with the chairman of the House committee on postal affairs, but cheaper postage would not come for years. Meanwhile Lieber painstakingly forwarded a considerable part of his correspondence through his acquaintances in Congress. They could receive mail free of charge and send it on with their congressional frank. The habit became so thoroughly engrained that Lieber continued it even during the Civil War when postage was only three cents.[8]

While the proposals for postal reform and the gathering of statistics had grown at least in part out of Lieber's difficulties in assembling data for the *Political Ethics,* his essay on legal interpretation was an unexpected adjunct to the major work. Originally Lieber had intended it to comprise two chapters, but though he tried to compress, "the subject was like a bladder—when pressed in on one side it would protrude on another." Sumner wrote a flattering introduction and inserted it in two numbers of the *American Jurist.* Thereafter Lieber enlarged it and persuaded Little and Brown to publish it.

The title was one of Lieber's unfortunate Teutonisms, or as he himself later styled such things, a "Lieberism": *Legal and Political Hermeneutics.* "Hermeneutics" was a perfectly valid word meaning the science of interpretation and explanation, but Lieber had unwisely borrowed it from theological rather than legal parlance, and it was sufficient to make most forthright American lawyers shy away from the work—as indeed they did. "What, in God's name, made you choose '*Hermeneutics'?*" William Kent, Chancellor Kent's able son, once asked Lieber. "Had you called your . . . book 'principles of Interpretation,' . . . many an honest fellow, now frightened away, would have read & enjoyed the writings." [9]

---

[8] Lieber to Matilda Lieber, July 10–11, 1841. Lieber, *Remarks on the Post Establishment in the United States, Reprinted from the Seventeenth Number of the New York Review* (New York, 1841), 22 pp. Cf. *PE,* II, 381.

[9] Lieber to Sumner, May 9, 24, 1837; William Kent to Lieber, December 19, 1843. Lieber, "Political Hermeneutics; or on Political Interpretation and Construction; and also on Precedents," *American Jurist,* XVIII (1837–38), 37–101; 281–94. Little and Brown reprinted the articles under the same title: *Political Hermeneutics . . .* (Boston, 1837), 78 pp. The standard edition, considerably revised and enlarged, was

Those honest and conservative lawyers who got beyond the title found the work as admirable for their purposes as the name was formidable. Lieber had overcome his lack of common-law background by long reading and pondering upon his subject. Indeed, he had first begun thinking about it shortly after his arrival in America when he had read a newspaper attack upon John Quincy Adams based largely on questions of constitutional construction.

Learnedly citing examples that ranged from the classics to recent legal decisions, Lieber set up a series of rules whereby lawyers could decide upon the meaning of documents. The need for these rules, he argued, arose from the very widespread ambiguity of words which had crept even into the Constitution itself. Often widely varying interpretations could be argued from a law. In autocratic countries, the state could govern by fiat through issuing its own interpretations; in democratic nations, the courts must decide.

Construction, while dangerous, was indispensable, and its leading stars should be good faith and common sense. Literal interpretation was one of the handiest tools of tyranny, and words should take their most probable sense. That which is inferior in a text cannot overrule what is superior; technical terms should receive technical construction; and the text itself should furnish, if possible, the means of interpreting its own doubtful words. At times common sense should overrule the text—no matter how clear. As an example, he cited Lord Bentinck's Order in Council, which abolished the whipping of native Indian soldiers. Despite the order, British officials had whipped a Sepoy and a drummer on the grounds that they had become Christians and were no longer entitled to the privileges of natives. Lieber would allow no such evasion of the clear intent of a document.

Cannily the political scientist guided his readers through the thickets and byways of argument by analogy or parallelism. He even took up the relative value of hearsay, spoken words, letters, journals, speeches, and other materials outside the text of a document. All this led to the general precept with which his readers

---

Lieber, *Legal and Political Hermeneutics* . . . (Boston, 1839), 240 pp. Cf. *New York Review*, V (1839), 508–509.

could well sympathize, that close construction ordinarily was most conducive to civil liberty.

Distinguishing carefully between construction and precedent, Lieber plunged into the legal jungle of *stare decisis*. He recognized that it possessed a fearful power for good or evil, and inveighed against a blind following of precedent for its own sake. "A precedent ought to be sound," and must not serve to perpetuate that which is unjust or injurious.

Reliance upon authorities was similar. The jurist must apply to them the rules of historical criticism: "Who is he? What opportunity had he to observe? What motive had he to give this account? What internal evidence of truth do we find in the account, and how far do those statements which we have in our power to compare with authenticated statements, agree?" [10]

Lieber laid down little that was new in his account of precedents and construction, but assembled and organized a body of information which heretofore had not been available. He permeated his essay with the leaven of reason, justice, and civil liberty. Yet Lieber's emphasis upon strict construction made it a conservative doctrine, one which must have pleased the state-rights advocates of the South.[11]

Lieber received many fine compliments upon even the first brief edition. Clay wrote so analytically that he demonstrated he had actually read the essay. He made several suggestions which Lieber later embodied in the new edition—among them that Lieber should insist "with more earnestness upon the obligation of the Legislative authority in a free country to conform to those expositions of its constitution, which may have been often & deliberately made." Clay was referring to the Democratic destruction of the Bank of the United States on the ground that it was unconstitutional.[12]

[10] This analysis is from the 1839 edition. The chapter on authorities was new. Lieber based his work on Coke, Blackstone, Kent, Pufendorf, Grotius, and a rich variety of American and European authors and codes. He used the classics for many of his examples, and demonstrated once more an encyclopedic grasp of his materials. Lieber carefully distinguished between interpretation of the meaning of a text and construction, "the drawing of conclusions respecting subjects, that lie beyond the direct expression of the text, from elements known from and given in the text— conclusions which are in the spirit though not within the letter of the text." Lieber, *Hermeneutics*, 56.

[11] *Ibid.*, 18–19.   [12] Clay to Lieber, February 12, 1838.

The legal patriarch, James Kent, to whom Lieber dedicated the second edition, was careful in his praise. "I have read with much pleasure & Profit your very learned, accurate & interesting Essay," he congratulated Lieber, but went on to confess that he had previously thought good common sense sufficed.[13]

Professor Simon Greenleaf of Harvard Law School thought on the contrary that the work was "eminently useful to our profession—not *merely* to students, but to men of long experience at the bar. . . . It is a valuable contribution to the law." One of the great English jurists, William Burge, wrote from Lincoln's Inn that he had read it "with very great delight. It is full of profound reflexions." To some lawyers it did prove useful. Rufus Choate told Lieber he had found the book helpful during the battle over the annexation of Texas, and Hillard in 1859 declared he frequently referred to it and within the year had cited it in an argument before the Supreme Court.[14]

Lieber's interest in words and their meanings was entirely in keeping with the interests of the German historical school in which he had received his training. It led him not only along paths of legal interpretation, but also into the byways of linguistics. Lieber had learned a smattering of the subject from Niebuhr; he followed closely the writings of William von Humboldt; and he was acquainted with the work of Jacob L. K. and W. K. Grimm and F. B. Bopp. But in a period when German scholars in a truly scientific spirit and with minute attention to detail were already building up the science of philology, Lieber never became more than a dilettante who helped to introduce Americans to a little-known study.[15]

After his arrival in the United States, Lieber gathered data on

[13] Kent to Lieber, December 1, 1837.
[14] Greenleaf to Little and Brown, July 3, 1838; Burge to Lieber, October 10, 1839; Lieber to Hillard and Sumner, March 12, 1845; Hillard to Lieber, May 11, 1859. The *Hermeneutics* (2d ed.) sold even more slowly than the *Political Ethics*. By 1847, Little and Brown had disposed of only 613 copies out of an edition of a thousand. In 1855, 169 still remained unsold. Little and Brown to Lieber, September 8, 1847; March 30, 1855. Lieber projected a third edition with William Curtis Noyes, but it never materialized. See draft title page, Lieber papers, Johns Hopkins University.
[15] Neither Lieber nor any of his American associates appear in Holger Pedersen, *Linguistic Science in the Nineteenth Century* (translated by J. W. Spargo, Cambridge, 1931). Lieber to Pickering, November 21, 1836, in Pickering, *Life of John Pickering*, 443; Lieber, *Miscellaneous Writings*, I, 457, 516, 520.

the Indian languages for Humboldt, and became acquainted with America's three leading students of philology: Pickering, Duponceau, and Gallatin. The Indian tongues fascinated Lieber, and in 1828 he proposed founding a society to promote their study. Then he discovered Pennsylvania German, and turned his interest largely to problems of language corruption and dialect building. He searched for evidences of new dialects among the Spanish and French Creoles of the West Indies, and planned a treatise on the corruption of languages. Especially he studied Pennsylvania German and prepared an unpublished essay upon it which preceded the first scientific study by thirty-five years.[16]

In his long discourse on American place names in the *Stranger in America,* Lieber had already demonstrated his love of words for their own sake. In his translation of Beaumont and Tocqueville's prison report and in the *Political Ethics* he had already begun the sport of word coining. One of his proudest achievements was the addition of a number of terms to the American vocabulary. About 1861, he prepared a list of words he had invented or first used. In addition to penology and jural, he claimed among others: nationalism and internationalism, individualism, city-state, interdependence, Rousseauism, commonwealth of nations, and Pan-American.[17]

In 1837 Lieber half playfully aired his philological erudition in a letter on "hipponomastics" or the naming of race horses in which he listed five axioms (with corollaries), six rules, and eleven name groupings. He even prepared, but did not publish, a companion piece on "The Theory of Naming Children." [18]

[16] Dr. Felix Reichmann has identified a paper by Lieber on Pennsylvania German as an important pioneer effort. Lieber had prepared it for inclusion in the *Reminiscences of Niebuhr,* but never published it. Reichmann, "Francis Lieber, Pennsylvania German Dialect," *American German Review,* XI (1945), 24–27. Quantities of other materials on philology, including notes, clippings, and correspondence, are in the Lieber papers. Pickering, *Life of John Pickering,* 443 ; Lieber to Delafield, November 15, 1831, Historical Society of Pennsylvania; Lieber to C. A. Heckscher, June 31, 1835 (contemporary copy) ; Lieber, proposal for a society to promote the study of Indian languages, January 21, 1828.

[17] Lieber, "What I have Done," [1861].

[18] Lieber, "On Hipponomastics . . . ," *loc. cit.* See ms., "The Theory of Naming Children," and a heavily revised interleaved copy of the "Hipponomastics," Lieber papers. Lieber wished to include the essay in his miscellaneous writings, but Daniel Coit Gilman, after Lieber's death, did not even list it among the scholar's publications.

Lieber sketched his theories of language origin and formation more seriously in another *Southern Literary Messenger* article. With simple illustrations, he pointed out how by combining indefinite word symbols one could create definite pictures.

The German-American scholar belabored his mentor William von Humboldt for calling combination words "agglutinations," and termed them instead "holophrastic" words, a new technical term which he impressed upon the vocabulary of American philology. Opposed to the "holophrastic" words (which expressed a whole complex of ideas) were "analytical" ones of limited meaning. Energy of style demanded the former, while for philosophical discourse and generalization one needed analytical terms. A rich language necessitated an abundant supply of both sorts of words, and none was better equipped in this respect than Greek.

Lieber aired his great respect for the classical languages. Modern languages were corruptions of Greek and Latin with the tongues of barbaric tribes. Hence one could not understand grammar without studying the well-rounded language structure of the ancients. Through knowledge of classical languages one could achieve "moral and intellectual expansion," the paramount object of all education. "Strengthen the mind, clear the intellect and give it sound knowledge in the general branches—develop it philologically never mind by what specific idiom." [19]

Though Lieber's essay on philology contributed but little to the science, it augmented Lieber's reputation as a scholar. Calhoun, whose interests ranged almost as broadly, commented specu-

---

[19] Lieber used few new arguments in favor of the study of the classics; his remarks on philology owed much to Humboldt, and were chiefly notable for their new phraseology. Lieber classified languages as holophrastic or analytical with regard to the meaning of words. He also divided them into synthetic, polysynthetic, parathetic, or inflective, according to the means used to arrive at the expression of a complex or a series of ideas. Lieber, "Remarks on some subjects of comparative Philology, and the importance of the study of Foreign Languages, especially of the Classic Tongues—In a letter to the Honorable *Albert Gallatin* . . . ," *Southern Literary Messenger*, III (1837), 162–72, 208. A profusely annotated, interleaved copy and a less heavily annotated one are in the Lieber papers. Gilman followed the latter in editing the essay for Lieber, *Miscellaneous Writings*, I, 499–534. Lieber's voluminous notes on languages indicate an unceasing curiosity about the reasons for changes in meanings of words, growth of languages, shifts in grammatical construction, and the odd or unusual. Like other American philologists of the period, he was more a word and vocabulary collector than a philosopher or scientist of language. This most strikingly appears in his incessant hobby of word coining.

latively upon the article: "It opens a wide field of comparison between the genius & character of various languages," he remarked. "It opens a new volume of the history of our race, in which many discoveries will be made, as geology does of the history of our planet." John Pickering, the lawyer philologist, also liked the essay, but hardly agreed with Lieber that it might form the basis for a separate volume—for, would the novel-reading girls peruse such a tome? [20]

Instead, Lieber turned out for profit an abridgment and translation from the German of Ramshorn's dictionary of Latin synonyms. He detested the task. "I have worked, positively like a horse, every day with all my other work, 10 nasty . . . pages of the syn[onyms]," he complained in the fall of 1838. "And what ugly work, copying, translat[in]g, &c.!!" [21]

Lieber headed the translation with a lengthy, discursive discourse on the study of foreign languages, particularly Latin, and sent it northward. He promised George Hillard and Luther Cushing each a gallon of Carolina "mountain dew" if they would put it through the press neatly. The interminable preface startled Hillard. "Don't you write such infernally long sentences," he counseled Lieber. "There is one . . . that is as long as an Anaconda or the Sea Serpent himself. Chop off their tails and bring them within moderate compass." Little and Brown were even more ruthless and lopped the preface to five and a half pages. Piqued, Lieber wanted his name removed from the title page, but the publishers insisted upon retaining it. The dictionary sold well, and in all it went through four printings—the last in 1870. Pickering boosted it in the *North American Review* as superior to any other in the English language.[22]

After he completed the dictionary of synonyms, Lieber shifted

[20] Calhoun to Lieber, April 8, 1837; John Pickering to Lieber, April 19, 1837.
[21] Lieber to Matilda Lieber, July 17, 1838; Lieber to Hillard, November 2, 1838.
[22] Lieber to Hillard, November 2, December 18, 1838; Hillard to Lieber, November 19, 1838, February 13?, March 22, November 20, 1839. Pickering, *Life of John Pickering*, 463. [Pickering], "Ramshorn's Latin Synonymes," *North American Review*, XLIX (1839), 467–77. Lieber (tr. and ed.), *Dictionary of Latin Synonymes, for the use of Schools and Private Students, with a Complete Index. By Lewis Ramshorn* (Boston, 1839), 475 pp. Subsequent printings appeared in Boston, 1841, 1856; Philadelphia, 1870. No evidence exists that Lieber obtained permission from the German publishers to translate the work, or paid any royalties to them. The unpublished preface is in the Lieber papers.

his interest largely to problems of language origin. During the 1840's he observed Laura Bridgman, a blind deaf-mute whom the talented Dr. Samuel Gridley Howe had taught to communicate through finger-language. Laura could not talk, but made many primitive vocal sounds which fascinated Lieber. He studied them carefully, and from them drew up a theory of a simple phonetic origin of all language. For illustrations he called upon the learning experiences of his own children and accounts of primitive tongues. Unfortunately, in drawing up his theories of language growth, he failed to consult the great European philologists of his day, and again his paper, which he persuaded the Smithsonian Institution to publish in 1850, was more significant as a pioneering American study than as a lasting contribution in the field.[23]

While Lieber was conducting his physiological study of language origin he was also following the researches of American ethnologists. In 1843 he read Alexander W. Bradford's *American Antiquities and Researches into the Origins and History of the Red Race,* the first sound study to appear, and pronounced it "one of the best books . . . that America has yet produced." Lieber seized avidly upon Bradford's hypothesis that the American Indian was of Mongolian origin and had migrated to America by way of Pacific islands. Bradford had adduced this in part through grammatical similarities of the Indian tongues and those of some Pacific islanders. Lieber had already pointed out the "holophrastic" nature of the Indian languages and those of some Pacific islanders, but he had failed to make any connection. Now he called Bradford's attention to the additional evidence and suggested further researches.[24]

In 1851 Lieber plunged with equal delight into a voluminous correspondence with Henry R. Schoolcraft, the learned student of Indian languages. From his files Lieber exhumed his material on philology, painstakingly debated his doctrines, and wound up pages later with an aside to the effect that the rather unprecise

[23] Lieber, *On the Vocal Sounds of Laura Bridgeman* [sic], *the Blind Deaf-Mute at Boston; compared with the Elements of Phonetic Language* (Smithsonian Institution Contributions to Knowledge, Vol. 2, Article 2, Washington, 1850), 31 pp. See interleaved, annotated copy, Johns Hopkins University, and enlarged version, Lieber, *Miscellaneous Writings,* I, 443–97.

[24] Lieber to Hillard, before February 23, 1843; Lieber to Bradford, March 20, 1843.

nature of all languages was one of his many arguments against "the very puerile theory of an inspired origin of language."

Schoolcraft was impressed by the letter and included it in his multivolumed study of the American Indian tribes, but piously retorted to Lieber that Hebrew, the language in which the Bible came to man, could be the result of nothing short of Divine inspiration. This indicated the treacherous ground upon which Lieber was treading, for while he later was to denounce the Darwinian theories, he was ascribing an humble origin and slow evolutionary development to languages. His Presbyterian neighbors in Columbia, who held fast to the Genesis account of the Tower of Babel, quickly detected the heresy in the paper on Laura Bridgman and wrote a stern refutation.[25]

It was symbolic of the perverse fate which dogged Lieber, that the serious philological study of Laura Bridgman, upon which he had worked long and hard, should bring him little but criticism from fundamentalists, while his entirely uninspired translation of the dictionary of synonyms sold merrily on year after year. Pleased by its success, Lieber in 1839 sought new faggots with which to keep his literary kettle boiling. He devised a new textbook scheme, a bit too advanced for the times, which in later years with other authors would prove highly successful: "Ten gentlemen of name in the various quarters of the Union, North, West and South, unite to publish a series of sound substantial schoolbooks—no Rollos at wheel-barrow—with the same publisher, uniform and with a fine title running through all, so that they become known as such."

Lieber could not interest Little and Brown in an entire textbook series, but he did persuade them to give him a contract for an ancient-history textbook. To stimulate interest, he obtained from Jared Sparks, who had assumed the history professorship

[25] Lieber to Schoolcraft, March 6, 14, 28, April 26, 1851; Schoolcraft to Lieber, March 10, 1851, Schoolcraft papers, Library of Congress; Schoolcraft to Lieber, March 22, May 6, 1851; Lieber to Schoolcraft, April 29, 1851, contemporary copy; Lieber to "a member of the SCC faculty," about 1851, contemporary copy, with clipping quoting the *Erskine Miscellany* attached, Lieber papers. Lieber, "Plan of Thought of the American Languages," Schoolcraft (ed.), *Information Respecting the History, Condition, and Prospects of the Indian Tribes of the United States . . . ,* 6 vols. (Philadelphia, 1851–57), II, 346–49. For favorable comments on the Bridgman article, see "Lieber, Nodheimer, and Donaldson on the Philosophy of Language," *Southern Quarterly Review,* XX (1851), 390–433,

at Harvard, a letter declaring that no suitable texts in ancient or modern history existed for use in American colleges or academies. Unfortunately, Lieber's product was to do little to remedy the situation.[26]

Eager to make money, he cast aside almost all of his own precepts, and, instead of writing a sound ancient history, threw together a handful of historical readings topped off with a moralizing preface entirely in keeping with banal American convention. He called it *Great Events Described by Distinguished Historians, Chroniclers, and Other Writers,* and announced in the preface that these inspiring accounts were a "means of forming strong character, awakening generous impulses, and invigorating the mind for future action."

Fifteen excerpts followed—ten of them accounts of battles, and the remainder equally dramatic. Among them were Herodotus' report of the Battle of Thermopylae, Plato's description of the death of Socrates, Livy's story of the impeachment of Scipio Africanus, Tschudi's legend of William Tell, Gibbon's analysis of the conquest of Constantinople, Southey and Napier's history of the siege of Zaragoza during the Peninsular campaign of the Napoleonic wars, and an eyewitness account of the sack of Rome in 1527. Lieber preceded each excerpt with a discussion of the historian and event. Though an occasional remark was instructive— he pointed out that Herodotus reported what he heard but Thucydides began historical criticism—most of the comment was discursive.[27]

Replete with Germanisms, the manuscript went to Boston in the winter of 1839–40 where the none-too-stable publishing firm of March, Capen, Lyon and Webb accepted it upon the stipulation that Lieber pay to have the English improved. Sadly the proud professor agreed, hoping the editing would not eat up all the royalties. Despite his forebodings, the book succeeded: its descriptions of violence were graphic enough to hold the interest of school-

[26] Sparks to Lieber, July 23, 1839, Harvard University. Cf. H. B. Adams' comments in Adams, *Life and Writings of Jared Sparks,* I, 427–28. Lieber to Hillard, August 19, 1839.

[27] Lieber, *Great Events, Described by Distinguished Historians, Chroniclers, and Other Writers* (Boston, 1840), 415 pp. Prescott praised the book warmly in a letter to Lieber, November 20, 1840.

boys at the same time that the introductions were moral enough to convince teachers of their educational worth. The publishers issued 1,500 copies, 1,000 of them in "The School Library Series." It was one of their few profitable productions and shortly they went bankrupt leaving Lieber without royalties. Eventually Harper and Brothers took over the plates and reprinted the *Great Events* four times between 1855 and 1871.[28]

With less profit and more publicity, Lieber maintained his vigorous interest in prison reform. He continued to correspond with his friends of the Philadelphia Society for Alleviating the Miseries of Public Prisons and with the German penologists, Mittermaier and Julius. Lieber promised Mittermaier that when he had finished the *Political Ethics* he would write a full-length work on criminal law and punishment. Although he gathered ample material for a substantial volume, he never wrote it. Instead he continued to collect questionnaires, clip newspapers, and turn out essays on his triple themes: "mild laws, firm judges, calm punishments." [29]

Lieber aimed these essays primarily against the foes of the solitary-confinement system, but in one of them, *A Popular Essay on Penal Law*, which he wrote at the beginning of 1838, he developed a theory of punishment in keeping with the concepts he had stated in the *Political Ethics*. Since the state was a society founded on right, interference with the rights of its component individuals or with the societal basis of the state necessitated protection. That could come only through lawful punishment. From the standpoint of the individual (the offender) punishment was

[28] Hillard to Lieber, May 5, 1841. W. Crosby and H. P. Nichols published a Boston edition in 1847; Harpers' reprinted the book in 1855, 1856, 1862, and 1871. Fragments of the manuscript and proofs are in the Lieber papers. In these years, Lieber also produced a "Geography of Ancient Asia," made up almost entirely of clippings, and never published.

[29] Lieber to J. R. Ingersoll, January 13, [1839], New York Public Library; Lieber to Mittermaier, April 9, June, 1835, translated copies. Among the prison statistics that Lieber collected in these years, see, "Pennsylvania Eastern Penitentiary, Statistical Report about the prisoners, showing ages, race, nativity, and parentage," enclosed in Wood to Lieber, March 22, 1838, and "Statistical Report about the prisoners showing sentences and crimes," enclosed in Wood to Lieber, April 20, 1838, and similar reports from Joseph A. Yard, warden at Trenton, and G. Barrett of Wethersfield, Connecticut. These and a great variety of materials on penology are in the Lieber papers, Huntington Library. Lieber's collection of pamphlets, together with a few clippings and several letters, comprise the larger part of seven volumes of "Pamphlets on Crime" in the University of California library.

"the obligation he owes to the state, [together] with the privileges he is entitled to." It "involves many and very valuable privileges and protections." [30]

From this, Lieber elaborated at length his prior ideas and developed a few new concepts. Much crime, he still felt, grew out of unsatisfactory environment. However, education and the removal of pauperism could not, as some utilitarians believed, entirely eliminate crime, since "the human heart will always remain a focus of passion, and . . . the more civilized a nation is the more intricate are its relations, which will always induce some to commit offences." As the variety of human activities grew, opportunities for crime increased.[31]

These theories brought little comment; nor was Lieber disappointed by their failure to do so. He had inserted them only as a fragment of a lengthy attack upon the foes of solitary confinement. His discourse was aimed directly at the twelfth annual report of the Boston Prison Discipline Society. Dwight had drawn a dire picture of suicide and despair resulting from the Pennsylvania system; Lieber's essay was a vigorous refutation.

Hillard carried Lieber's crusade within the very bastions of the Boston Society by summarizing the essay in the *North American Review*. He quoted in entirety a list of nineteen advantages of the Pennsylvania system and the almost equally numerous objections to the Auburn plan. The Bostonians fostered a potent reply. President Francis Wayland of Brown University in a subsequent number of the *Review* pointed out the fundamental fallacy of Lieber's warm arguments for the solitary system: Lieber declared the prisoners could not at all communicate with each other, yet admitted they listened to the sound of their neighbors' shuttles and competed with each other in swiftness. Dwight went further and reported that the prisoners talked to each other in "low, vulgar, obscene language" through the heating and drain pipes. Was

---

[30] Lieber, *A Popular Essay on Subjects of Penal Law*. With additions Lieber made as late as the 1850's, the parts of this essay concerning theories of punishment are in Lieber, *Miscellaneous Writings*, I, 471–94. In addition to setting forth his own ideas, Lieber discussed and discarded earlier theories based on expiation, necessity and expediency, deterrence, special prevention, warning, contract, correction and reform, and retaliation. Lieber, *A Popular Essay on Subjects of Penal Law*, 11–26. Reviewed in *New York Review*, VI (1840), 124–41.

[31] Lieber, *Miscellaneous Writings*, I, 486 et *passim*.

Lieber being naïve in assuming that the solitary system with its nineteen enumerated virtues actually did keep the prisoners solitary? [32]

If Lieber failed in rebuttal against Wayland and Dwight, he at least effectively refuted a dolorous tale that Charles Dickens had included in his *American Notes*. In his description of Eastern Penitentiary, Dickens sentimentally pictured a mulatto girl, who with moistened eyes "spoke most touchingly on the gnawing griefs of solitary confinement." This, Lieber retorted, was nonsense. He reported in detail his own conversation with the mulatto in which she had told of kind treatment and declared herself reformed.[33]

While Lieber could scarcely compete with Dickens stylistically, he could count upon strong public support for his castigation. Americans were roaring with rage over Dickens' stinging quips in the *Notes*. Yet, during the English author's visit, he had been lionized, and Lieber had joined the acclaim, for Dickens had with great publicity advocated another of Lieber's favorite reforms, international copyright. Both British and American authors were intensely interested in bringing about reform. Americans were especially interested, since lack of an international copyright enabled publishing houses to glut the market with cheap pirated editions of well-known English authors. The publishers preferred these to American books, since they did not have to pay royalties other than an occasional pittance for advance sheets.[34]

Lieber plunged into the controversy. In the *Political Ethics* he had proposed not only international copyright, but copyright

---

[32] [Hillard], "Lieber's Essay on Penal Law," *North American Review*, XLVII (1838), 452–64; [Wayland], "Prison Discipline," *North American Review*, XLIX (1839), 1–43. Wayland declared temperately that the weak points of the Pennsylvania system were its expense and the difficulty of actually isolating the prisoners; the Auburn system was weak because it did not effectually prevent conversation in the workshops. He did not, like Dwight, stress the psychological damage of solitary confinement. For Lieber's arguments in favor of the Pennsylvania system, upon which he later embroidered, see *post*, Ch. VI.

[33] Lieber, "A Letter from Dr. Lieber. Charles Dickens and the Silent System," *The Inquirer and National Gazette*, Philadelphia, November 15, 1843, reprinted as "Dr. Francis Lieber's Letter on the 'Attack of Chas. Dickens on the Eastern Penitentiary,' published in the 'Saturday Courier' December 9, 1843," in Teeters, *They Were in Prison*, 503–505.

[34] For a bibliography of the early movement, see Frank Freidel, "Lieber's Contribution to the International Copyright Movement," *The Huntington Library Quarterly*, VIII (1945), 200.

throughout the lifetime of a man and his heirs or perhaps even for a century. "It strikes every one now-a-days, as very barbarous, that in former times, commodities belonging to any foreign nation were considered as good prize"; he pointed out, "Yet we allow robbing in the shape of reprint, to the manifest injury of the author." [35]

The publicist showed no reticence in taking these ideas from the study to the forum. In 1839 he urged Clay, who three times had presented an international copyright bill, to continue the fight. The Whig senator counseled a campaign to enlighten public opinion and Congress; so Lieber tried to enlist the aid of William H. Prescott, the historian of Spanish America, and Senator William C. Preston.[36]

Logically, Lieber determined to give impetus to the measure through his favorite palliative, a pamphlet. In March, 1840, he addressed to Preston a long essay in which he elaborated the theory of property in literature. Man created property through personal and individual activity, and this property right appeared nowhere more clearly than in a literary production. "If there exists any species of property not made by government, but existing by spontaneous right, and which requires only to be acknowledged by way of protection on the part of the government, it is literary property; if there is any property which does not trench upon the rights of others, and exists without any sacrifice of theirs . . . it is literary property."

Scathingly the scholar tore to pieces the arguments defending literary piracy. Resorting to history, contemporary incident, and analogy, he pointed out the ethical and theoretical desirability of international copyright and the practical necessity to protect American authors.[37]

The professor sent the manuscript and accompanying notes for Senator Preston to use in debate. Subsequently, after each of six publishers rejected it, Lieber printed it at his own expense and

[35] Lieber to Sumner, August 27, 1837; Lieber, *PE*, I, 113, 121–24. Lieber translated the Prussian copyright law for the *Law Reporter*, II (1839), 129–33.

[36] Clay to Lieber, June 19, December 28, 1839; Prescott to Lieber, November 26, 1839, February 10, 1840; Preston to Lieber, March 1, 1840.

[37] Lieber, *On International Copyright, in a Letter to the Hon. William C. Preston* (New York, 1840), reprinted in Lieber, *Miscellaneous Writings* II, 329–67. See annotated copy in the Lieber papers.

hoped that the investment would bring him a little acknowledg-ment. It did bring that, but came too late to affect the Senate, which in July, 1840, had ordered Clay's bill laid on the table. From New Orleans to Boston to Berlin, the pamphlet created comment and helped revive waning interest in international copyright.[38]

Most of the reviews were quite favorable, though the Boston *Courier*, candidly admitting it opposed international copyright, quoted lengthily from the introduction solely because it liked Lieber's sound ideas on property. Henry Wheaton, the eminent writer on international law, and American minister to Prussia, strongly favored the movement because he himself had suffered from literary piracy. He told a student of Lieber's that he thought the essay completely settled the matter.[39]

Beverley Tucker of William and Mary College gave the treatise his warmest blessing. Tucker roundly cursed not only piratical bookmongers, but in addition "editors" who attempted "to monop-olize theft by adding half a dozen ill considered notes to a foreign work," so that they could obtain an American copyright. "It is the art of him, who . . .

> 'Creeps thro' the window from a Whore
> But points the rogue who takes the door.' "

Tucker promised to give a copy of the pamphlet to President John Tyler, an old boyhood friend, and discuss it with him over a friendly bottle of wine. Apparently Tucker won Tyler's aid, for in April, 1842, the President sent to the House of Representatives a copy of the correspondence with Great Britain concerning inter-national copyright.[40]

Although the pamphlet provoked much comment in newspapers and magazines, Lieber felt discouraged. He received a letter which underscored the futility of his campaign. A student at Davidson College in North Carolina who was going to participate in a liter-

---

[38] Lieber to Sumner, August 10, 1840; Thorvald Solberg, *International Copyright in the Congress of the United States 1837–1886* (Boston, 1886), 34–35.

[39] "Lieber on International Copyright," Boston *Courier*, August 6, 1840; W. C. Moragné to Lieber, August 25, 1841; Wheaton to Lieber, January 25, 1843.

[40] Tucker to Lieber, June 20, 1841; J. D. Richardson (ed.), *A Compilation of the Messages and Papers of the Presidents 1789–1897* (Washington, 1899), IV, 150.

ary society debate on international copyright requested information from him—on the negative.[41]

Nevertheless, Lieber continued his efforts. In 1843 he joined an international-copyright association and prepared a petition for American booksellers to send to Congress. Again in 1848 he co-operated when John Jay petitioned Congress, but for decades the publishers continued vigilant and prevented the international-copyright bills from even coming to a vote.

Throughout his lifetime, Lieber sustained his interest, and toward its close presented the same arguments he had used in 1840 before a new group of men, the members of the newly formed International Copyright Association. This was in 1868, and some of these men after a drawn-out struggle were to see passage of the long-desired measure, the Chace Act of 1891.[42]

With equal zeal and similar lack of success, the publicist wrote legislators and memorialized Congress in 1842 urging a revision of the highly illogical tariff on books. Books, like herrings or hemp, paid duties on a poundage basis. Those printed before 1775 or in languages other than English, Greek, or Latin were charged a nominal four cents per volume, but importers must pay fifteen cents a pound on classical-language works, and thirty cents a pound on ones in English.

Congress did allow colleges and learned institutions to import books free of charge. This, Lieber reasoned, showed an acknowledgment of the principle that books were conductors and promoters of knowledge, and of benefit to American civilization. He suggested that Congress further aid scholarship by admitting large

[41] W. T. Caston to Lieber, October 7, 1842; Lieber to Hillard, November 12, 1841. For periodical reviews of Lieber's pamphlet, see *Allgemein Press-Zeitung*, II (1841), 238–39; *American Jurist*, XXIV (1840), 246–48; *North American Review*, LI (1840), 513-15; *Revue étrangère de Législation et d'économie politique*, VIII (1841), 170; [D. K. Whittaker], "Lieber on International Copyright," *Southern Quarterly Review*, I (1842), 252–58. The latter, an attack upon Lieber, was refuted by the Charleston *Mercury*, April 13, 1842.

[42] Lieber to Hillard or Sumner, April 17, 1842; Cushing to Lieber, January 1, 1843; Lieber to Matilda Lieber, September 14, 1843; Jay to Lieber, May 11, 1848; A. D. Sims to Lieber, May 25, 1848, Lieber papers. Lieber to ?, September 26, 1843, Johns Hopkins University. L. H. Houtchens, "Charles Dickens and International Copyright," *American Literature*, XIII (1941), 18–28. *International Copyright. Meeting of Authors and Publishers, at the Rooms of the New York Historical Society, April 9, 1868, and Organization of the International Copyright Association* (New York, 1868), 20–24.

numbers of noncompeting books duty-free, especially after the elapse of reasonable time limits. Remaining book duties should be *ad valorem* rather than upon the ridiculous poundage basis. The well-organized publishers' lobby found this reform as easy to block as international copyright, and Lieber was so irritated that he sneered at one of the leading protectionist houses, Harper and Brothers, as the "hangers-on" of the nation.[43]

This was only a minor matter. It was not often that Lieber's solid economic ideas were so distinctly at odds with the dominant propertied groups. Indeed, at this very period, and through the very presses of Harpers', he struck one of his strongest blows in defense of property, the *Essays on Property and Labour*.[44]

Lieber worried over the extent to which restless intellectual Americans were listening to radical social doctrines during these unsettled depression years. Many an unconventional thinker felt that the growth of industrial wealth and the accompanying impoverishment of the urban masses were incompatible with social justice. Albert Brisbane for seven years had been preaching Fourier's French socialist doctrines; even a few New Englanders were tasting the giddy philosophy in their search for transcendental truths. In the spring of 1841, George Ripley headed a group of adventuresome souls who experimented with co-operative living on a tract of poor land near West Roxbury, Massachusetts, which they named the "Brook Farm Institute of Agriculture and Education." [45]

That same spring, Lieber, deeply alarmed by these portents, decided the time had come to indite a strong counterblast. Especially he felt the need to refute Orestes Brownson's latest proposal

[43] Lieber to Sumner, [June 16], 1841; Rufus Choate to Lieber, January 9, June 20, 1842; Lieber, *Memorial . . . Praying a Modification of the Tariff in Regard to the Duties on Books* (27 Cong., 2 Sess., Senate Document No. 59), 8 pp.

[44] Lieber, *Essays on Property and Labour as Connected with Natural Law and the Constitution of Society* (New York, 1841), 225 pp. An interleaved, annotated copy is at Johns Hopkins University. For an incisive critique, see Dorfman and Tugwell, "Francis Lieber: German Scholar in America," *loc. cit.*, 176–79. Joseph Dorfman, *The Economic Mind in American Civilization, 1606–1865*, 2 vols. (New York, 1946), II, 865–80, contains a thorough analysis of Lieber's economic ideas.

[45] For significant discussions of these movements, see Curti, *Growth of American Thought*, 368–80; Tyler, *Freedom's Ferment*, 47–224; and A. M. Schlesinger, Jr., *The Age of Jackson* (Boston, 1945), 361–68.

to abolish hereditary property—albeit the proposal had been most tentative. The Whigs had widely and effectively circulated it as the work of a Democratic writer during the Hard Cider Campaign recently past. Lieber, who had old scores to settle, chose to make much of it. Brownson's most pungent criticisms of the *Political Ethics* had been aimed at Lieber's pious regard for individual property rights. "It is apparent," Brownson had emphasized, "that the right of society is throughout *paramount*, that society possesses and exercises, under all forms of government, a discretionary power over the *whole* produce of the labor of its members, levying upon it at discretion, in the first place, the amount wanted for its own use, and then determining at discretion the principles on which the rest shall be held and distributed." [46]

At this type of statement Lieber aimed his refutation. Long since he had been shocked by reading in a speech of Webster's that property was the creature of government. If the people willed, the conservative senator's theory could lead startlingly to undue government interference, or even to Brownson's radical plans. The obvious solution was to place property rights upon a foundation so fundamental that even the government could not disturb them. Already Lieber had thought in that direction. In a draft of the *Political Ethics* he ascribed a high place to property, but Sumner thought his theories of property origin too similar to Locke's. So, while lurching in a stagecoach through Connecticut, Lieber worked out more definite doctrines. These appeared first in the *Political Ethics*, and later even more emphatically in the *Property and Labour*.[47]

"The origin of property can be referred to no fixed point of time," Lieber stated. "It grew up with man, as language, as government did. It was the necessary and unavoidable effect of his physical and moral nature. The first two human beings could not but feel the import of Mine and Thine." The progress of civiliza-

---

[46] Brownson, *The Laboring Classes* . . . (Boston, 1840), 3. Schlesinger, *Orestes Brownson*, 88–111. [Brownson], "Manual of Political Ethics," *Boston Quarterly Review*, II (1839), 120. Lieber, interleaved *Property and Labour*, opposite 1, Johns Hopkins University; Lieber, "Lectures on Polit. Phil. Phonographically reported by H. H. Bond," ms.; Lieber to Sumner, September 15, 1841.

[47] *PE*, I, 108–26. Lieber to Sumner, August 27, 1837, September 15, 1841.

tion demanded greater and greater property accumulation, since "civilization cannot take place without increase of population, and population cannot increase without increased production, increased accumulation and exchange of products." Since property was one of the most fundamental components of civilization, government must function to protect it. "Property is not the creature of government," he reiterated. "Property precedes government, and the latter arises out of the former . . . government is the creature of property." [48]

Subsequent to publishing the *Property and Labour*, Lieber applied these ideas to the English and American Revolutions and decided they had broken out over violations of property rights. "The noblest struggles for rights and liberties generally begin . . . with a struggle for property," he argued. "Not that the people could not be moved by any other motives than sordid ones, but because property is the most palpable reflex of man's independence, individuality, rights and liberty, the mirror of his personality, and if all previous cases of oppression allowed of doubt . . . the attack on property presents the oppression or the abandonment of duty on the part of government, palpably, and incontestably." [49]

While the government passively stood guard over property, all progress would come through an intensification of industrialization and the free working of the economic laws so wisely described by Adam Smith, Ricardo, and Say. Any tampering with these through price fixing, wage fixing, high tariffs, prohibition of large fortunes, or legalization of unions would result inevitably in destroying capital or driving it from the country.

Lieber admitted he could not fathom the new radical "labor theory of value," which he interpreted as placing a premium upon mere brawn. Obviously, labor should receive only the share it could receive on the open market; capital likewise. "Any attempt to force up the value of one and depress the other," he warned, "must create ruin and mischief. Wages are no more an invention than property itself. They are the natural and necessary effect of

[48] Lieber, *Property and Labour*, 28, 41–42, 70–71.
[49] Interleaved *ibid.*, opposite 193, Johns Hopkins University.

THE LIFE OF FRANCIS LIEBER

the state of things—of the relation of man to the things around him."

Labor unions which by means of strikes tried to alter the natural state of wages were not only engines of economic destruction, but positively immoral. Lieber was shocked the year after his *Property and Labour* appeared when Chief Justice Shaw of Massachusetts declared in the case of *Commonwealth* v. *Hunt* that unions legally could organize to raise wages. Lieber called this decision contrary to common law and "startling" in view of "the deplorable consequences of Trades' Unions by engendering habits of idleness, promoting the lazy, intemperance, insufferable tyranny, cruelty, misery, &c. &c." [50]

The honest laboring man should foreswear unions and stand guard against false friends like the unnamed Mr. Brownson, who would destroy incentive to accumulate capital through abolishing inheritance or in similar sinister ways. Inequality of property and the existence of wealthy persons were no detriment to the laborer. Quite the contrary. Equality would only produce stagnation, presumably because it would destroy the incentive to exchange and make difficult large capital accumulations necessary for modern industry. The builder of a great fortune hurt no one, for he created values which had not hitherto existed. He aided the entire community through employing his capital to create additional opportunities for laborers.

"If it be true," Lieber subsequently mused, "that overgrown fortunes are dangerous and inexpedient, it is equally true . . . that one of the greatest blessings of a people consists in a great number of substantial private fortunes, and that values which collectively can be used productively to the highest advantage for the labourer and the community at large, melt away if slivered into small proportions. . . . Let *all* men, therefore, rejoice whenever they see that one more of their fellow-creatures has succeeded in honestly accumulating a substantial fortune." Contrariwise, "Every disturbance of property is a proportional blow to indus-

[50] Interleaved *ibid.*, opposite 180, Johns Hopkins University; *ibid.*, 187–88. Lieber to Hillard, August 24, 1842. Lieber castigated both unions and employers' associations in the *PE*, II, 198–204. He used Say's text in his classes. His heavily annotated and interleaved copy is at Johns Hopkins University. Jean-Baptiste Say, *A Treatise on Political Economy* (6th American ed.; Philadelphia, 1834).

try," and the result "no farther increase of capital . . . , no increase of property, no advance of civilization." [51]

Lest his readers be deluded by the apparent success of communist experiments within the United States, Lieber emphasized that they were not valid examples of the working of socialism. They were too circumscribed by peculiar religious tenets or too limited in scope. Anyway, regardless of the arguments in favor of socialism among the miserable industrial population of England, there was no excuse for it in America. "Never before has a country existed in which industry, honesty, and frugality were so sure of success in acquiring a fair livelihood and an honourable standing in the community as in our own." The poor workingman must be contented. Neither should he fear the influence of the rich upon the government. "Are our richest men politically the most influential? No one will seriously assert it." [52]

No one actively challenged Lieber's premises. By the standards of a period when industrial consolidation had scarcely begun, he could with fair justice consider himself something of a liberal. Only a few radical experimenters were advocating drastic schemes, and their followings while spectacular were insignificant in numbers. Lieber, though he pleaded for the rising capitalist class, felt himself no foe of labor. Indeed, the gulf between him and the open partisans of the laboring class was incredibly narrow. William Leggett, the most able urban advocate of Jacksonian democracy, enunciated *laissez-faire* dogma no less wholeheartedly. Leggett defended the labor unions stanchly in their fight against monopolies and currency manipulation (evils beyond Lieber's understanding), but felt as did Lieber that wages would inevitably respond only to the laws of supply and demand. [53]

The only notable attack upon the *Property and Labour* came not from the left, but the right. Professor John McVickar, who stirred much scripture into his political economy, denounced as dangerous Lieber's doctrine that property preceded government and received its sanction from natural law. God, not man, he sharply reminded

[51] Lieber, *Property and Labour*, 96–97 *et passim;* interleaved *ibid.*, opposite 96–97, Johns Hopkins University.

[52] *Ibid.*, 221–22 *et passim.*

[53] Richard Hofstadter, "William Leggett, Spokesman of Jacksonian Democracy," *Political Science Quarterly*, LVIII (1943), 581–94.

THE LIFE OF FRANCIS LIEBER

everyone, created both government and property. This was the only Christian and safe theory which would cut "by the roots, all infidel schemes directed against the foundations of government and society." [54]

Lieber's views received phenomenally wide circulation. Through the offices of the Reverend Alonzo Potter of Union College, who wrote an introduction conservative even by comparison with the text, he sold the manuscript to Harper and Brothers. Harpers' issued an initial edition of 15,000 and reprinted the *Property and Labour* three times in the following six years. Ten thousand of the first printing were for school-district libraries—a forerunner for adults of free public libraries. The remainder appeared in the "Family Library" series priced at fifty cents. Lieber's compensation was $275.[55]

The ambitious professor was fully aware of how strongly he was plumping for wealth and privilege. Unlike Elbert Hubbard of a later generation, his profit was small, but he realized he deserved more. "I firmly believe," he confided, "that men like Astor, Lawrence and Appleton ought to print my Property Mss. and give me a handsome douceur, for I know it is good, and if disseminated will aid in counteracting evil writings and mischievous theories." Or better still, he envisaged a worker-education program: "Men like Appleton, Lawrence . . . should club together to issue a series of 'tracts for the people,' written by the most competent men of the land in a truly instructive and attractive manner on a number of important subjects as on Government, obedience to the Laws, Property, Labor, Social (Political) Economy, Trades' Unions, Liberty, Commerce, Marriage, Patriotism, Our Advantages, Emigration, Contentment &c. . . . Each tract to fill one sheet. . . . Sound tracts, well written, succeeding each other according to a judicious plan, and properly directed, are like shot, cleverly aimed and perseveringly fired." [56]

[54] *New York Review*, X (1842), 236–39. For favorable notices, see the *Knickerbocker*, XIX (1842), 194–95 and Charleston *Mercury*, April 13, 1842.

[55] Potter to Lieber, April 12, after August 19, 1841; Lieber to Matilda Lieber, August 21, 24, 1841; Lieber to Sumner, [September 3, 1841]. The book was 16mo. in size, and additional printings appeared in 1842, 1843, and 1847. Sam Ward read proofs. Ward to Longfellow, September 11, 1841, Longfellow papers, Longfellow House. Lieber to Sumner, September 15, 1848.

[56] Lieber to Ruggles, September 14–15, Lieber papers, Library of Congress. Lieber

But this scheme worked out no better than Lieber's many others. He directed all of them toward his two ultimate objectives: an honorable position in the North and an independent income. Certainly Lieber "cleverly aimed and perseveringly fired," but his projects took no more effect than a charge of buckshot rattling off a New England granite boulder.

to Matilda Lieber, July 11, 1841; Lieber to Sumner, February 17, 1842. Lieber sent copies to Nathan Appleton, Amos Lawrence, and other wealthy men. Lieber to Sumner, August 30, 1841.

197

X
Escape Fails

DESPITE the success of the *Political Ethics* and *Property and Labour,* Lieber found the North still more ready to praise him than to reward him. Buried deep in "Nigritia," as he termed it in letters to Northern friends, he could see no future for himself. When President Barnwell of South Carolina College resigned, no one considered him as a possible successor.[1]

Long since, one of his fellow professors had told him he would not feel at home in the South until he built a summer home in the sand hills, and a smokehouse in which to cure his own hams and sausages. Matilda now toiled in the smokehouse—but a home in the sand hills, never. The adventurous young man, the lover of daring and action, was now past forty—graying and growing heavy around the waist. The would-be-reckless Schill gallantly charging the enemy, the spellbinding Clay, holding forth to an awe-stricken Senate: such roles as these were mere elusive dreams. By riding hard through the woods on his mare Nausicaa, the recondite professor tried to forget his grandiloquent ambitions and shake out of his mind the specter of the classroom and strictures on his style.

"Shall a professor, engaged in the honourable pursuit of instructing young men in a college, consider himself degraded because he must acknowledge that the spheres of action in which a leader of the House of Commons, or a commanding general who rescues his country, moves, are infinitely superior to his?" queried Lieber in his *Property and Labour.* Sternly he heaped upon his readers admonishments meant for himself: insisting that "due

[1] Lieber to Hillard, April 8, 1840, Lieber papers, Henry E. Huntington Library. All manuscripts referred to in this chapter, unless otherwise identified, are from this collection.

contentment, proper resignation, absence of envy and jealousy, and a resolute endeavour to enjoy the blessings given to us by Providence to the best of our powers, without frittering away our means and embittering our lives, is true manliness." [2]

Unwavering moralist to the public, to his wife Lieber showed himself a disheartened man. "Do you know, my dearest Matilda," he sighed characteristically, "that I feel like a watch which has lost the elasticity of the spring? I cannot help it; it is so. Life passes on, year after year, nothing changes, nothing brightens, nothing opens, and with all the acknowledgment that meets me, what is it? . . . The place I have seems the very highest point I can ever obtain, and there every furious parson overtowers me." [3]

Summer after summer, Lieber had traveled to the North in search of advancement. He secured publication of his manuscripts, angled futilely for posts at Harvard, Columbia, and Girard College, and urged his projects upon Congress. His inability to persuade even Whig politicians to grant him an appointment was due, of course, to politics. He commanded no votes in South Carolina. The failure of his publications to gain him a Northern professorship may have been partly due to his exotic way of writing. Every pamphlet he published brought derogation, though seldom as devastating as a blast in the *Southern Quarterly Review*: "His style is frigid, jejune, angular, thorny, and indigestible. His sentences march into the columns they occupy, one after another, like undisciplined militia-men, without grace or order, and arrayed in as checkered a costume as Fallstaff's [*sic*] men 'on a training day.' " [4]

Lieber's personality may have been another bar in polite Brahmin circles. He talked slowly but incessantly, always holding the center of attention in every salon he frequented. With a remarkable frankness, Lieber was willing to heap high praise or scathing criticism upon either himself or his acquaintances. His compliments were effusive and personal in the continental manner—often so much so as to cause embarrassment. Even in the household of Baron Bunsen he occasioned comment. One of the daughters des-

[2] Lieber, *Property and Labour*, 197–98, 201–202.
[3] Lieber to Matilda Lieber, July 11, 1841.
[4] [Whittaker], "Lieber on International Copyright," *loc. cit.*, 252.

cribed "Lieber, from America, with his fixed, melancholy, sentimental look, joining nevertheless in conversation with great zest and interest, always mixing in strange outlandish compliments."

Just how out of the ordinary these compliments could be is well illustrated by a note he penned to one of the loveliest of Boston belles: "When I said last night, my dear Miss Fanny, how well you look this evening, you answered in a manner which sufficiently showed, that my observation . . . was, in your mind, on a level with all of the same character which ever may have been addressed to you. I observed then that beasts and men drink but that there was still a great difference between the lapping of a dog and the sipping of fine wine by the delicate lips of the connesseur [sic]."

Close friends were always ready to accept the unconventional husk of Lieber's conversation in order to savor the rich kernel of thought. After he returned to the South in 1849, Hillard remarked, "We all voted that you had never been so winning and so attractive before." Mrs. George Ticknor wrote the Boston lawyer: "I hope Lieber has been with you. I was delighted to see him on Saturday, and was more than ever struck with the vivacity, the force of his thoughts, his instant application of illustration, analysis, investigation, to every subject that came up, and the spiritualizing tendencies of his mind. He is very interesting, not only from power, but from his deep feeling, and simplicity, or rather, I should say, directness. I wish he was established among us." [5]

Unfortunately, the warm appreciation of sympathetic friends did not counteract the coolness of some chance acquaintances, and Lieber was sometimes hurt to find Beacon Street doors closed to him. Intellect was a poor substitute for conventionality in formal Boston society.

In Lieber's own estimation his foreign birth was the greatest bar of all. He swallowed the bitter draught of seeing Philadelphia-born Alexander Dalles Bache, a grandson of Franklin, appointed president of Girard College and sent to Europe on the very mission Lieber had strongly advocated. Fruitlessly he angled for one of the Lowell lectureships recently established in Boston, and in a moment of disillusion cried: "It is too good a thing to be given to

[5] Lieber to Fanny Appleton, [August, 1838]. Frances Bunsen, *A Memoir of Baron Bunsen* . . . , 2 vols. (London, 1868), II, 270. Hillard to Lieber, October 12, 1849.

MATILDA LIEBER

Photograph taken about 1885

a foreigner. I donot say this in anger . . . but it is natural. Family and town connections and associations must be powerfull; it cannot be otherwise or society would not be society." Yet, a few years later, the Lowell trustees brought to America the great Swiss naturalist, Louis Agassiz.[6]

Whatever the current difficulty, Lieber did manage upon one pretext or another to travel northward almost every summer. In 1837 he warmly congratulated Joel Poinsett of South Carolina upon his new post as Secretary of War, and in his next breath frankly asked an appointment to the Board of Visitors at West Point so that he might get north to push his statistical project. Poinsett complied. Other summers, other opportunities arose.[7]

Lieber traveled alone. One year he sent Matilda to Germany, but usually he left her behind with the three children. Once she sadly pictured herself vacationing in the sand hills of South Carolina: "*Scene.* A farmers house, 3 or 4 miles distant from every other human habitation. . . . Matilda, alone in a little room containing a bed, table and chair, baggage of every description suspended on nails about the room, amongst the rest a huge calico sunbonnet a yard deep with a ditto flounce, windows large enough to admit the sun and all species of bugs, but not the air. Air all together being a mere name without a meaning at this time of year in South Carolina. . . . My nature has ever been of a quiet retiring kind, but *now* in all social intercourse, I am dull, heavy, gloomy." [8]

To melancholy Matilda, Lieber wrote long and detailed letters describing his gaiety. Boston to him was a happy intellectual paradise. He occupied himself from eight in the morning until midnight with "two things—my science and people belonging to that sphere, and women." He frequently visited Prescott, Longfellow, Felton, Greenleaf, or Story, but most often he would talk through the day with the brilliant young lawyer-scholar Sumner and his retiring, aristocratic partner, Hillard. "Sumner is one of the finest men I know," Lieber declared in 1837, "he has the true [inspiration of knowledge], studies hard & *deep,* and is withal

[6] Lieber to Sumner, November 19, 1836.
[7] Lieber to Poinsett, March 21, 1837, Historical Society of Pennsylvania.
[8] Matilda Lieber to Fanny Appleton, August 26, 1838.

enthusiastically devoted to me. He verily loves me. He loves literature, fine arts and is a noble piece of God's creation." [9]

When Lieber again saw Sumner in the summer of 1840 after the young man had returned from his lengthy European travels, he was even more enthusiastic. Sumner had been so feted and praised by the nobility of England that Professor Greenleaf feared he might no longer be "the simple, whole-souled, transparent, generous fellow we all love." Lieber found these qualms ungrounded. He was soon so intimate with Sumner that he declared exuberantly: "I wish I could remain here for weeks and months. We have talked literally until the dawn of day reminded us that it might be time for talkers to go to bed when workers rise. I not only found him unchanged but much improved, more manly yet as child-like and simple . . . as ever." Lieber stanchly defended Sumner from Fanny Appleton's criticisms that he was unaesthetical and crammed with "musty law." "He is full of noble enthusiasm, true to the inmost fibre of his heart, without guile, ardent very ardent in the pursuit of knowledge for knowledge's sake, *empfänglich* for everything good and noble, he is persevering, he freely soars above utility, and is well stocked and firm with much knowledge." [10]

In marked contrast to these intellectual companions were the belles of Boston with whom Lieber often whiled away his evenings. In 1837 he lavished his attention upon the Inglis sisters, one of whom as Madame Calderon de la Barca was later to delight America with her travel reports of Mexico. Lieber spent many a lively hour at the Inglis home: "Fine music, fine singing, happy dancing, racy joking, beautiful figures, elegant embroidering, playing cards, witty remarks, children, girls, maids, mothers and matrons, fun laughing, shawl dance, all mixed with punch and this or that, like the disordered profusion of spring's flora." When not at Inglis', Lieber was with Fanny Brooks or Sally Newton—and to Matilda he reported everything. [11]

The following year he shifted his attention to the daughters of Nathan Appleton, the cotton magnate. Fanny and Mary, grown tall and lovely, were recently returned from a sojourn in Europe,

[9] Lieber to Matilda Lieber, August 12, 1837.
[10] Lieber to Fanny Appleton, July 20, August 2, 1840.
[11] Lieber to Matilda Lieber, August 12, 1837.

and Lieber could not help hearing rumors that in Switzerland young Professor Longfellow had fallen head over heels in love with Fanny, to no avail. Fanny was "a most graceful girl and noble," and Mary even finer looking; both were statuesque. Every evening Lieber went to the Appletons' to enjoy the superb moonlight on their balcony; in the daytime he walked with them. On one of the lovely evenings, "I proposed to Gossler [a German friend] to fetch from his house a bottle of champaigne, ice & tumbler & drink it in the Commons, in beautiful moonshine, so we did. While we were enjoying the moon and ice and wine, we heard a serenade. We went, and I said: if we only could find out whether they are amateurs or not, and whether we could serenade the Appletons. We addressed them, and after much palabring, and four different serenades, they go with us, and we serenaded Mrs. Brooks and the Appletons. Mary came to the Window and her beautifully shaped head was seen as long as the music lasted. . . . Now we had become hungry, and went back to Gossler, where we ate Hamburg Bologna and drank exquisite Burgundy, and at 4 o'clock I went home." [12]

With mock seriousness, Sumner gave Lieber a stern warning to deliver to his wife upon his return home from one such summer: "Permit me to suggest, by way of inquiry, what I know cannot be expressed too delicately. We have all been surprised at the extent to which yr. husband allows himself to be occupied by young girls. Old & valued friends, men of learning & sagacity, like Mr. Pickering & Judge Story, were neglected that he might find another hour for chat with these *ephemerae* of society. . . . And since he has been in New York, I understand he has besieged the mansion of a lovely Trinity of damsels." [13]

The "Trinity of damsels" were the Ward sisters, who lived with their brother Sam, the almost profligate son of the pious banker who had been treasurer of New York University. Sam, a highly talented and wholly misdirected young man, was just the sort of gay soul whom Lieber found most congenial, and his sisters, "the

---

[12] Lieber to Matilda Lieber, July 4, 6, 17, 1838. Regarding Longfellow, Lieber wrote Sumner, April 21, 1839: "Fanny and Mary talked with me about him, when they related their journey to me; but as they would speak of anyone else; as you may imagine."
[13] Sumner to Matilda Lieber, September 22, 1842.

three graces of Bond Street," were among the most popular of New York belles. Lieber especially took delight in the eldest, Julia, "a rare girl. She speaks German as if she had grown up near one of the 'lovely German mill-brooks.'" Lieber enjoyed discoursing to her on German philosophers, as she remembered years later when she was the famous Julia Ward Howe.[14]

Often at Ward's house, as Sumner reported, Lieber was "glad with good dinners, a good library & the pop-pop-pop of corks." "In an hour we sit down," Ward wrote reproachfully to the absent Longfellow, "—Champagne, Moselle, Johannisberger, Madeira, Sherry, Burgundy, & Lafitte all will flow without your lending a mouth to help them down hill." And the wine brought forth many a pungent story. One of Lieber's, Ward thought so good that he repeated it to the absent Longfellow: "a middle aged lady in Germany went near an Iron German stove to warm herself & nobody being in the room she raised her dress to remove all obstacles to the genial Warmth. Coming too near the Stove its embossed date 1769 was burnt upon a certain part that shall be nameless. . . . A Leech was summoned to provide a healing balsam. But when he saw the date 1769—he said he could do nothing for so old a complaint." [15]

When the hour of midnight arrived, and Lieber started homeward from Ward's, the seemingly policeless state of New York City alarmed him. After twelve, "the rowdies have complete possession of Broadway; the prostitutes are ten times more offensive than ever before; gunpowder explosions, tar barrels burning, yelling, shuffling &c. &c." Yet the evenings were unmitigated successes. Ward reported to Longfellow concerning Lieber, "I like him much better than I did last Summer—. There is a vast deal of good in him." And the poet replied, well pleased, "He is a strong man; and one whose conversation, like some tumultuous mountain brook, sets your wheels all in motion." [16]

[14] Lieber to Sumner, August 13, 1840; Lieber to Fanny Appleton, September 5, 1840; Lieber to Matilda Lieber, September 1, 1840, Lieber papers. Sumner to Longfellow, after August 2, 1840, Longfellow House. Perry (ed.), *Lieber*, 146. For an account of a similar conversation in 1866, see L. E. Richards and M. H. Elliott, *Julia Ward Howe, 1819–1910*, 2 vols. (Boston, 1916), I, 240.

[15] Ward to Longfellow, August 20, 27, 1841, Longfellow House. Lieber to Matilda Lieber, September 1, 1841.

[16] Ward to Longfellow, September 11, 1841; Longfellow to Ward, September 17, 1841, Longfellow House. Lieber to Sumner, September 6, 1841.

Gradually Lieber's companionship was taking on a more masculine cast. By the summer of 1840, Mary Appleton had married an Englishman and sailed overseas; Fanny Brooks's husband objected to Lieber's protracted tête-à-têtes with his wife and made the visits unpleasant. Aside from the Ward sisters, only Fanny Appleton remained—clever, cool, stately Fanny. To her Lieber poured out his heart in letter after letter. They were entirely proper and brought comforting replies. Lieber had read *Hyperion* in which Longfellow had but thinly disguised the story of his long, unsuccessful suit for Fanny, but the professor respected the proprieties and in his written comments on the novel for a long while did not mention the possible originals of the characters. Nor did Fanny show by word or deed that she in the slightest favored the bold Longfellow. To her Bostonian admirers she seemed to have an aspect almost glacial.[17]

Another Fanny, the sensational Viennese ballet dancer Fanny Elssler—a veritable Fanny of fire rather than ice—was melting the hearts of New Yorkers that summer. Not until the arrival of Jenny Lind was America to know a greater theatrical sensation. As a table topic she competed even with Old Tippecanoe and the Hard Cider Campaign. Lieber, in common with all his friends, fell "up to his neck" in love with her, as Sam Ward put it. "A married man dares not get over head and ears." Lieber confided to Sumner, "She is one of the loveliest pieces of poetry in my life." He vied with his friends in composing extravagant compliments: "that wonderful woman who makes one understand what dancing is. . . . She revels as the maddened mocking bird revels, loud, bold, crazy, yet ever graceful—a nightingale drunk with champaign."[18]

The gay scholar further poured out his admiration for Fanny in a poem. When he brought it to her the next morning, she was delighted and clapped her hands with pleasure. "Good God," Lieber exclaimed, "that woman ought to have a statue." Indeed, one could obtain a small plaster Fanny Elssler, and carefully the naughty Sam Ward packed one off to Longfellow so that he could

---

[17] Lieber to Fanny Appleton, May 14, 1840; Prescott to Lieber, November 26, 1839; Lieber to Hillard, August 19, September 8, 1839.

[18] Ward to Longfellow, August 24, 1840, Longfellow House; Lieber to Sumner, [August 22], September 3, 1840. George C. D. Odell, *Annals of the New York Stage* (New York, 1927—), IV, 358 ff., 440–42.

have Fanny spend the week end with him. The flesh-and-blood Fanny shortly thereafter arrived in Boston and Sumner also succumbed. "We are in *two fevers* here," Sumner exclaimed at the height of the Log Cabin Campaign, "the Election & the Ellsler fever. Some have both; I have only one—the more graceful. I have seen much of Fanny; & like her more & more. . . . Think of the author of Polly Ethics writing verses on a dancer. I have drawn all the hornets of scandal about my ears, by calling upon Fanny E. & dining with her since." [19]

Tactless Charles, in paying his respects to Fanny mentioned to her within earshot of her husband-manager Wikoff that Lieber had written mentioning the proportions of her bust and waist. When Sumner left the room, the jealous manager followed and asked an explanation of Lieber's liberties with the danseuse. Only by showing the manager the letter in which Lieber raved about Fanny's figure and dancing could Sumner quiet him. The following summer, Lieber found his access to Fanny's dressing room blocked. "Wikoff seems to be an ass," he complained to his wife.[20]

When Lieber was not sitting with Sam Ward drinking wine and elaborating praises for Fanny Elssler, he found time to visit Ward's father-in-law, gruff old John Jacob Astor, retired magnate of the fur trade and owner of much of the most valuable real estate in Manhattan. Far and above the wealthiest man in America—worth about twenty millions—he retained traces of his lowly German origin, and still spoke with an accent. Astor received Lieber most kindly and had Lieber's books read to him, but to the scholar's disappointment showed no inclination to endow a chair for Lieber at Columbia College. Within a few years Lieber decided the penurious Astor was a great bore and dodged invitations to

[19] Lieber to Sumner, [August 22, 1840], Lieber papers. Sumner to Lieber, September 23, 1840, Harvard University. Lieber may have been the coauthor of a printed poem in the Lieber collection, Huntington Library, *A Fanny Elssler, Alemanna, Visitante Rapidamente L'America, La Primavera Del 1840. An Fanny Elssler, Aus Deutschland, auf Ihrem Kurzen Besuche in America Im Frühlinge des Jahres 1840.* The poem is dated New-York, June 8, 1840, which was a month before Lieber's arrival, but he may have prepared the German version. Both Lieber and Sumner, fundamentally highly proper, would have been shocked had they known of Fanny Elssler's liaison a decade earlier with the Austrian statesman, Friedrich von Gentz. Cf. Paul R. Sweet, *Friedrich von Gentz: Defender of the Old Order* (Madison, Wis., 1941), 288–93.

[20] Lieber to Matilda Lieber, August 24, 1841.

dine. "If I could talk anything of interest with the old man, about his intended library &c, I should like it," he explained, "but thus as it is, I might as well look at the outside of a cask of ducats." [21]

Other wealthy New Yorkers impressed Lieber more favorably. He became acquainted with a Mr. Parish, a New York merchant, and twice accompanied him on trips to his summer home at Ogdensburg on the St. Lawrence River. The splendor of these expeditions was impressive, for Parish took with him "his old servant, a French cook, 2 German chambermaids, a German scullion, 75 boxes with heaven knows what all, an English water closet with a man to place it! ! !" [22]

Through all the revelry, Lieber was pursuing his serious task of searching for a Northern position—and each time as he failed he returned reluctantly to the South. In New York, in early September of 1840, he was awaiting his wife's arrival from Germany when he met two South Carolina College students in the street. "I first felt hot, and then shivering cold," he confessed. "Imagine what my feelings are at the appro[a]ching return to Columbia, and dragging poor Matilda back." [23]

Through the 1840's, deliverance from the South seemed always imminent. That it did not take place was by no means the fault of Lieber's friends, and none worked harder for him than the serious, crusading Dr. Samuel Gridley Howe. Lieber's and Howe's orbits had frequently crossed prior to 1841, and since Howe, the same age as Lieber, had also campaigned in Greece he might have been expected to be most congenial. But somehow the physician had at first taken a dislike to the pompous professor. The dislike began to evaporate when Lieber seized upon reports of Howe's phenomenal work at Perkins Institution for the Blind, and wrote an account of the unprecedented manner in which Howe had taught the blind deaf-mute, Laura Bridgman. Howe's new respect ripened into warm friendship in 1841 when the professor took him and two of his students into the Lieber home and helped Howe persuade the South Carolina legislature to send South Carolina's blind children to Perkins Institution. After the zealous reformer had left

[21] Lieber to Matilda Lieber, September 8, 1838, September 1, 1841.
[22] Lieber to Hillard, September 8, 1839; Lieber to Matilda Lieber, August 24, 1841.
[23] Lieber to Fanny Appleton, September 5, 1840.

Columbia, Hillard reported, "You & your wife have planted yourselves deeply in Howe's heart & that is a heart worth having a place in." [24]

Generous Howe tried to repay Lieber's good services. By the spring of 1842 the professor was in difficulties. Far from being in a position to obtain the vacant presidency of South Carolina College, he feared his own chair was in jeopardy. The hints that the trustees might oust him grew so loud that he even wrote Senator Preston, who reassured him that he had never heard the slightest intimation of them from any quarter. Still the rumors persisted, and while the trustees seemed to know little of the matter, the hints spread from among Lieber's fellow faculty members. In particular they seemed to emanate from Professors Henry and Ellet. Dr. Ellet and his authoress wife established themselves in the summer circle at Boston. "I did not like her," forthright Sumner snorted. "I do not like women who have written books & articles. . . . Mrs. E. seemed to think nothing of me, because I had never written a book. She has a scowl like the horseshoe of Redgauntlet." [25]

Professor Ellet made the grave error of repeating the gossip to the even more forthright Dr. Howe, who indignantly relayed the whole story to Lieber. Steal a march on your enemies, Howe counseled the harassed professor. Therewith the reformer sketched a delightful proposal: he detested Louis Dwight, the religious-minded secretary of the Boston Prison Discipline Society and violent opponent of solitary confinement. Why should not the scholar have Dwight's position? He promised to give Lieber his vigorous support.[26]

Lieber's answer was a hearty aye. He had been trying to endure a summer of Southern heat but now he could resist temptation no longer. He dashed northward to glower at the "wagging and

[24] Howe to Lieber, August 7, November 30, December 15, 17, 1841; Lieber to Sumner, April 26, 1841; Lieber to Hillard, December 10, 1841; Hillard to Lieber, December, 1841.

[25] Sumner to Lieber, June 3, 1841, Harvard University; Preston to Lieber, March 20, 1842.

[26] Howe to Lieber, August 17, 1842. Howe reported Ellet as saying that the ostensible reason for abolishing Lieber's chair was to establish in its place a course of modern languages; "the real cause was want of power of appreciating your talents and acquirements . . . and want of good will towards you personally on the part of some of the Trustees. He himself spoke of you in warm, and even eulogistic terms."

grinning" Ellet, to save his professorship if he could, and if not to help Howe oust Dwight. Another possibility existed too. When Astor dashed Lieber's hopes for a chair at Columbia College, he had given as his excuse the fact that a fund already existed. Chancellor Kent, ever on the lookout for a New York post for his friend, wrote in April that a German professorship at Columbia would materialize. It would pay no more than $1,500, but he was sure Lieber could get it. Kent's clever son, Judge William Kent, who had already sipped wine with Lieber at Sam Ward's wrote immediately to the leading trustees—Philip Hone, a New York merchant, and Samuel B. Ruggles, a retired lawyer. Boldly Lieber wrote Ruggles—whom he had barely met—and applied for the possible opening. Thus began a glowing friendship which was to last the remaining thirty years of his life.[27]

When Lieber arrived in the North, both Ruggles and William Kent were exceedingly friendly. They declared that Lieber was the very man to stir up the moribund college, and set about to win a majority of the trustees to their views. Lieber was so encouraged that for a while he even considered resigning his South Carolina College professorship. Fortunately, he did not, for Columbia was slow to act. At the end of the following January, Ruggles had to admit to Lieber that out of sheer poverty, "The old College sits like a leaden statue with its lack lustre eyes slowly awaiting the Advent of old Gebhard's legacy." When the German chair finally did materialize, the trustees quickly appointed an impecunious young immigrant who would accept it for far less than would Professor Lieber.[28]

Lieber continued a witty correspondence with Ruggles. A professorship at Columbia, like the dream that he and Sumner would both be law professors at Harvard, was for years an alluring mirage just beyond grasp. The scholar's hopes for the secretaryship

[27] James Kent to Lieber, April 13, 1842; William Kent to Lieber, May 9, 1842; Ruggles to Lieber, May 31, 1842; John McVickar to Lieber, June 24, 1842, Lieber papers. Lieber to Ruggles, May 19, June 7, 1842, Library of Congress. For an analysis, with lengthy excerpts, of the Lieber letters to Ruggles in the Lieber papers, Library of Congress, see L. M. Sears, "The Human Side of Francis Lieber," *South Atlantic Quarterly*, XXVII (1928), 42–61. D. G. Brinton Thompson, *Ruggles of New York, A Life of Samuel B. Ruggles* (New York, 1946), 164.

[28] Ruggles to Lieber, July 7, August 2, 1842, January 31, 1843; William Bard to Lieber, July 16, 1842; Lieber to Matilda Lieber, September 8, 20, 23, 1842, Lieber papers. Lieber to Ruggles, July 14, 1842, Library of Congress.

of the Boston Prison Discipline Society underwent a similar rise and fall. With almost fanatic zeal, Howe worked to pry Dwight out. He campaigned all fall for an improvement in the treatment of lunatics confined in country prisons and for an investigation of the Prison Discipline Society. However, Dwight, with his insistence upon appropriations for prison chaplains, was very solidly entrenched with the religious people of Boston; indeed the Society existed almost solely for his benefit.[29]

Lieber's disappointment was tempered by the fact that at least he had succeeded in retaining his professorship at South Carolina College. The dismissal movement dwindled out of existence, and the professor was heartened by the cordial support he received from one of the alumni, John N. Frierson, a planter and former member of the state legislature.[30]

Another compliment came Lieber's way in the fall of 1842, though it took a full eighteen years to reach him. An elderly Massachusetts woman, Eliza Lee, in translating a life of Jean Paul Richter, the German sentimental writer, came upon a letter addressed to Franz Lieber, and wrote to the South Carolina professor asking if he were that person. Lieber replied he did not know, that he had never received a letter from Jean Paul. Mrs. Lee sent a copy of the letter, and indeed it was to Lieber, in answer to some poems he had once sent the novelist. Richter had written kindly and encouragingly, but Lieber had fled from Berlin before the letter arrived, and had assumed the silence to mean disapproval. Now, the letter from the grave made him wonder if he should indeed have followed a literary career, and he let loose a veritable flood of bad German verse.[31]

While he himself was inditing vast quantities of doggerel, Lieber was engaging in sharp controversy with his friends over the poetic merits of Henry Wadsworth Longfellow. Lieber had known Longfellow since at least 1835 when he had given the young poet-professor letters of introduction for a trip to Europe. When, at the end of the thirties, Professor Longfellow returned to America

[29] Howe to Lieber, October 29, 1842, Lieber papers; Sumner to Lieber, [December 8, 1842], Harvard University.

[30] Frierson to Lieber, October 29, 1842.

[31] Eliza Lee to Lieber, February 28, October 15, 1842, Lieber papers. Lieber to Ruggles, October 25, 1842, Library of Congress.

after vainly wooing Fanny Appleton, Lieber wrote the poet's close friend, Sumner, "The little I have seen of Longfellow has pleased me; more so still what I have read of him, by him."[32]

Lieber's mildly benevolent feeling gave way to violent disapproval when he read Longfellow's new book of verse in January, 1842. Save for the "Wreck of the Hesperus," he thought it a dismal failure. "How could he print those awful would-be hexameters," he exclaimed. "Make a cow dance a minuet, and you may make hexameters in English. . . . [They] did not grate my ear but positively boxed them." A bit more temperately, he appraised the reason for the success of the contents. "The Americans," he posited, "are just now a peculiarly sentimental nation. . . . A consequence is that the minor sentimental poem (which in its way may be excellent) stands at the top of our poetic efforts. In this Longfellini [sic] partly succeeds, and consequently he succeeds with the great number—girls, boys, women, men all can feel that and at once understand it." But as for Lieber, "they taste to me like diluted Wieland with a little haze of Jean-Paulism about it." Longfellow's friends came strongly to his defense, but the bludgeoning critic, thoroughly enjoying the controversy, continued the attack for several years.[33]

In the early spring of 1843, a strange leaven was at work. Dr. Howe stole away from his blind wards to pay his respects to the graceful damsels on Bond Street, New York. From beautiful Louisa he switched his attentions to "Julia intellect," and did not stop like Dr. Lieber with a kiss upon her brow, but proposed matrimony. More breathtakingly, Fanny Appleton amazed Boston by capitulating to Longfellow. Gallantly Lieber proclaimed an armistice. He promised Sumner that if the Bostonian would give up extravagant praise, he would cease his retorts—and hope for great poetry.[34]

"I always rejoice," Lieber had declared graciously, "when a literary man, a scholar, an author gets one of the choicest tidbits,

[32] Longfellow journal, [December] 12, [1835], Longfellow House; Sumner to Lieber, November 17, 1836, Harvard University; Lieber to Ticknor (copy), May 2, 1835; Lieber to Sumner, April 21, 1839.
[33] Lieber to Sumner, January 21, February 24, 1842.
[34] Francis and Matilda Lieber to Fanny Appleton, May 28, 1843, Longfellow House; Lieber to Sumner, June 7, 1843.

and shows that merchants and lawyers are not the only ones who stand a chance of carrying home the noblest girls." Nevertheless, Lieber in New York was none too happy when he heard from Sumner: "Tomorrow Longfellow weds Fanny. Both are happy—very happy. Fanny is deeply in love, & the tides of her soul rush in warm currents." Lieber's soul seemed to be at ebb tide. He refused Sam Ward's invitation to come to Boston for the wedding, though Ward offered to pay all his expenses. "To say the truth," Lieber rationalized to Matilda, "being present at weddings is always a stupid affair and in this case—You know, I donot think Longf *the* poet, and a poet who is not the poet, is worse than a common prose fellow." [35]

Lieber quickly recovered his poise. A few days later he called on the honeymooning Longfellows at Nahant, and read them some of his poems. Longfellow praised them, and Lieber's estimate of him instantly soared. When the honeymooners, bound for the Catskills, asked him to accompany them, he trailed along. Soon Longfellow was "Henry" to him, but despite the poet's great friendliness and kindness, Lieber withheld praise.

"I have now seen a good deal of Lfgw.," he confided to Matilda. "I have never seen any man of a poetic glow (not to speak of poets) who seemed to care less for the beauties of nature; to have less sense for them, to be more womanish indolent. . . . I see now how it is: he is not the poet of action, not of history, not of nature, not of the masses, not of the towring genius, not of the hero, but the versifier, possibly the poet of sentiment." [36]

While Lieber dallied with the Longfellows in the summer of 1843 he busily tried to raise an endowment for a law chair for himself at Harvard. Justice Story offered to write letters of recommendation, and his hopes were fired once more. Yet he had suffered disappointment so often that he began to wonder if perhaps his greatest opportunities lay not in the North but in his native Prussia. If nothing were forthcoming at New York or Boston, which would be the lesser evil—to live in a section which

[35] Lieber to Sumner, June 7, 1843; Lieber to Matilda Lieber, July 13, 1843, Lieber papers. Sumner to Lieber, July 12, 1843, Harvard University. Even to the bride, Lieber confessed his irritation. Lieber to Fanny Appleton, [July 13, 1843], Longfellow House.
[36] Lieber to Matilda Lieber, August 8, 13, 16, 1843.

idolized slavery, or in a country which foreswore democracy? [37]

Already, Lieber had taken steps to settle his differences with the Prussian government. In the summer of 1841 he had called upon Baron von Roenne, the Prussian minister at Washington, whom he found sympathetic. When the new king, Frederick William IV, had come to the throne, he had granted a general pardon to all political offenders in Prussia. Being in America, Lieber was excluded, and found that should he return to Prussia he would have to stand trial. In the fall of 1841 he addressed a long petition to Frederick William pleading for a pardon. He admitted that in his youth he had written some "foolish and absurd political essays," but spoke of his knowledge of the plotting of Major von Fehrentheil at Erfurt as "nothing but idle gossip." He wholeheartedly recanted a bitter letter he had addressed to Minister von Kamptz after his flight to London, and vowed he still loved his fatherland with all his heart. He no longer wished to feel that "of all the countries in the world, the land of my birth is . . . the only one from which I am excluded." [38]

In the early spring of 1842, a pardon arrived from the King of Prussia, and Lieber began to wonder whether or not to try for a position in Germany. To do so would mean the sacrifice of the American civil liberty he had grown to cherish. "My lot is without question one of the hardest," he complained. "Why have I this burning love of liberty and of country at the same time?" He knew perfectly well that a denunciation of American democracy would go further than anything else to attract favorable notice in Berlin, "But may God strike my tongue with palsy if ever I say a word against liberty to advance my interests." Instead he prepared a paper in German on a thoroughly harmless subject, public and private executions—extramural and intramural he called them. He sent this to Dr. Julius, who had suggested it to him, to lay before the King and Savigny's committee on law revision. [39]

[37] Lieber to Matilda Lieber, July, August 26, 27, 1843.

[38] Perry (ed.), *Lieber*, 153; Lieber, petition to His Majesty the King of Prussia, November 4, 1841, contemporary copy in German in Lieber's hand, Lieber papers; translation in Perry (ed.), *Lieber*, 159–60.

[39] Friedrich Wilhelm IV to Lieber, January 15, 1842; Lieber to Sumner, September 11, 1843. Lieber enclosed a summary of the paper in his letter to Sumner. The German manuscript is in the Lieber papers.

During the fall months, Lieber pondered ways to obtain a trip to Europe without cutting his ties with South Carolina College. He talked over his plans carefully with the professors and his old friend, William C. Preston, now president of the college. Ultimately he won them to his proposal that he receive a leave of absence in return for teaching double time both before and after the trip.[40]

The request granted, he hastily gathered letters of introduction from Webster, Choate, Sumner, Wilde, Ticknor, and many others. Secretary of State Upshur sent Lieber a most useful one. It not only commended him to the American ministers and consuls abroad, but made him a bearer of dispatches in order to exempt him from customhouse annoyances. Francis Markoe, Upshur's assistant, enlisted Lieber's aid in behalf of the National Institute. He persuaded Lieber to write a letter for the *National Intelligencer* commending the institute, and from a list the professor prepared, made out certificates conferring membership upon distinguished Europeans. Lieber delivered the certificates while on his travels.[41]

Only one cloud darkened the jubilant scholar's horizons. All Europe, and England especially, was feeling strongly anti-American at the moment because during the recent depression many states and municipalities had repudiated their bonds. Other Americans recently returned from England had felt that hostility among the British investing classes. Lieber fumed. Stanch defender of property that he was, he had written violently against repudiation in American periodicals, had lectured against it, and had included a whole chapter on monetary honesty in the *Political Ethics.*[42]

Indeed, the fuss did mar Lieber's sojourn in England. "Brougham behaved absolutely crazy to me," he mourned. "Our repudiators have done more harm than I thought. . . . Wherever I go I meet the insult of silence on my country. Unless people are

[40] Perry (ed.), *Lieber,* 178; Lieber to Sumner, after December 2, 1843; Matilda Lieber to Fanny Longfellow, December 18, 1843.

[41] Webster to Choate, December 15, 1843; Lieber to Hillard, December 17, 1843; Secretary of State Abel Parker Upshur, letter of introduction, December 26, 1843.

[42] Ticknor to Lieber, January 6, 1844; Lieber to Ticknor, January 15, 1844; Lieber to Fanny Appleton, January 31, 1844.

intimate they abstain from talking of America, as we would avoid mentioning a man's mother in his presence when she has forfeited the esteem of the decent." Hillard tried to end Lieber's lamentations by reminding him that "in the eyes of a God of mercy & justice the conduct of England towards the Chinese [the Opium War] involves moral guilt of a deeper dye." [43]

Except for the embarrassment over repudiation, Lieber's days in England were a happy round of famous places and personages. He became acquainted with Joseph Adshead, a British penologist who favored the Pennsylvania system, and found he stood high in that gentleman's esteem. With his letters of introduction and Institute certificates, he called on the celebrities: "Saturday I breakfast at Hallam's with Macaulay. My dinner coat is blue with guilt [sic] buttons and velvet collar—my tailor . . . Prince Albert's." Lord Morpeth, who had taken a great liking to Sumner, now extended many courtesies to Lieber. The American professor dined with the great editor Lockhart, breakfasted with Sir Robert Inglis and Archdeacon Wilberforce, and heard Sir Robert Peel speak in Parliament. He wrote to Chevalier Bunsen, Niebuhr's secretary when he was in Rome and now Prussian minister to England, to inquire what prison reforms Prussia might institute, and whether he might hope for a position in the program. Subsequently he renewed a warm friendship with Bunsen, whom he found surprisingly liberal.[44]

Tocqueville and Beaumont extended a cordial welcome when Lieber arrived in Paris in the middle of May. Paris was "quiet, sedate, orderly, calm in comparison" with London. "It is impossible to imagine that this orderly Paris is the Paris of the Revol[ution] [the] Paris of so much vice and crime." Indeed, Paris was quiet, and was not to undergo a revolution for another four years. In the meantime the premier was F. P. G. Guizot, the conservative historian, with whom the admiring Lieber had dinner. Toward the end of the summer, he returned to Paris to visit the galleries. "I have lived ten days in this world of art called the Louvre," he gloated to Sumner. "Ah! and what delight when

---

[43] Lieber to Sumner, June 2, 1844, Harvard University; Hillard to Lieber, August 1, 1844.

[44] Lieber to Matilda Lieber, April 8, 19, 23, May 5, 1844; Everett to Lieber, April 20, 22, 1844; Lieber to C. K. T. Bunsen, May, 1844, translated copy.

nearly every day, I found my way past all the schools and that mass of beefy Rubenses . . . [to] the Titians and Coreggios and Raphaels. . . . I live the life of a long dried sponge thrown into water." [45]

In June, just twenty-nine years since he had campaigned under Blücher, he returned to Belgium, retraced the marches he had made at Waterloo and Namur, picked a few flowers at the spot where he had been wounded, and felt exceedingly sad and sentimental. Then he went on to Hamburg where he joyously met Matilda and his three sons, who had preceded him. He had not seen Oscar, the eldest, for five years.[46]

Berlin was Lieber's major objective, and with considerable qualms he arrived there toward the end of July. To his delight, he found himself the center of attention everywhere. He had acted wisely in sending ahead the manuscript on public executions. It had arrived just as the law-reform committee was discussing punishment by death and it impressed them profoundly. Savigny told Lieber that though his ideas were novel, the committee would adopt them. Lieber was so pleased that he opportunistically set to work writing in German a general sketch of his views on the entire field of penology and solitary confinement.[47]

In his capacity as a great American authority upon prison reform, he went to Potsdam Palace to see Frederick William IV. "The king came in," Lieber remembered, "wearing common undress, no star or order, his cap and handkerchief in hand." He invited Lieber into his cabinet, and declared: " 'I am sorry you are going away again. I thought that we might be able to keep you here. It is a great pity.' I replied: 'Your Majesty, I have a wife and children, and no fortune, and must depend upon my salary.' "

The King questioned Lieber about South Carolina, slavery, commerce, and emigration. Finally the subject came around to

---

[45] Lieber to Matilda Lieber, May 18, 29, September 2, 1844, Lieber papers. Lieber to Sumner, September 9, 1844, Harvard University. Lieber arranged to contribute articles on America to Tocqueville's newspaper.

[46] Lieber to Matilda Lieber, June 11, 22, 1844.

[47] Lieber to Matilda Lieber, July 27, 31, August 2, 1844. Lieber, *Ueber Hinrichtungen auf Offenem Felde, oder über Extramuran-und Intramuran-Hinrichtungen* (Krit. Zeitschr. f. Rechsw. u. Gesetzg. d. Ausl. XVII, B. 1. H., 1844 or 1845), 30 pp.; Lieber, *Bruchstücke über Gegenstände der Strafkunde, besonders über das Eremitensystem* (Hamburg, 1845), 48 pp. See Lieber's annotated copy of the former, Lieber papers.

penitentiaries, and Lieber set forth his views. He favored the Pennsylvania system, he told the King, but thought it would need modification in Germany, since the people were of a more desponding nature. "The King agreed to this, and said it was worse in the north than in the south of Germany. I asked why it was so, but knew the reason perfectly well. It is the natural consequence of two causes—the national German character, and the absence of all public life and liberty of practical discussion."

Lieber begged Frederick William to put an end to scandalous public executions. "The King replied: 'Only think at the last execution forty thousand people were present, and made a great uproar. . . . I have now given an order that the executions shall take place in Spandau.' " He expressed a wish to appoint Lieber to a prison inspectorship, and hoped that their paths would cross again.[48]

Following his flattering interview with Frederick William IV, Lieber angled carefully for a position. He suggested to the cabinet ministers that they create a chair of penology at the University of Berlin, and couple with it an inspectorship of prisons. They responded favorably, and urged Lieber to fill the post. Upon his departure from Berlin at the end of October, they told him that an offer would be forthcoming.[49]

From many leading Berliners Lieber received high compliments. Alexander von Humboldt was very friendly, and suggested to Lieber that he write the King about public administration of justice and trial by jury. Lieber found his old friend, the rising lawyer Knoblauch, was now a high official, "a regular G[e]H[eim]rath all over, who nevertheless loves me." He met barons and baronesses aplenty, and the more courteous they were, the higher his estimation of himself soared.

"I begin to regret that a Prussian minister has been appointed for the United States because I see that they have really a good opinion of me here," he boasted to Matilda. The thought of a fine position appealed to the ambitious Lieber; the prospect of returning permanently to Prussia did not. He would have been delighted if he could have obtained the office of "Consul-general of the German League in the U.S.," for then he could have lived

[48] Perry (ed.), *Lieber*, 185–88.   [49] *Ibid.*, 190.

in New York or Washington. As for being a professor at the University of Berlin and an inspector of prisons, he exclaimed: "Oh, Berlin stinks so!" "Things stand here, in many respects most deplorably and if I have a place in which teaching is the cheaf [*sic*] part and I cannot speak truth, I would rather be anywhere else." "If you ask me, whether I found Prussia better than I thought," he declared flatly, "I must distinctly answer *no.*" "The whole present tendency of Prussia is a most melancholy one; it is at war with everything most noble in our time, and must therefore become worse and worse." [50]

Consequently it was with some relief that Lieber left the stiffness and formalism, the repression and petty airs of Berlin. But he liked Austria little better. There a high government official pounced upon him as a prison authority, and dragged him from one Staatsrath and Count to another, until even the protocol-loving Lieber cried enough.

"I dislike exceedingly travelling in Austria," he complained. "[One has]to have a *permit* from the police to travel more than 2 German miles, each time one wishes to go!" Indeed, the only part of the German-speaking realms which Lieber truly enjoyed was Heidelberg, where he visited Mittermaier, the outstanding authority on criminal law, who for years had been a correspondent of Lieber's. Mittermaier was an affable host, and talked expansively of a professorship of *staatswissenschaft.*[51]

After that Lieber returned to his family at Hamburg to await the offer from the Prussian government. "I warn you not to be surprised if after all that has preceded the whole should end in a very thin and insufficient thread," he counseled Matilda. And such it was: a temporary appointment with the remuneration of one thousand thalers annually, as inspector and manager of prisons of detention, until a more satisfactory appointment developed. It served one salutary end: Lieber could boast from one end of America to another that the King of Prussia had offered him an excellent position, but that out of his loyalty to his adopted country and his deep-seated love of liberty, he had refused His Majesty

[50] Lieber to Matilda Lieber, July 22, 27, 31, August 2, 13, 19, and [22], 1844.
[51] Lieber to Matilda Lieber, September 14 (translated copy), September 26, 1844. While traveling in Austria, Lieber met the wife of the Russian governor of Warsaw, who painted a deplorable picture of Russian serfdom.

Frederick William IV. Actually, he wrote the King that the stipend was too small, and that he would return to America while awaiting a suitable offer of a permanent position in Prussia.[52]

Lieber crossed to England and embarked for America on the Royal Mail Steamer *Hibernia*. After a phenomenally fast passage of only twelve days, he arrived in Halifax, and two days later was in Boston. There he saw Longfellow, and noted happily, "That hearty shake and beaming eye with which he received me gave me real joy, for I felt it was genuine." He greeted Hillard and Sumner with even greater delight, and inquired with great solicitude after Charles's health, for the preceding summer the young lawyer had been deathly ill. Now he was entirely recovered, but, though as zealous as ever in his friendship, was strangely changed. Sumner was beginning to follow the lead of his close friend, Samuel Gridley Howe, and to subordinate aesthetic and scholarly pursuits to active espousal of reforms. Moreover, his wholehearted plunge into reform was leading him to dabble tentatively in politics.[53]

If Sumner was undergoing rapid ideological change, Lieber as yet was not. He found the South in the spring of 1845 as distasteful as ever, and American politics even more so. The country had abandoned Whiggery to return to Democratic heresies, which as personified by President Polk meant Manifest Destiny. The first move had been the annexation of Texas which brought the United States not only a vast new slave territory but also an almost inevitable war with the outraged people of Mexico. Lieber thought he might almost as well be in Germany, and most of his New England friends were equally despondent. Fanny Longfellow mourned that with the admission of Texas her patriotism had "almost died a natural death." [54]

Lieber clearly saw what annexation would bring. He termed the resolutions admitting Texas: "A disgrace! And all without the slightest preparations for a possible war. The government has been fooling with the Texas question as a [moron] with a razor.

[52] Lieber to Matilda Lieber, October 16, 1844; Ernst von Bodelschwingh to Lieber, December 18, 1844.
[53] Lieber to Matilda Lieber, January 26, February 3, 1845, and subsequent letters, Lieber papers. Lieber to Sumner, February 21, [1845], Harvard University.
[54] Fanny Longfellow to Lieber, March 16, 1845.

. . . The only reason why the South demands annexation was to perpetuate slavery and to insure their ascendancy in the Senate. . . . I advised [a congressman] to propose an amendment, conditionally granting 15 or 20 millions to the President, [in] case of war. I hoped it might open the eyes of some. If they wished to dance, it was well to know how much the piper would cost. But all was too late." [55]

With trouble imminent in the South, clearly the time had come to get out at all costs. Yet Lieber, with his high standard of living, was not yet ready to make a sacrifice in order to move. In the late spring a second offer came from Prussia. Besides the thousand thalers stipend, Frederick William offered three hundred thalers for lectures, principally upon penology, and eight hundred thalers for moving expenses. Lieber felt the salary was still too low, though by Prussian standards it was high, and utilized the offer solely as a means of spreading through the newspapers a further advertisement of his desirability.[56]

He followed it up that summer with a most determined drive to raise the necessary endowment for a law chair at Cambridge. With the able assistance of a merchant, John Eliot Thayer, who had long professed a great admiration for him, he actually seemed at last to be on the brink of success. He planned long and seriously with Justice Story and Sumner until the plans seemed at the point of fruition. But Story became ill, and early in September, Howe wrote, "Bad news for you, my Dear Lieber, bad news for all of us!

"I saw Thayer yesterday, & he seemed most sanguine of success: Lowell was confident he could raise the money, & we agreed that the general gratulations on Story's recovery would furnish a fit occasion for pushing the matter to a termination.

"Today a cloud is over every thing; Story is sinking perhaps he is now dead!" [57]

Indeed, kindly, conservative Joseph Story was dead—prematurely dead from overwork—and gone with him were all Lieber's hopes of obtaining a chair at Harvard. Sumner, Howe, and Thayer

---

[55] Lieber to Bunsen, April 16, 1845.
[56] Ludwig von Thile to Lieber, May 22, 1845.
[57] Howe to Lieber, September 10, 1845.

tried faithfully to revive the project and push it through, but the one man who could have made it succeed was missing.[58]

"I feel Judge Story's loss deeply; I feel almost less at home in America. This is all in all a very sad time for me—I think the most oppressive of my life," Lieber confessed. Well it might be, for soon those around Harvard were absorbed in plans for building an observatory and with speculations as to who might fill Story's professorship. Lieber was not among those considered.[59]

Depressed, Lieber tried to reconstruct his future. Sumner was most considerate and tried to lead the exiled professor off into other schemes. There was, for instance, the possibility of founding a school for boys somewhere in the North. Everyone thought it would succeed—Hillard, Longfellow, Felton, and Detmold, a leading New York German-American. Lieber had no stomach for more disciplining of adolescents, and was too disappointed to be either kind or polite. When, after a period of some silence, he heard from Sumner, he replied rather curtly that he was glad Sumner bethought himself of "the economy of friendship." Loyal Howe, who had even proposed that Lieber should write notes and comments to a book Howe would prepare about Laura Bridgman, could not brook this testiness. "There is the sensitive, generous Sumner, the best friend you have," Howe chided, "he treats you delicately, & you abuse him." [60]

Poor Lieber, like Job, was finding all of his afflictions visiting him at once, but Lieber was endowed with none of Job's fortitude. His rasping temper wore the affectionate coating from his friendship with Sumner—and it grew more cutting, not only over disappointment in the North, but through worry for fear he would lose his chair at South Carolina College. Two influential members of the Board of Trustees agitated openly for the abolition of his chair. They carried their onslaught even into the press.

Lieber wisely held his tongue, and his friends and students came to his aid. The students held a mass meeting at which they resolved unanimously that they wished to keep him as an instructor; his

[58] Howe to Lieber, September 14, 1845; Thayer to Lieber, September 11, 1845; Greenleaf to Lieber, November 10, 1845.
[59] Lieber to Sumner, September 19, 1845; Greenleaf to Lieber, November 10, 1845; Thayer to Lieber, September 20, 1845.
[60] Lieber to Sumner, December 6, 1845; Howe to Lieber, December 29, 1845.

friends demanded a serious inquiry of the charges against him. In the end, all but three of the trustees voted for his retention. Instead of censuring him, they added to his chair the department of political philosophy. "And how I will hammer at the S.C. boys," Lieber crowed. He took great solace in his victory: some people told him he was one of the strong men of the state. Probably without even realizing his shift, he began to dream of attaining the presidency of the college, and tentatively began to make a few adjustments to South Carolina.[61]

[61] Lieber to Sumner, December 6, 1845.

XI

Abolitionist or Apologist?

PROFESSOR LIEBER in the spring of 1847 candidly wrote: "*As to Mexico.* The war is bad, thoroughly so, which I repeat a hundred times a day, to prevent me from applying for a commission." So wrought up that he lapsed into German accent, he added, "for, Ruggles, did I follow my feelings I should sit on an officer's nag, and not in a professor's share [*sic*]; I should help making history instead of teaching it. Good heavens! To teach political economy when those boys—but no more about it. It is an unrighteous war and I believe to *volunteer* in such, is taking the moral responsibility." [1]

The bellicose Lieber deliberately tried to subordinate his love for war to his strong Whig principles. He endeavored to put the conflict out of his mind during the excitement of 1846. Taking a strong stand against Polk's administration on all matters except tariff reduction, he had predicted that Manifest Destiny would surely bring war. At first, as Western congressmen vied in hurling warlike epithets at Great Britain, he thought it would come over Oregon. "Can anything be more low and contemptible than the vulgar braggadocio which is eructated," he queried. "The truth is that we are drunken with prosperity and need to be scourged by Providence and if we undertake to take John Bull by the horns, we shall come by the handsomest of lickings. And I don't see what is to prevent a collision." [2]

England compromised, but in May came war with Mexico.

---

[1] Lieber to Ruggles, April 23, 1847, Lieber papers, Library of Congress. He wrote similarly to Hillard, April, 1847, Lieber papers, Henry E. Huntington Library. All manuscripts referred to in this chapter, unless otherwise identified, are from this collection.

[2] Lieber to Hillard, January 12, 1846.

Lieber kept quiet—singularly quiet—and in the summer went to Ohio to deliver an oration on the *Character of the Gentleman* before the students of Miami University. His yardstick for the measurement of the gentleman was, of course, the *Manual of Political Ethics;* at South Carolina College the art of politics was almost synonymous with the code of gentlemen. Thanks to entertaining stories, the discourse was clever as well as soundly conservative, and in printed form it brought Lieber compliments from Princeton to New Orleans. Most significantly, not one word in the speech bore upon the war with Mexico.[3]

Everywhere in the West the German-American publicist aired his throughgoing Whiggery. At Cincinnati he met Justice John McLean of the United States Supreme Court, who was working quietly for the presidential nomination. Although Lieber was a total stranger, the jurist proposed buying the leading Whig paper of Cincinnati to serve as his personal campaign organ in order to install Lieber as editor. The scholar was astounded, and asked his wife, "Is this not strange, upon the whole, and would not the simple fact in my Life were it ever written which it will not, read remarkably?" It was not remarkable, for Lieber had forgotten the tide of Germans already pouring into the Ohio and Mississippi valleys.[4]

After delivering his speech in Ohio, the peripatetic professor crossed into Kentucky and spent two delightful days at Lexington, talking and smoking with aging Henry Clay. Lieber noted that Clay spoke calmly, but did not try to disguise his disappointment over the loss of the presidency, "and that too by illegal votes—as he at least thinks and I believe." "You know how much I have always cherished him," Lieber added admiringly; "my affection is

---

[3] Isaiah Little to Lieber, May 25, June 27, 1846; E. D. MacMaster to Lieber, May 24, 1846. Lieber, *The Character of the Gentleman: An Address to the Students of Miami University, on the Evening before Commencement. August, 1846* (Cincinnati, 1846), 31 pp. An edition appeared in Columbia, S.C., the following year. A pirated version appeared in the United Kingdom during the Civil War: *The True Character of the Gentleman . . . with preface by E. B. Shuldham* (Edinburgh, 1862), viii, 12–90 pp., 2d ed., enl. This caused Lieber greatly to expand his original essay, and reissue it with Lippincott (Philadelphia, 1864), 121 pp. See an interleaved copy with letters of laudation, Johns Hopkins University, and a review in the Washington *National Intelligencer,* July 17, 1847. It is reprinted in Lieber, *Miscellaneous Writings* I, 225–79.

[4] Lieber to Matilda Lieber, August 30, 1846. F. P. Weisenburger, *The Life of John McLean: A Politician on the United States Supreme Court* (Columbus, Ohio, 1937).

now increased. Politics, history, anecdotes, balls, blood horses, slavery, everything was talked of, except tariff, for, having the very opposite views to his, why should I have discussed [that] with him?" [5]

Why, indeed? Lieber in his free-trade views was going beyond most of his Southern Whig friends of the forties, and in the face of his silence on the slavery issue was making it the dominant theme of his public writings. It helped greatly to ingratiate him with the people of South Carolina. He was so actively writing and publishing on the subject that he was coming to receive notice as one of the great American apostles of free trade—not the greatest, as he liked to remember the extravagant-tongued Robert J. Walker had once termed him—but one important enough to receive a warm letter from England's free trader, Richard Cobden. "Your country has indeed nobly entered upon the same path," hailed Cobden overoptimistically as American tariffs went downward in 1846, "—a path which I fervently believe will conduct the nations of the earth to the goal of peace & universal brotherhood." [6]

Though on Henry Clay's veranda Lieber might keep the conversation turned toward blooded race horses, to John C. Calhoun he would write emphatically in praise of free trade. He pointed out to Calhoun—who exceeded even Lieber's ultraconservative views on labor—the falsity of the industrialists' claim that a protective tariff maintained the high living standard of American workingmen. "I am much gratified to learn," the South Carolina senator replied, "that you are prepared to attack protection under its new Sophism, the rights of labour." [7]

For his friends, the McCords, who were violently proslavery and antitariff, Lieber wrote an introductory letter to a translation of Bastiat's *Sophisms of the Protective Policy*. The crux of his

[5] Lieber to Matilda Lieber, September 3, 1846. Lieber also spent a day in the Mammoth Caves, taking copious notes, which are in the Lieber papers. Upon his return, he wrote a lengthy poem extoling the glories of the prosperous trans-Appalachian empire: *The West: A Metrical Epistle* (New York, 1848), 30 pp.

[6] Cobden to Lieber, September 23, 1846. Walker, a Democrat, declined Lieber's offer to write free-trade articles for his newspaper. J. A. Woodward to Lieber, July 15, 1846.

[7] Calhoun to Lieber, November 11, 1846. Lieber also feared the cost of the war would lead to a higher tariff. Lieber to G. F. Holmes, March 14, 1847, Holmes papers, Duke University.

argument was that free trade meant cheaper goods and a consequent higher standard of living. America could cease the uneconomical manufacture of exotic products behind a high tariff wall, and confine herself to what she could most cheaply produce. Free trade, Lieber emphasized, was analogous to improvement in machinery or transportation, or any "other abridgment of toil. . . . All have but this one end, to get as much for as little labor as possible, so that the labor thus saved may be applied for the attainment of other objects, and that capital be not wilfully wasted." [8]

Through letters to the South Carolina press Lieber kept up a constant peppering at tariff proponents. Hiding behind the pseudonym "Columbiensis," he even published a violent attack upon his friend Clay for denouncing the "temerity" of nations which adopted free trade. He suggested to Calhoun that delegates be sent to a world free-trade convention at Brussels, and started a newspaper movement to name them.[9]

In that mentor of King Cotton, *DeBow's Review,* Lieber set forth his elaborate philosophical arguments in favor of unrestricted trade between nations. After all, it was but a further step in "the widening course of civilization," and to restore free trade would be merely to return to "one of the first rights of a free man." He elaborated the ideas he had already suggested to Calhoun: At first American protectionists had pointed to the need of a tariff to protect American capital, which bore higher rates of interest than in Europe. Otherwise, the products of the United States could not compete with cheaper British goods. Jacksonian democracy had brought the ballot to the common man, to whom arguments based upon the protection of capital were quite unsavory, so the protectionists had quickly proclaimed their love for American labor. Wages were higher in the United States; an influx of

---

[8] Lieber wrote a letter for the McCords almost as long as their little book. The original manuscript (Lieber to McCord, January, 1848) and McCord's comments (McCord to Lieber, February 6, 1848) are in the Lieber papers. A highly abridged version is in Mrs. D. J. McCord (tr.), *Sophisms of the Protective Policy by Fr. Bastiat . . . With an Introductory Letter, by Dr. Francis Lieber* (New York, 1848), 182 pp., 5–14.

[9] [Lieber], "Temerity," Columbia *Palmetto-State Banner,* December 1, 1846; [Lieber], "Free Trade, World Convention at Brussels in the Month of September Next," Columbia *South Carolinian,* June 22, 1847; McCord to Lieber, June 19, 1847; Calhoun to Lieber, June 27, 1847.

inexpensive foreign goods would curtail production and lower the worker's return. Yet, Lieber cannily pointed out, a protectionist sincerely interested in aiding labor would also try to prevent the immigration of cheap foreign workers. None of the high tariff exponents had mentioned bars against immigrants.

"There seems to be but one real mode of protecting American or any labor," Lieber concluded characteristically. That was the assurance "that the laborer shall be able to obtain for his wages all the consumable commodities he is entitled to, in the natural unhampered order of things—the *whole* amount of all he may obtain in *free* exchange for his labor or wages." He failed to mention the great advantages which free trade offered the cotton South as opposed to the industrial North.[10]

Lieber's free-trade stand was completely sincere. He had accepted the *laissez-faire* creed without the slightest reservation, and had married into a family of international merchants. In a letter to the North, he became so emotional that he labeled protection "nothing but a veiled . . . communism, an anabaptist heresy." Indeed, faith in free trade, like his nationalistic ardor, seemed imbedded in his very marrow. Two decades later he was still earnestly shouting his discordant war cry against tariffs, from well up in the ranks of the ultraprotectionist Republicans.[11]

Lieber was fortunate indeed to have one safety valve in free trade. With a caution almost equal to his circumspection about slavery, he kept his views on the Mexican War out of the newspapers. During the exciting spring months of 1847, they gradually began to creep into his letters to friends, and came to be more in keeping with the Southern viewpoint. By then Lieber had deserted more conservative Northern Whigs, like Robert Ingersoll of Pennsylvania, and had come openly to favor annexation of California. He defended this on grounds previously suggested in his *Property and Labour:* the soil was rich; the Mexicans and Indians were making no use of it. Therefore, though it might be inconsistent with the rest of his well-rounded theories, he decided that energetic, industrious Americans who would make the best

10 [Lieber], "Free Trade and Other Things. A Philosophical Tutti Frutti," *De-Bow's Review,* XV (1853), 53–65.

11 Lieber to Hillard, November 9, 1848; Lieber, *Notes on Fallacies Peculiar to American Protectionists. . . .*

possible use of the land as God had intended, held a "natural right" to it! [12]

This was a dangerous deviation from Lieber's carefully formulated doctrine against "common conquest," but that applied solely to the eternal foolish, medieval cravings of European powers to conquer already well-cultivated lands. "If we take California we rob no one," he rationalized. "The Mexican government does not *own* it; it gives no strength to it; we donot rob the inhabitants; indeed we would *give* it to mankind." [13]

Lieber feared his argument would fall into the hands of those who sickened him "with their coarse cry of conquest and halls of Montezuma and all that low verbiage." Indeed, he fought vehemently against the proposals to hold all of Mexico which certain adventurers tried to make reality. Years later General Winfield Scott confirmed to Lieber that a group of these had offered him a huge sum to assume the presidency of Mexico, make over the American army into a Mexican one at liberal salary increases, and plan for ultimate American absorption. Lieber did not know this in 1847–48, but feared it, and wrote a newspaper article lauding Calhoun's temperate stand against overaggrandizement.[14]

All Lieber wished to see was the annexation of Mexico's unoccupied northwestern domain, the exaction of a favorable trade treaty, and the acquisition of the right to dig an isthmian canal. He expected a great re-orientation of the world's commercial centers as a result of the acquisition of California. When word arrived in December, 1849, that the first vessel from China laden with tea, silk, and chinaware had arrived at San Francisco, he predicted enthusiastically: "This is the first pulsation of the chick in an egg, now hatching, and from which a mighty bird will come. . . . St. Francisco will be more than Lisbon was after the sea route around the Cape of Good Hope had been discovered." [15]

[12] Lieber, *Property and Labour*, 142–50.

[13] Lieber to Ruggles, April 23, 1847, Library of Congress.

[14] Lieber to Ruggles, April 23, 1847, Library of Congress; Lieber, "Mr. Calhoun's Speech on the 4th January 1848," Columbia *Daily Telegraph*, 1848 (clipping in Lieber papers); Calhoun to Lieber, February 6, 1848; Scott to Lieber, December 17, 1852. Cf. C. W. Elliott, *Winfield Scott: The Soldier and the Man* (New York, 1937), 579–80. J. D. P. Fuller, *The Movement for the Acquisition of All Mexico, 1846–1848* (Johns Hopkins University Studies in Historical and Political Science, Series 54, No. 1) (Baltimore, 1936).

[15] Lieber, California Scrapbook, Bancroft Library, University of California.

The professor waxed poetic upon the possibilities of a ship canal across the lower part of Mexico or at Panama. Would not Longfellow tune his lyre to this great theme and thus win the hearts and support of congressional leaders and cabinet officers? He would not. Therefore, in 1847 Lieber raised his none-too-melodious voice:

Rend America asunder
And unite the Binding Sea.
That emboldens Man and tempers—
Make the ocean free

. . . .

Long indeed they have been wooing,
The Pacific and his bride;
Now 'tis time for holy wedding—
Join them by the tide.

. . . .

Must the globe be always girded
'Ere we get to Bramah's priest?
Take the Tissues of your Lowells
Westward to the East.

For twenty-three verses the bard pleaded on. Boston aesthetes groaned; Fanny Longfellow, trying to be kind, praised the ode as the epithalamium of the waters; and newspaper and magazine editors, not knowing any better, printed and reprinted the ode on "The Ship Canal." It began its career in 1847 in Polk's paper, the Washington *Union,* and flourished thenceforth. The Democratic Boston *Post* exulted: "This is a good sign, as the Dr. distinctly realizes the mighty mission of the unthralled Saxon. Wherever a whig has soul and sense enough to elevate him above the slough of his party, his mind attains at once the natural scope and grandeur of democracy." At the time of Lieber's death in 1872, he was urging Longfellow to prevail upon *Harpers'* to print the effusion a second time.[16]

[16] Lieber to Ruggles, May 2, 1847, Library of Congress. Many letters and clippings in the Lieber papers refer to the canal and poem. See "The Ship Canal," Columbia *South Carolinian,* December 31, 1847, and innumerable other copies, Lieber papers. Boston *Post,* February 1, 1848, cited in Fuller, *Movement for the Acquisition of All Mexico,* 98.

Lieber also lifted his lyre in the summer of 1847 to extol America's generosity to Europe in the face of Europe's petty canting against the United States. He sang the praises of the American warship *Jamestown,* which Congress sent loaded with food to succor famine sufferers in Ireland and Germany. With characteristic energy, he went on to organize famine relief in his area. From the small group of Germans, mostly shoemakers, who lived in and around Columbia, he recruited a band, the Philharmonians, "who with wonderful industry have made themselves able musicians." Acting as their manager and press agent, he arranged a concert and raised $2,100 in the South Carolina Piedmont. His pleas for relief appeared in newspapers as far away as Cincinnati.[17]

The terrible famine caused the tide of Germans going to America to swell into a torrent. Lieber watched their arrival with deep interest, for he had long favored German immigration. In the early thirties he had solicited Mathew Carey's opinion on how to facilitate it, and at the beginning of the forties had aided Representative Caleb Cushing in blocking congressional plans to restrict naturalization. While he was opposed to entrance of criminals, the diseased, and those likely to become public wards, he welcomed immigrant settlement on the broad prairies of the West. "Every productive emigrant creates a new market with his product and actually presents the U. St. with the choice gift of so many acres of cultivated land," he reasoned. "What the United States became as wealthy customers to England, the West has become to the East in our country and California will become to the West. The emigrant who hangs about large towns and opens a grog shop is a real loss indeed." [18]

Many Americans did not look upon immigrants so enthusi-

[17] Matilda Lieber to Fanny Longfellow, June 13, 1847; Monitz Mayblum to Lieber, June 11, 1847; Henry Muller to Lieber, June 17, 1847; MacMaster to Lieber, July 6, 1847; Lieber to Hillard, April, 1847; Lieber to Sumner, March 15, 1847, Lieber papers. Lieber to Ruggles, May 2, 1847, Library of Congress. See four different articles by Lieber, all titled, "Musical Entertainment for the Relief of Famine in Germany," *Palmetto-State Banner, South Carolinian, Chronicle,* and the *South Carolina Temperance Advocate,* Columbia, S.C., June 3, 1847; "The Philharmonians," Columbia *South Carolinian,* June 22, 1847, clippings in Lieber papers.

[18] Lieber to Mathew Carey, September 16, 1832, Historical Society of Pennsylvania. Lieber queried similarly in a letter to Francis Markoe, December 28, 1843, Library of Congress. Cushing to Lieber, January 9, 25, 1840, January 1, 1843; Lieber, undated note of about this period in Lieber papers.

astically. This was especially true in the South, to which few of them came. Not many South Carolinians shared the regret Calhoun expressed to Lieber that the German tide did not come their way. On the contrary, they launched their barbs against Lieber, and made him squirm. A Charleston paper had termed his *Political Ethics* excellent, but had regretted that it was the work of a foreigner.[19]

"Why should a German draw South Carolina salary in Columbia," Lieber had found written on the blackboard one day when he entered his classroom. Quickly he thought of General Johann Kalb who had died near by during the Revolutionary War. He took the chalk and quietly wrote under the quip, "Because South Carolina drew German blood at Camden." The students cheered.[20]

In the forties Lieber launched a strong newspaper attack upon Nativism. He wasted no sympathy upon those naturalized citizens who gave basis to Native American denunciations by parading at election time as "True Sons of Erin," or the "Noble Sons of Germany." He warned sternly that "in any way to bring a feeling arising out of a common and foreign extraction to bear upon election falls little short of treason." He laid the major guilt upon native-born politicians—Lieber did not mention that they were usually Democrats—who in order to gain votes "flatter, feast, fuddle, bribe and seduce the needy foreigner or stolid pauper." The solution was not that proposed by Nativists, overlengthy periods of naturalization or laws excluding foreigners, but the relatively simple one of sound, strictly enforced election rules.

Lieber scoffed at antiforeign bias. The only claim to superiority on the part of the Native American party was priority of arrival —and the Indians had been in the New World long before their forebears. One should measure the worth of all men solely on their ability, not their place of birth; some of the ablest and most patriotic citizens of most modern nations had been foreign. "Has any native Spaniard done for Spain what Columbus the Genoese did? . . . What British monarch was so English as King William the Dutch? . . . What Frenchman more French than Napoleon the Italian. . . . Has Gallatin not redeemed his citizenship

---

[19] Calhoun to Lieber, June 27, 1847.
[20] Lieber, No. 2549; Lieber to Ruggles, January 14, 1842, Library of Congress.

pledge? Did Hamilton less service than any statesman or general born within the limits of this country?"

Many of America's ablest farmers, artisans, barristers, and statesmen were foreign-born. Were they not capable within a few years of sufficient affection for and understanding of the American government to warrant citizenship? "The government of the United States is no more a mystery than that of any other country." Indeed, the best account of the workings of the organic laws of the United States was by a Frenchman, Tocqueville. "If I am answered: All emigrants are not . . . DeTocquevilles, I reply: Nor are all native citizens Marshalls, Jeffersons, Calhouns, Clays or Websters." [21]

Lieber's well-wishers greeted the tremendous German influx with enthusiasm. They were sure that he, being influential in the press and well established in America, would be able to step into a position of political leadership over this large new segment of the national polity. His sage shepherding would bring them safely into the Whig fold. Less ambitious or more wise than the forty-eighter, Carl Schurz, Lieber made no pretense of being able to capture the new German vote for the conservatives.

Ruggles had glowingly sketched a plan for him. Lieber should assume the low-salaried Columbia professorship, which Johann Louis Tellkampf had botched, and combine with it the editorship of a German newspaper. "Surely, amid the floods of German population now pouring into our Continent, there would be thousands and tens of thousands who would read with delight and with instruction such a journal as *you* could edit," Ruggles predicted exuberantly.

"Politically speaking," the New York lawyer added, "it would be of enormous importance in this early stage of German colonization to give its infant mind the proper bias and direction. . . . Surely much may be written and said . . . to resist or at least to modify the torrent of democratic sentiment that this stream of German population is hourly rolling into our country. . . . We are to be *Teutonized.* . . . Come then and take command of the

[21] Lieber, "On Foreigners in the United States," Columbia *South Carolina Temperance Advocate,* January 8, 1846; New York *Semi-Weekly Courier and New York Enquirer,* January 15, 1846; Newport (R.I.) *Herald of the Times,* March 19, 1846, clippings in Lieber papers. Lieber, No. 2549, Library of Congress.

invading host by taking the direction of their sentiments and opinions." [22]

The German-American received the proposal coldly. Most of the Germans coming to America, he pointed out, were freed peasants and "rabid democrats—novices and therefore fanatics in politics." Lieber felt he could become their leader only by "Out St. Justing St. Just himself." He added with some alarm: "All these fellows have two odd ideas or trains of ideas. On the one hand they are democrats of the Bancroft style, whose creed is: attack is great and 3 is more than 2, therefore the 3 have a right to slit the noses of the 2.; on the other hand they think America must be un-Englished, and German nationality must swamp the U.S." [23]

"I love my country—I would lay my life down for it any day," Lieber declared, "but when they talk of Germanizing America I spurn the idea. The German character furnishes stuff to make a nation of, that might be good enough for the Lord's grenadiers, but what *is* it. Germany has no institutions, has no popular Common Law, no tradition of liberty. . . . *Transplanted* nationality can consist in institutions only, and where are the German institutions! The princes have knocked every one on the head. Indeed, I would like to found an Anglico-German College, but that would be only for the two-fold object of promoting assimilation, and helping to bring over German knowledge and education." [24]

Lieber had trouble enough stretching himself between Northern and Southern institutions without plunging into the vortex of the German-American whirlpool. New England's great protectionist, Daniel Webster, came to Columbia in the spring of 1847, and the task of providing suitable fetes fell in part on Lieber. The professor, now wise in Southern lore, realized that the Carolinians, in keeping with their concept of gentlemanliness, would receive the Northern statesman with great cordiality. He himself counted Webster a friend, since two summers previous with Ruggles he

---

[22] Ruggles to Lieber, April 18, 1847.

[23] Lieber to Ruggles, April 23, May 2, 1847, Library of Congress.

[24] Lieber to Ruggles, April 23, 1847, Library of Congress. Lieber's views did indeed disqualify him from becoming a German leader. Quite typically, Karl Heinzen disliked him "because he advocated the complete cultural assimilation of the German immigrant and because he was a conservative in all matters, including slavery." Carl Wittke, *Against the Current: The Life of Karl Heinzen (1809–80)* (Chicago, 1945), 124.

had visited the senator at Marshfield, and had thoroughly enjoyed the fishing and yarn swapping. So he set about energetically
to prepare a soiree in Webster's honor.[25]
The godlike Daniel arrived in one of the moods he sometimes
assumed—dour, curt, and uncommunicative. About two hundred
attended the Liebers' party; Mrs. Webster was affable and the
students excited and enthusiastic, but with keen disappointment
Lieber lamented: "Mr. Webster did not make himself agreeable
here. The students illuminated their houses, the chapel windows
and public buildings, had bonfires music and a torchlight procession, but he remained cold, torpid like an aligator [sic] and was
in all his intercourse absent to a degree of discourtesy which
many, I believe, consider rudeness. The speech he made to the students was frigid and bore the stamp of one prevailing thought
from beginning to end, namely: I donot know what to say." [26]
The sensitive Carolinians felt slighted, and Lieber, who quite
unnecessarily felt that he stood sponsor, winced at the bad impression. Later Hillard reassuringly declared that Webster's "torpor
and indifference of manner has long been noticeable here," and
Ruggles reported that the Massachusetts senator, far from being
intentionally rude, had written warmly of Lieber's reception.[27]
If it was arduous for Lieber, as sectional feeling heightened,
to entertain a great Northern acquaintance in the South, it became even more difficult for him to justify his Southern position
among his Northern friends. Since Sumner's dangerous illness in

[25] Webster to George Grennell, July 19, 1845; Ruggles to Lieber, August 6, 1845;
Perry (ed.), *Lieber*, 198–99.

[26] Lieber to Ruggles, April 23, 1847, Library of Congress; Lieber to Hillard, April,
1847; Lieber to Sumner, May 22, 1847. For an interesting student account of the
Lieber's party, see Patterson, *Journal of a Southern Student,* 55. The evening of
Webster's arrival, Preston gave a party, and invited only Seniors; the second evening
the Liebers entertained the Juniors. "Webster . . . graced the room with his presence
but a short while. The old Doctor had provided for us well in lemonade and cake and
claret, ice-creams, strawberries, etc.—quite a treat."

[27] Hillard to Lieber, May 28, 1847; Ruggles to Lieber, June 14, 1847. Webster had
traveled South to combat the growing popularity of Zachary Taylor. Claude Fuess
concludes that he ate and drank too much and did not sleep enough, "that he was
a victim of Southern hospitality." Fuess, *Daniel Webster* (Boston, 1930), II, 176.
See Fuess, "Senator Webster Goes South—a Study in Hospitality," *Proceedings of
the Massachusetts Historical Society,* LXII (1929), 161–71. Webster's own account
of his visit to Columbia was quite favorable, but he barely mentioned Lieber. Hennig, *Columbia,* 267; E. L. Green, *History of the University of South Carolina* (Columbia, 1916), 52.

1844, the young lawyer had rapidly undergone a radical meta-morphosis from a scholarly young aesthete into a militant abolitionist-politician. The change brought about a gradual cool-ness between the two old friends. Lieber, from his long residence in the South, saw in varied shades of gray the issues which to Sumner appeared in the most dazzling white and diabolical black.

Slavery had concerned Lieber ever since his arrival in America. He had disliked it intensely but his overweening respect for the American legal system which protected slavery had served as a substantial counterbalance for the strong personal revulsion that swept him when he saw the notorious auction blocks of the District of Columbia.

This respect for the law probably as much as any other factor kept Lieber from joining the professional abolitionists during the lean years in Philadelphia. In *The Stranger in America* he set forth clearly his disgust with slavery and his corresponding awe for the system which maintained it. He sent a questionnaire to officials at Sing Sing penitentiary where confined Negroes and white men lived under identical conditions. Their answers led him to believe that Negroes were little inferior to whites either physically or mentally. Although many of them were capable of the responsibility of political equality, it would be meaningless without social equality, and that surely would not follow. Social equality implied race amalgamation, an idea repugnant to Lieber's Anglo-Saxon mind. The Southerners understood best their local problems; hence Lieber would not dispute the state-rights stand that emancipation was not a question for Congress to settle, but one belonging entirely to state legislatures. The only solution might be a gradual amelioration of the plight of the Negro until he had achieved the status of serfdom or peasantry.[28]

During many years of residence in South Carolina and of care-ful study, Lieber retained his early views almost unchanged. He hid them behind a discreet silence, but back of this protective bar-rier he assembled in systematic fashion data on every conceivable

---

[28] Lieber, *The Stranger in America*, II, 188–210. "Queries and answers respecting the colored convicts in the Sing-Sing State Prison," August 19, 1833, with answers by Robert Wiltse and Dr. Hoffman, and note by Lieber. Frank Freidel, "Francis Lieber, Charles Sumner and Slavery," *Journal of Southern History,* IX (1943), 75–93.

aspect of "this nasty, dirty, selfish institution." He clipped newspaper accounts of lawsuits involving Negroes, copied into commonplace books anecdotes and opinions of his friends and associates, and set forth his own observations on the social, economic,
and political aspects of slavery.[29]

The scholar carried on his study not only as an outside observer,
but also as a master and owner. Shortly after his arrival in Columbia, he rented a fourteen-year-old slave boy named Tom, for
whom he paid $4.50 a month. Sentimentally, Lieber contrasted the
position of his own children with that of Tom, who brought with
him only a single shirt and a blanket.[30]

The following January, Lieber became the owner of two female
slaves, Betsy and her daughter Elsa, whom he purchased from a
North Carolina dealer. Faithful Betsy and feckless Elsa were the
first of a succession of Lieber slaves, almost all of whom brought
trouble or sorrow to their professorial owner. Some were lazy or
dishonest, but Elsa's troubles were of a different kind. To Lieber's disgust, he discovered in the spring of 1841 that Elsa was
pregnant. In the summer she suffered a miscarriage and died. The
stern professor was both touched and horrified. He had followed
with pain the progress of her pregnancy; upon her death he felt
afflicted. Though he winced at the pecuniary loss he had sustained,
"fully one thousand dollars—the hard labor of a year," he did
not in the least blame the poor girl for her troubles. "As to Elsa
herself, why she is better off. If there is immortality she must have
gone to a better state." [31]

[29] See scrapbook and notebooks on slavery, together with quantities of notes and
newspaper clippings, Lieber papers. The following notes on hired-out slaves in
Columbia, made about 1837–40, are indicative of the contents: "Carpenters here,
and bricklayers, receive from their master 25 cts. to find themselves, but when sick
they go home.

"Two dresses i.e. shirt, jacket, pantal. shoes (about 4 pair) hats irregular. The
master earns by them if mechanics 30 $ a month.

"Cooks from 7 to 10 $, generally 8 a month.

"House maid $7—for which they are clothed and medicine by the master.

"About ½ lb of bacon a day, besides the meat from the table, and four &c.

"The servants are very slow—dirty of course.

"Slovenly—forget everything.

"They know and think probably more than people believe they do."
[30] Perry (ed.), *Lieber*, 109–10.
[31] Notebook entitled "Slavery"; Lieber to Matilda Lieber, August 24, September
1, 1841. Numerous other letters between the Liebers during the summer of 1841 refer
to Elsa, whom Lieber had regarded as inoffensive.

The German-American was not alone in his moral repugnance toward slavery. He had early discovered that many a prominent upcountry planter and professional man shared his disgust. With delight he recorded the remarks of Senator William C. Preston, Professor Nott, William DeSaussure, and numerous others. Like them, Lieber also fell in with the general undercurrent of feeling that the economic lag of the South was due to the wastefulness of slavery. He agreed with the general consensus that the refusal of the South to improve the legal status of slaves was a natural reaction to abolitionist pressure from the North. Senator Preston had told him how John Randolph of Roanoke had detested the sight of slave gangs, with their clanking chains, being marched to the markets at Georgetown. Randolph had prepared a bill calling for the abolition of the slave trade within the District of Columbia, but Northern agitation had prevented him from ever presenting it. Finally, Preston declared, Randolph had passed on the bill to Senator Thomas Hart Benton, who likewise had waited many years without finding an opportune time.[32]

All these things the scholar had reported to his Massachusetts friends—and his detailed reports fired Sumner's imagination. Lieber, intensely discontented with his Southern position, had pleaded with Sumner in letter after letter to find him more suitable work in the North. In these letters he so incessantly harped upon the degrading effect of slavery upon all Southern life and economy that it was hardly surprising that Sumner replied roundly in 1841, "A curse upon slavery!" Soon Sumner began to surpass Lieber's steady

[32] Perry (ed.), *Lieber*, 108; Lieber, notebook on slavery; note in scrapbook on slavery, October 31, 1848. Another entry in the scrapbook reads: "I returned from the West in Sept. 1846 when I met young Davis our Librarian at Branchville, he returning from the North which he had seen for the first time. His first word was: Dr, I return, not an abolitionist but deplore slavery. So! that North!. They beat us in every thing. Oh, if we could get rid of this unfortunate slavery."

"I met Wm. DeSaussure in the street. Well, how have you been &c &c. I praised the West and *he* exclaimed: Ah slavery, slavery, slavery!

"Mrs. DeHassell told me yesterday that Mrs. Preston, Wm. C. Preston's wife said to her she prayed every evening that God in his wisdom might devise some means to do away with this unhappy institution. . . .

"Ah Sir, said Dr. Sill once to me, when wagon & a number of emigrating negros passed by, there goes our misery our misfortune."

Lieber wrote Sumner, October 27, 1835: "Now, about 10 years ago there was not a man in the South, who did not allow that slavery is an evil; at present I believe that there are few that do allow it."

237

surreptitious dislike, and with his characteristic wholehearted enthusiasm began to attack slavery in bombastic Garrisonian terms. This, like all Sumner's exaggerations (excepting those praising Lieber), annoyed the professor. After reading one of the perorations, he chided gently, "It seems to me slavery may be attacked without fiction." [33]

Sumner was hurt, not impressed, by Lieber's criticisms. By the fall of 1846 he had allied himself strongly with those Whigs who were trying to carry the party over to abolitionism. To both Lieber and Hillard this was a great disappointment, since they had always pictured the scholarly Sumner as holding a chair at Harvard where he could give himself over to the meditation and broad generalizing for which he was so well suited. His reform tactics had ended any remaining chance for a law professorship.[34]

While Sumner moved toward the vehement stand of his friend Dr. S. G. Howe, Lieber tried to define his own views on slavery. Amidst the turbulence of national politics and wrangling over whether the territorial spoils of the Mexican War should be slave or free, Lieber sat in his study in Columbia, and under the pen name "Tranquillas" addressed to John C. Calhoun a set of open letters which he was never to publish.[35]

Although Calhoun more than any other single man had helped build a Chinese wall around slavery, Lieber nevertheless keenly admired his conservative, analytical mind. The great Southern statesman assumed an almost Marxian view of the struggle between capital and labor, but looked to slavery rather than communism as the solution. After the Civil War, the scholar recalled that Calhoun had once told him, " 'Do you not agree that slavery contains all that is good in communism, and discards what is bad?

[33] Sumner to Lieber, September 6, 1841; Lieber to Sumner, June 14, 1846, Lieber papers. Lieber sharply criticized Sumner's eulogy of Story, Pickering, Allston, and Channing because he did not "sufficiently reign in the prancing steed of laudation." Lieber to R. C. Winthrop, September 22, 1846, Massachusetts Historical Society. Sumner, *The Scholar, the Jurist, the Artist, the Philanthropist* . . . (Boston, 1846). Lieber noted many exaggerations in his copy, University of California.

[34] Kent to Lieber, September, 1846, Lieber papers. Greenleaf to Lieber, May 5, 1838, inserted in "Pamphlets on Crime," vol. 6, University of California.

[35] Several sets of the five draft letters to Calhoun under the pen name "Tranquillas" are in the Lieber papers. With Lieber's plan for remedy omitted, fragments appear in Perry (ed.), *Lieber*, 228–37.

Slavery in this, as in so many other cases, solves problems which cannot be solved otherwise.' " [36]

In 1846, Lieber seriously contemplated issuing an appeal to Calhoun. It would urge him to head a movement to modify the Southern slaveholding system, wasteful and unprofitable as it was, by introducing a system of serfdom—the word "sharecropper" had not then been invented—through which the more ambitious slaves could gradually win certain rights and privileges.

Three years later, Lieber drafted more open letters on slave extension into the territories: "I know what every Southern citizen knows, if neither blinded by the love of theory nor by political extravagance, that an overwhelming majority of your portion of the country consider slavery a heavy burden and grievous evil," Lieber asserted. He reminded Calhoun of a view the statesman had earlier expressed that slavery was a scaffold to rear the fabric of civilization in new countries. Surely by now, the scholar argued, civilization firmly existed in the Southern states and change was due. Shifting to humanitarian grounds, he inquired: "Would you like to be a slave? . . . Would you grieve to see your daughter enslaved? . . . Would you vote slavery into existence did it not already exist?" Then flatly he stated his basic objection: Slavery was eminently a state of degradation which as much as the vilest communism disavowed the two greatest elements of progress and civilization, the institutions of property and marriage.

The scholar charged that Southerners were fighting the Wilmot Proviso, which would prohibit slavery in the new territory, less to expand the institution than to preserve their distorted property rights. In defending these they overlooked the fact that a slave was more than a chattel; he was also a human being whom the law protected from his master's cruelty. If, because of soil exhaustion, slavery must constantly expand, like any institution which incessantly demanded "more, more," it contained the seed of death.

[36] Lieber, *Miscellaneous Writings*, II, 427. For an analysis of Calhoun's social theories, see R. N. Current, "John C. Calhoun, Philosopher of Reaction," *Antioch Review*, Summer, 1943, 223–34.

The Ottoman and Napoleonic Empires, nurtured through conquests, ultimately died when they met reverses. The argument of Governor McDowell of Virginia, that the admission of California as a slave state would not mean an extension of slavery, since no free person would become enslaved, was fallacious. "Free men," Lieber emphasized, "would become subject to all the ills of the institution." The slaves would increase; the white laborers would be circumscribed.

The South had no right to regard the Wilmot Proviso as a breach of its natural rights. Slavery could not exist in conquered territory until established there by positive legislation, since it depended for its existence upon municipal law, not natural right. The Southern delegation in Congress, including Calhoun, was wrong in its demand that the slaveholder be allowed to take his human belongings anywhere in the Union. Lieber asserted that slaves, because of their status as human beings, could not go into an area where slavery was not a municipal institution. He supported this assertion with case after case. The institution of antislavery in the North, he pointed out, was no less positive in character than the slavery of the South. The Southern view that the prohibition of slavery in the territories was an unfair restriction which would keep citizens from their section from migrating there was fallacious, since millions of white people in the South possessed no slaves.

Southerners must not use the taunts of the abolitionists as a pretext to rigidify slavery. Like every other institution, it must undergo development. The South must admit the necessity of change and allow dicussion. Calhoun as its leader should consider the more lenient provisions of the slave codes of other lands: legalize marriage, declare a "quinteroon" white and free, allow a slave to own property, permit him to buy himself through work in leisure hours, give land to a slave after a certain number of years of work, and with limitations admit his testimony in court.

Lieber challenged the South to defy orthodoxy and consider these modifications. Men like Calhoun must end the terrorism of a minority within the South and inaugurate constructive criticism. Perhaps Lieber was aware that this rigidity had been im-

240

posed by the large planters to protect themselves from a latent hostility within the upland South—a hostility which in the 1820's had taken the form of an attack upon slavery. He was well aware of the hostility, but may not have seen its connection with the pro-slavery argument or the issue of white supremacy. He did see the psychological basis for terrorism by a minority, and granted that every great change went through such a period of control "because the existing state of things . . . is so interwoven with ancient associations . . . that [it] is easy to raise the hue and cry of heresy against every one who thinks different or doubts." Timidity, lack of concerted action, and fear of appearing in favor of the enemy could keep the majority quiet for a long time. "It was so in the two centuries preceding the reformation. But what a gush when once the dam was broken!"

Solemnly, the professor warned the South that everywhere else the progress of civilization had gradually modified slavery into serfdom and thence through various stages to freedom. The worst promoters of disorder were those who clung to what existed merely because it existed. If the South were to avoid violence it must allow discussion and undertake wise and gradual modification. "It is not the *North* that is against you," thundered Lieber, "It is mankind, it is the world, it is civilization, it is history, it is reason, it is God, that is against slavery." [37]

Had Professor Lieber published these letters, he could hardly have remained in South Carolina. He considered proclaiming his views regardless of consequences, and even hoped at times that he would be discharged over the slave issue since he could then leave the detested South with a clear conscience that he had not deliberately thrown away his livelihood. Nevertheless, caution overruled his emotions; he accepted the advice of his colleague, Professor Matthew J. Williams, a Unionist mathematics instructor, and withheld the first letter. The later set also remained bur-

[37] Draft letters to Calhoun, signed Tranquillas. On the relationship between the large planters and upland farmers, see W. B. Hesseltine, "Some New Aspects of the Pro-Slavery Argument," *Journal of Negro History*, XXI (1936), 1–14; K. M. Stampp, "The Southern Refutation of the Proslavery Argument," *North Carolina Historical Review*, XXI (1944), 35–45; and Stampp, "The Fate of the Southern Antislavery Movement," *Journal of Negro History*, XXVIII (1943), 10–22.

ied among his papers, a mute protest against the bellicose defenders of the slavery system.[38]

Yet these emphatic views, with which Sumner was familiar, for Lieber showed the letters to his Northern intimates, were not extreme enough to hold the abolitionist's respect. Perhaps this was because Sumner knew none of Lieber's private thoughts about slavery crept into his public life in South Carolina. Rather, there he was the slaveowning, antitariff German, not quite one of them, but beyond question a partisan of the Palmetto State. In the local newspapers he gloated over his aid in developing a new use for cotton—a most sinister one—in the early months of the Mexican War. He had read in a German periodical of the invention of guncotton, the basis for nitroglycerine, and had translated the details for Dr. Ellet, the chemistry professor. Ellet had not only duplicated the process but improved upon it for mass-production methods.[39]

Neither did Lieber write about slavery to Longfellow, who took all his political views intact from Sumner. Rather, in the winter of 1848, he stiffly criticized *Evangeline*. He disliked the hexameters and preferred to read the epic poem as metrical prose. He even objected to the section in which the sleeping Evangeline felt her lover pass; it was supernatural and out of place.[40]

Lieber's criticism of the hexameters rather rankled Longfellow, who quipped that the German-American "thinks that because he made a great many bad ones when 'in prison in Köpnick' I cannot make any good ones when *not* in prison in Cambridge." The innumerable poems Lieber constantly sent for criticism were even more irritating. When Fanny Longfellow referred to the "Ship Canal" as the epithalamium on the marriage of two oceans, Lieber's enthusiastic response had been to open the floodgates of

[38] Lieber to Matilda Lieber, September 18, 1847. See Williams to Lieber, undated, together with note by Lieber, July 24, 1849, stating that he never published the letter drafted in 1846, in Lieber papers. Perry (ed.), *Lieber,* 228, creates the impression that the Tranquillas letters were printed, but the present writer has found no evidence that Lieber ever published any of them. However, he did show them to friends in the North.

[39] Lieber, "Dr. Lieber's Article—Gun Cotton.—Dr. Ellet's Recent Experiments," Columbia *Palmetto-State Banner,* November 24, 1846.

[40] Lieber to Hillard, April 3, July 9, 1849; Lieber to Fanny Longfellow, February 27, 1848, Lieber papers; Lieber to Longfellow, February 6, 1848, Longfellow House.

verse. Manfully Longfellow swam through the torrent and even jotted in his journal that he liked one Lieber had written upon the departure of Oscar for Freiburg, "because he dipped his pen in his heart instead of his brain." [41]

Longfellow had repaid Lieber's caustic criticisms with compliments, both to him and to mutual friends, but finally even his kindly and gentle nature could stand no more. He fumed to Hillard abroad: "Since your departure *Lieber* has singled me out as his victim. He has taken to the indicting of English verse, and sends me great quantities, not *asking*, (he never asks) but demanding my candid opinion, and criticism in detail. His letters are like the second chapter in Gil Blas;—an old soldier, a lamentable voice, two cross-sticks and a blunderbuss! He has already sent me six poems in three months! . . . I like Lieber very much—as you know; but I cannot undergo what you and Sumner have undergone." [42]

Longfellow quickly regained his good humor and took a generous tone when he wrote to the scholar praising the verse. As tactfully as possible, he tried to stem "the great paper avalanche" by inviting Lieber to visit that summer so Longfellow could give him detailed personal criticism. [43]

Even before Longfellow wrote his reply, Lieber had switched his attention sharply from sentimental verse to the rapid succession of revolutionary fulminations in Europe. Louis Philippe had lost his throne, and all the Germanic states seemed about to overthrow absolutism. "What glorious tidings from Europe!" Longfellow rejoiced. "Where are the dreams of your youth, O Götz von Berlichingen! that your heart does not rejoice more in this heaving off those old nightmares called 'monarchical institutions'! I for one say with all my heart,

[41] Longfellow to Sumner, October 1847, Longfellow House. Longfellow Journal, [February] 15, [1848], Longfellow House.

[42] Longfellow to [Hillard, about April, 1848], New York Public Library, photostat in Longfellow House.

[43] With more sentimentality than critical acumen, Longfellow wrote Lieber in this same letter that the verses on Oscar's departure were "a very tender, beautiful poem; and I cannot read it without my heart swelling into my throat, and tears coming into my eyes. I do not know that I ever saw a parting scene so truly and touchingly described." Longfellow to Lieber, April 8, 1848, Lieber papers.
At some time in this period, Longfellow translated one of Lieber's poems, "To a

Sweet Phosphor! bring the day!
Light will repay
The wrongs of Night;
Sweet Phosphor! bring the day!" [44]

Indeed, when news came of the uprisings in Germany, Lieber's heart did fill to overflowing. He so choked with joy upon hearing the news that he wept in the classroom. Speechless, he waved out the students, who stopped only to give a cheer for good old Germany. Earlier, the French overthrow of Louis Philippe, the bourgeois king, had inspired him only with trepidation. It was "Blowing a King out of a Kingdom as we are apt to blow a down from our sleeve." A French republic was an impossible anomaly. To be sure, for some years the French might have a kingless government, but not a republic, since that required the democratic institutions which France lacked. The very manner in which the city of Paris

---

mocking bird who just sang perhaps his last song before my window in Columbia. For Oscar. November 15, 1849." [Copy.]

Du süsser Vogel, singe mir	Sweet bird, sing unto me once more
Noch einmal deine Weise,	Once more thy carol sprightly;
Vermisst du unsern lieben Freund,	Say, dost thou miss our darling friend
Und singst darum so leise?	And therefore sing so lightly?
O könntest du zu ihm dich schnell	O would that thou couldst fly to him
Von deinem Zweige schwingen	Swift from thy bough up-springing
Und ihm des Vaters Herzengruss	The greeting of a father's heart
Voll treuer Liebe bringen!	Full of affection bringing.
Doch zwischen uns wallt auf und ab	Alas! between us rolls a sea
Ein Meer mit weiten Wogen	With ceaseless undulations;
Das hat auch unser grosser Aar	A sea, that never eagle yet
Noch nimmer überflogen.	Hath crossed in his migrations.
Kann sich der grosse Aar auch nicht	But though the eagle has not power
So weit und fernhim wagen	To cross such vast dominions
Kann weiter doch der Liebe Flug	The flight of love can wing its way
Als alle Schwingen tragen.	Beyond the flight of pinions.
Zu dir, au dir, mein Knabe süss	To thee, to thee, my gentle boy
Wär auch das Meir viel breiter	Though wider were the ocean,
Zu dir fliegt meine Liebe stets,	To thee my love flies evermore
Und wohntest du viel weiter!	With ever fond devotion.
Zu dir, wo du auch immer seist	To thee, wherever thou mayst be
Strebt sie mit stetem Triebe	It strives with constant yearning;
Gott segne dich geliebtes Kind	God bless thee, my beloved boy
Und gieb uns Lieb für Liebe.	My love with thine returning.

[44] Longfellow to Lieber, April 8, 1848, Lieber papers.

could so quickly effect a revolution and persuade the rest of the nation to accept it was an important indication.[45]

Germany too lacked democratic institutions, but in his first enthusiasm the professor envisaged better things for her. The distant but ultimate result would be "a brighter sky and healthier air. . . . Much blood, much violence, much woe must be gone through." He could only hope against hope that his own son would not be a casualty of that violence, for Oscar had hastened to Berlin, and by coincidence, on his father's birthday had participated in fighting along Breite Strasse, the very street where Lieber had been born.[46]

Lieber prayed anxiously for the safety of his son and the consummation of a German nation. He hoped against hope that events would sweep out the thirty-three petty German states and leave one government "equal to her great destiny, whether monarchical or republican."

"All this fearful struggle will last a long time, and be bitter indeed, and a thousand rending follies must run their race," Lieber realized, but nevertheless confessed his excitement: "In all this foaming and boiling, I cannot remain here. I must see with my own eyes. Possibly I may be of good use there with my experience and study of republicanism of near a quarter of a century, possibly I may be of no use at all, for I may find the sea lashed by very tempests." He disliked waiting for vacation, but did not quite dare "cut the cable" at South Carolina for fear he would find no future for himself in Germany.[47]

More like a tourist than a warrior, the professor sailed from New York toward the end of June, taking with him specimens of dried river mud for a German savant and a large American flag presented to him by the ladies in the Ruggles family.[48]

Even before he reached Germany, all of Lieber's soaring dreams had died. In England he read with deep dismay that the Parliament at Frankfurt had toadied to Austria by electing the Arch-

[45] Lieber to Sparks, March, 1848, Harvard University; Lieber to Hillard, November 9, 1848.
[46] Matilda Lieber to Fanny Longfellow, May 5, 1848.
[47] Lieber to Sumner, [April 21], 1848; Lieber to Howe, April 8, 1848; Perry (ed.), *Lieber*, 213–14.
[48] Lieber to Ruggles, May 15, 1848, Library of Congress; Lieber to Matilda Lieber, June 20, 29, 1848.

duke John Vicar-general. He felt so low and disgusted and poor that he wished he had his passage money back. Sick at heart, he arrived at the home of his sisters-in-law near Hamburg to find that if only he had arrived sooner he easily could have been elected to the national assembly.[49]

The unpreparedness of the German people to participate in governmental activities appalled Lieber, now so used to American ways. "Of the utter and almost absolute want of all political culture here you can have no idea," he snorted. "They don't even understand here the first a.b.c. This is the consequence of that miserable bureaucratic principle." The only lighthearted phase of the trip was his visit with Oscar at Göttingen, where he went sight-seeing, talked, and ate a fine venison dinner. Unfortunately, the beer gave "Papa" a headache.[50]

German politics gave Lieber an even worse headache. There was only one exception: a visit to old Hitzig, whose home he had frequented when he was a young blood in Berlin. Now palsied on one side, blind in one eye, "this wreck of a man said to me, his tears streaming down, so that his very spectacles were bedewed with tears, 'Yes my dear Lieber, we are going yet to have a great time.' "

Knoblauch and all those younger men who had won their positions under absolutism wailed and condemned the revolution. Lieber brushed them aside and went to Potsdam to see Humboldt, who was quite ill and confined to his bed. While Lieber was on the stairs, the King came, and to the professor's relief, was too nearsighted to recognize him. "I was glad," Lieber exclaimed, "for it would have been painful to me to talk with him on late affairs. I pity him from my soul." [51]

Then Lieber plunged into the welter of politics at Frankfurt. The situation was very complex. He could not foresee unification without an exclusively national army and handling of foreign affairs; the assembly must throw the princes overboard. A majority of the people seemed to oppose this, and the Landwehr, both

[49] Lieber to Matilda Lieber, July 4, 12, 1848.

[50] Lieber to Matilda Lieber, July 2, 12, 1848; Oscar Lieber to Matilda Lieber, July 2, 1848.

[51] Lieber to Matilda Lieber, July 24, 1848.

army and militia, had torn down the German cockade and replaced it with an even larger Prussian one.

For the time being, Lieber reported: "The Princes are quite down, and if there were a man among them, bold and grasping their Time as Cromwell, Napoleon or Frederic the Second did theirs, the play would be easy, but such a man does not exist." The confused assembly was drifting toward French radicalism, he lamented. It regarded England and America as insufficiently democratic, so was adopting untried Gallic regulations rather than the well-tested English or American ones. It made no great difference; Lieber did not think even the Anglo-American laws would work since "they presuppose a people well skilled, trained and formed in the politics of liberty."

Frankfurt was filled with old acquaintances, fellow students, and fellow prisoners. Even *Turnvater* Jahn was there, but Lieber found few who agreed with him politically. The extreme left were of a younger generation and wanted French liberty. Those of the right and right center looked down on Lieber as having lived too long in a republic. Indeed, Lieber did feel strangely a foreigner in his native land. He was clumsy with the German idiom and realized he would need time and practice before he could make speeches in his mother tongue. "You cannot conceive how I long for you and America," he confessed to Matilda, "for to you belongs my heart, to America my soul."

Rather cynically Lieber watched a tangible German government slowly materialize. It lacked a constitution, so its relationship to the single German states was not defined, and when it would be defined, "then the difficulty will only begin." Nevertheless, Lieber hoped for some good from the government for himself. A brother of his New York friend Heckscher had gained the portfolio of foreign affairs; Lieber keenly regretted that he was not a member of the assembly, since then surely Heckscher could have appointed him the first German minister to the United States.[52]

[52] Lieber to Matilda Lieber, August 8, 1848. Lieber commented: "I will give you an instance of the enormous ignorance in state affairs here, with reference to the U.S. A member of the cabinet talked with me of the importance of a close intercourse between Germ. and the U.S. Yes, said he, we want an alliance of offence and defence with the U.S. e.g. now we would ask them to bombard Copenhagen for us! This beats everything!"

Instead, he persuaded the Minister of Foreign Affairs to propose him to the cabinet as a special emissary to the President of the United States to inform him of the change of government in Germany. The cabinet was divided on the nomination. Soon Lieber saw that the assembly was interrogating it sharply, realized that the cabinet would have to choose an assembly member in order to maintain its prestige. He began packing his bags. The appointment went as he had expected, and he left for home.

As Lieber departed, he saw clearly that he had come too late to be a part of the fabric of the new government, and that he belonged to neither of the two main contending factions. "I must consider my life as closed," he sadly concluded, "that is to say, I cannot join in here, and must content myself with earning my modest livelihood." [53]

As for Germany, Lieber could see that the princes would not yield, but in the face of an impotent, wrangling parliament, would coalesce against the people to regain their shaken powers. "I take with me the clear conviction, that Germany cannot be great, strong or happy with her many princes," he predicted to Mittermaier from aboard ship, gazing for the last time at German shores. "She could be a great country if united under one government; . . . the many sovereigns will be abolished . . . and the sooner this is done the better it will be." At the end of the following year, Mittermaier sadly admitted that all Lieber's predictions as to the fate of the national assembly and the revolution had been right.[54]

The year 1849 was heart-rending for Lieber. The revolutionary movements gradually fizzled out, but not without stiff street fighting. Eighteen-year-old Oscar fought for three or four days on the barricades of Dresden. "He always stepped forward when volunteers were called out; he defended a rickety barricade against pouring attacks; he served . . . the cannons. His coat was rid-

[53] Lieber to Matilda Lieber, August 30, 1848.

[54] Lieber to Mittermaier, September 15, 1848 (translated copy); Mittermaier to Lieber, December 5, 1849. For a definitive account of the revolution, see Veit Valentin, *Geschichte der deutschen revolution von 1848–49*, 2 vols. (Berlin, 1930–31), in abridged translation as *1848 : Chapters of German History* (London, 1940).

dled; his powder flask perforated; the hat shot into, but God has protected the ardent lad." [55]

For many months a cloud hung over Lieber's mind and he thought of his career as nipped and closed. "My life *is* done," he continued to mourn. "I know I was made to act, to do something for my native country . . . yet I *can* do nothing. . . . I have no hold in the North, no hope to be removed. My name is worth nothing in the Northern market." [56]

He was upset also because he heard that Sumner was growing steadily more violent. Hillard had moved out of the office he had shared with his old friend because it was "such a place of rendezvous for abolitionists, free soilists and all other *ists,* that it was quite impossible to think of doing any business there."

Lieber did not write to Sumner for more than a year. Then he sent a single sheet, undated, unaddressed, without beginning, end, or explanation—telling of Oscar's fighting and simply initialed "F.L." [57]

Aggrieved, Sumner wrote to find out in what way he had offended, for Lieber had written to all their mutual friends, but had not so much as acknowledged the publications Sumner had sent. He pointed out to Lieber how assiduously he had continued to labor for a Northern opening. [58]

The disappointed German-American was gradually becoming himself again. From the beginning of February, 1849, he acted as president of South Carolina College during the illness and absence of William C. Preston. He carried out the duties successfully, enjoyed the increased prestige, and naturally hoped that the position might become permanent. This was not to be, for in 1851 James H. Thornwell, the strongly Calvinistic professor who for ten years had been Lieber's closest neighbor on the campus, left the pulpit he had briefly occupied, to return as president. [59]

Meanwhile Lieber, still acting president, went northward with

---

[55] Lieber to Sumner, [July, 1849]; Lieber to Hillard, June 24, 1849.
[56] Lieber to Hillard, April 3, 1849.
[57] Hillard to Lieber, December 5, 1848; Lieber to Sumner, [July, 1849].
[58] Sumner to Lieber, July 17, 1849.
[59] Lieber to Hillard, June 24, 1849, Lieber papers; Q. D. Blanding to Lieber, December 4, 1851, University of South Carolina.

his family in the summer of 1849. When the Liebers visited the Longfellows at Cambridge in the early autumn, Sumner came to dinner, and the gulf between the two old friends was only too painfully apparent. "We had a vigorous discussion of Slavery," Longfellow noted.[60]

Vigorous it was indeed—so vigorous that for years its memory stung in the minds of both disputants. The quarrel had developed over slave atrocities. Lieber maintained that the plantation Negroes were better treated than those in the West Indies. "I said . . . that as to physical treatment the slaves were upon the whole well off in the South, and that the general feeling of humanity toward the blacks in the South makes slavery additionally burthensome to the master, inasmuch as in most cases the owner has very little control over house slaves." [61]

Sumner refused to forget the argument, and with tenacity for months and even years strove to prove his point by culling through abolitionist papers for slave atrocity stories with which to plague the sensitive Southern professor. At the time when the Compromise of 1850 hung in the balance, Lieber protested bitterly: "Does not that unfortunate institution surround me with all its worrying adhesions night and day, day and night, without friends taking my finger and putting it on this and that unpleasant thing?" Worse still, Charles's incendiary papers which he mailed to the Southern professor attacked the proposed Compromise and even the very structure of the Union.[62]

Sumner shared the journals' frightening views. He informed Lieber in August, 1850: "Good men here rejoice in the defeat of that Clay & Foote patchwork. We are determined to push our cause, & establish the *policy of freedom,* instead of the *policy of Slavery,* which has controlled for years the Nat. Govt. On this there will be no flinching: cry, bully & brag, though the slaveholders may." Lieber frankly informed Sumner that he deeply regretted this bellicose spirit—and he was equally upset over the militancy of the secessionist fire-eaters of South Carolina.[63]

[60] Longfellow Journal, [September] 14, [1849], Longfellow House.
[61] Lieber to Hillard, April 6, 1850, Lieber to Sumner, draft, May 2, 1853; Lieber to Dorothea Dix, April 18, 1858.
[62] Lieber to Hillard, February 24, 1850.
[63] Sumner to Lieber, August 3, 1850, Harvard University; Lieber to Sumner, August 26, 1850.

Longfellow had reported in the late fall of 1849: "Sumner and Hillard are well; working in separate shafts of the dark dirty political coal mine." Lieber could feel no such detachment as this might imply. Rather, he agreed with Sumner's estranged friend, Professor Felton: "A great insane hospital is the only fit place for Toombs & co., and in an adjoining apartment should be shut up Charles Sumner . . . Philips and the other partners in this philanthropic concern." [64]

As North and South battled over whether California should be admitted as a free state, Lieber's one fervent desire was to preserve the Union. The tragedy of the Frankfurt failure had only heightened his fervor. He disliked slavery, but would rather accept it than see his adopted country "suffer nearly all the misery and disgrace under which Germany has staggered for centuries." He analyzed his position for Webster: "I find that I feel far deeper upon this subject of the Union than very many of the native citizens, perhaps *because* I am not a native American, and therefor naturally and necessarily a *Pan-American,* and because I am a native German, who knows by heart the commentary which his country has furnished and is furnishing for the text of querulous, angry, self-seeking, unpatriotic confederacies." [65]

In the summer of 1850, the Union still seemed to hang in the balance, and Lieber went to hot, dusty, tired Washington, where the congressional leaders debated on and on, trying to work out a compromise. Never before had the capital seen such an array of political leaders—those who had dominated for the past three decades and more were still active, while the men who would loom great in a new era pressed hard on their heels. Lieber seemed to know them all. He dined with Webster, saw Clay repeatedly, and hobnobbed with Justice Benjamin Curtis, who a few years hence was to hand down a dissenting opinion in the Dred Scott decision.

"Yesterday I dined at Benton's where I met Mr. Seward," he noted. Jessie Benton Frémont, the Missouri senator's daughter, was extremely cordial. The ambitious wife of an adventurer whose aspirations exceeded his talent, like Justice McLean she miscalculated Lieber's potency with the German voters. Frémont was

[64] Longfellow to Lieber, November 18, 1849; Felton to Lieber, May 6, 1850.
[65] Lieber to Webster, June 6, 1850, Webster papers, Library of Congress.

also friendly, and made fine promises of a career in the West to Lieber's geologist son, Oscar. Though Oscar waited hopefully an entire winter, Frémont failed to make good his offer.

With Matthew Fontaine Maury, the great oceanographer and "an excellent unpresuming man," Lieber went picnicking to the falls of the Potomac. "Genl Scott, the other day, received me most kindly and respectfully, when Mr. Seaton . . . introduced me," he recorded. "I have become much acquainted with Senator Foote. . . . He has taken a great fancy to me, asks my opinion on a thousand points, seizes upon arguments and says 'I must make use of this.' " Foote obtained a permanent seat on the floor of the Senate for Lieber, where the scholar carefully followed the debates.[66]

Compromise seemed nearer fruition when suddenly President Taylor died, elevating to the presidency Millard Fillmore, whose name Lieber could not even spell correctly. The professor called upon the new President, who said he was ashamed Lieber had thought it necessary to bring a letter of introduction, as though he were not thoroughly acquainted with Lieber's name.

Lieber cautiously appraised the situation: "Matters stand bad here. Still I donot by any means believe the Union is in immediate danger, but what I fear is that there is so much shaking and pulling at the old post, that it will get looser and looser like an old tooth, [so] that ultimately it may become impossible for any dentist to fasten the grinder again." [67]

Despite Toombs, Sumner, and company, the Congressional dentists did save the molar, but the compromise by no means ended agitation in the Palmetto State. There hotheads agitated for secession with or without the rest of the South. Radicals in the state legislature pushed through a call for a Southern congress to be followed by a South Carolina state-rights convention.[68]

During the campaign for delegates to the state convention, the fidgety Lieber through the insistence of his friends remained

[66] Lieber to Matilda Lieber, July 10, 30, August 2, 9, 1850.
[67] Ibid.; Lieber to Ruggles, September 9, 1850, Library of Congress.
[68] Philip M. Hamer, The Secession Movement in South Carolina, 1847–52 (Philadelphia, 1918); Melvin J. White, The Secession Movement in the United States, 1847–52 (New Orleans, 1910).

a silent onlooker. It was just as well, for the small vote had shown that South Carolinians were ready to wait until the rest of the South would secede with them.

This apathy frightened Lieber, who appraised the situation for Daniel Webster: "To be passive when boys fire crackers near a powder magazine shows an amazing callousness, which in politics always means the game may be taken in hand by a few trading politicians and a number of reckless editors. . . . I find now tens and even hundreds who frankly say that separate state secession would be folly, for one a few months ago. Almost everyone is for Southern Separation, but we must be thankful for small favours. State Secession once given up, and we are safe, whatever amount remains on the score of morality and duty."

The state's stanchest Unionist, James L. Petigru, regarded the light vote as a sign of returning sense, and commended the professor for having kept out of the contest. The realistic Petigru, who was no foe of slavery, saw in secession a threat to the social structure of the South. After separation the slave agitation would have to begin all over again in the Southern Confederacy. "The rights of the slave-holder are now sustained with unanimity at home; because it is a constitutional right, and as between us and the north, every man whether slave-holder or not feels that his own rights are at stake: but after a separation the interests of the free labourer would clash with those of the Masters of the Slaves. But people see nothing of this nor a thousand things that lie on the surface of disunion." [69]

Lieber had already seen this issue clearly. A year earlier he had commented: "If the Union breaks up, mark me, . . . the old process will begin again—an antislavery party will rise in Virginia, and spread to N. Carolina." During the campaigning for a second election, he realistically played upon the antagonism between the Piedmont and low country. This election, scheduled for October, 1851, was to elect delegates to a Southern convention. Once again, only "co-operators"—those who wished to wait for the remainder

[69] Lieber to Webster, February 13, 1851, Webster papers, Library of Congress; Petigru to Lieber, February 11, 1851, Lieber papers; Lieber to Benjamin Franklin Perry, February 15, 1851, Alabama Archives. The present writer is indebted to Dr. Lillian A. Kibler, for calling his attention to Lieber's letters to Perry.

of the South—stood opposed to the advocates of immediate secession.[70]

The first battle of the campaign came on the South Carolina College campus. Egged on by DeSaussure, one of the trustees, some students led by young Calhoun sought to form a Southern Rights Association. Others opposed the step and asked "a professor" to draw up a set of denunciatory resolutions for them. This Lieber did, and it was the only part, he claimed, that any faculty member played in the affair. At a grand meeting the student body voted down the resolutions as tending to censure the University of Virginia students who had called upon them to form an association. Nevertheless, those opposed to the association triumphed by pushing through a set of resolutions declining to join because they were not yet citizens and therefore should not meddle in politics. Thus, crowed Lieber, the matter was "as dead as a horse." [71]

The Unionist professor celebrated too soon. The townspeople were irate with him for his role in blocking the secession organization. While his friends pointed to his complete silence, his enemies retorted that the Southern Rights Association had failed due to his indirect influence on the students as a teacher of Unionist heresies. Not until many years later did Lieber find out how close he had come to having his home raided by a mob of angry townsmen and students.[72]

Within three weeks after the initial failure, the firebrands brought sufficient pressure to bear to win. One hundred and ten students, practically the entire student body, formed a Southern Rights Association and drew up as incendiary a set of resolutions as the most determined secessionist could desire.[73]

Regardless of the risk, the dogged Lieber stayed in the fight. At Greenville in the Piedmont, Benjamin Franklin Perry, as uncompromising a Unionist as Petigru, founded in mid-February of 1851 the *Tri-Weekly Southern Patriot,* the only Unionist paper in

[70] Lieber to Hillard, December 29, 1849.

[71] Lieber to Perry, February 15, 1851, Alabama Archives.

[72] "Only a week ago a person wrote me from S. Carolina, that he quelled a rising and projected mobbing me and my family by the students and others at that time, and later," Lieber to Garfield, March 12, 1869, Garfield papers, Library of Congress.

[73] *The Address of the Southern Rights Association of the South Carolina College, to the Students in the Colleges, Universities and to the Young Men, throughout the Southern States* . . . (Columbia, 1851), 16 pp. The address is dated March 6, 1851.

all South Carolina. Perry had been a member of the state legislature, and through his interest in penological affairs had met Lieber. As soon as he founded the paper, he began to receive a steady flow of contributions from the scholar.

Trying hard to be discreet, Lieber sent his contributions under the pen name "Suburanus." He did not question the issue of slavery, but instead with an abundance of facts, statistics, and clever arguments, pointed out the stupidity, futility, and ridiculousness of a separate Republic of South Carolina tied to the skirts of England or France. Astutely Lieber carried "state rights" arguments one step farther to play one section of the state against the other. He warned that "despotic centralization" was as great a menace within the state as within the Union, and invoked up-country passions against secession by labeling it a trick of the politically dominant Charlestonians.[74]

While lending his pen to try to keep South Carolina in the Union, Lieber was writing to his friends in Massachusetts that he wished he had sufficient influence to keep Charles Sumner out of the Senate. Sumner, with his splendid oratory and infectious enthusiasm, had become the darling of the free-soilers. Through a political coalition they elevated him to a six-year seat in the Senate.

Lieber shuddered at the news, and asserted: "I consider it bad for Sumner, for Boston, for your state, for Congress, for the Union, for the country. I detest this whole buseness [sic], and really think that if people must have slaves it is their affair to keep them." Sumner and his cohorts were "Fifth Monarchy" men and "Jacobins" of a brand of fanaticism which followed one principle blindly and ignored another equally important. This "has never gained the ultimate victory though often a battle, and has never sown, planted, gathered, blessed, but always destroyed, embittered, ruined and cursed." [75]

[74] Lieber to Perry, February 18, March 2, April 19, June 1, 1851, Alabama Archives. See Lillian A. Kibler, *Benjamin F. Perry, South Carolina Unionist* (Durham, N.C., 1946). Among Lieber's articles were: "Some Questions on Secession Answered, The Strength of Armies & Navies etc.," twenty-page draft in Lieber papers; "The Strictures on the Inequality of Representation . . ."; "Patriotism"; and "Centralization," all in the Greenville (S.C.) *Tri-Weekly Southern Patriot,* undated clippings in Lieber papers.
[75] Lieber to Hillard, April 28, 1851.

To his former protégé (who had been busy all that spring trying to obtain Harvard's history chair for Lieber), the professor painfully wrote: "I cannot, and if worlds depend upon it, be a hypocrite. Yet, it is true, I donot rejoice at your election. Believe me, my old and dear friend, that I feel it very bitterly not to be able freely and fully to rejoice when for the first time 'one of the family' rises to high honours. But I cannot. . . . *My* feeling toward you has never altered since that day when Story brought us to-gether. . . .

"I believe I can say Secession is dead—at least dying; but I cannot say what labour and anxiety it has cost us, and will long cost us, often increased to a fearful degree by doings in other regions." [76]

It was bad enough to write thus to an old, beloved friend. The thought of facing him in Boston was unbearable; yet Lieber could not stand South Carolina summers. The solution came in a most tempting letter from Chevalier Bunsen urging Lieber to come to London and visit him while attending the great exhibition in the Crystal Palace. Lieber weakened and went, leaving behind him a final summing up of his Unionist stand for Perry to read at a Fourth of July celebration. Casting caution aside, he sent it under his own name. "Dont [*sic*] be frightened if people come and tell you how sorry they are that I have written it and that I must undoubtedly go," he counseled his wife. "They will not send me away so easily. To be sure my salary might not be voted in December. Well, then we go somewhere else and must see how we fight our way." [77]

In England, Lieber put slavery politics out of his mind. He talked over German affairs with Bunsen, who seemed completely out of sympathy with his home government's reactionary policies. He visited the Crystal Palace and prepared an account for home

[76] Lieber to Sumner, May 20, 1851.

[77] Lieber to Hillard, May 4, 1851; Lieber to Dorothea Dix, May 27, 1851; Lieber to Matilda Lieber, July 10, 1851. Lieber sailed from Boston and did see Sumner once. That same spring, Lieber wrote a public letter which, if he had signed his name, would have caused a much greater furore in South Carolina. In it he favored a college for Negroes in Liberia and ridiculed the idea that Negroes were incapable of higher education. Their intelligence level on the average, he believed, was below that of the average white—but as a scientific historian he rejected the idea of white supremacy. [Lieber], "Education in Liberia," Boston *Evening Journal,* June 6, 1851; Greenleaf to Lieber, April 26, 1851.

newspapers ridiculing the poor American exhibit. He even gazed upon Queen Victoria and her spouse, "Prince Albert, who by the way has become an overgrown, stout, fat, square-shouldered German, so that he and the queen, who is purple red and fat like an innkeeper's wife, donot represent royalty by very dignified terms."

Lieber also made a short visit to Paris, where he attended a session of the Institute, to which Tocqueville had secured his election. He discussed seriously with the French theorist the new regime of the upstart Louis Napoleon, and in September headed homeward. Upon his arrival he found that thanks to his Fourth of July message he had been far from neglected in his absence.[78]

Throughout the South, newspaper after newspaper published Lieber's remarks, and wherever they appeared, people read and pondered. Graphically he stressed the realities of separation as it existed in his fatherland, "that living, yet bleeding, ailing, writhing, humbled commentator of Disunion." He pointed the fallacy of the Southern dream that they could break up the Union and form a new confederacy with the ease and precision with which a glazier cuts glass. A country has never "broken up or can break up in peace, and without a struggle commensurate to its own magnitude; and when that vehement passion dashes down a noble mirror, no one can hope to gather a dozen well-framed looking-glasses from the ground."

Lieber's faith in legalism peeked out as he warned that the Constitution of the United States did not condone secession, nor could the constitution of a Southern Confederacy allow that much sovereignty to a constituent state. To secede necessitated revolution, and revolution meant war. Secession "must either kindle a general conflagration, or we must suffer single-handed the consequences of our rashness"—the economic weakness of a particularistic group of countries.[79]

<hr/>

[78] Lieber to Matilda Lieber, July 21, 28, August 15, 1851. For a fortnight of his sojourn, Lieber was quite ill. Before he went, he wrote "The London Exhibition," Washington *National Intelligencer,* July 3, 1851; his descriptions appeared in "The Crystal Palace," Columbia *South Carolinian,* and New York *Journal of Commerce,* 1851, clippings in Lieber papers.

[79] Lieber, "Address of Prof. Francis Lieber, Read to the Union Convention in Greenville . . . ," Greenville *Tri-Weekly Southern Patriot,* undated clipping in Lieber papers. The *National Intelligencer* reprinted the speech in entirety and, according to Oscar Lieber, so did many Southern papers. The Lieber papers contain a clipping

These were strong words, and upon his return to Columbia in October, 1851, Lieber wondered if the fire-eaters would win the election and demand his dismissal. He queried Perry: "Will they kick me out of the college?" I am prepared for it. Of course, the presidency is gone for ever, if indeed it was ever obtainable by one who was not born in the empire of S.C. . . . But what is all this, compared to the great struggle!" [80]

As election time neared, Lieber was in a precarious position since there was not even a Union ticket. His letter had "the doubly damnatory character that it is against single secession and un-qualifiedly for the Union." But the co-operators, willing to wait for the rest of the South, were victorious with an overwhelming two-thirds majority. Lieber felt his political sins whitewashed, and like the mathematics professor, the only other Unionist on the campus, he could have exclaimed, "Elections all glorious! I can scarcely keep myself down. I feel like making all sorts of noises and cutting all sorts of capers." [81]

---

of the address from a Tuscaloosa, Alabama, paper. In 1865 Lieber reprinted it as a propaganda pamphlet, *An Address on Secession, Delivered in South Carolina in the Year 1851* (New York, 1865), and it appeared in the *Independent* during the secession crisis. It is also in Lieber, *Miscellaneous Writings*, II, 125–36.

[80] Lieber to Perry, October 7, 1851, Alabama Archives; Lieber to Dorothea Dix, October 2, 1851.

[81] Williams to Lieber, October 16, 1851.

XII

Metamorphosis

I A M astonished that you even mentioned the apathy or dullness which prevents certain people here from acknowledging certain acts of yours," Lieber exclaimed in the late fall of 1851 to the New England humanitarian, Dorothea Dix, who was working valiantly for improvements in the prisons and insane asylums of South Carolina. The lack of interest, the disillusioned professor reminded her, was "a striking feature of S. Carolina—the effect of her eternal warfare with the general government, which absorbs her whole attention, and of her uninterrupted grumbling with all the world."

Sadly Lieber pointed to his own experience: "I have not yet been able to interest one solitary minister in the cause of prison discipline or penal law reform; what is our school system. I could mention a hundred things. We are lacking here all the joyful inspiriting of nationality, of the consciousness of belonging to a vast country and of the hearty good will to join the great chorus of our times and our peculiar era." [1]

Lieber's failure to distinguish himself in South Carolina as a prison reformer had been one of his continuing sorrows. He had decided rightfully in the 1830's that the state needed a new penal code and penitentiary system. Even the stanchest partisans of the Palmetto banner would at least grant this. Governor Pierce Butler in a message to the general assembly castigated the existing code as "a chaos of confusion unequal and frequently unintelligible." The code was more in keeping with Elizabethan than

---

[1] Lieber to Dorothea Dix, November 12, 1851, Lieber papers, Henry E. Huntington Library. All manuscripts referred to in this chapter, unless otherwise identified, are from this collection.

259

nineteenth-century standards, but the legislature ignored Butler's recommendations for revision.[2]

Governor Patrick Noble in 1839 requested Lieber to prepare a study on penitentiaries for the legislature. The penologist complied enthusiastically with an impassioned plea for the moderation of the antiquated, harsh, but unenforced laws. "Are we more blood-thirsty than others," he inquired. "Are our offenders, even the merest pilferers, so inveterate villains that they must be cut off at once?" Humanely, Lieber denounced hanging for petty crimes and the outmoded whipping, pillorying, and branding. In their place, the state should introduce a prison system on the Pennsylvania plan.[3]

The solitary system was very costly, and while Major B. F. Perry, the upcountry chairman of the legislative committee, liked Lieber's ideas, the overwhelming majority of the lawmakers had no desire to expend tax money on even the most inexpensive type of prison. They received the report with a listlessness as stifling as the heat of a South Carolina summer. Probably because of their apathy, Lieber dropped his plans for a comprehensive study of penology to follow the *Political Ethics*.[4]

During the forties South Carolina's apathy turned to profound distrust. What previously had failed in part because of indolence and even more through the unwillingness of the planter-legislators to tax themselves for the general welfare now was opposed far more vehemently as Northern humbuggery. Many of the Northern prison reformers, in common with Howe and Sumner, were anti-slavery men, and the South with alacrity bundled almost every reform into its violent repudiation of abolition.

Nevertheless, Lieber hoped Dorothea Dix could succeed where he and others had failed. "You donot excite the same opposition," he explained to her in 1846; "no one can suspect you of ambitious

[2] *American Jurist*, XX (1838), 236.

[3] Lieber to Fanny Appleton, November 10, 1839; Patrick Noble to Lieber, November 11, 1839. Lieber, *Letter to His Excellency Patrick Noble, Governor of South Carolina, on the Penitentiary System* (Printed by order of the Legislature, pp. numbered 35–62, Columbia, S.C., 1839), 28 pp., 36.

[4] Lieber to Ingersoll, January 13, [1838?], New York Public Library. Ultimately Lieber's and Perry's recommendations were accepted. W. M. Geer, "Francis Lieber at the South Carolina College," *The Proceedings of the South Carolina Historical Association*, 1943, 16. Kibler, *Perry*, 230–31.

party views and—you can dare more because people donot dare to refuse you many a thing which they would not feel ashamed refusing to any one of our sex." [5]

Lieber's optimism proved justified, for in the spring of 1851 Miss Dix prevailed upon the South Carolina legislature to approve a large expansion and reorganization of the state insane hospital in Columbia. During her sojourn she stayed with the Liebers, who gloried in the presence of this "wayfaring missionary of humanity." When she left to carry on her work elsewhere, Lieber sent her with a warm letter of introduction to Major Perry, and wrote Southern newspapers explaining and lauding her work in order to mitigate the cloud of anti-Northern feeling hampering her.[6]

The professor labored diligently with the board of regents to draft plans for a new South Carolina insane-hospital building. Still his work in the field of penology, which continued unabated, found acceptance only in the North and in England; it caused not a ripple within his own state. For Joseph Adshead, the leading British penologist, he prepared a strong rebuttal to Elizabeth Fry's questioning of the solitary-confinement system. For the New York Friends of Prison Discipline, of which he was a corresponding member, he gathered telling statistics, and wrote a powerful paper against the misuse by governors of their pardoning privilege. The New York legislature published it as a document; it reappeared in the Washington *National Intelligencer;* but not even sympathetic B. F. Perry could find room for it in his South Carolina newspaper.[7]

Save for his continued interest in care for the unfit, Lieber was himself becoming rabidly antireform and anti-"ism." He proclaimed that his "inmost aversion to all humbug, flammery, chicken-philanthropy, wishy-washy politics, and all that sort of thing," led him to despise both the "Sumner-Howe" abolitionists

[5] Lieber to Miss Dix, November 5, 1846, Harvard University.

[6] Lieber to Miss Dix, [March], April 24, 25, May 27, 1851; Miss Dix to Lieber, April 27, 1851; Lieber to Hillard, April 1, May, 1851, Lieber papers; Lieber to Perry, April 10, 11, 1851, Alabama Archives. See Helen E. Marshall, *Dorothea Dix, Forgotten Samaritan* (Chapel Hill, 1937).

[7] Lieber to Miss Dix, April 24, May 17, December [15], 1852, January 9, 25, about February, 1853. Lieber, "On Abuse of the Pardoning Power," *Civil Liberty* (3d ed.; Philadelphia, 1874), 431–50.

and those "dirty drunken vagabonds" of the South who proclaimed white supremacy.[8]

Lieber groused at the extension of prohibition to Massachusetts in 1852: "I [loathe] the coarse drinks and low American bar habits; I consider drinking a national calamity in the U.S., but I assure you that I should feel nettled and irritated under such a law. And what will men like Webster do? . . .

"Must sober, genial fellows give up the blessed glass of Margeaux with a bosom friend, or the pungent poetry of iced champaign with a lovely woman, because the low brutes could not keep their muzzle from the coarse poison? It is the fanaticism of the iconoclasts, the fury of the Shakers against love and marriage. And with what a bestial rush they [the drinkers] will return to the swill!" [9]

Even more vehemently, Lieber castigated the Latter Day Saints, those hard-working and deeply religious followers of Brigham Young who had dared digress from accepted custom by adopting polygamy. Proclaimed the publicist in *Putnam's Monthly,* "Mormonism, from its very beginning, has been encrusted with vulgarity, jugglery, license, and muddy materialism." Like the Reign of Terror and the vice and crime of the court of Louis XV, it made one ashamed to belong to the same race. The licentiousness of the Mormons, he concluded, should most certainly prevent Utah from attaining statehood.

In the course of his tirade, Lieber took a side-thrust at the Oneida Community which held even more unconventional views on marriage. The Oneidans quickly counterattacked with an article in their newspaper, *The Circular.* They scoffed at Lieber's denunciation of the Mormons: "There is evidence that something . . . equally distant from pure 'wedlock,' and considerably less respectable than polygamy, is tolerated among the plantation patriarchs. That a man should live silent in a slave-holding Community and raise his voice against Mormon morality . . . is certainly strange." This merely amused the scholar, who privately insisted that the Oneidans were "religio-prostitutionists." [10]

8 Lieber to Hillard, May 21, 1851.   9 Lieber to Hillard, June 5, 1852.
10 [Lieber], "The Mormons. Shall Utah be Admitted into the Union?" *Putnam's Monthly,* V (1855), 225–36; *The Circular,* IV (1855), 30. Lieber to Miss Dix, January 12, 1852; Timothy Jenkins to Lieber, March 23, 1852, Lieber papers. Lieber

The publicist plunged just as enthusiastically into public controversies outside the field of reform. With greater vigor and far more significance, he aired his disgust over the downfall of the conservative bourgeois government of France. When the Revolution of 1848 swept out King Louis Philippe, whom Lieber earlier had considered an ideal monarch, the scholar prepared an article sharply contrasting Anglican and Gallican liberty. Scornfully he wrote of the concentration of power which characterized the French. Their liberty rested in the government, not the people, and they sought to develop organizations, not individualism. While the British followed patterns of orderly evolution, the French drifted into eddies of stagnant institutionalism. All this came about because the French confused democratic absolutism with genuine civil liberty.[11]

From 1848 until his death, Lieber warred almost constantly upon the French. He felt all his worst expectations realized when Louis Napoleon rose to power. The new emperor achieved his position through a *coup d'état* followed by a plebiscite through which the French people overwhelmingly approved his seizure of power —or so the vote would indicate. Lieber was not so sure, and made a careful statistical analysis.

"We abstain from giving our opinion on the infamy of first breaking down a whole government by a brutal soldiery, and then forcing a nation to vote *yes* or *no* on the proposition which it pleases the chief of political brigands to propose," Lieber prefaced his findings. "A whole nation is unmuzzled just to cry out 'Oh, gag me, Saviour of my country,' " but in the gagging process, Lieber proved cleverly, the officials lied by their own figures.

The French claimed a vote of seven and a half million in favor of the *coup d'état* out of a total electorate of a mere eight and a half million. Only 372,000, or one out of every twenty-three or

---

to Ruggles, April 1, 1855, Lieber papers, Library of Congress. See Lieber, *Civil Liberty*, 99–100.

[11] Lieber, "Memorandum for Norman," September 1, 1859; Lieber, "Anglican and Gallican Liberty," Columbia *Telegraph*, June 7, 1848, reprinted in expanded form in Lieber, *Miscellaneous Writings*, II, 371–88. Lieber similarly contrasted the two forms of liberty by comparing Washington and Napoleon in an anonymous article, "Was Napoleon a Dictator," *Putnam's Monthly*, V (1855), 12–21, reprinted as *Washington and Napoleon. A Fragment* (New York, 1864), and in Lieber, *Miscellaneous Writings*, I, 413–41.

twenty-four, abstained from voting. On the basis of every known election statistic, Lieber pointed out, this miniscule percentage of abstainers was ridiculous. In American presidential polls, rarely more than half the electorate participated. In Algiers, in the same election, out of 68,000 voters, more than 50,000 abstained and a majority of the remainder voted against Napoleon III. The answer, said Lieber, was that the French had not bothered to manipulate the returns from North Africa. The American press widely copied Lieber's findings, and published numerous rebuttals to which Lieber energetically replied with new statistics and further examples to show from every conceivable basis the falsity of the high percentage of affirmative votes.[12]

Lieber went deeper still, and made perhaps the first thorough investigation of the voting habits of electorates. He not only gathered statistics on the percentages, but speculated into the reasons why some elections brought out more voters than others. At the same time, through the newspapers he continued his warfare on the "Democratic absolutism" of France.[13]

Surging emotional currents—partially caused by his hatred of French absolutism, but mainly by the constant pulling and tugging between New England and South Carolina going on within him—threw Lieber into a fit of depression. At the beginning of 1853 he was ill with what he termed "brain fever," and complained of feeling two egos within himself so separate and distinct that he could not tell which was truly he. This feeling soon faded, but he was left with an intense desire to put on paper, as a foil to the French and to all like them who would strip away governmental checks and balances, an explanation of the workings of Anglican

---

[12] Lieber, "The Late Vote in Favor of Louis Napoleon Bonaparte Proved to be a False One," Columbia *Daily State-Rights Republican,* February 17, 1852; "The 7,500,000 Votes in Favor of Louis Napoleon Bonaparte, Proved a Falsehood," *Republican,* February 20, 1852; "The Presidential Vote in France Once More," *Republican,* March 12, 1852; "Some More Election Statistics. France and Massachusetts," *Republican,* March 19, 1852; "Election Statistics, Or How People Make Use of their Right to Vote," *Republican,* April 6, 1852. These articles were widely copied. A typical rebuttal appeared in the Washington *Union,* March 4, 1852.

[13] Lieber published his survey of voting habits as an appendix to the *Civil Liberty,* 3d ed., 413–30. He wrote at least a dozen newspaper articles against the French government between 1848 and 1853, and a comparison of the 1853 and 1859 editions of the *Civil Liberty* shows that his anti-French bias heightened during the intervening years.

liberty. Probably, too, as a warning to those in both South and North who would welcome the breakup of the Union, he wished to delineate the true pattern and function of the federal system.[14]

Lieber's ideas crystallized, and he began with almost superhuman effort to put on paper his interpretation of the federal union. Day after day he wrote at top speed until midnight or later, then rose to deliver a six o'clock lecture before prayers and breakfast. Lieber wrote sadly: all about him were merely biding their time before setting to work deliberately to pull South Carolina from the Union. Not much more could be said for Sumner and his Northern friends. He wrote regularly only to Hillard, who remained steadfast in his old beliefs. With Longfellow he had too little heartfelt sympathy; Howe out of loyalty to Sumner had cut off all communication between his family and the Liebers. Sumner wrote only occasionally, and returned Lieber's Greenville letter on the Union without a word. By this act, and by Sumner's perorations in the Senate, Lieber deduced painfully that his old friend felt none too great a loyalty to the Union. That feeling sickened his heart but sped his pen.[15]

The Southern professor felt that Sumner's actions were intolerable—Sumner faced an audience as most men did a mirror, and sent Lieber paper after paper in which he had carefully marked passages most extravagantly laudatory to himself. To Lieber (who enjoyed comparing himself with Grotius and Montesquieu) such conceit was disgusting. Worse, Charles continued for a full three years to pelt Lieber with slave-atrocity stories. Sometimes the professor found the papers had been peeked into, and feared dire reprisals would follow. He did not even dare send letters addressed to Sumner through the Southern mails. Rather, he enclosed them in envelopes addressed to Miss Dix or other mutual friends. As a crowning insult, Sumner did not once send the Congressional documents for which the scholar incessantly asked.

By March, 1853, after a full three years, Lieber was thoroughly angry. "What does he mean keeping these papers flinging at me?"

[14] Lieber to Hillard, January 11, 1853.

[15] Lieber to Hillard, April 4, 1852; Lieber to Miss Dix, November 11, 1852; Lieber papers; Lieber to S. G. Howe, June 9, 1854; Lieber to Julia Ward Howe, September 27, 1855, No. 1917, Library of Congress.

he exclaimed with more heat than rhetoric. "Is it nothing to me that Fate has put me hither and that I spend my life with a smarting pain the whole day and year; have I made slavery?" Lieber sent Sumner a letter requesting him please to stop sending abolitionist materials. The doughty abolitionist retorted that Lieber had no reason to complain, for he had become an "apologist of slavery." Another interchange followed. It was no more satisfactory, so Lieber decided to end the correspondence. Sadly, he hoped Sumner would come to his senses and that a few years hence under happier conditions they could resume their friendship.[16]

Heartache or not, the hard-driving professor whipped his manuscript into shape, took it to Philadelphia in the summer of 1853, and, despite extreme heat, read proofs, emended, and saw his new book through the press of J. B. Lippincott and Company. He was highly satisfied with their work, and henceforth they were to serve as his publishers.[17]

The *Civil Liberty and Self-Government,* forged on the anvil of the most strident turmoil America had yet known, tempered in the bitter wisdom of one torn between Germany and America, South and North, came out straight and true. It was the masterwork of Lieber's maturity, when out of his own pain he came to perceive most clearly the political institutions of Europe and America. It was the product of his period of greatest lucidity, for he was no longer blinded by naïveté and inexperience, nor yet ready to

[16] Sumner was more sensitive than Lieber and apparently never discussed his side of the break with Lieber. The details of the last interchanges of correspondence are from the Lieber-Hillard letters, since the Sumner-Lieber letters both at Harvard University and the Huntington Library end with the year 1852. Lieber to Hillard, April 4, 1852, March 16, 1853, May, 1853; Hillard to Lieber, June 2, 1853; Lieber to Sumner, draft, May 2, 1853. Lieber to Dorothea Dix, April 18, 1858, contains a detailed account of Lieber's side of the quarrel. Reprinted in Perry (ed.), *Lieber,* 296–98, it brought a sharp retort from Edward Pierce in his biography of Sumner. Apparently the touchiness and ultimate break grew out of the long disassociation of the two men, rather than jealousy over Sumner's rise to "high distinction," as Pierce implies, *Memoir and Letters of Charles Sumner,* 4 vols. (Boston, 1877–93), III, 34. Lieber thought too well of himself to consider Sumner's position more exalted. In personality the two men were quite similar—in itself sufficient to make a quarrel likely under the circumstances. Both apparently would have gladly patched it over if they could have done so without loss of dignity. In 1854 Lieber noted with great pleasure that Sumner had called upon Matilda Lieber and been most affable; yet a few years later, at the sculptor Crawford's funeral, Lieber rushed up to Sumner only to receive so cold a greeting that the breach remained unmended until 1861.

[17] Lieber to Matilda Lieber, July 29, 1853.

compromise civil rights to obtain the great end of nationalism.[18] As America's leading political weekly, the *Nation,* pointed out in 1874, at the heyday of Lieber's influence, the publication of the *Civil Liberty* (and the *Political Ethics*) had "marked an era in the political literature of the United States." The only prior account at all exhaustive or scientific, said the *Nation,* was the *Federalist,* and it was based on classic examples not entirely valid for nineteenth-century America. Lieber had enunciated significant principles well beyond the ken of the ancients and the founding fathers, for he had based his study upon contemporary political systems. The scarcity of other treatises also helped lend this one an authoritative weight for many years.[19]

The *Nation*'s wholehearted endorsement of the *Civil Liberty* was symptomatic of the dilemma of Liberal Republicans in the post-Civil War period. The very constitutional limitations which they continued to laud as the means of blocking political aggrandizement led to an equally ominous hegemony of the industrial leaders. The *Civil Liberty* was a lengthy and elaborate paean for limited government: institutional self-government through federalism, checks and balances, separation of powers, limitations of the bill of rights, the common law, and the conservative guardianship of judicial review. Lieber fervently believed that thus and thus alone could a free citizenry avoid "democratic absolutism"—prevent the masses from tendering all power to a dictator.

---

[18] Lieber, *On Civil Liberty and Self-Government,* 2 vols. (Philadelphia, 1853). This was the best-selling of Lieber's three treatises on political theory. Richard Bentley published it in London in a single 552-page volume in 1853; Lippincott issued a single-volume enlarged edition of 629 pages in 1859 and reprinted it in 1869. After Lieber's death, Theodore D. Woolsey edited a third revised edition (Philadelphia, 1874), 622 pp. A London version of this appeared in 1877. The American edition was reprinted in 1875, 1877, 1880, 1881, 1883, 1890, and 1911. The last printing contained an introduction by President Nicholas Murray Butler of Columbia University. The son of Lieber's correspondent Mittermaier prepared a German translation, but because of its strong anti-French tone, found a publisher only with difficulty. An Italian edition also appeared. Lieber to Ruggles, not dated, Library of Congress; Lieber to Samuel Tyler, May 21, 1860; Franz M. Mittermaier to Lieber, March 9, 1861. An American promoter purchased and successfully distributed copies of both the *Political Ethics* and *Civil Liberty* in Argentina. Victor L. Johnson, "Edward A. Hopkins and the Development of Argentine Transportation and Communication," *Hispanic American Historical Review,* XXVI (1946), 33. Hereafter, unless otherwise indicated, all references are to the third edition and *Civil Liberty* is abbreviated *CL.*
[19] "Lieber's *Civil Liberty,*" *Nation,* XVIII (1874), 396–97.

Lieber based his diagnosis upon the plight of France writhing in the web of Napoleon III as contrasted with the free condition of wealthy, conservative England, which had easily sloughed off the menace of Chartism. He hinted, and only hinted, at dangers facing the United States, for basically he aligned it with prosperous, safe Great Britain. France had failed because she lacked the bulwark of guardian institutions. Their lack left the masses free to vote all power to Napoleon; Great Britain and the United States, blessed with safeguards, proceeded along the peaceful middle course of gradual, very gradual, evolution. All that remained was to delineate in detail these magnificent limiting institutions.

Lieber's *Civil Liberty* appeared a mere five years before Karl Marx's *Das Kapital*, yet almost no strident overtones of proletarian struggle or economic unbalance complicated Lieber's elementary diagnosis of European politics. Considering the utter simplicity of his formula, his prescience was remarkable. He warned against the menace of a professional noble military class as typified by the *Junkers* of Prussia. Alarmed at the extreme despotism in Russia, he predicted to a friend in 1851: "This will create ultimately a convulsive explosion and give for a time, fearful power to Communism, Socialism and all other sorts of French democratic absolutism." [20]

The smoke and murk of the embryo ironworks and the drabness of the houses around Pittsburgh had no greater significance for Lieber than to make him nostalgic for his beloved England; his economic concepts remained permanently anchored at the level of the *Essays on Property and Labour*. He could not see that the governmental limitations (with Hamiltonian digressions) that so well suited the relatively small merchant and manufacturer of the period in which he wrote were to prevent vital regulation in a new and complex age.[21]

The infant industries of America, nurtured on government protection, were to grow fat on the contracts of the Civil War and to emerge a formidable behemoth. They were to feel few restrictions, for the shackles on government which Lieber had glorified as serv-

[20] Lieber, *CL*, 118; Lieber to Hillard, March 11, 1851. Of course, Lieber's governmental program was that of the middle-class liberals, which could exist only where the middle-class controlled. He wrote only of the institutions, not the class.
[21] Lieber to Matilda Lieber, August 9, 1846.

ing to prevent a popular despotism functioned pre-eminently well to block the regulation which might quell the new industrial despotism. The tragedy was that liberal leaders of the postwar era so long paid homage to Lieber's dogma.

During the second Grant administration, the *Nation* warmly advocated the widespread study of the *Civil Liberty* as a high-school and college text. It would serve as a salutary remedy for positivism and other "political heresies which, under the garb of an advanced liberalism, are spreading in England and have begun to show themselves even in our own country—heresies which would destroy the very institutions that in all constitutional governments, have proved to be the only safeguards of civil liberty by being the only possible checks upon irresponsible power." [22]

"To my former pupils," Lieber inscribed the work, and indeed it was to them and their kind that he addressed his message—not to the common man, but to "the future law-makers of a vast and growing commonwealth." To them in a startling and dangerous age he gave counsel and warning.[23]

They should mark with profound gratitude their political blessings and beware of the pitfalls of Continental Europe. "We belong to the Anglican race, which carries Anglican principles and liberty over the globe, because wherever it moves, liberal institutions and a common law full of manly rights and instinct with the principle of an expansive life accompany it," Lieber declared with profound complacency. "We belong to that race whose obvious task it is, . . . to rear and spread civil liberty over vast regions in every part of the earth." [24]

Students might visit Continental Europe to study art, music, or science, but to learn liberty they would have to come to America or England. These two nations alone truly understood the concept. "There is an immense difference," he pointed out, "between admiring liberty as a philosophical speculation, loving her like an imaginary beauty by sonnet and madrigal, and uniting with her in real wedlock for better and for worse. Liberty is the loved wife and honored companion, through this earthly life, of every true

---

[22] *Nation*, XVIII (1874), 397.   [23] Lieber, *CL*, 1st edition, I, v.

[24] Lieber, *CL*, 21, 53. Lieber was unwilling to include the German people in his term "Anglican race."

American and Englishman, and no mistress for sentimental sport or the gratification of spasmodic passion, nor is she for them a misty nymph with whom a mortal falls in love, nor is she the antiquated portrait of an ancestor, looked upon with respect, perhaps even with factitious reverence, but without life-imparting actuality." [25]

How had Great Britain and the United States achieved this felicitous state? How had it come about, even though, in the United States especially, the franchise had become very broad? This it was important to answer, since historically the unchecked masses had aided the princes against the barons, and in modern times through universal suffrage they might vote all power to a dictator. "Uninstitutional universal suffrage," Lieber warned, would "turn the whole popular power and national sovereignty . . . into an executive, and thus fearfully . . . confound sovereignty with absolute power, absolutism with liberty.[26]

"Yet the idea of all government implies power, while that of liberty implies checks and protection. It is the necessary harmony between these two requisites of all public vitality and civil progress which constitutes the difficulty of establishing and maintaining liberty." [27]

The only solution—and here Lieber came to the crux of his theory—was "a well-grounded and ramified system of institutions, checking and modifying one another, strong and self-ruling, with a power limited by the very principle of self-government within each, yet all united and working toward one common end." Their "number supports the whole, as the many pillars support the rotunda of our capitol." These the United States and Great Britain possessed in abundance, and these gave vitality to their constitutions.[28]

What was an institution? Lieber laid down a careful definition. It was "a system or body of usages, laws, or regulations of extensive and recurring operation, containing within itself an organism by which it effects its own independent action, continuance, and generally its own farther development. Its object is to generate, effect, regulate, or sanction a succession of acts, transactions, or

25 *Ibid.*, 157, 295.   26 *Ibid.*, 357, 368–69.
27 *Ibid.*, 357.   28 *Ibid.*, 340, 359.

productions of a peculiar kind or class. The idea of an institution implies a degree of self-government. Laws act through human agents, and these are in the case of institutions, their officers or members . . . single laws or usages . . . are institutions, if their operation is of vital importance and vast scope, and if their continuance is in a high degree independent of any interfering power." [29]

Institutions to foster civil liberty were those which, applied to political man, protected against "undue interference, whether this be from individuals, from masses, or from government." Again: "The highest amount of liberty comes to signify the safest guarantees of undisturbed legitimate action and the most efficient checks against undue interference." [30]

The greater part of the *Civil Liberty* was a study of these institutional checks. In most of them Lieber saw only unalloyed good. He lavished praise upon the common law, not in the least doubting its capacity to keep apace of rapid economic changes, for it was "all the time expanding and improving." Judicial precedents were a corollary benefit. He asserted, "everything that is a progressive continuum requires the precedent." He pointed out to critics that courts could overrule, or legislatures enact laws, to invalidate bad precedents. As for judicial review, not even the Dred Scott decision was to alter his praise for that "very jewel of Anglican liberty, one of the best fruits of our political civilization." [31]

The Bill of Rights received a similar apotheosis, though Lieber made several assertions that were to embarrass him when the Civil War altered his ways of thinking: he opposed the soldier vote and denied emphatically the presidential right to suspend the writ of habeas corpus.[32]

Lieber did advocate a few moderate changes, notably, alteration of the unanimity principle in jury decisions. He granted that nothing was so convenient to despotism as the hulls of old institutions—for example, purportedly free elections in which all the ballots were marked "yes." "Hollow institutions in the state are

[29] *Ibid.*, 300; see 310.
[30] *Ibid.*, 34–40. For a more comprehensive definition of civil liberty, see 24–25.
[31] *Ibid.*, 164, 208–14. However, he tempered his praise during the Reconstruction period. See Ch. XVII.
[32] *Ibid.*, 108, 118.

much like empty boxes in an ill-managed house. They are sure to be filled with litter and rubbish, and to become nuisances." These, together with all institutions bad from the start, must be eradicated. Still, one should not abolish them thoughtlessly, for they might possess a preventive value. "Antiquity is prima facie evidence in favor of an institution." [33]

On the whole, Lieber viewed the system as it stood with deep affection. He stood in dread of revolutionary change. In his second edition he lashed out at Richard Hildreth and other moderate writers as "those who follow the French view, and who . . . strive above all for union of force"—which by remarkable logical progression would bring them to the support of a "democratic Caesar"! [34]

Change should come through gradual evolution within the institutions. This development frequently came about through internal clashes of interests or powers, which Lieber regarded as an unpleasant but salutary phenomenon. For all their revolutions, none of the Continental powers were achieving such constant and vast changes as the United States and England, "for the very reason that [the latter] are institutional governments . . . they move within their institutions." [35]

"Institutional self-government distinguishes itself above all others for tenacity and a formative, assimilative, and transmissable character." This was why England could stand the cataclysms of the Puritan revolution and the later Stuart period without losing its civil liberties, why the United States, unlike Latin America, could change presidents without bloodshed, and why the people of California and Oregon formed new governments almost identical to those of the older states. This should stand also as a check to keep a nation on the path leading to its greatest destiny, the "intensive improvement of its institutions." [36]

Without this balance, "a large and active nation, which therefore instinctively seeks a political field of action for its energy . . . generally turns its attention to conquest . . . the most debilitating fever of a nation and the rudest of glories. . . . The sword does not plough deep." [37]

Deficiencies in self-governing institutions did not excuse a na-

---

[33] *Ibid.*, 238, 317–18, 342.   [34] *Ibid.*, 213–14.   [35] *Ibid.*, 342.
[36] *Ibid.*, 329, 351.   [37] *Ibid.*, 351.

tion for lacking civil liberty. It should start building them, even though it must expect partial failures during the earlier stages. "Liberty may be planted where despotism has reigned," Lieber believed, "but it can be done only by much undoing, and breaking down; by a great deal of rough ploughing. We cannot prepare a people for liberty by centralized despotism, any more than we can prepare for light by destroying vision. Nowhere can liberty develop itself out of despotism. It can only chronologically follow the rule of absolutism; and if it does so, it must begin with eliminating its antagonistic government. Every return to concentrated despotism, therefore, creates an additional necessity of revolution, and throws an increased difficulty in the way of obtaining freedom." [38]

Lieber addressed almost all of his criticisms against the new French Empire, but obviously at many points he also had the South in mind. He pointedly denounced the fever of Manifest Destiny which gripped such a large part of the planter population, and assuredly was thinking of slavery when he wrote that any "institution unquestionably results in part from, and in turn promotes, respect for that which has been established or grown. This leads occasionally to a love of effete institutions, even to fanaticism." [39]

In arguing against the proverb *"Vox populi vox Dei,"* Lieber's reference was superficially to France, but he wrote of the tyranny of the majority over the minority with a fervor reminiscent of his unpublished letters on slavery: "To differ from the dominant party or the ruling majority appears almost like daring to contend with a deity, or a mysterious yet irrevocable destiny. To dissent is deemed to be malcontent; it seems more than rebellious, it seems traitorous; and this feeling becomes ultimately so general that it seizes the dissenting individuals themselves. They become ashamed, and mingle with the rest." [40]

In keeping with Southern patterns of thought, Lieber emphasized the necessity for local self-government. It should manage

[38] *Ibid.,* 335, 348.
[39] *Ibid.,* 340–41, 351. Lieber referred in a footnote, though not by name, to an ultraexpansionist pamphlet which had shocked him: [John M. Galt], *Political Essays* [1844], copy with comments by Lieber, University of California.
[40] *CL,* 408.

everything it could handle without general inconvenience, but should not obtain control over the whole federal system. "One of the dangers of a strongly institutional self-government," He warned, "is that the tendency of localizing may prevail over the equally necessary principle of union, and that thus a disintegrating sejunction may take place." As an example, he cited the Dutch Republic. He declared even more sternly that the local self-government "may impede measures of a general character," and that to seek liberty through giving a vetitive power over the whole to "each class or circle, interest or corporation, would simply amount to dismembering instead of constructing." Lieber referred to Poland, but clearly had in mind Calhoun's concurrent majorities.[41]

The moderate professor stood equally afraid of localization and centralization. The citizens must seek a balance, and the only salutary one was in the federal system provided by the Constitution. Lieber left no doubt of his nationalism: "We must have national states (not city-states); we must have national broadcast liberty (and not narrow chartered liberty)." The people could achieve this only through the proper frame of government. In addition to protecting the individual, a good constitution must define and delimit the powers of each branch of the government so that each could move harmoniously in its own orbit free from encroachment. The branches must all "work abreast, like the horses of the Grecian chariot, public opinion being the charioteer." This was Lieber's concept of the federal union.[42]

Lieber had not expressed himself fully upon some aspects with which he was deeply concerned. He had said nothing about slavery other than to point out the racial bars against the Negro in both South and North, and he reserved his belief that legally the Union was indissoluble. He was still a professor in a Southern college, and he did not wish to lose his position; after he moved to the North, he filled in these gaps with lectures and essays.

Meanwhile his silence upon the great issues, together with his long years in the South, seemed to make him suspect in the North.

41 *Ibid.,* 321, 337, 358–59. C. B. Robson, "Francis Lieber's Theories of Society, Government, and Liberty," 248–49.
42 *CL,* 337, 360–61.

At first the *Civil Liberty* made scarcely a ripple there. The pace-setting *North American Review* ignored it completely, and most Northern magazines gave it no more than a paragraph of brief and empty praise.[43]

The treatise began slowly to attract Northern attention. Lieber's friends were prolific in their compliments. Hillard compared it to *The Federalist* and the writings of Adams, Hamilton, and Jefferson, while Ruggles declared it was far ahead of Montesquieu and fully the equal of Tocqueville. George Ticknor Curtis praised the book warmly not only in conversation but also in a footnote to his constitutional history. It was introduced as a text at Yale, and seniors were asked on their final examinations, "Show what is defective in any four of the definitions objected to by Lieber," or "Characterize the French idea of liberty, as distinguished from the Anglican." Ultimately the work spread from the classroom to the pulpit; the elderly father of Professor Noah Porter preached a Fourth of July sermon in 1856 frankly based almost entirely upon the *Civil Liberty*.[44]

A few weeks later the president of Yale, Theodore Dwight Woolsey, who had never met Lieber, published a careful, analytical review of the *Civil Liberty* in the *New Englander*. He whole-heartedly accepted and endorsed Lieber's basic ideas and interpretations, but pointed to the obvious flaws of style and organization and noted numerous minor errors. This rankled the South Carolina scholar who wrote Woolsey's colleague Porter complainingly. Porter showed the letter to Woolsey, who at once apologized in such highly complimentary terms that Lieber, more than satisfied,

[43] Hillard, "Dr. Lieber's New ·Book," Boston *Daily Courier,* January 13, 1854. In typical, brief reviews, *Harper's New Monthly Magazine,* VII (1853), 860, declared, "It is a profound, elaborate, and comprehensive discussion of the subject, and needs a larger space to do justice to its merits than we can now command," and *Putnam's Monthly,* II (1853), 566, termed it "a profound and analytical inquiry. . . . Dr. Lieber is a warm friend of popular rights, grounding his attachment upon sincere and intelligent convictions."

[44] Hillard, "Dr. Lieber's New Book," *loc. cit.;* Ruggles to Lieber, November 17, 1853; Lieber to Allibone, April 29, November, 1856; Hillard to Lieber, September 24, 1856; "Biennial Examination Senior Class (No. 4) Yale College, May 31, 1855," and June 4, 1857, printed copies in Lieber papers. Noah Porter, *Civil Liberty, A Sermon Preached in Farmington, Connecticut, July 13, 1856* (New York, 1856) ; G. T. Curtis, *History of the Constitution* I, 488. Curtis lauded Lieber's "profound and admirable work." "Whoever will follow that very able writer in his masterly exposition of the principles of Anglican liberty, will become satisfied that the American branch of it is more strictly a system of 'self-government' than any other."

commented: "It is a kind, manly thing, and I trust he does not think me a thin-skinned fellow." [45]

Hillard reported that Woolsey was a superior man and an excellent Greek scholar. "He is rather hard, Calvinistic, New Englandish, angular, and unprepossessing in person and manner, but a strong, clear, learned, and true man." Woolsey was to become Lieber's close friend and ardent disciple. To Lieber he dedicated his *International Law* text; in his lectures and writings he spread Lieber's ideas; and upon the scholar's death, edited new editions of the *Political Ethics* and *Civil Liberty*.[46]

Lieber struck up a friendship with another ardent admirer, Samuel Tyler, a philosopher. In the *Princeton Review* for October, 1858, Tyler praised both Tocqueville and Lieber in the highest terms, but declared that of the two Lieber was by far the more profound political philosopher. He considered the *Civil Liberty* the most important contribution of the century to political science, and asserted, "There is not a political idea, much less a principle of political science propounded by DeTocqueville [in *The Old Regime*] which Lieber had not before announced in his 'Civil Liberty.' " [47]

This was heady praise, but Lieber had already reached a similar conclusion. Two years earlier, in 1852, he had informed his wife: "The other day I was asked whom I considered the greatest living political philosopher. I answered that if the question meant: who is the most statesmanlike, substantial, earnest, historical, faithful, and analysing, I could not easily distinguish between two, who seemed to me decidedly at the head, viz. de Tocqueville and Lieber. This was very cool, but it is the truth which makes it still cooler. My interrogant said: I had the answer in mind—Lieber." [48]

[45] Woolsey, "Lieber on Civil Liberty and Self-Government," *New Englander*, XIV (1856), 329–44. Lieber objected most strongly to Woolsey's misstatement that he had "made submission" to the proslavery element in South Carolina. Lieber to Allibone, October 9, 30, 1856, Lieber papers; Lieber to Ruggles, October 23, 1856, Library of Congress.

[46] Hillard to Lieber, October 30, 1856; Woolsey, *Introduction to the Study of International Law* . . . (2d ed.; New York, 1864), 3.

[47] [Tyler], *De Tocqueville and Lieber as Writers on Political Science from the Princeton Review for October, 1858* (n.n., n.d.), 7. See also the Lieber-Tyler correspondence in the Lieber papers.

[48] Lieber to Matilda Lieber, August 9, 1856. He wrote Allibone, the bibliographer,

To Lieber's deep satisfaction, lawyers began to dip into the *Civil Liberty* for legal arguments, and judges began to cite it in decisions. Jurists utilized his stanch defense of property rights and personal liberty in preparing their briefs against state prohibition laws. Lieber was delighted to find that the New York Supreme Court referred to him when it placed strictures upon their state law. Justice Samuel P. Douglass similarly used the *Civil Liberty* in a Michigan case. The New York decision was based on a violation of property rights; the Michigan one on the grounds that the state legislature had unconstitutionally delegated its authority by ordering a referendum. Lieber heartily approved the latter decision because "the reserving of the ultimate passage of a law for the approval of the people at large is a dangerous confusion of ideas which might easily have become general." [49]

Lieber's delight knew no bounds, when at a banquet, Horatio Seymour, the Democratic governor of New York, turned to him and remarked that he had dipped into the *Political Ethics* and *Civil Liberty* in preparing a message vetoing a prohibition law. "And Sir, continued Mr. Seymour [according to Lieber], the message has generally met with a very favourable reception. It is exclusively due to you." [50]

The impact of the *Civil Liberty* in England was quite the reverse of that in the North. It received immediate hearty and copious praise in the reviews, then sold so scantily that the publisher wished he had his money back. The British were far more aware of the French than the self-absorbed Americans. Nothing could have pleased them more than the vigorous manner in which Lieber truncheoned Napoleon III and lauded Anglican institutions.[51]

"Nothing can possibly conduce to such a mutual understanding"

October 19, 1856, "The two highest statesmanlike political philosophers . . . now living are De Tocqueville and Lieber." Again, "Perhaps I write more [in] a philosophical and historical spirit . . . than any of my predecessors, unless Aristotle be excepted, but the historical spirit could only show itself in him as a spirit of grasping reality." Lieber to Hillard, November 29, 1853.

[49] Lieber to Allibone, July 9, 1856; Samuel P. Douglass to Lieber, April 17, May 17, 1854, and clipping from Detroit *Free Press*, April 10, 1854, with comment by Lieber. New York *Times*, March 26, 27, 1856. The opinion of Judge Comstock as published in the *Times* did not mention Lieber. For other citations of Lieber in law cases, see *Williams* v. *the State*, 10 Ind. 503; *The State* v. *Dunning*, 9 Ind., 25.

[50] Lieber to Allibone, September 15, 1856.

[51] Bentley to Nicholas Trübner, December 8, 1853.

between Great Britain and America as "books and lectures like Dr. Lieber's," the London *Globe and Traveller* pronounced glowingly. They demonstrate "how much more the political institutions of England and the United States have in common, in source and substance—than distinct, in detail and superstructure." [52]

John Bull compared the *Civil Liberty* to Montesquieu's *Spirit of the Laws*, and asserted that "for closeness of coherence and perspecuity of argument [it] stands preeminent among works on political science." The *Athenaeum* termed it a thoroughly practical antidote for the many dangerous theories and disturbing doctrines then afloat.[53]

More critically, the *Westminster Review* hinted that "perhaps [Lieber's] interpretation of other nations and times is too much narrowed to his own Anglo-Saxon point of view." It pointed out his garrulity and lack of organization, and declared he lacked the divining philosophical power of Niebuhr—all of which Lieber contested hotly in private correspondence. On the other hand, the *Westminster Review* praised him warmly for his clearness and heartiness, sense of historical appreciation and intuitive soundness of political judgment.[54]

British scholars were quick to accept Lieber's institutional theories. Sir Edward Creasy, author of *Fifteen Decisive Battles of the World* and professor of history at the University of London, praised the *Civil Liberty* in a treatise on the English constitution. He wrote Lieber: "I have caught from it a leading idea of infinite importance for the course of Lectures on Ancient History, which I am now delivering at University College. It is this—Test the value of a particular nation's history and the amount of study that you should devote to it, by the degree of Institutional Energy which that nation has displayed." [55]

Only the London *Daily News* was unkind. It not only joked about Lieber's wordiness, but probed his sorest wound: "The most remarkable feature of Dr. Lieber's work is the omission, in

[52] London *Globe and Traveller*, November 7, 1853.
[53] *John Bull*, XXX (1853), 732; *Athenaeum*, June 29, 1839, Nos. 609, 483.
[54] *Westminster Review*, V (1854), 250–51; Lieber to Hillard, April 15, 1854.
[55] Creasy to Lieber, December 12, 1853; Lieber to Allibone, December 1, 1855; Sir Edward Creasy, *Rise and Progress of the English Constitution* (2d ed.; London, 1854), 40. Lieber wrote the preface for a German edition of Creasy's book.

a treatise professing to discuss the nature, limits, advantages, and disadvantages of liberty, of all mention of negro slavery! A stranger to America and its history might read the whole 530 octavo pages without discovering that such a thing as Negro slavery existed, or that it existed in South Carolina in particular." [56]

Lieber prepared for South Carolina newspapers an anonymous summary of the British reviews which he wrote in the third person. In it he did not even dare mention the content of the *Daily News* attack. He declared only that the paper "speaks of him as if he were little better than the merest tyro. We suppose Dr. Lieber will be able to bear the censure with fortitude." [57]

As for the Southerners, they almost overlooked the omissions, and enthusiastically greeted the *Civil Liberty* as another brick for their bulwark. Professor Holcombe of the University of Virginia, whom Senator Preston characterized as "most thoroughly states rights in his constitutional doctrines," introduced it as a law text at the University of Virginia. The South Carolina Court of Appeals added it to the list of readings required of candidates for the bar. [58]

The *Southern Literary Messenger* in a lengthy review gave the *Civil Liberty* its full approbation. It termed Lieber's writings "models of patient research and clear analysis," and commented appreciatively upon his comforting political theories. [59]

A long discourse in the *Southern Quarterly Review* by Lieber's banker-planter friend, David J. McCord, illustrated how the South regarded the treatise. McCord criticized Lieber only for his failure to mention the Virginia and Kentucky Resolutions and the state-rights essays of Thomas Cooper and John Taylor of Caroline. With bombast, he proclaimed: "In these days of Communism, Spiritualism, Fourierism, Negrophilism, . . . Odism, Odylefluids, Mesmerisms, and Millenarianisms, it is comforting to meet a book full of good, sound, wholesome principles, entirely free of all that

---

[56] London *Daily News,* November 2, 1853.

[57] No. 423, Lieber papers, Library of Congress. See also clippings, Lieber papers, Huntington Library. The content of the *Daily News* attack remained so clear in Lieber's mind that he mentioned it in a letter to Sumner, February 8, 1862.

[58] Preston to Lieber, December 19, 1858, University of South Carolina; Lieber to E. H. Duyckinck, August 17, 1854, New York Public Library; Lieber to Hillard, June 27, 1854.

[59] "S.," "Lieber's 'Civil Liberty and Self-Government,' " *Southern Literary Messenger,* XIX (1853), 713–21.

abominable, political and philanthropical cant . . . which now threatens to undermine all the old and most valued institutions, moral and political, of civilized life." [60]

Though by no means a substitute for a proslavery diatribe, the *Civil Liberty* did help convince most South Carolina leaders as it did McCord that Lieber was the sturdy foe of all humbuggery, certainly abolitionism included. In short, he was, as always, "safe."

Under the circumstances, Lieber still could not make up his mind whether to leave the langorous, slave-ridden South for the free, cold climate of the North. Though he was only in his early fifties, the years were beginning to weigh upon him. While Senator Preston referred to him as a "hearty and solid old German gentleman," B. F. Perry remembered him as not only a walking encyclopedia, but "a stout and heavy man, formed for strength and labor. He is not very graceful in his person, though genteel. Nor is he very spruce in his dress. His great massive mind soars above such considerations." In a facetious moment the professor referred to himself as "that fat, broad-backed blubber-scholar, yclept Francis Lieber." [61]

By 1854 Lieber was thinking of old age—he felt his race was run. He contemplated bidding "adieu to Columbia, South, niggery and all," and retiring to the North, but he dreaded the climate. "Yes I have become old," he confessed, "I avow it, I dread the long winters, the rubber caloshes, [*sic*] the heated rooms and bone cutting blast." Still, he wrote some friends that he planned to move to Connecticut in two years. There he would live in simplicity and augment his livelihood with his pen. Perhaps he would edit a universal dictionary, a sort of condensed one-volume encyclopedia. He actually started such a project with a reporter for the *Wall Street Journal*, but after receiving some months' pay, the writer withdrew, leaving Lieber with a never-to-be-completed manuscript. The ex-professor might become editor-in-chief (not working very hard) of a new American encyclopedia, he might buy into a news-

---

[60] McCord, "Lieber's Civil Liberty and Self-Government," *Southern Quarterly Review*, IX (1854), 300–32.

[61] Preston to Mrs. McCord (copy), University of South Carolina; Perry, *Reminiscences of Public Men*, 2d series (Greenville, S.C., 1889), 147; Lieber to Duyckinck, October 26, 1855, New York Public Library.

paper, obtain a diplomatic post abroad (this time it was Switzerland), or gain a chair at Columbia.[62]

These were little more than evanescent daydreams and, while Lieber continued to spin them, he worked hard to ingratiate himself in the South, especially through newspaper articles in which he proposed a series of schemes to bolster the regional economy. By 1852 he realized clearly, as did everyone else, that the Southern seaboard was lagging far behind the rest of the nation. Cotton was a false ruler; it depleted the soil too rapidly and new areas in Latin America, Africa, and India could begin to compete. The South must abandon its single-staple economy and the system of "letting the hogs eat up all the crops, and the negroes all the hogs." It must introduce diversified farming.[63]

Olive oil might become one significant alternate product. Where olives could not grow, planters could put in fields of sunflowers whose seeds also produced a fine oil. Or they might raise commercial bamboos, which Commodore Perry, recently returned from Japan, assured Lieber could be introduced into South Carolina.[64]

While one remedy to Southern economic ills would be crop diversification, another might be improved methods of financing. This could come in part through building and loan associations, and Lieber heartily advocated one which began operations at this time in Columbia.[65]

None of these projects offered solutions to the basic problems of the South, but they did demonstrate to the Carolinians that Lieber wished to be considered one of them. He should be worthy of candidacy if a suitable high office were to become vacant. Just that happened at the end of 1854 when James H. Thornwell handed in his resignation as president of South Carolina College, to take effect a year later. Lieber keenly aspired for the presidency, for in state opinion it ranked in prestige next only to the governor-

[62] Lieber to Hillard, January 15, November 10, 1854; Lieber to Allibone, about 1857. See also the Lieber-J. B. Auld correspondence, Lieber papers. Lieber to Ruggles, September 22, 1854, Library of Congress.
[63] See Lieber's notes on slavery, Huntington Library.
[64] Lieber, "The Importance of Olive Trees," Columbia *Daily States-Rights Republican,* February 27, 1852; Lieber, "Sunflower," clipping from a South Carolina paper, about 1852; Perry to Lieber, March 12, 1856.
[65] Lieber, "Building and Loan Associations," Columbia *Daily States-Rights Republican,* May 22, 1852.

ship, United States senatorship, or chancellorship of the state courts. Although he had grumbled over the added duties, Lieber had savored being acting president from 1849 to 1851. Now he longed to obtain the position permanently, even though it would mean spending the remainder of his days in South Carolina.

With a pessimism born of long disappointment, Lieber at first viewed his chances with a wary eye. "Everyone looks toward me, many trustees have told me that I am their man," he reported. "But, . . . I shall not have the appointment. Many side winds are worse than one keen blast. One will say: 'Oh yes, of course, but he is a foreigner'; another will say: 'No doubt, but he always goes in the vacations to the North'; another still: 'Why, no one has such claims, but why has he never said a word on slavery?' and still another, 'Lieber is the man, but then you know that Greenville Letter. Now that was so national!' " [66]

When papers throughout the state began to nominate Lieber for the presidency, he quickly lost his equilibrium. Some of the editors were his former pupils—indeed he was able to prepare a list of some thirty-three who had been in his classes. While the low-country press remained silent, *"every up-country* paper, nearly, has nominated me with a heartiness and zeal of which I had no idea, and which is not in all cases even very discreet." This indicated to Lieber one further proof that "the low-country is the real seat of our anti-national fever and furor." Lieber counseled himself against optimism—Thornwell might not carry out his resignation; the trustees might resent the newspapers taking over their prerogative; some trustees might look upon the nominations as "a latent hostility toward hyper-Calvinism." But he could not be truly cautious at such a time—the movement filled his soul with joy.[67]

"The reputation of DR. LIEBER (*confined not alone to the American continent*) as a finished scholar, historian and political philosopher, reflects honor upon the age in which he lives," proclaimed the *Independent Press* in Abbeville, well to the West. "We

[66] Lieber to Ruggles, December 24, 1854, Library of Congress. Lieber wrote Hillard, December 22, 1854, that the presidency would increase neither his comfort nor his income, but not to receive it would be "a pointed neglect."

[67] Lieber to Ruggles, January 14, 1855, Library of Congress; Lieber to Hillard, January 21, 1855.

hope the State will take pleasure in tendering to one, whose name is so bright with literary distinctions, the Presidency of her beloved institution of learning." Other newspapers followed with equally warm endorsements. "In the College," one editor pointed out, "we believe, he has always been popular with the young gentlemen, and greatly esteemed and appreciated by them in after life. He is pleasant and agreeable in his manners, cordial and affectionate in his disposition, and firm and determined in his purposes." [68]

Lieber read these editorials and turned his attention increasingly, but not entirely, toward South Carolina. He still wrote learnedly on education to Peter Cooper, a wealthy New York merchant and manufacturer who was about to organize an institute which would need professors. Also he felt his old pangs of isolation when Bancroft failed to invite him to the semicentennial celebration of the Massachusetts Historical Society. Even Simms, the Charleston novelist, had received an invitation. However, in the fall of 1855, when Bancroft came to Columbia, to Lieber's surprise he was very friendly and exchanged books and compliments. [69]

Lieber's position was basically comfortable. Although not an able disciplinarian, he was a success as a teacher and never the object of those explosive student outbursts that occasionally harried his colleagues. Despite his long feud with the Ellets and unfavorable comments in letters to the North, Lieber got along well with his fellow faculty members. Even the next-door neighbors, the Thornwells, were personally pleasant. He loved to give German or French lessons to the daughters of William Preston and other associates, and the little girls often left flowers at his doorstep.

Often in discussions Lieber appeared too stern or dogmatic, or bewildered his friends as he did his classes, with his voluminous outpouring of knowledge. At parties he was gay and witty, even as in the North. At a fete on a warm April evening in 1856 he worried "a handsome and modest lady by pitying her with the many robes in such hot weather as we have, she being desirous to convince me that on the contrary these amplitudes are very cool (in

[68] Clippings, Lieber papers.
[69] Lieber to Hillard, February 12, May 24, June 21, 1854; June 30, 1855; Lieber to Allibone, October 16, 1855; Bancroft to Lieber, October 15, 1855.

as much as they wear nothing under it, which she could not well say) and I always pretending that they have 20 dresses beneath, the neighboring ladies smiling, which of course I did not perceive." [70]

Through the fall of 1855 Lieber worked hard for his election. He inspired favorable newspaper comment, and even pressed the Duyckinck brothers of New York, who were preparing a biographical dictionary, to send their laudatory sketch of him for publication in the local journals. One paper attacked him as a Unionist, but the way seemed almost clear. A majority of the trustees, fellow faculty members, and most of the upcountry people seemed in his favor. There was only one cloud on the horizon—the ardently Presbyterian Thornwell and his friend, the violently secessionist Governor Adams.[71]

Lieber's dislike for Thornwell was acute. It covered not only his stern theology but even extended to the hint that Thornwell was lazy and liked to sleep all morning. Probably personal jealousy entered strongly into the animosity. Lieber enjoyed the national and international reputation that Thornwell lacked, but within South Carolina, Lieber was a puny figure compared with the theologian's towering stature.[72]

Lieber argued for conservatism in ambiguous legalistic terms which only by assumption covered slavery and state-rights. Thornwell, on the other hand, had used the pulpit to heap imprecations upon meddlers with all the fervor of a Calvin. He had gloried at the threat of secession in the spring of 1851, and had urged South Carolina College men to prepare to do their duty under the Palmetto banner. In his sermons, with devastating logic and potent emotional content he placed the church foursquare against abolitionism and all other tinkering with the status quo. Indeed this defender of the South almost fashioned a new theology.[73]

[70] Lieber to Ruggles, April 17, 1856, Library of Congress.
[71] Lieber to Allibone, October 6, 1855, Lieber papers; Lieber to Duyckinck, October 29, November, 1855, New York Public Library; "The Great Publicist of Modern Times—Dr. Lieber," Camden *Weekly Journal*, December, 1855, clipping, Lieber papers.
[72] Lieber to Matilda Lieber, August 15, 1854. Garber, *James Henley Thornwell;* Palmer, *Life and Letters of James Henley Thornwell.*
[73] Hennig (ed.), *Columbia*, citing J. B. Angell, *Reminiscences of James B. Angell* (New York, 1912), 55.

When Lieber went to church he attended the Episcopal rather than Thornwell's Presbyterian services—though most often he would stay home: "For all the sermons I could hear would be either fiery like Chinese dragons or drowsy like stuffed serpents." [74]

"I went to the chapel," the professor commented acidly in 1854, "heard a furibund sermon of our president's and feel sorry that after many months going to another church I ventured once more within the pale of bitter, biting, acrid, scratching, tearing, grating, grinding, harrowing, infaming Hyper-Calvinism, that seems to forget that Saviour means healer and religion ought to be balm, hope and confiding love. For my soul Christ's religion centers most in that sublimest and purest of all that exists in words—the sermon on the mount." Once when an enthusiast declared there had been no man like Thornwell since Calvin, Lieber commented dryly, "I hope so." [75]

On the eve of the election, President Thornwell wrote the Reverend Mr. Barnwell, a former president, and other trustees, urging the candidacy of another professor, Charles F. McCay. McCay's single year at the college had been a failure, but he was a good Presbyterian. No one expected him to win the election, but Thornwell through the introduction of a second faculty candidate might be able to swing the trustees to a dark horse by convincing them that neither of the two professors would work well under the presidency of the other. Lieber labeled it a low election maneuver, but granted that it might well succeed.[76]

Although Thornwell's objections to Lieber seemed mainly to have a theological basis, the Presbyterian worthy found a strong political ally in Governor James H. Adams, who was shortly to win notoriety through advocating the re-opening of the African slave trade. Both could have made strong political capital from a remark Lieber wrote northward the very week of the election: "Measures are making to get Fremont nominated for the presidency of the U.S. Donot let this slip into the papers. . . . I wish he were elected, simply to have a decent man in the White House."

[74] Lieber to Hillard, July 9, 1849.
[75] Lieber to Hillard, February [12], 1854, December 25, 1851.
[76] Lieber to Hillard, December 1, 1855. See Green, *History of the University of South Carolina*, 61.

For a similar statement, B. S. Hedrick was driven out of the University of North Carolina.[77]

With no more than a suspicion of the direction of Lieber's sympathies, his enemies triumphed. For the first few ballotings, Lieber stood in the lead. Then all the whispered things about him turned the tide, and triumphantly the Thornwell faction voted in McCay by the margin of a single vote.

The news left Lieber bitter and crushed. He felt humiliated, not only because the trustees had passed him over, but "because a professor, unknown to the trustees, and utterly incapable to rule this institution has been elected, and because the College will go to ruin. I am too old to play the College constable for another man." [78]

Before even a day had passed, he addressed himself to the Governor of South Carolina: "I do myself the honour respectfully to request you that you will lay before the Hon. Board of Trustees, my resignation as professor in the South Carolina College, to take place a year from this time according to the College law." [79]

For a week Lieber grieved in silence; then he launched a grand campaign for a Northern position. To Samuel Austin Allibone, the Philadelphia bibliographer, Samuel Tyler, the Maryland philosopher, Evert Augustus Duyckinck, the editor, and to all his old friends, Ruggles, Hillard, Longfellow, and many more, he wrote of his resignation—his defiance of slavocracy, which certainly should make him more desirable in Northern eyes. "I am now a mason out of work and must look out for some building running up, where I may get fair wages," he reminded them gaily, and begged them to insert notices of his resignation in the newspapers.[80]

[77] Lieber to Hillard, December 1, 1855. Eaton, *Freedom of Thought in the Old South*, 202–204.

[78] Lieber to Allibone, December 13, 1855. Petigru attributed Lieber's defeat to the bigotry of the Calvinists and defenders of slavery, who could not tolerate Lieber's middle-of-the-road stand. Petigru to Lieber, March 21, 1857. Perry, who deeply regretted Lieber's failure, noted the widespread stories that he was an unsuccessful disciplinarian. Perry, *Reminiscences of Public Men*, 2d series, 145–47. Concerning his continued thick accent, see J. H. Easterby (ed.), *The South Carolina Rice Plantation As Revealed in the Papers of Robert F. W. Allston* (Chicago, 1945), 110.

[79] Lieber to Gov. James H. Adams, December 5, 1855, University of South Carolina.

[80] Lieber to Ruggles, December 13, 1855, Library of Congress. See also, Lieber to Duyckinck, December 14, 1855, New York Public Library; Lieber to Sparks, December 14, 1855, Harvard University; Lieber to Mrs. George Ticknor, December

"You are astonished that I could stand a 20 long years' residence here," Lieber commented to Ruggles. "The answer is simple: They paid me a salary. With all my friends and all the people at Cambridge saying they want me, I have never had an offer."[81]

Lieber wondered where and at what he could find employment or partial occupation. At his age, and with the plans for a Columbia University going ahead so slowly, he doubted if he would ever be able to find another professorship. He did hope for some literary labor and lectureships. He could not even decide where to settle. Perhaps he could spend a year in Europe before establishing himself somewhere in the North; he debated the relative merits of Philadelphia, Boston, New York, and even Cincinnati. Up to the time when he began to pack to leave at the end of 1856, he still felt completely at loose ends.[82]

More than once, Lieber and his wife wished he had not been so impetuous about handing in his resignation. "It is true," admitted Matilda, "that we have become more reconciled to our life at the South and less anxious for change which is the natural consequence of having lived here 21 years and formed our circle of duties." Perhaps it was not too late to reconsider; Lieber skillfully probed here and there with a newspaper article to keep public opinion muttering against the trustees.[83]

"They are still anxious to keep me," he asserted to Ruggles. "My resignation is to be acted upon in May. They will suggest to me to withdraw it. I certainly shall not do it without some conditions, and even then reluctantly. Besides matters I tell you stand very badly. I am no alarmist. It lies in the cursed thing, the slavery itself. Now if we Separate . . . I want to be with you, and not here."[84]

Even as Lieber had predicted, McCay was an utter failure as president. The students thought him incompetent both as an instructor and disciplinarian. They gave ear to stories that he had

---

14, 1855; Choate to Lieber, December 29, 1855; Longfellow to Lieber, December 17, 1855; Samuel Tyler to Lieber, April 30, 1856.

[81] Lieber to Ruggles, December 30, 1855, Library of Congress.

[82] Lieber to Duyckinck, November 17, 1856, New York Public Library; Lieber to Hillard, April 5, May, 1856.

[83] Matilda Lieber to Fanny Longfellow, February 16, 1856.

[84] Lieber to Ruggles, January 20, 1856, Library of Congress.

not been completely honest, and that Thornwell too had not been "perfectly truthful." Even tales of McCay's meanness were bruited about, especially that he accepted $100 from one of his Negroes to help purchase the slave's wife. Drinking and disobedience flourished among the students, who finally made a general and open declaration that they wished McCay to retire. They rioted in town and acted so violently that for some weeks the college suspended operations.[85]

The delighted Lieber accepted the revolt as vindication, and expected the trustees to reorganize the faculty at their next meeting. "The personal conduct in my classroom has been uninterruptedly good," he reported maliciously to President McCay and the trustees. But before the trustees' meeting, Governor Adams pulled an ace from his sleeve.[86]

"I think I may as well let you know, my dear Cross Bones," the frustrated professor wrote Ruggles, "that an attack has been made upon your unworthy friend for—what do you think? Keeping a mulatto girl? That would be a trifle! For having killed a person? Pshaw! we don't talk of bagatelles here. For high treason? Why, that might recommend me. No, for *ABOLITIONISM* on the ground of an article published in *1828* in the Americana. Yes, mark that down! I have been asked to reply. I would as lief reply to a question in the papers what I think of a plurality of wives, or how I tuck away my shirt between the legs." [87]

The trustees met, and accepted Lieber's resignation.

Lieber's private views were so militantly nationalistic that he could not have remained much longer in South Carolina, and the attack upon him was really most fortunate. It was so ridiculous

[85] Lieber, "Causes of the Present Discontent &c.," ms. in Lieber papers. The trouble continued throughout 1857 and, only when the college had nearly been disrupted, came to an end with the ousting of McCay. Green, *History of the University of South Carolina*, 62–64.

[86] Lieber, Report to President Charles F. McCay, May 7, 1856, University of South Carolina.

[87] Lieber to Ruggles, May 9, 1856, Library of Congress. Lieber declared that a Columbia paper controlled by Governor Adams had picked out of the *Encyclopaedia Americana* all the statements hostile to slavery and attributed them to Lieber. Lieber to Hillard, April 30, 1856. LaBorde upheld Lieber, but later retracted part of his defense. New York *Tribune*, May 12, 1856, cited in W. M. Geer, "Francis Lieber at the South Carolina College," *loc. cit.*, 16.

that it attracted almost no attention in South Carolina where even the fire-eating Charleston *Mercury* ignored it. Yet Lieber was able to spread stories about it throughout the North. These served not only to counteract suspicions that he favored the slavery system, but clothed him with the aura of a martyr. For such a hero, a good position must be forthcoming.[88]

By coincidence, disaster for Sumner quickly followed Lieber's downfall. Following a violent speech in the Senate, he was severely caned by a South Carolina representative, Preston Brooks. At first a wave of jubilation swept the Palmetto State. "Now they *collect money here to reward Mr. Brooks by Some Pieces of plate!*" the shocked professor reported. "It is to hide one's face." "Sometimes nations go on so that nothing but a war will make a period of reason possible. And so I think it is now with the South and North." [89]

In the North that summer, Lieber even persuaded himself that the people might elect Frémont. The Republican candidate and his clever wife wooed the wavering publicist. "I want you to remember," said Frémont according to Lieber, "that you have strong friends in the North, to which you belong, and who will take care of you if they come into power. I shall not let you go, should I be elected." [90]

Though Lieber would not go as far as his Brahmin friend Hillard and boost Fillmore and conservatism, he did heap maledictions upon both main parties because both seemed to threaten the continuance of the Union. Then, with the victory of the "dough-

---

[88] Lieber exaggerated: "theoretically, I have been tarred and feathered for abolitionism . . . . this affair has added a spoonful or two of castor oil to my cup here." Lieber to Hillard, May, 1856. In reporting the trustees' meeting, the Charleston *Mercury* did not even mention the acceptance of Lieber's resignation. Charleston *Mercury*, May 12, 15, 1856.

A number of the distinguished alumni of South Carolina College passed resolutions expressing regret over Lieber's departure, and presented him with an engraved pair of silver pitchers. J. H. Hudson to Lieber, December 2, 1856. During the Civil War, Lieber noted the anomaly that the taxes he was paying on the pitchers were being used to wage war on the very persons who had given them to him. In the 1930's, Lieber's granddaughter, Miss Mary Lieber, presented one of the pitchers to the University of South Carolina, where it is now on exhibit.

[89] Lieber to Dorothea Dix, May 25, 1856, Lieber papers; Lieber to Ruggles, June 5, 1856, Library of Congress.

[90] Lieber to Matilda Lieber, July 11, 28, August 14, 1856.

289

face" Buchanan and the Democrats, he dramatically shifted to the conclusion that disunion would be preferable to a nation held together through toadying to the South.[91]

Stung by his own failure to win the college presidency, upset by the assault on Sumner, and cut loose at last from his Southern economic moorings, Lieber assumed a violent stand against slavery. His deep respect for the Constitution and Union no longer fettered his moral repugnance. Since 1853 he had felt that the conflict between the North and South was irrepressible and that the two sections were divided by a broader abyss than the slavery controversy:

"The ill-feeling against the North of those Southerners who are the leaders of the malcontents is owing in a great measure to the malaise which is always felt in a period in which the centre of power, or influence or the hegemonia is removed—when wealth, population, knowledge, renown or anything that is power shifts. This is the case with the South." [92]

Now, with the election of Buchanan, he lashed forth at the exponents of slavery extension in a truly Garrisonian spirit: "The victory of Southern bullyism; the acknowledgment of Northern men that, right or wrong, they yield because the South threatens to secede, will inflame and inflate proslavery to such enormity and obscene tyranny over the free states, and madden it in its ungodly course of extending slavery within the U. States and into neighbouring countries . . . [that] you, I, every man that has muscle enough left to heave his breast will all out: Let us part, come what may." [93]

Lieber clearly realized when he wrote these conclusions to Hillard that they might cost him their friendship. "Let us never secede," he implored.[94]

"No, my dear Lieber, we will not secede," the Bostonian reassured him. "It would be hard for you to lose Sumner because you were not antislavery enough, and me because you were too antislavery." [95]

The stakes were far higher than Hillard's friendship. They were

[91] Lieber to Hillard, October 23, 1856. [92] Lieber to Hillard, April 20, 1853.
[93] Lieber to Hillard, October 23, 1856. [94] Lieber to Hillard, October 23, 1856.
[95] Hillard to Lieber, October 30, 1856.

no less than the affection of Lieber's beloved son, Oscar, who had become a promising geologist. Except for his years of schooling in Germany, Oscar had grown to maturity in the South and had completely accepted the regional views on slavery and state rights. To Lieber's alarm, an acute political gulf was threatening to separate him from his son, and he pleaded, "let us solemnly resolve to remain closely attached friends to our deaths." [96]

[96] Lieber to Oscar Lieber, September 5, 1856, in Perry (ed.), *Lieber,* 289.

XIII

The Conservative Revolution

FRANCIS LIEBER, ex-professor, arrived in New York City in January, 1857, and established himself in a boardinghouse. Though almost fifty-nine years of age, he was not discouraged by his lack of employment, since his reputation as a political scientist was at its height. He began promoting two possibilities: an appointment to the institute Peter Cooper was founding, and a professorship in Columbia College, which was being transformed into a university.[1]

In 1855 Cooper had sent the scholar a set of the Institute plans to criticize, remarking, "I have read in part your books and find in them much to admire. Your views harmonize more nearly with mine than any work I read." Although Lieber prepared recommendations and over a long period advised Cooper, he considered the millionaire a bore. Ruggles felt similarly, and wittily described an omnibus conversation: *"Cooper—* . . . I have just been reading the book that your Mr. L*y*ber,—(L*ee*ber! do you call him?) has written about government—and he hits my notions *to a hair!"* [2]

While Cooper was slowly planning his institute, the timid, conservative trustees of Columbia College were taking tentative steps toward reorganization. The new president, Charles King, a sound businessman, prodded them to increase the emphasis upon practical arts and the social sciences. In 1856 they appointed a committee on reform which Ruggles persuaded to consult Lieber. The committee submitted 180 questions covering the entire field of

[1] See Lieber-Ruggles correspondence, Lieber papers, Library of Congress.

[2] Peter Cooper to Lieber, March 15, 1855; Ruggles to Lieber, March 17, 1855. Lieber's plan for Cooper Institute is in the Lieber papers, Henry E. Huntington Library. All manuscripts referred to in this chapter, unless otherwise identified, are from this collection.

education, which the scholar reluctantly condescended to answer in the hope that he would thus ingratiate himself. "I dare say, I would not reply without proper fee," he commented, "were not the question about settling me in some shape seriously moved." [3]

In the spring of 1857 the trustees began to move slowly in the direction Lieber had indicated. They introduced two elective courses open to freshmen, and split McVickar's tremendous chair which covered all morality, polity, and literature into three new professorships, one of which was to be a chair of history and political economy. Lieber's name, together with that of Parke Godwin and a Professor Green were put in nomination for the positions. Lieber received a majority of the votes; the ballot was made unanimous. His salary was to be $3,000 and a dwelling, or (as he elected) $3,000 and not over $1,000 per annum for house rent. Ruggles wrote a friend, "The Chair needed Lieber quite as much as he needed the Chair." [4]

The aging professor rejoiced over the news and prepared to set up a permanent residence. He purchased a large brownstone house on East Thirty-fourth Street, a short distance from the present Empire State Building. Busily he moved in his books and papers, named the sections of his library after favorite writers, and inscribed in his anteroom, "Patria Cara, Carior Libertas, Veritas Carissima." His Puerto Rican niece, Clarita, presented him with a piece of German sculpture, "Die Studiende Owle." He hung it over the doorway, and promptly dubbed his new home "The Owlry." [5]

Although Lieber had finally achieved his thirty-year goal, a professorship in a leading Northern college, the driving ambition of three decades had built up habits which continued unabated. Hardly had he received notice of the chair than he wrote to Hamilton Fish, the chairman of the board of trustees, asking that his

---

[3] Lieber's efforts to obtain a position in Columbia College, and the situation within the institution at that time receive careful and detailed treatment in Dorfman and Tugwell, "Francis Lieber: German Scholar in America," *loc. cit.*, 267–74. Lieber to Ruggles, August 19, 1856; Lieber, "Suggestions Columbia University," February, 1857, Lieber papers, Library of Congress; Lieber to Matilda Lieber, July 20, August 14, September 5, 1856.

[4] Minutes of the Board of Trustees, Columbia College, 5:215–23, Columbia University; Lieber to Hillard, March 5, 1857; Thompson, *Ruggles of New York,* 165.

[5] Lieber to Hillard, May 19, August 12, November 3, 1857.

new title be changed to "Professor of History and Political Science," because it would sound so much better to his European friends. The trustees complied.[6]

Next the scholar wrote an eloquent four-page memorandum to President King, listing many reasons why he should escape teaching freshmen. He accompanied this petition with a lengthy report, stressing the amount of time he spent preparing lectures, pointing out that he never delivered the same lecture twice, and begging the trustees not to pile onto him the customary teaching load of twenty hours per week. He could not possibly teach more than fifteen hours without making his classes little more than uninspired quizzings.[7]

That fall, the trustees assigned him classes in "Modern History, Political Science, Natural & International Law, Civil & Common Law." Even before the formal assignment, he had asked President King to reduce the two-hour history course to a single hour in order to increase political economy to two hours. He could not teach "an entirely new branch for the class, and so comprehensive and important a one, in one hour a week," and he promised to give "substantial and expansive lectures."[8]

During the years at Columbia College, petition followed petition in unending succession—some granted, most ungranted. Altogether, Lieber did not teach many hours—seven to eleven a week—and his salary of $4,000 was higher than that of almost any college professor outside New York City. As famous a scientist as Louis Agassiz, professor at Harvard, had to open a girls' school in Cambridge to augment his $1,500 salary. Lieber never faced such straits, though during the inflation of the Civil War he complained mightily of the rising cost of living and a temporary salary cut.[9]

In February, 1858, Lieber delivered an inaugural address in

[6] Lieber to Fish, May 20, 1857, Columbia University. Minutes of Board of Trustees, Columbia College, 5:272.

[7] Lieber to Charles King, June 24, 1857; Lieber to Board of Trustees, August, 1857, Columbia University. The latter is reprinted in Harley, *Francis Lieber,* 195–98.

[8] Lieber to King, August 14, 1857; Minutes of Board of Trustees, Columbia College, 5:272.

[9] The many petitions and letters, covering even matters like painting and remodeling of his classroom, together with his official reports, are in the Columbiana Room, Columbia University.

which he brilliantly expounded the value of history, political science, and economics. Roughly the concepts were about the same as those he had stated upon assuming his chair at South Carolina College, but twenty-three years of teaching and observation had molded them into a well-rounded philosophy. The inaugural was his most lucid and concise statement of his views.

Except that he emphasized more than ever his ardent nationalism, Lieber added little to his previous statements on political and economic thought. He did present a far more matured philosophy of history. Political science and history, the scholar stated, treated "of man in his social relations, of humanity in all its phases in society." He described the continuous nature of society, and defined history as "that science which treats of men in their social relations in the past, and of that which has successively affected their society, for weal or woe." He scorned false historical schools— the one which tried to trace great events to insignificant causes or accidents, and another which "seems to believe that nothing can be right but what has been." Finally he deprecated the "philosophical school" of absolutist thinkers which sought out "a predetermined type of social development in each state and nation and in every race, reducing men to instinctive and involuntary beings and society to nothing better than a bee-hive. . . . In their

<hr>

According to the report to the trustees, November 1, 1858, Minutes of Board of Trustees, Columbia College, 5:393–96, Lieber's program was:

"[Seniors:] In *History*, the two Schools of Letters and Jurisprudence attended Prof. Lieber two hours weekly, in the last period of Modern History, beginning with the French Revolution & ending with the year 1848. The Instruction was by lecture, with the use of 'Weber's general outline' as text book.

"The School of Jurisprudence one hour weekly pursued with Professor Lieber the Study of Political Economy by lecture, with Jay as a text. . . .

"[Juniors:] In *Modern History*, the class attended Prof. Lieber two hours weekly. The mode of instruction was by lecture, using as with the other, Weber's Outline; the period was from the age of Maritime discoveries, and the Reformation down to the age of Louis XIV using Russell's Epitome for the latter portion of the year. The Revolution of the Netherlands and of England, and portions of the English Constitution as developed thereby formed a large portion of the Course. . . .

"[Sophomores:] In History the class attended Prof. Lieber one hour weekly; studying the period from the downfall of the Roman Empire to the Reformation, using Weber as the Text book; the instruction being by lectures; and in all the classes being partly oral; but chiefly by written exercises in the lecture-room, which are taken by the Professors and examined at home."

That year, Columbia University had 26 seniors, 36 juniors, 50 sophomores, and 41 freshmen. Lieber's salary was reduced to $3,600 in June, 1861. Minutes of Board of Trustees, 5:648.

eyes every series of events . . . becomes a necessity and a representative of national predestination."

The great teacher of history must avoid the blandishments of these schools and eschew bending facts to fit a theory. He must demonstrate "the great connection of things, that there is nothing stable but the progressive . . . that there is the microcosm of the past in each of us." He should "foster in the young an institutional spirit," an ability to distinguish between good and bad, growing and dying institutions. "A wise study of the past teaches us social analysis, and the separation of the permanent and essential from the accidental and superficial, so that it becomes one of the keys by which we learn to understand better the present." [10]

Lieber's inaugural struck sparks in diverse places. John Lothrop Motley, historian of the Dutch Republic, some years later commented lengthily and approvingly on Lieber's philosophy of history. Prescott, who was approaching the close of his life-span, exclaimed that he had "scarcely ever read a more suggestive little work—one that puts the reader more upon thinking." Charles Francis Adams, Jr., beginning his fruitful career, was conscientiously searching standards by which to set his course. He had sickened of the blasé manner in which Harvard professors "sneered at zeal or enthusiasm," and seized upon Lieber's fervent pages: "It seemed the production of one who believed in his science & wanted to make others believe—there was something tangible and earnest in it," he informed the author. "In it I found a knowledge of the broad field to work in,—a belief in the pursuit & a desire to propagate that belief . . . after all a belief & earnestness in something besides the accumulation of wealth is the crying want of America—Cambridge has proved herself unable to supply that want." [11]

Lieber brought to bear on his new duties all the vigor that young Adams had sensed in the inaugural. He lectured profoundly, and quickly gained a reputation for working the students hard. He

[10] Lieber, *History and Political Science Necessary Studies in Free Countries* . . . (New York, 1858), reprinted in Lieber, *Miscellaneous Writings*, I, 329–68.

[11] Motley to Lieber, June 12, December 3, 1866; Prescott to Lieber, June 18, 1858; Charles Francis Adams, Jr. to Lieber, June 13, 1858, Huntington Library. See also Preston to Lieber, July 3, 1858, and Mitchell King to Lieber, February 15, 1860, University of South Carolina.

did not find the leisure he had cherished in South Carolina, but enjoyed and found favor with his students. They sent him baskets of flowers on his birthday and the seniors singled him out from among all the faculty members to sit for his photograph that they might each have a copy. In addition he gained the confidence of the trustees and influenced them in the planning of the university.[12]

Only Lieber's public lectures were a failure. They dealt with interesting subjects, such as the history of commerce; they drew detailed accounts in the New York newspapers, and Mrs. Frémont read summaries of them in San Francisco. But in the lecture hall, the famous Dr. Lieber addressed empty benches. Perhaps it was because, as he commented after hearing the phenomenally successful Beecher, he loathed "that curse of American oratory of the present time—pityful sayings to make the audience laugh." Once he mentioned having an audience of only "7½" but gradually he assembled about fifty auditors. A small nucleus, he boasted, were prominent lawyers and deep thinkers who listened appreciatively.[13]

"I hope ultimately to see from you some fruits of the greater freedom of thought your present position affords you," young Adams had frankly commented to the transplanted professor. Adams did not have long to wait. Lieber's interests were as heterogeneous as ever: he participated vigorously in prison reform; delivered a reminiscent address on Alexander von Humboldt; and actively promoted Dr. Hayes's Arctic expedition. Yet increasingly he channeled his major attention into the exciting political currents of the late 1850's.[14]

[12] Lieber to Hillard, April 11, May [22], 1858; George F. Allen to Lieber, December 24, 1858.

[13] Lieber to Duyckinck [about 1858], February 19, October 8, 1859, New York Public Library; Lieber to Gulian C. Verplanck, December 29, 1859, New York Historical Society; Lieber to Hillard, January 25, 1859; Lieber to Allibone, November 16, December 25, 1859; Lieber to Henry Drisler, December 4, 1859, Huntington Library.

[14] C. F. Adams to Lieber, June 13, 1858. Lieber's activities on behalf of the Hayes expedition are detailed in the Lieber-Alexander Dalles Bache correspondence in the Lieber papers and Rhees papers, Huntington Library. See also Lieber to Allibone, March 10, July 5, August 22, 1860; Lieber to Drisler, March 11, June 9, 1860; Lieber to Tyler, June 28, 1860; and Senator J. H. Hammond to Lieber, April 19, 1860. Lieber, "The Proposed Arctic Expedition," New York *Independent,* March 29, 1860. American Geographical Society, *Humboldt Commemoration* (New York, 1859) 230–

At the opening of an 1859 lecture course at Columbia, Lieber proclaimed his absolute liberty as a teacher of politics: "No government, no censor, no suspicious partisan watches my words," he exulted. "No party tradition fetters me; no connections force special pleading on me. I am surrounded by that tone of liberality, with that absence of petty inquisition which belongs to populous and active cities." [15]

Even before Lieber left South Carolina he had been moving secretly toward Republican party doctrines. In the North he heartily espoused them, at first privately in correspondence, and by the fall of 1860, openly from the hustings. While Kansas bled, he compared the "Lecompton fraud" to "Göthe's progress of shame in Faust." He predicted that the South would establish a protectorate over Mexico. Indeed, an independent Confederacy would encircle the Caribbean with a chain of slave dominions. Even mad John Brown was a hero. As he swung from the gallows, Lieber proclaimed, "He died like a man, and Virginia fretted like a woman." When Chief Justice Roger B. Taney published an opinion in the Dred Scott case that all territories were open to slavery, the political theorist fulminated to friends that Taney's statement was "illegal, unjuridical, immoral, and disgraceful." [16]

A traveler's account of a supposed Fijian custom of roasting one's wife inspired Lieber to launch an especially telling attack upon slavery. First he fashioned verses to amuse his friends, then prepared a biting prose satire for the *Atlantic Monthly* of March 1859: "A Plea for the Fijians; Or, Can Nothing be Said in Favor of Roasting One's Equals?" With flawless logic, Lieber applied the proslavery argument and Taney's reasoning in the Dred Scott decision to the institution of cannibalism. One could make as good a case for it as for Negro slavery, and a better case than for intro-

---

38; *Tribute to the Memory of Humboldt* . . . (Pulpit and Rostrum, No. 6, New York, 1859), 117–52; "Dr. Lieber's Address," *Journal of the American Geographical and Statistical Society*, I (1859), 230–38. The address also appeared in the New York *Century* and the *Courant* and is reprinted in Lieber, *Miscellaneous Writings*, I, 389–404.

[15] Lieber, *The Ancient and Modern Teacher of Politics. An Introductory Discourse to a Course of Lectures on the State* . . . (New York, 1860), reprinted in Lieber, *Miscellaneous Writings*, I, 369–87.

[16] Lieber, note, "Senator Douglas' Minority Report on Kansas"; Lieber to Hillard, March 23, 1857, February 9, March, April 20, May 1, July 5, 1858; Lieber to Drisler, December 4, 1859; Lieber to Allibone, January 16, 1860.

ducing slavery into territories free under positive law. Cannibalism was scarcely more immoral than the pronouncement of a Southern seer-statesman (probably George Fitzhugh) that "Capital ought to own, and has a divine right to own . . . Labor; and that, since Labor constitutes the whole humanity of the laboring man, it clearly follows that he himself must be owned." Answered the indignant publicist: "Would you own the bird without its cage? Generous gospel of the rich! Blessed are the wealthy!" [17]

During the crisis year 1860, Lieber's vehemence increased. Still, he was so upset that he could not sleep nights when his former South Carolina friend, Senator J. H. Hammond, wrote in April that he, in common with most senators, had been forced to the expedient of putting a loaded pistol within easy reach in the drawer of his Senate desk. To top off this bravado, Hammond added that the Union cramped the South. "I firmly believe," he announced, "that the Slave-holding South is now the controlling *Power* of the World—that no other power could face us in hostility." [18]

Although Lieber foresaw the breakdown of the Union, he felt no personal responsibility and was unwilling to take any steps to prevent the tragedy. Denouncing those Northern Unionists who prostrated themselves before the Southern disunionists, he snorted, "The Union is not my *end* or God." Indeed, he was beginning to believe that a bloody war similar to that which fell on Prussia in 1806 might be the only means of national regeneration: "When nations go on recklessly as we do, dancing, drinking, laughing, defying right, morality, justice, [engaging in] money-making and murdering, God in his mercy has sometimes condescended to smite them and to smite them hard, in order to bring them to their senses and make them recover themselves." [19]

Since Lieber welcomed the irrepressible conflict, he was ready, secretly at first and then openly, to help swing the German vote to the Republican cause. Although he counseled Seward in 1858 on means of winning the Germans, he recognized the difficulties the Republican leader outlined to him. "Sometimes I despair,"

---

[17] Anonymously published in the *Atlantic Monthly*, III (1859), 343.
[18] Perry (ed.), *Lieber*, 309; Hammond to Lieber, April 19, 1860.
[19] Lieber to Allibone, January 16, July 12, 1860.

Seward declared. "The natural course for the Germans is to sustain free labor. But except myself all our free labor public men either directly or indirectly join the Know nothings in persecuting Germans while the Democrats having patronage subsidize the Presses which the Germans rely on for information and guidance."[20]

Nevertheless, during the campaign of 1860 the Republicans persuaded many Germans to come over to their standard. They depended especially upon the spellbinding qualities of a young forty-eighter, Carl Schurz. Lieber sat enraptured in Cooper Institute as he listened to this "fearful logician" attack Douglas. "It was the most effective speech . . . I have ever heard in America," he exclaimed. "It was literally clawing."[21]

The Republicans, well aware of Lieber's sympathies, invited him to preside over a German meeting at Cooper Institute a month later. It was supposed to be a nonpartisan meeting at which the redoubtable Schurz would debate Chris Kribben, a German Douglas Democrat. But only Schurz attended the gathering, and thus Lieber, who only four years earlier had been a professor at South Carolina College, found himself chairman at an enthusiastic Lincoln rally. He reminded the audience that it was the anniversary of the Battle of Leipzig and expressed the hope that the present great battle for freedom would result as gloriously for the German name.[22]

New York papers carried the news; from South Carolina College came the echo. The Euphradian Society struck Lieber's name from its membership list and his portrait became the target of so many student penknives that the officials took it down and hid it away. Oscar Lieber wrote North with pained dismay to ask his father's views. Only "the thread of parental and filial affection" remained between father and son, and Lieber wrote painstakingly for fear even that would snap:[23]

[20] William Henry Seward to Lieber, May 7, 1859.

[21] Lieber to Allibone, September 19 and 22, 1860. Lieber's active participation in Republican politics is further shown by his platform proposals to William Curtis Noyes, prominent New York attorney, who was one of the delegates to the Republican convention. Noyes to Lieber, [1860].

[22] New York *Tribune,* October 19, 1860. The *Herald* did not, as Lieber declared, carry a sensational account of his participation in the meeting.

[23] Lieber to Allibone, November 25, 1860; Lieber to Oscar Lieber, draft, November 2, 1860; Lieber to Hillard, December 27, 1860.

"My dearest Boy, and if I knew a more endearing term, that term I would use now to address you. I feel your grief most bitterly. . . . I have often thought what heart-burning there must have been in many a family in the time of the Reformation . . . heart-burning, the greater the more truthful and upright the members of the household are that may differ. . . .

"After very mature consideration I have decided to vote for Mr. Lincoln. . . . As to the threat of dissolution of the Union should Mr. Lincoln be elected . . . I believe [it] is made in good earnest and that it is quite possible to carry it into execution . . . if the Union depends upon such conditions it is virtually dissolved; . . . some gush of wind or other must come and blow down the rotten tree. The sooner we are then, separated the better. Who would not prefer living in a house of moderate dimension, in peace,. to dwelling in a mansion in daily bitter and empoisoning strife? . . . It sometimes has occurred to me that what Thucydides said of the Greeks at the time of the Peloponnesian war applies to us. The Greeks, he said, did not understand each other any longer, though they spoke Greek. Words received a different meaning in different parts." [24]

Despite the tone of his letter to Oscar, the aging scholar did not in the least expect or desire peaceful separation. When South Carolina retorted promptly to the election of Lincoln by passing an ordinance of secession, Lieber referred to it with more scorn than surprise as a "barbarous relapse." He dug into his files for the warning against disunion that he had addressed to the people of South Carolina in 1851, and reprinted it without emendation in Tilton's *Independent*.[25]

One pregnant sentence stood out in the 1851 address: "To secede, then, requires revolution." Lieber fortified it with two lectures on the nature of the Constitution which he delivered to his

[24] Lieber to Oscar Lieber, draft, November 2, 1860. Lieber was quoting from memory a passage from Thucydides, iii, 70–85, which he had included in the *PE* (2d ed.), II, 262–63, with the comment: "Party spirit may run so high that the greatest link and tie of humanity, language, loses its very essence, and people cease to understand one another, when even the best-intended words, as in the theological controversies of religiously excited times, are unintentionally yet passionately or wilfully wronged, misconstrued, wrung from their very sense."
[25] Lieber to Allibone, November 25, 1860; Lieber to Hillard, January 10, 1861, Lieber papers; Lieber to Parke Godwin, December 18, 1860, New York Public Library; Lieber, "Secession," New York *Independent*, January 10, 1861.

evening law class in January, 1861. In these, he did not touch upon the economic or political expediency of coercion, an issue which split his powerful friends. Lieber would not publicly choose between ex-Governor Fish who accompanied a union committee to Washington and William Curtis Noyes who went as a stanch anticompromise delegate to the National Peace Convention. Instead the professor laid down elaborate constitutional arguments to justify coercion should it come.[26]

Lieber addressed his audience with solemn earnestness, for he felt war inevitable. Indeed in early January, when Charlestonians fired upon the *Star of the West* to prevent it from reinforcing Fort Sumter, he was sure he heard "the boom of civil war . . . of the most factitious and therefore the most unrighteous civil war." That sound in his ears heightened his customary nationalistic ardor. "Some people have charged me with inconsistency," he asserted as he prepared his talks, "yet if I am invulnerable on any point it is that from the day when my father was obliged to remove me from the window, because my sobbing attracted the attention of Napoleon's soldiers . . . to this, when I shall lecture . . . on Secession, my heart has warmly beaten, and unflaggingly for Liberty . . . true liberty requires a *country*." Yet as he elaborated his theses, it sickened him to realize that he was lecturing on architecture while the flames of conflict roared and crackled through the national edifice.[27]

The political theorist marshaled all the customary refutations against the Southern claims to the right of secession. He met the contention that the constitution was a contract broken by the North and therefore void with the arguments against the social compact expounded in his *Political Ethics*. The Constitution was more than an agreement between states. Lieber pointed to the words "We the people" in the preamble and noted the decree within the Constitution that all laws made pursuant to it should be the supreme law of the land.

This and other provisions proved that: "The Constitution is a law, with all the attributes essential to a law, the first of which

---

[26] Lieber, *Miscellaneous Writings*, II, 133. Philip S. Foner, *Business and Slavery* . . . (Chapel Hill, 1941), 248–49, 267–68.

[27] Lieber to Fish, January 11, 1861, Columbia University; Lieber to Hillard, January 10, 1861; Lieber to Allibone, February 26, 1861.

is that it must be obeyed, and that there must be an authority that can enforce obedience. . . . the provision that the national government has no rights but those which are granted to it, cannot mean that it must allow itself to be broken up whenever it pleases any portion possessing the 'reserved rights' to do so. . . .

"It is a national fundamental law, establishing a complete national government,—an organism of national life. It is not a mere league of independent states or nations. . . . It is an organism with living functions."

Except for the concluding remark, this was no more than a clear summarization of well-known legal arguments. Unfortunately, it was the part of the lectures which drew the greatest approbation. Although Lieber utilized these conventional doctrines, he went beyond them to lay down a dictum implicit in his theories of institutional self-government. The United States was more than a government set up under a constitution. It was a nation, and even before the Constitutional Convention it had been a nation. One people settled the thirteen colonies. They brought with them a single language, common customs and institutions, professed allegiance to one crown, and considered themselves to be a distinct and separate people.

"The national current flowed here," and deepened as the difficulties with Britain intensified. With the coming of the Revolution, "we were attacked as one country, we defended ourselves as one country, and we proclaimed our independence as one country, and called the government of that country the Union." With that government sovereignty rested. Even during the Confederation period when internally the states were supreme, from the viewpoint of foreign countries only the central government was sovereign.

The existence and divinely prescribed mission of the United States as a nation far transcended all narrow legalistic interpretations of the Constitution. "The normal type of modern government is the National Polity," Lieber reminded his auditors. "The highest type . . . is the organic union of national and local self-government." Only upon this basis could the American nation fulfill its destiny.[28]

[28] Lieber, *What is Our Constitution,—League, Pact, or Government?* . . . (New

"Oscar, probably on his march to Virginia, under that flag of shame; Hamilton, in the Illinois militia at Cairo; Norman writing to-day to Presdt. Lincoln for a Commission in the U.S. army." [35]

Even before Fort Sumter, Lieber learned in part the frightful price the conflict would exact from him. News came that his beloved Oscar had joined Wade Hampton's Legion in South Carolina. Staggered, the father finally steeled himself to write: "I shall not touch, in this letter upon any public topic, nor speak of the dark cloud which over-shadows my mind, and will darken the remainder of my years, because that has appeared to my first born son as the path of his duty, which appears to his father in so different a light. I merely write because I can no longer delay it; and I have delayed so long because I turned from the task with a bleeding heart." There he ended abruptly and put the letter aside, unsigned and unsent.[36]

Anguish over Oscar's decision impelled rather than deterred the elderly scholar in his determination to be of maximum service to the Union cause. Spurred equally by patriotism and ambition, he sought means by which he could contribute to the war. Obviously one of the most effective would be to regain Charles Sumner's ear.

After the clash in Charleston Harbor, Sumner abandoned his long-standing pacifism in favor of the militancy which made the Republican party so attractive to Lieber. This closed the last crack in the ideological crevasse which had separated the two friends. Moreover, the zealous Senator with his potent abolitionist following and his chairmanship of the Committee on Foreign Relations was to mold policy on both the destruction of slavery and the conduct of diplomacy. Through Sumner, Lieber could gain a hearing for his ideas in both these vital fields. Therefore in May, 1861, he swallowed his pride and wrote a conciliatory note.

Sumner replied immediately and graciously; he had always drawn heavily upon Lieber's intellect and was pleased to do so again. Moreover, the Senator worked as willingly as of old to do favors for his friend. He ultimately obtained an army appointment

[35] Lieber to Hillard, May 11, 1861.
[36] Lieber to Oscar Lieber, March 5, 1861 (draft, apparently never sent).

for Norman which Lieber requested in his second letter. Conversely, the Senator was soon utilizing the professor's ideas on paroling prisoners of war. The correspondence became prolific. The deep personal feeling of early years was gone, but politics, which had originally separated them, now drew them together into a mutually profitable partnership.[37]

Before the end of the year, Sumner wrote: "I shall value any suggestion from you—especially of a practical character. Write me freely. Have you any propositions—? Let me have them. We have the majority now &, of course, corresponding responsibilities. We can put into law what ought to be law." [38]

The ambitious professor rejoiced in his renewed friendship, but sought additional means to exert influence. As soon as classes ended in June, he hurried to the capital to seek a niche in the new administration. Washington was confused and hectic with military preparations. It was crowded, hot, and dusty, plagued with flies and drunken officers, and reminded Lieber painfully of the South—"everything is massive, greasy, half-finished, or half-gone." [39]

Lieber went to the White House in his official capacity as a Columbia University professor to confer an honorary LL.D. degree upon President Lincoln. When Secretary of State Seward introduced him to the President, the solemn German was not quite sure the strange person he met was a statesman. "He is far better than people think him, but oh! so funny," Lieber reported to his wife. "When we went away Gov. Seward said: 'I shall return with Lord Lyons; you had better put on your black coat. You ought to have put it on for Dr. Lieber.' 'I intended to do so, but the Dr. will excuse me, I was not aware it was so late.' " [40]

A few days later, the bellicose professor again talked to Lin-

[37] Lieber to Sumner, May 24, 1861, Huntington Library; Sumner to Lieber, May 30, 1861, Sumner papers, Harvard University. Laura White, "Charles Sumner and the Crisis of 1860-61," Avery Craven (ed.), *Essays in Honor of William E. Dodd* (Chicago, 1935), 131-93. This is a careful and unassailable evaluation which reverses previous interpretations of Sumner's stand on coercion.

[38] Sumner to Lieber, December 16, 1861, Harvard University.

[39] Lieber to Matilda Lieber, June 26, July 7, 9, 10, 1861.

[40] The Columbia University Committee on Honours recommended the degree May 20, 1861. Columbia University, Minutes of Board of Trustees, Columbia College, 5:631. Lieber declared Lincoln was quite pleased with the honor. Lieber to Matilda Lieber, June 26, 1861.

coln, and at the close of the conversation asked, "well Mr. President wont you give us at least a little fight?" Lieber reported that Lincoln replied, "Well, I'll see and he turned away evidently pained at the idea. He is thoroughly a kind hearted man—too much so I fear." [41]

Though Lincoln had delighted him by praising the lectures on the Constitution, Lieber listened rather critically to the Message to Congress. "Why did the Presdt. not give his message to some one to correct the language," he exclaimed. It "begins with a blunder. But what he says is good—not elevated, but very popular." [42]

Carefully the opportunistic scholar renewed or made other acquaintances he thought might be of value. Aged, heavy General Winfield Scott, who to Lieber's disappointment was still general in chief of the army, gave him a letter of introduction to that most remarkable of all the political generals the war produced, cross-eyed, disputatious Benjamin F. Butler. Lieber set out to visit him in company with New York's moderate Republican leader, Thurlow Weed, and Sumner's Massachusetts colleague, Henry Wilson. On the way, they visited another political general, ex-Governor N. P. Banks of Massachusetts, who commanded at Fort Mc-Henry.[43]

Upon his return to Washington, Lieber held several long conversations with his old acquaintance, General John C. Frémont, who was soon to snarl his Western Department into helpless confusion. Frémont was quite cordial, and in August urged him to rush experienced European artillerymen to St. Louis. Lieber

[41] Lieber to Matilda Lieber, July 5, 1861. On July 10, Lieber wrote Matilda he had seen Lincoln again at a levee. "He at once introduced me to Mrs. Lincoln and her companion against the rule." Lieber wrote H. B. Smith, August 15, 1861, "Lincoln seems to me a peculiarly truthful simple hearted man."

[42] Lieber to Matilda Lieber, July 7, 1861; Lieber to Norman Lieber, July 5, 1861. A suggestion of Lieber's had found its way into Lincoln's hands, presumably by way of Seward. Lieber proposed that the President's message include a factual statement "of the amount of treasonable acts carried on under Mr. Buchanan, for instance the number of arms and the amount of ammunitions carried to the South." Lieber to King, May 15, 1861, Lincoln papers, Library of Congress. Lincoln declared in the message, "A disproportionate share of the Federal muskets and rifles had somehow found their way into these States and had been seized to be used against the Government." Richardson, *Messages and Papers of the Presidents* . . . , VI, 20.

[43] Lieber to Fish, April 24, 1861, Columbia University; Lieber to Matilda Lieber, June 28, 30, July 10, 1861.

scoured New York but could find none, for General Daniel Sickles had already enlisted them.[44]

General John A. Dix of New York, who had recently helped stiffen Buchanan's cabinet by serving as Secretary of the Treasury, promised to help obtain a commission for Norman. The new head of the Treasury Department, the Ohio abolitionist, Salmon P. Chase, was equally cordial. He urged the professor to write often, and Lieber considered him one of the "master-minds" of the government. However the friendship soon chilled. Probably one reason for this was the warm and valuable association Lieber quickly formed with Chase's rival, Attorney General Edward Bates. Bates, a Missouri moderate of Whig background, had been one of Lincoln's competitors for the Republican nomination. As a member of the cabinet he was to represent border-state opinion as vociferously as Chase did the Middle Western Radical Republicans.[45]

The publicist dined at the Bates home and found to his delight that Mrs. Bates was a sister-in-law of his dear friend Senator Preston. The Attorney General, already beginning a frantic search for precedents to justify Lincoln's war measures, welcomed Lieber's acquaintance, and soon drew him into a long and sustained correspondence on technical points of law.[46]

The self-assumed role of unofficial adviser to the Attorney General placed Lieber in a somewhat uncomfortable position. America's most widely quoted defender of civil liberties now labored diligently to aid Bates in ferreting out legal justification for the administration's political arrests. At the end of April Lincoln had reluctantly suspended the writ of habeas corpus in the turbulent area between Washington and Philadelphia. This meant the denial of normal court processes of arraignment and jury trial to suspects held for disloyalty.

A furore of protest quickly arose. Radical Republicans in Congress who wished to see the power vested in their hands, and Demo-

---

44 Lieber to Matilda Lieber, July 5, 1861; Frémont to Lieber, August 5, 1861; Lieber to Sumner, August 13, 1861.
45 Lieber to Norman Lieber, July 5, 1861; Lieber to Matilda Lieber, July 5, 1861.
46 Lieber to Matilda Lieber, June 26, 1861. See the Lieber-Bates correspondence, Huntington Library. Howard K. Beale (ed.), *The Diary of Edward Bates* (American Historical Association, Annual Report, 1930, vol. 4, Washington, 1933).

crats who feared the suspension as a potential weapon against them, joined forces to assail the order. Significantly, when Congress on July 13, 1861, gave blanket approval to Lincoln's other extralegal steps, it omitted mention of the habeas corpus.[47]

Chief Justice Taney in *Ex Parte Merryman* asserted that the right to suspend the writ belonged only to Congress. The power had rested solely with the legislature both in England and the colonies and the clause relating to suspension was incorporated in a section of the Constitution placing restrictions upon Congress.[48] Lincoln replied in his message to Congress that he had acted in the interest of public safety. Since the Constitution was silent as to whether the executive or Congress should exercise the power, he had stayed within the limits of the fundamental law. Attorney General Bates elaborated upon this in an opinion that the three branches of the government were co-ordinate. Hence the President could not be subordinate to the judicial writ if he were to carry out his duty to protect and defend the Constitution. That justified him in suspending the writ to help suppress the rebellion.[49]

Lieber wholeheartedly agreed that the end well justified the arbitrary means. Yet he seemed to feel that the arguments of Lincoln and Bates were hardly adequate to refute Taney's formidable opinion. He himself had foreshadowed the line of thought of the Chief Justice with a blunt assertion in the *Civil Liberty* which soon came back to plague him: "It is obvious that, whatever wise provisions a constitution may contain, nothing is gained if the power of declaring martial law be left in the hands of the executive. . . . that this cannot be done by the president alone, but by congress only, need hardly be mentioned." [50]

Before Lieber left Washington, General Frémont, about to take

[47] For a definitive discussion, see J. G. Randall, *Constitutional Problems under Lincoln* (New York, 1926), 118–39. See also, G. C. Sellery, "Lincoln's Suspension of Habeas Corpus as Viewed by Congress," *Bulletin of the University of Wisconsin* (Historical Series 1, No. 3), 213–86.

[48] *Ex Parte Merryman*, 17 Fed. Cas. 144: Randall, *Constitutional Problems under Lincoln*, 120–21.

[49] U.S. Department of Justice, *Opinion of the Attorney General on the Suspension of the Writ of Habeas Corpus* (Washington, 1861), reprinted in Series 2, *War of the Rebellion: Official Records* . . . (Washington, 1880–1901), II, 20–30; Randall, *Constitutional Problems under Lincoln*, 121–24.

[50] Lieber, *On Civil Liberty and Self-Government* (Philadelphia, 1853), I, 130–31; (3d ed.), 108.

command in seething Missouri, consulted him upon the legal justification for martial law. For once the scholar's prolific juristic
imagination failed him and he had little to suggest. On his way
home, he stopped at Philadelphia to visit sage old Horace Binney,
whom Sumner considered America's foremost lawyer. Binney in
a half hour outlined what seemed a telling refutation of each of
Taney's arguments.[51]

Lieber was delighted and urged the octogenarian to prepare his
opinion in written form. Binney complied with a long letter which
the scholar copied for Frémont and loaned to Bates. This formed
the basis for three pamphlets which Binney subsequently published at Lieber's persuasion. They contained probably the best
rationale for presidential suspension of the habeas corpus. The
defense attracted wide attention—at least ten pamphlets appeared
in direct refutation—and Attorney General Bates expressed his
warm approval and admiration.[52]

Binney pointed out that in England the writ had been a bulwark against the despotic monarch; in the United States there was
no need for it to be a restriction upon the already weak President.
Since the Constitution did not specify which arm of the government should suspend the writ, why should not the President do
so as well as Congress? Presidential suspension was less dangerous
than congressional, since the single executive could not avoid blame
for misdeeds while members of Congress enjoyed the irresponsi-
bility of divided authority. Lieber liked the pamphlet and gloried
in the fact that the distinguished jurist dedicated it to him.[53]

[51] Lieber, prefatory remarks to contemporary copy of Binney to Lieber, July 29,
1861; Lieber to Bates, July 31, 1861. Lieber had carried on an earlier correspondence with Binney, Lieber to Allibone, March 10, 1860; and Sumner admired the aged
lawyer, Pierce (ed.), *Memoir and Letters of Charles Sumner,* IV, 138. Lieber queried
Andrew Johnson for a full report of his remarks on the habeas corpus, July 29, 1861,
Johnson papers, Library of Congress. In addition to Binney's arguments, Lieber
esteemed those of the Solicitor of the War Department, William Whiting. See Whiting, *The War Powers of the President and the Legislative Powers of Congress in
Relation to Rebellion, Treason and Slavery* (Boston, 1862). Lieber's copy is in the
University of California library.
[52] Lieber to Bates, July 31, August 5, 8, 27, December 2, 3, 1861; Bates to Lieber,
December 19, 1861, May 6, 1862. Binney, *The Privilege of the Writ of Habeas Corpus
under the Constitution* (Philadelphia, 1862). Parts II and III were printed under
the same title the same year. The Library of Congress catalogue lists ten pamphlet
rebuttals.
[53] Binney to Lieber, July 29, 1861 (contemporary copy); Binney, *Privilege of the
Writ of Habeas Corpus;* Randall, *Constitutional Problems under Lincoln,* 125–27;
Lieber to Sumner, [January 9, 1862].

Senator Sumner's glowing enthusiasm for Binney overbalanced his desire as a Radical Republican to wrest authority from Lincoln. He predicted without qualification that Binney's "conclusions will stand as law," but apparently modified his position by January, 1863, when the Radical stand had become more distinct and pub-lic opinion strongly incensed over the large number of political prisoners being held without trial. At that time, he queried Lieber on his views.[54]

The professor replied that he still subscribed to his earlier be-liefs (which he presented in an eleven-point outline). However, he granted that the constitutional clause was bungling and that "a good law might and ought to be passed insuring *revision* and *examination* of cases of imprisonment without the H[abeas] C[orpus]." After much wrangling, Congress did pass such a law in 1863. It also authorized the President to suspend the writ, but did not in the least decide whether or not he had already possessed the authority. Lincoln effectively strengthened his position through an able public letter in which he inquired, "Must I shoot a simple-minded soldier-boy who deserts, while I must not touch a hair of a wily agitator who induces him to desert?" He directed his secretary to send a copy to Lieber. A "sterling letter," the publicist replied; he would propose that the Loyal Publication Society print ten thousand copies, if funds were available.[55]

Lieber's stand brought frequent charges of inconsistency against him. Those who opposed the arbitrary policies of the administra-tion proclaimed with delight the earlier doctrines of this political theorist, now so high in the Republican ranks. Wendell Phillips, who fought for civil liberty with all the eloquent passion with which he attacked slavery, reminded a New York audience in December, 1861, "Lieber says that *habeas corpus,* free meetings like this, and a free press, are the three elements which distinguish liberty from despotism. . . . But today, Mr. Chairman, every

[54] Sumner to Lieber, January 8, [1862], Harvard University; Lieber to Sumner, January 8, 1863.

[55] Lieber to Sumner, January 8, 11, 1863. This measure had passed the House the previous July. Randall, *Constitutional Problems under Lincoln,* 129. Lieber to Lin-coln, June 16, 1863, Lincoln papers, Library of Congress. The Loyal Publication Society did not publish the letter (Lincoln to Erastus Corning and others, June 12, 1863, Lincoln papers, Library of Congress), but the Philadelphia Union League issued it as *President Lincoln's Views* . . . (Philadelphia, 1863).

one of them is annihilated in every square mile of the republic." [56]

A few weeks later, Lieber addressed another New York audience in earnest defense of that annihilation. Critically but most respectfully an erudite writer for the New York *World*—Lieber suspected it was his former friend, George Ticknor Curtis, the historian of the Constitution—contrasted the political theorist's former and contemporary views.[57]

If Lieber was now right, he warned, "we have no security for our liberties except in times of perfect tranquility; the times when safeguards against illegal violence are least needed." He lamented the theorist's drift from "his earlier, and we think sounder, opinion. We appreciate the motives of patriotic support of the administration to which we ascribe this change; but we had counted on finding him the consistent advocate of the views which he had deliberately formed when there was nothing in passing events to disturb the equipoise of his judgment." [58]

Lieber's defense was, of course, that he had not thought in terms of an insurrection when he outlined his precepts on civil liberty: "People forget that a treatise on Navigation is not written for cases of ship wreck." Only through abrogation of normal constitutional privileges could the government save his beloved country and its sacred institutions. He was steadfast in his determination to preserve the nation. When the political principles that had protected it changed, he espoused the new doctrines as wholeheartedly as he had the old. His consistency ran deep—far deeper than mere constitutional principles.[59]

The political theorist's role in formulating official rationale for the presidential suspension of the habeas corpus had been minor but heart-warming. Also he relished greatly the respectful manner in which Bates consulted him on minor technicalities. The At-

[56] D. S. Alexander, *A Political History of the State of New York* (New York, 1909), III, 19.
[57] A lengthy summary of Lieber's lecture appeared in the New York *Times,* March 17, 1862; the notes from which he spoke, "Law and Usages of War," are at Johns Hopkins University. In both this lecture and his correspondence, Lieber closely followed Binney's arguments. "Dr. Lieber on the Habeas Corpus," New York *World,* March 18, 1862. Lieber to Bates, March 30, [1862], misdated 1863.
[58] New York *World,* March 18, 1862.
[59] The quotation is the comment Lieber wrote on Leonard[?] Bacon to Lieber, March 5, 1864.

torney General submitted a definition of the word "constitution" for Lieber's comment, and debated with him the complexities of the term "citizenship." Could it cover a Negro? Naturally, Lieber argued in the affirmative. Again, Bates queried, "Can a nation *blockade* its own seaport?" The scholar answered pragmatically that regardless of what terminology a nation used, it could close its own ports—and could do so without acknowledging the sovereignty of the Confederacy.[60]

Throughout 1862, the erudite professor sent frequent suggestions to Bates. The Attorney General respected his judgment, but did not depend upon it in major matters. Although Lieber's views were taking on an increasingly Radical Republican cast while Bates budged but little from his old border-state Whiggery, the relationship remained cordial. As late as 1864, the Attorney General read several of Lieber's minor writings, but he no longer agreed with the Radical scholar on the issues of the war. He commented in his diary in the fall of 1863 upon an article Lieber had sent him proposing the suppression of slavery: "The Dr. *theorises* very well, he suggests ends, perhaps good in themselves, but wholly ignores the principles and means of their attainment." [61]

At the same time that Lieber gave legal advice to the Attorney General, through Sumner he exerted some small influence on foreign affairs. The powerful Senator carried on intimate personal correspondence with a number of important European statesmen, and Lieber was one of a circle of friends to whom he sent bundles of these letters to peruse.[62]

This confidential relationship with Sumner stimulated the

[60] Bates to Lieber, October 12, 21, November 22, December 1, 1862; Lieber to Bates, November 9, 20, 22, 25, 29, December 3, 1862. U.S. Department of Justice, *Opinion of Attorney General Bates on Citizenship* (Washington, 1863).

[61] Beale, *Diary of Edward Bates,* 308. Lieber to Bates, September 19, 1863; Bates to Lieber, October 8, 1863. In the latter letter, Bates wrote of the article on slavery, in contrast to his diary entry: "In common with all your works that I have read, it exhibits depth of learning & a breadth of thought which would be invaluable to a founder of political society—one who is about to erect a fabric of Government, intended for the common good, & therefore guided by policies whose only object is, the attainment of the most enduring & the most diffusable social benefits. In that point of view, I don't see how your propositions can be minded." Bates read Lieber's *Niebuhr, Character of the Gentleman,* and *Washington and Napoleon.* Bates to Lieber, February 13, 1864 (Huntington Library); April 23, 1864 (Johns Hopkins University); Beale, *Diary of Edward Bates,* 332, 359, 368.

[62] See, for example, Lieber to Sumner, February 16, 25, 1865.

scholar's thinking on foreign problems and caused him to develop an increasing interest in international affairs. He wrote the Senator frequently and urgently when the United States came dangerously close to war with Great Britain over the *Trent* incident late in 1861. Captain Wilkes had stopped the British ship *Trent* and removed two Confederate commissioners, Mason and Slidell. While the North, Lieber included, wildly applauded the act, the British government denounced it as completely unjustifiable under international law. Competent jurist though he was, Lieber insisted that the United States had justice on its side, but concurred with Sumner that conflict with England would be disastrous.

Sumner, like President Lincoln, with whom he frequently conferred, hoped for arbitration. He turned to Lieber for concrete suggestions upon how to bring it about. The scholar recommended Prussia as arbiter and proposed a congress of nations, similar to that held at Paris at the close of the Crimean War. The congress could prevent future crises by drawing up clear rules of maritime international law. Sumner thought the plan excellent in theory but unlikely to win favor with the traditionally isolationist legislators of the United States. Lieber quickly saw the point and shifted to the view that an informal congress of noted authorities on international law might serve almost as well.

Cooler councils prevailed on both sides of the Atlantic and made arbitration unnecessary. At a cabinet meeting on Christmas Day, Sumner read conciliatory letters from the British Liberal leaders, Richard Cobden and John Bright, and Seward prepared a statement agreeing to release the Confederate envoys. Within a few weeks the affair was almost forgotten, but it had helped inoculate the previously pro-British Lieber and Sumner with an Anglophobia which constantly grew more virulent. On the positive side, it left Lieber with a dazzling new idea which he pushed almost to fruition by the time of his death in 1872. From 1861 on, he worked steadily for a private congress of publicists and authorities on international law to draw up codes which would possess the same weight of authority in the law of nations as the treatises of Blackstone, Kent, and Story in the realm of common law. Lieber's idea ultimately materialized much as he had hoped.[63]

[63] J. G. Randall, *The Civil War and Reconstruction* (Boston, 1937), 463–68;

By December, 1861, just five years had elapsed since Lieber left his chair at South Carolina College, a half decade which had marked a tremendous revolution in his own life and that of the nation. He had abandoned his muted minority position in the plantation South to join the vanguard of the new industrial North and help press into execution his nationalist political theories. He could function less as a mere professor expounding abstractions to schoolboys and more as an influential publicist molding governmental policy. He liked the title "publicist"; indeed he himself had coined the word, and increasingly he served as a publicist to the conservative revolution.

C. F. Adams, "The Trent Affair," *American Historical Review*, XVII (1912), 540–62. Lieber to Sumner, December 26, 1861; Lieber to Bates, December 2, 3, 1861 (copy); Lieber to Sumner, December 19, 27, 1861, Huntington Library; Sumner to Lieber, December 19, 24, 1861, Harvard University. Beale, *Diary of Edward Bates*, 213–17. Lieber wished to settle the many technicalities involved in visit and search: were ambassadors immune and generals not, should no neutral vessel be searched, or only no neutral vessel proceeding between neutral ports? Should, as Lieber wished, private property of belligerents be declared safe and free on the high seas? Should financial obligations continue uninterrupted by war? Lieber recommended the omission of the questions of a permanent court of arbitration and of compulsory arbitration before recourse to war. Lieber to Sumner, January 17, 1862.

XIV
Codifying the Rules of War

THERE are but these alternatives before us," Professor Lieber pointed out midway through the Civil
War, "either the North simply and plainly conquers
the South . . . or the North must submit in abject, vile serfdom."
The struggle for hegemony was regrettable, but since it was under
way, the only practical question was which section should grind
the other under its heel. "We must conquer the South," he insisted,
"not for a crown, as a province, but for the *country* and the *National* constitution." [1]

Thus, the publicist came to interpret clearly the emerging pattern of civil conflict and to foster his war aims in newspaper letters, pamphlets, and private correspondence. From the beginning
he proclaimed the preservation of the Union as a divine mission.
"God has given us this great country for great purposes," he had
assured Attorney General Bates in the summer of 1861. "He has
given it to us, as much as He gave Palestine to the Jews."

Lieber wished to fortify as well as to preserve the Union, and
hoped fervently that the war would strike a deathblow to the state-
rights shibboleth in the North as well as in the South. He conceded
to his old Brahmin friend Hillard that the "doctrine has cropped
out in almost every region of our country at some time or other,"
but emphasized, "This will be a great period if we can settle,
plainly and avowedly, that allegiance is due to the U.S. and to no
one else." [2]

This overwhelming nationalism, combined with a loathing of

---

[1] Lieber to General Henry Wager Halleck, March 4, 1863, Lieber papers, Henry
E. Huntington Library. All manuscripts referred to in this chapter, unless otherwise
identified, are from this collection.
[2] Lieber to Bates, July 3, 1861, copy; Lieber to Hillard, May 20, 1861.

slavery, induced Lieber to abandon one of his firmest positions. He reversed his thirty-year contention that slavery, deplorable though it might be, was a state institution with which the Federal government had no right to tamper. "If only two things be clearly carved out by this struggle," he asserted in June, 1861, "the . . . nationalization of this country and the wiping off of slavery from Maryland, Virginia and Kentucky and Missouri—all the struggle and heartburning would be like a breeze." He was by no means certain how this might come about. Perhaps the government should spend a hundred and fifty million or two hundred million dollars to emancipate slaves in border states so that they could settle as free laborers in the British West Indies. By the end of the year he was so confident that Negro servitude in the upper South would disintegrate that he predicted, "American slavery will lose itself in the tropics." [3]

In the following three years, Lieber encouraged and advised Sumner's Radical onslaught against slavery. Slowly the program became more ambitious until it embraced freeing all slaves, enlisting Negro troops, and even extending the vote to former slaves. Step by step, the scholar kept pace and his advice became increasingly important as the abolitionist Senator's role grew larger.

Lieber's influence on the army program, first through Attorney General Bates then through General in Chief Henry W. Halleck, was more direct and significant. Here again his views slowly shifted, always a trifle more moderately than the Radical Republicans'. Although the aging scholar did endorse Lincoln's suspension of the habeas corpus, it was not easy for him to slough off overnight his long-standing insistence upon civil liberties and property rights. Necessity forced him to regard them as secondary to the restoration of the Union, but only secondary.

Occasionally the emotional professor lost his balance in the enthusiasm of the moment. He lamented that the government could not confiscate the Newport summer homes of rebel women who were openly gloating over the reverse at Bull Run, and he urged Bates to take action against a hostile New York German-language newspaper, *Das Journal*. Normally he pursued a far calmer course.

[3] Lieber to Hillard, June 12, 1861; Lieber to Sumner, June 1, 1861; Lieber to Bates, December 19, 1861.

He admitted regretfully that any official curb upon James Gordon Bennett's barbed attacks on the administration in the New York *Herald* would probably result disastrously, and in the summer of 1862 he cautioned Sumner against drafting a sweeping confiscation act. Nor did he agree at first with Sumner's "state suicide" theory of secession, which would revert defeated Southern states to the condition of territories.[4]

Although this moderation placed Lieber on the right fringe of the Radical Republicans, it added weight to his pronouncements since sometimes they could serve as useful compromises. The elderly professor's eminent position gave him some authority, for he was highly regarded by a public which looked upon his writings with more respect than knowledge. He gained additional prestige be creating the impression that he was above petty politics. Especially on military questions he rarely trimmed his sails to the breezes from the Capitol; he preferred to strike a somewhat pompous pose as the stern and honest old soldier turned elder statesman. He was only half joking when he reminded Sumner of his qualifications for a brigadier generalship, and an ember of envy burned through his words when he boasted that he would make at least as good a general as Carl Schurz.[5]

This attitude led Lieber to coincide with the most vociferous Radicals in his demand for a vigorous prosecution of the war. He lamented in January, 1862, that no traitor or spy had been hanged; and unlike some Radicals, he longed also for the prosecution of "that herd of infamous cattle," the dishonest war contractors. He called for rivers of blood because only thus could the war come to a crushing uncompromising conclusion. "I also long, . . . most heartily for an end of this repulsive shedding of blood," he pointed out, "—so wanton, so wicked, so aimless, so fiendish on the side of the South." [6]

All three of Lieber's sons were in the war, one on the Confed-

---

[4] Lieber to Bates, August 27, 1861; April 8, July 8, 18, 1862; Lieber to Sumner, March 23, April 29, 1862.

[5] Lieber to Sumner, December 19, 1861; Lieber to Norman Lieber, April 13, 1862. In the latter letter, Lieber declared: "I tell you, I ought to have had the offer of a brigadiership. I would have done as good service as many others and quite as good or better as Carl Schurtz [*sic*]."

[6] Lieber to Sumner, January 28, February 12, 1862; Lieber to Norman Lieber, April 20, 1862.

319

erate side. That was an important reason for the father's desire to see the conflict end as quickly as possible. Some Radical Republicans, especially those who dominated the Congressional Committee on the Conduct of the War, seemed more interested in supporting commanders with "correct" views than those who could merely win battles. Lieber joined these in excoriating the cautious and dapper General McClellan, a Democrat, but was just as quick to label their darling, General John Pope, a braggart on the basis of his first sweeping proclamation.[7]

Military problems fascinated the bellicose scholar, and during the first confused months after the outbreak of the war, he turned his intellect to the clarification of one hazy question after another. The most significant of these concerned the treatment of the foe on the field of battle. The foes were rebels, and according to the reasoning of many, when caught should pay the penalty for treason. This would, of course, have resulted in the unspeakable shambles of a no-quarter war.

When the Confederate armies bagged a sizable number of Union troops at the Bull Run debacle, the problem shifted from theory to reality. Obviously both armies must follow the ordinary rules of war, but could the Union forces exchange prisoners or work out parole agreements without recognizing the Southern Confederacy? Washington officials seemed to think it impossible.

The skillful Lieber delved into treatises on international law and came up with a formula. For humanitarian reasons, even in times of rebellion, the customary rules of warfare and treatment of prisoners should continue. Precedents proved this did not involve either the recognition of the rebels nor a foregoing of the right to try rebels for treason after the rebellion was crushed. Lieber published his interpretation as an open letter to the Attorney General, who expressed his approval. Since the dictum was sound international law and backed by a general humanitarian sentiment, it became the official viewpoint.[8]

[7] Lieber to Bates, July 18, 1862. For a complete account of the war aims of the Radicals and their strategy for obtaining them, see T. Harry Williams, *Lincoln and the Radicals* (Madison, 1941).

[8] W. B. Hesseltine, *Civil War Prisons. A Study in War Psychology* (Columbus, Ohio, 1930), 1–15. Lieber's article, in the form of a letter addressed to Bates, appeared in the New York papers in August, 1861. Bates termed it a "terse and excellent article." Bates to Lieber, July 23, 1861. Lieber, "The Disposal of Prisoners," New

Though Lieber favored exchange, he vigorously opposed parole —the release of prisoners upon their pledge not to take up arms again. Even as he expected, it led soldiers to lay down their arms too easily in the expectation that they could sign a pledge not to fight again, return to their own lines, and go home.[9] The scholar wrote with equal enthusiasm on problems of lesser import. He extolled military reviews as a morale-building factor, and urged through the press that commanders conduct more of them. He addressed an open letter to Secretary of the Treasury Chase on the pressing need for a government-operated army savings bank. It would enable the soldiers to send home their pay, provide additional funds for the war, and soften the depression after the war. The publicist pressed the proposal vigorously upon both Chase and Sumner, but without success.[10]

Lieber had not hesitated to work through Washington acquaintances to obtain a regular army appointment for his son Norman, but almost immediately thereafter he complained eloquently to Sumner that political appointments were leading to the selection of very poor-quality officers. These seldom received their commissions on the basis of ability, and were often as ignorant of military matters as the privates. As a twofold reform, the publicist suggested a board of review to examine the qualifications of all candidates, and the Federal appointment on a merit basis of all officers above the rank of captain.[11]

York *Times*, August 19, 1861; Lieber, "The Exchange of Prisoners," *ibid.*, October 21, 1861. On December 11, 1861, Congress passed a resolution in favor of exchanges. General H. W. Halleck succinctly stated the same principle as Lieber's to General George Brinton McClellan, December 3, 1861: "This exchange is a mere military convention. A prisoner exchanged under the laws of war is not thereby exempted from trial and punishment as a traitor. Treason is a state or civil offense punishable by civil courts; the exchange of prisoners of war is only a part of the ordinary *commercia belli.*" Series 2 *Official Records*, III, 150–51, cited in Hesseltine, *Civil War Prisons*, 14–15.

[9] Lieber to Sumner, August 20, 1861, Lieber papers; Sumner to Lieber, August 24, 1861, Harvard University. Hesseltine, *Civil War Prisons*, 74–77. New York *Times*, August 19, October 21, 1861.

[10] [Lieber], "Military Reviews," New York *Times*, August 17, 1861; [Lieber], "The U.S. Treasury an Army Savings Bank," New York *Times*, September, 1861, clippings in Lieber papers. Two decades earlier, Lieber had proposed an army savings bank. Lieber to Alonzo Potter, November 10, 1842, Historical Society of Pennsylvania. See also Lieber to Sumner, September 14 and 15, December 14, 1861.

[11] Lieber to Sumner, July 27, 1861. Fred A. Shannon, *The Organization and Administration of the Union Army*, 2 vols. (Cleveland, 1928), I, 45, 46, 154–65.

Congress and the War Department ignored the plea for this essential reform which would have been valuable to the army and detrimental to the patronage-hungry politicians. At the same time they were ready to listen to Lieber's mistaken warning that the combination of the regular and volunteer forces might lead to the evils of a European-type permanent standing army.

The scholar warned, "Make our present large army a homogeneous, vast democratic army . . . let some striking victory knit them well together, men to men, and then to the general, and every person versed in the analytical chemistry of History will tell you that a Bonaparte, dictating after a Lodi is unavoidable. No Congress, no Parliament can keep under an organized vast democratic army." [12]

The chairman of the committee considering the merger liked Lieber's critique, Sumner reported, "& said that it came in time." Already Radical Republicans in Congress had started at the specter of a potential dictator in General McClellan, the "Young Napoleon." More important still, patronage stalked in the guise of state rights to prevent the amalgamation. While the Massachusetts politician Ben Butler became a major general in the first year of the war, Phil Sheridan remained a captain of the regulars until May, 1862. Congress smashed the merger plan and the small body of regulars which could have worked as a training leaven in the enormous mass of volunteers remained intact and comparatively useless. [13]

Political questions similarly intrigued the publicist. He greeted General Frémont's proclamation of August, 1861, with elation and trepidation. The political-minded general had made a strong bid for Radical Republican support by issuing an order emancipating the slaves of all disloyal Missourians. While antislavery factions acclaimed the proclamation, President Lincoln viewed it with consternation as a threat to the skittish border states. Lieber felt strongly that the fugitive slave who entered the Union lines must be received and become *ipso facto* free, but he did not

[12] Lieber to Bache, December 14, 1861, contemporary copy enclosed in Lieber to Sumner, December 14, 1861.
[13] Sumner to Lieber, December 16, 1861, Harvard University; Shannon, *Organization and Administration of the Union Army*, I, 164–65, 191–92.

seem sure whether the power to proclaim this policy resided in a field commander, the President as commander in chief, or Congress.[14]

President Lincoln sent Frémont a letter of admonition; Lieber studied it with some bewilderment and concluded that Congress must pass an act to authorize military emancipation. Sumner agreed, but complained that since it meant that "Slavery shall only be touched by Act of Congress & not through *Martial Law*," it weakened the armies. The political theorist was too familiar with problems of military discipline to concur entirely. While he disliked Lincoln's cautious policy, he feared that to allow a single general to "Napoleonize" a "grand manifesto" on slavery or any other subject would demoralize the forces.[15]

The varied treatment of fugitive slaves coming within the lines typified the chaotic nature of the rules of war devised by Union commanders. Some ordered slaves returned to their masters; others like Ben Butler declared them "contraband of war" and put them to work upon fortifications; many dodged the issue by doing nothing. Lieber's perplexity at the time of Frémont's proclamation was trivial compared with that of the ordinary volunteer officer as he faced the complexities of military field law. The scholar was learned in the laws of war; to the average general officer they were no more than rhetorical expressions to justify one's own conduct and damn the enemy's.[16]

Lieber began to agitate for co-ordinated rules because he wished to see the Union army become a smooth-functioning, efficient military machine. He confided to several friends, "I desire to write a little book on the Law and Usages of War, affecting the Combatants—some 200 pages 12mo., but nothing of the sort having ever been written, so far as I know, it would require a good deal of hunting up, and God has denied me the two delectable things— a saddle horse and an amanuensis. Otherwise I would try to write

---

[14] Lieber to Sumner, February 12, 1862.

[15] Lieber to Sumner, September 14 and 15, December 19, 1861, Lieber papers; Sumner to Lieber, September 17, 1861, Harvard University. Williams, *Lincoln and the Radicals*, 39–40, 48–49.

[16] Randall, *The Civil War and Reconstruction*, 478–80. A few officers consulted the standard treatises on international law, especially those by Halleck, Kent, Wheaton, and Vattel. See Randall, *Constitutional Problems under Lincoln*, 347.

something which Congress might feel inclined to recommend to the army." [17]

Congress was not interested, but nevertheless the indefatigable professor began gathering materials for a course on "The Laws and Usages of War." For many years it had been his ambition to teach the subject at West Point. Failing that, in the winter of 1861–62 he delivered the lectures in the Law School of Columbia University. Basically an elaboration upon his chapter on war in the *Political Ethics,* they were rich in solid precepts, thought provoking and clear.[18]

The War Department was not yet ready for standard rules to govern armies in the field: not enough battles had been fought and not enough Confederate territory occupied to make them a necessity. Only one general took note of Lieber's lectures. That was Henry Wager Halleck, who had succeeded to the command of the western armies. Meticulous, a sound authority on military law, and a good organizer, Halleck was author of a treatise on international law of which more than two thirds was devoted to the laws of war. Upon his arrival in Missouri he had promulgated a series of able regulations that quickly brought order out of the confusion Frémont had left. Nevertheless, he asked Lieber for a brief of the lectures, which he hoped might aid in the solution of some difficult problems.[19]

Before Lieber could send a copy of his lectures, he learned his son Hamilton had been wounded at Fort Donelson. In his resultant trip to the West, he met General Halleck, who was most kind and even promised the convalescent Hamilton a place on his staff. The trip not only built a personal bond of friendship

[17] Lieber to Sumner, August 19, 1861; Lieber to Allibone, August 19, 1861.

[18] Lieber, "Laws and Usages of War," and "Twenty-Seven Definitions and Elementary Positions Concerning the Laws and Usages of War," Lieber papers, Johns Hopkins University. Lieber delivered this series of eight lectures between October 21, 1861, and February 6, 1862. Some of them appeared in condensed form in the New York *Times,* January 13, February 10, 16, March 17, 1862. On Lieber's desire to teach at West Point, see Lieber, draft letter, May, 1862; Lieber to Halleck, March 10, 1864; Halleck to Lieber, March 14, 1864.

[19] Lieber to Halleck, January 30, 1862; Halleck to Lieber, February 3, 11, 1862. Halleck, *International Law or, Rules Regulating the Intercourse of States in Peace and War* (New York, 1861). General Orders 8, 13, *General Orders, Department of the Missouri,* 1861. George W. Cullum, "Biographical Sketch of Major-Gen. Henry W. Halleck," Halleck, *International Law* (4th ed.; London, 1908), xiii–xiv.

between the general and scholar, but gave Lieber new insight into the problems of the conflict. "I knew war as [a] soldier, as a wounded man in the hospital, as an observing citizen," he commented, "but I had yet to learn it in the phase of a father searching for his wounded son, walking through the hospitals, peering in the ambulances." [20]

Hamilton had lost an arm; his father took deep pride in his heroic behavior under fire and after he had been wounded. Lieber had never been able to understand this son, who was not bookish and voluble like his father and brothers, but large, blond, stolid, exceedingly shy, and filled with a deep love of the soil. He had become an Illinois farmer rather than a naval officer as his father had hoped. Now, wounded, he assumed the stature of a character from Plutarch.

The professor returned to ponder what he had seen and heard: prisoners from the Tennessee back country who had expected death upon capture; Northern men who told him that Southerners whittled Yankee bones into souvenirs; Union and Confederate officers who received equal treatment in the hospital where Hamilton lay. Firsthand he saw some of the practical problems of occupying hostile territory, and even returned to the question Sumner so frequently posed: How best could Congress eliminate slavery? [21]

The stress and strain of following his three sons in battle endowed Lieber with a realistic approach to the international law of war; even more, it developed in him a strongly humanitarian feeling. In the spring of 1862 he waited for the coming campaigns below Washington with the deepest apprehension. He would not read the letters Oscar sent through Puerto Rico, but knew nevertheless that his son was in the Confederate army moving out onto the Yorktown Peninsula to meet McClellan's impending thrust toward Richmond. Norman's Union regiment would participate in the attack, and with bloody battles taking shape, Lieber found

[20] Lieber to Sumner, February 18, 19, March 23, 1862; Matilda Lieber to Norman Lieber, February 27, March 27, 1862; Lieber to Matilda Lieber, March 3, 1862.
[21] Lieber to Sumner, March 23, 1862; Lieber to Norman Lieber, March 4, 1862. Apparently Hamilton had written his father earlier about the bones and Lieber had communicated the story to Sumner. Sumner to Lieber, [January 8, 1862], Harvard University.

himself with a son on each side likely to fight in the same engagements. "Hard, hard, to think so," he mused, "but it does not change one jot in my feelings. Our cause is a just one, and we belong after God, to our country, not to a state or paltry province." [22]

The severe fighting soon began, and the father anxiously joined the crowds reading the casualty lists as they appeared on the bulletin board outside the *Tribune* offices. To his intense relief, he learned that Norman came through uninjured. After the Battle of Williamsburg, he wrote in a self-congratulatory mood: "O'Riley . . . was expressing his joy that his son had received 'no scratch' . . . when a man sitting near him said: Why here is the name of your son, pointing to a list of 'Killed.' The poor man stared, read, and his face and hands moved convulsively. It was heart rending."

Ironically, Lieber did not learn until much later that he too had lost a son at Williamsburg. Oscar had been wounded mortally, but the news came through in driblets, and it was months before the heartbroken Lieber was forced to accept the hard fact of Oscar's death. Then the crushing story came that his beloved eldest son had died deliriously raving against his father and the North.[23]

Mellowed by grief, but more anxious than ever to press upon the army his interpretation of the laws of land warfare, Lieber applauded General Halleck's promotion to the position of general in chief. In actual fact, Halleck was little more than a military adviser. He had become a hero by quieting turbulent Missouri and transforming one of the worst-run military departments into probably the most efficient. He also gained glory from his subordinate U. S. Grant, who won victory after victory in the field.

[22] Lieber to Norman Lieber, April 19, 1862.

[23] Lieber to Bache, May 24, June 18, 26, July 1, 1862, Rhees collection, Huntington Library; Lieber to Matilda Lieber, August 6, 1862. When, December 16, he finally learned the details of Oscar's death, he wrote his wife: "Your letter has made me very meditative and sad yet you are wholly mistaken if you think there is any ill will—I cannot say so to a departed one—any resentment in my breast. All I can feel occasionally, for a moment is toward the South as if it had robbed me of my son's Kindliness toward me. But that too, is merely passing. I can lay my hand on my heart and say that unconditionally as I desire the South to be subdued and most wicked as I hold her cause to be, I know at the same time that God alone can weigh and judge each individual."

Jealous of Grant, "Old Brains" took active command before Corinth and showed himself to be a hypercautious textbook commander.

Halleck's flair for organizing and his knowledge of the laws of war made him an asset in the War Department, which, even following the removal of Cameron, remained thoroughly inefficient. In politics he had formerly been a Democrat and had issued an order in Missouri banishing fugitive slaves from the Union lines on the grounds that the Confederates were using them as spies. This earned him the fury of the Radical Republicans, who were far from pleased at his elevation. Soon they learned that Halleck was ready to co-operate with their plans to stamp out slavery, but he was so ineffectual that his proposals bore little weight with Stanton above or field commanders below. The enmity of the Radical Republicans turned largely to scorn; Senator Ben Wade expressed it crudely when he sneered, "Put Halleck in command of twenty thousand men and he will not scare three setting geese from their nests." [24]

Radical dismay at Halleck's new appointment was matched by Lieber's delight. With an expert in military law as general in chief, he saw at last a chance to contribute to the settlement of the confusion concerning treatment of Negroes, guerilla bands, and a score of kindred matters. Moreover, he was still anxious to lay down a clear-cut army rule based on international law which would free the Negroes of seceded states as they came within the jurisdiction of the Union army.

The political theorist had warmly denounced on one ground or another almost every Negro policy instituted by either reactionaries or radicals. A stickler for precision in legal matters, he had scorned General Butler's use of the makeshift term "contraband" to justify retention of escaped slaves, because it incorrectly gave them the status of property. He was furious when he heard reports that General McClellan had not only returned runaways, but had promised to use the army to put down slave revolts if they should materialize. When he read in the newspapers that General David Hunter had issued a proclamation emancipating all slaves in three

[24] Williams, *Lincoln and the Radicals*, 50–51, 149–51; W. A. Ganoe, "Henry Wager Halleck," *Dictionary of American Biography*, VIII, 151–52.

seaboard states still largely in Confederate control, and that Edward Stanley, the military governor of North Carolina, was returning runaways to their masters and disbanding schools for Negroes, he wrote an indignant article castigating both officials.[25]

General Hunter, he declared, had completely overstepped his authority within the military hierarchy by issuing an order rightfully in the province of his superiors. Moreover, the order was a travesty since it was based upon martial law which could extend only as far as the actual force of the army. Lincoln was entirely right in repudiating it.[26]

On the other hand, Lieber's wrath against Governor Stanley knew no bounds. The publicist once more pronounced slavery to be a creature of municipal law, mixture of property and personality. It arose from being taken captive in war; fleeing fugitive slaves for centuries past had been free once they had crossed beyond the jurisdiction of the municipal law. Consequently, if the United States were fighting a belligerent state, whether recognized or not, slaves from the hostile territory immediately upon entering the Union lines obtained all the rights and privileges of freemen. Governor Stanley's restrictions upon Negro education were highly immoral; the citizen army would refuse to serve as "beedles of an institution which is the cause of our civil war." [27]

Professor Lieber sent a copy of the letter to General Halleck, who himself was veering slightly toward the Radical position on the conduct of the war. The General in Chief replied that he fully endorsed Lieber's stand: "Our people and Government are only beginning to understand *martial* law and its effect on *municipal* and civil courts." [28]

Halleck saw the opportunity to make use of this prolific jurist whose ideas so nearly coincided with his own. Lieber had com-

---

[25] Lieber to George William Childs, July 23, 1863. By no means all the antislavery people sided with General David Hunter. Sumner's close friend E. L. Pierce complained that the general's proclamation and his forced recruitment of Negro troops would ruin Pierce's government-sponsored project for running abandoned plantations. Shannon, *Organization and Administration of the Union Army*, II, 152–54; Series 3 *Official Records*, II, 50.

[26] For Hunter's and Lincoln's proclamations, see Series 3 *Official Records*, II, 43.

[27] Lieber to Bates, June 8, 1862, published in the New York *Evening Post*, June 17, 1862, under the title, "The Duty of Provisional Governors."

[28] Lieber to Halleck, July 23, 1862; Halleck to Lieber, July 30, 1862.

mented that he was studying the guerilla question. The General in Chief still felt the lack of clear-cut precepts to guide field officers who must cope with this kind of warfare in the border areas, and told Lieber he anxiously awaited the treatise. "It has now become an important question in this country and should be thoroughly investigated," Halleck wrote encouragingly. "I know of no one who can do it as well as yourself." [29]

Delighted by the prospect of obtaining official sanction for his project, the professor quickly prepared a dissertation. When the work appeared in August, 1862, General Halleck gave it his high approval and ordered five thousand pamphlet copies for army distribution.[30]

The essay on guerillas was remarkable for its brevity and clarity. It was only sixteen pages long—short enough not to wear the patience of an overworked or unschooled field officer—and a felicitous combination of historical and legal scholarship with sound common sense. By no means hard and fast dictum, it afforded latitude for reasonable discrimination.

As a preliminary, Professor Lieber clarified the problem by setting up categories of irregulars. He defined guerillas according to contemporary American usage as "self-constituted sets of armed men, in times of war, who form no integrant part of the organized army, do not stand on the regular pay-roll of the army, or are not paid at all, take up arms and lay them down at intervals, and carry on petty war (guerilla) chiefly by raids, extortion, destruction, and massacre, and who cannot encumber themselves with many prisoners, and will therefore generally give no quarter."

American army officers tended to lump into the guerilla classification other types which Lieber sharply distinguished. Partisans, which were a part of the army detached from the main body to engage in guerilla tactics, were entitled to the privileges of the laws of war as long as they did not transgress them. Free corps, troops not belonging to the regular army but raised by authorized individuals, were entitled to similar treatment unless they pillaged or refused quarter. In that case they should be treated on the basis

---

[29] Halleck to Lieber, July 30, 1862.
[30] Lieber to Halleck, August 1, 1862; Halleck to Lieber, August 6, 20, 1862.

of retaliation. Armed peasants or *levies en masse* against invading armies were entitled to the full benefits of the laws of war as long as they openly opposed the invader in respectable numbers and were raised in yet uninvaded or unconquered areas. The absence of a uniform was of no significance unless it was for the purpose of concealment or disguise.

Provided they conducted themselves properly, these groups were entitled upon capture to treatment as prisoners of war. Other categories should receive harsher treatment. Brigands, soldiers who detached themselves from their units to commit robbery or to assail the enemy without or against the authority of their own government, were subject to death if caught. The spy, the war rebel who renewed war in an occupied territory, and the conspirator who planned to renew war were all subject to the death penalty no matter how patriotic and self-sacrificing they might be.

Bushwhackers or armed prowlers were giving especial trouble to the Union army. The Confederates were trying to protect them through threatening retaliation, but they were not entitled to be prisoners of war simply because they had taken up arms for the defense of their country in answer to a Confederate proclamation.

Lieber tried to formulate a rule of reason for the treatment of guerillas and bushwhackers. If they were captured in fair fight and open warfare, they should be prisoners of war until definite crimes or the killing of captives was proved against them. If they were captured in a district fairly occupied by military force or in the rear of the army, they were clearly brigands and not prisoners of war.

At the conclusion of his paper, the scholar pointed out that all his observations applied to the international law of war in general and not to civil war, the rules of which were dependent upon municipal law. Whether in a civil war the regulations should be more or less severe was a problem for the executive or possibly the legislative power. "So much is certain," he emphasized sternly, "that no army, no society, engaged in war, any more than a society at peace, can allow unpunished assassination, robbery, and devastation, without the deepest injury to itself and disastrous consequences, which might change the very issue of the war." [31]

[31] Lieber, *Guerilla Parties Considered with Reference to the Laws and Usages of*

Professor Lieber could now feel that he occupied a semiofficial status in the War Department. Not only did the General in Chief distribute his paper on guerilla parties among the troops, but Secretary of War Edwin M. Stanton encouraged him to submit memoranda on two of his schemes. Consequently he prepared an outline of rewards for military merit similar to European decorations, and a proposal for the establishment of Negro battalions. Able-bodied men not used as teamsters, cooks, or servants could form armed working companies of about two hundred each, similar to those in the Prussian army.[32]

Stanton apparently made no use of the memoranda, but these projects brought the professor into such close association with the army leaders that he felt himself in a position to press upon them his long-dormant proposal for a code. In November, 1862, he carefully drafted a formal letter to General Halleck:

"Ever since the beginning of our present War, it has appeared clearer and clearer to me, that the President ought to issue a set of rules and definitions providing for the most urgent cases, occurring under the Law and Usages of War, and on which our Articles of War are silent." The President, Lieber proposed, should appoint a committee to draw up a code defining the acts or offences and in some instances stating the punishment under the laws of war. The chairman should be General Halleck himself.

The committee should define "the spy," "paroling," and all like matters; it should establish penalties for sundry military offences. By way of example, Lieber queried, "Who shall be treated as prisoner of war?" If the President did not possess sufficient authority to proclaim the rules of war for the American forces, Congress might enact them.[33]

At first Lieber received no decisive answer; Halleck said he was

---

War . . . (New York, 1862), reprinted in Lieber, *Miscellaneous Writings*, II, 277–92, and Series 3 *Official Records*, II, 301–309. Notes used in preparation, and manuscript drafts and copies are in the Lieber papers.

[32] Lieber to Matilda Lieber, August 7 [should be 6], 1862. Lieber, "A Memoir on the Military Use of Coloured persons, free or slave, come to our armies for support or protection, written at the request of Hon. Edwin M. Stanton, Secretary of War"; Lieber, "A Memoir on Rewards for Military Merit and Marks of Distinction in the Army of the United States, chiefly for Privates and Non-Commissioned Officers," both enclosed in Lieber to Halleck, August 10, 11, 1862.

[33] Lieber to Halleck, November 13, 1862.

temporarily too busy to consider the proposal. The professor continued to press him and began to prepare a sample chapter on paroling.[34] With unexpected suddenness Lieber received a reward for his persistence. Early in December the General in Chief wired him to come to Washington at once to spend a month or more. When he arrived, Halleck appointed him to a special board created by the War Department "to propose amendments or changes in the the Rules and Articles of War and a code of regulations for the government of Armies in the field as authorized by the laws and usages of War." [35]

The aged and eccentric General Ethan Allen Hitchcock, to whom Stanton had earlier offered McClellan's command over the Army of the Potomac, presided as the highly competent chairman of the Board. The remainder of the members were well-qualified general officers; Lieber was the only civilian. With the exception of Hitchcock, who unwittingly was serving as a tool for the Committee on the Conduct of the War, the generals were decidedly conservative in their leanings.[36]

The Board cautiously sent a form letter to officers asking for suggestions. Meanwhile Lieber, glorying in his new role, submitted to his colleagues a memorandum proposing that they under-

---

[34] Halleck to Lieber, November 15, 23, 25, 1862; Lieber to Halleck, November 20, 1862; General N. P. Banks to Lieber, November 23, 1862. Williams, *Lincoln and the Radicals*, 274–77.

[35] Lieber to Halleck, December 7, 9, 1862; Lieber to Allibone, December 12 and 14, 1862; Lieber to Matilda Lieber, December 14, 1862. Lieber received eight dollars a day—the salary and mileage of a member of the House of Representatives. Lieber to Matilda Lieber, December 20, 1862. Adjutant General's Office, U.S. War Department, Special Orders No. 399 [Extract], December 17, 1862, Series 3 *Official Records*, II, 951.

[36] W. A. Croffut (ed.), *Fifty Years in Camp and Field; the Diary of Major-General Ethan Allen Hitchcock, U.S.A.* (New York, 1909), 437–40; Ernest Sutherland Bates, "Ethan Allen Hitchcock," *Dictionary of American Biography*, IX, 73–74. Other members of the Board were George L. Hartsuff, John H. Martindale, and George Cadwalader. Hartsuff had been a West Point instructor as well as a field commander; Martindale, a distinguished lawyer, was military governor of the District of Columbia. Cadwalader, a lawyer with Mexican War experience, had been rumored to be Lincoln's choice to succeed Ben Butler. Greeley attacked him as "a Philadelphia Democrat of the extreme Breckinridge school" who would follow a proslavery policy in New Orleans. New York *Tribune*, September 1, 1862. Cadwalader presided, and Martindale sat on the military court which, at the same time that the code was being drafted, cleared General McDowell of Radical charges and censured Senator Wade. Series 1 *Official Records*, XII, part 1, 327.

take comprehensive reform of the entire military system. They should discuss punishments, military distinctions, improved uniforms, creation of new ranks—especially of general officers, promotions on a seniority basis, a new militia law, revision of the curriculum at West Point, and a publication of these changes for the guidance of the army in the field. Nothing came of these startling suggestions. Instead, the Board undertook the rather staid task of revising the antiquated articles of war, and assigned to Lieber the task of drawing up a code of rules of land warfare.[37]

The experienced political theorist quickly prepared a draft code during the first few weeks of 1863. He drew heavily upon his chapter on the international law of war in the *Political Ethics* and delved into his recent lectures on the laws of war, texts on international law, newspaper clippings, and miscellaneous notes. As usual, he called upon his scholarly associates to elucidate obscure classical or historical points. In a helter-skelter fashion he threw together sound and substantial precepts, which in February he took to Washington for approval.[38]

The Board ordered Lieber to print his draft "as manuscript" with copious margins and blank space at the end upon which army

[37] Hitchcock, printed circular letter, December 22, 1862; Lieber to the Board, undoubtedly enclosed in Lieber to Halleck, December 31, 1862, Lieber papers. Lieber to Childs, July 23, 1863, Historical Society of Pennsylvania. The revised articles of war failed to pass Congress, so the only product of the Board was Lieber's code. *Congressional Globe*, 37 Cong., 3 Sess., 1179, 1323; 38 Cong., 1 Sess., 262; Halleck to Lieber, February 23, 1863; Hitchcock to Lieber, March 6, 1863.

[38] Lieber, *Manual of Political Ethics*, 2 vols. (rev. ed.; Philadelphia, 1874), II, 426–59. Lieber made greatest use of Halleck, *International Law*, although privately he considered it inferior to August W. Heffter, *Das Europäische Völkerrecht der Gegenwart* (3d ed.; Berlin, 1855). Of the classic treatises, he also consulted Hugo Grotius, Cornelius van Bynkershoek, and Samuel Pufendorf, but scorned "old" Vattel as "Father Namby-Pamby." Lieber to Halleck, October 3, 1863; Lieber to Sumner, memorandum [1863 or 1864]. Among the contemporaries, he strongly disapproved of William Beach Lawrence's edition of Henry Wheaton, which he considered too state rights. Lieber to Sumner, December 4, 1863. The works of the following were in his library or referred to in his writings: C. S. Zachariae, Adolf Trendlenburg, G. F. von Martens, Robert Phillimore, Sir James Mackintosh, William Whewell, J. J. G. Foelix, Robert von Mohl, Johann K. Bluntschli, Montague Bernard, C. M. Kennedy, Johann Ludwig Klüber, M. S. Pinheiro-Ferreira, James Kent, and Theodore Dwight Woolsey. See catalogue of the Lieber Library, 1859, in the Lieber papers. Most of Lieber's copies of these books are now in the University of California law library. Unfortunately, they are almost entirely lacking in marginalia. Numerous notes and clippings on the laws of war, some probably used in preparation of the code, are in the Lieber papers, Huntington Library and Johns Hopkins University.

officers and other critics could note suggestions. Few army men responded, but Lieber did receive excellent ideas from General Halleck, Hamilton Fish, and a few others. Many of these he embodied in a new revision which he soon sent to the Board for its inspection.[39]

General Halleck considered the need for the sections on paroling and exchange so great that he did not await the final action of the Board, but smoothed them out, clarified them, and issued them on February 29 as General Orders No. 49.[40]

By the end of March the Board was ready to consider the revised code, and Lieber spent several days conferring with its members. Most of its few emendations were the work of General Hitchcock, the chairman. At the suggestion of General Halleck, Lieber gingerly added a section on civil war, rebellion, and insurrection—"ticklish work, that," he commented. The addition was characteristically prolix, but the General in Chief reduced it without loss of content from six pages to a few succinct paragraphs.[41]

Finally, with a few more modifications after it had left Lieber's hand, the code appeared in final form in May, 1863, as General Orders No. 100. It was entitled "Instructions for the Government of Armies of the United States in the Field," and bore the approval of the President of the United States, who commanded that it "be published for the information of all concerned." It was not at the time a binding army ordinance, but as General Halleck

[39] Copies of the various drafts of the code are in the Huntington Library and Johns Hopkins University. A complete and excellent survey of these materials by Charles Robson is in the Huntington Library manuscripts. The letters containing suggestions are in the Lieber papers: "Uncle" to "Willie," February 27, 1863; W. W. Howe to Lieber, [1863]; N. B. Buford to Lieber, April 10, 1863; Halleck to Lieber, February 23, 28, 1863; Lieber to Halleck, March 4, 1863; Fish to Lieber, March 10, 17, 1863; Lieber to Fish, March 19, 1863, copy; C. E. Detmold to Lieber, February 25, 1863; Bache to Lieber, February 25, 1863; John Palmer Usher to Lieber, February 26, 1863. The "printed draft," not to be confused with the finished code, was Francis Lieber, *A Code for the Government of Armies in the Field, as Authorized by the Laws and Usages of War on Land* ([New York], 1863), 23 pp.

[40] Adjutant General's Office, War Department, General Orders No. 49, Series of 1863, Series 2 *Official Records*, V, 306–307; Lieber to Halleck, March 16, 1863; Lieber to Fish, March 19, 1863. For the reception of this order, see Hesseltine, *Civil War Prisons*, 92 et seq.

[41] Lieber to Halleck, March 22, 1863; Lieber to Matilda Lieber, March 26, 1863. [Lieber], *Section X, Insurrection.—Rebellion.—Civil War.—Foreign Invasion of the United States* [n.p., 1863], 6 pp.

pointed out, a statement of "general principles which apply only in the absence of a special agreement," and which could be tempered at the discretion of the President, the War Department, or commanders in the field.[42]

Part propaganda and part expediency, but almost entirely sound international law at the core, the code was, like its chief author's personality, an admixture of military sternness with basic humanitarianism. In keeping with Lieber's lifelong beliefs, it was a stanch defense of property rights, except for property in slaves. It was a practical formulation of the Radical Republican philosophy of the war, tempered by a respect for legal institutions and a compassion toward the enemy often lacking among the Radicals. Indeed the code could serve as easily to curb a too-zealous Radical as to censure an overly-moderate proslavery commander. Moderate though it was, the code was acceptable to the Radical Republicans since it was a two-edged sword which Confederate authorities could wield against the Union army.[43]

Perhaps one of the greatest merits of the order was its form, highly characteristic of Lieber's writing. It was less a rigid legal code than a persuasively written essay on the ethics of conducting war. This made it usable for tough-minded Union officers, unschooled in the laws of war, who must be convinced rather than ordered. It was realistic in its view that vigorous prosecution of war could most speedily bring peace, yet so humanitarian compared with treatises of earlier epochs that one over-zealous Lin-

---

[42] Adjutant General's Office, War Department, General Orders 100, Series of 1863, Series 2 *Official Records*, V, 671–82, republished in Lieber, *Miscellaneous Writings*, II, 247–74, and in innumerable editions in many languages. Though not released until mid-May, the order bore the date April 24, 1863. For Halleck's interpretation, see Halleck to Hitchcock, August 12, 1863; Halleck to General S. A. Hurlbut, June 22, 1863, Eldridge papers, Huntington Library. For an able summary of Lieber's activities during the war, with especial emphasis upon General Orders 100, see Brainerd Dyer, "Francis Lieber and the American Civil War," *The Huntington Library Quarterly*, II (1939), 449–67. See also Frank Freidel, "General Order 100 and Military Government," *Mississippi Valley Historical Review*, XXXII (1946), 541–56.

[43] The order was transmitted to the Confederates with the information that it went into effect against the United States as of the day of issue (April 24) and against the enemy on the date of its delivery, May 22. The Confederates wished immediately to apply it against Federal troops which purportedly had committed outrages in Virginia. Series 2 *Official Records*, V, 689, 744, 755; Hesseltine, *Civil War Prisons*, 95.

coln lover flatly asserted in the 1930's that it must obviously be directly from the pen of the President. In sum, General Orders 100 was a logical outgrowth of the conflict, a guide for its conduct, and an interpretation of its meaning.[44]

"Men who take up arms against one another in public war," Lieber insisted in the order, "do not cease on this account to be moral beings, responsible to one another, and to God." Wars were not their own end, but the mode of obtaining great ends of state. Hence ridiculous restrictions of chivalry no longer held, "but the law of war imposes many limitations and restrictions on principles of justice, faith, and honor."

The code listed these in detail, then handed to the officers two great means of negating its humanitarian principles: military necessity and retaliation. Military necessity allowed destruction or capture of the enemy, armed and unarmed, and of his property, the withholding of sustenance, or use of deception where it did not involve bad faith, providing these things were indispensable to obtain the ends of the war. It did not admit cruelty, maiming, or wounding except in fight, torture to extort confession, use of poison, wanton destruction of a district, nor ordinarily "any act of hostility which makes the return to peace unnecessarily difficult."

These were strong prohibitions, but so loosely framed as to admit Sherman's wide swathe of destruction through Georgia. Four decades later American army officers operating under General Orders 100 pleaded exoneration from charges of torturing Filipinos on the basis of this selfsame "military necessity."[45]

Retaliation, the second loophole, also received official sanction. Lieber termed it "the sternest feature of war," and warned it was a most stringent device which could rapidly lead to "the internecine wars of savages."

From these broad precepts, Lieber went into a detailed discussion of the treatment of property and citizens in occupied terri-

[44] Emanuel Herz, *Abraham Lincoln: A New Portrait*, 2 vols. (New York, 1931), I, 277–79.

[45] For a British criticism of Sherman on the basis of G.O. 100, see J. M. Spaight, *War Rights on Land* (London, 1911), 171. Elihu Root, *The Military and Colonial Policy of the United States* . . . (Cambridge, 1924), 65–69, 106–107; Moorfield Story and Julian Codman, *Secretary Root's Record "Marked Severities in Philippine Warfare"* . . . (Boston, 1902), 14, 109 *et passim;* P. C. Jessup, *Elihu Root*, 2 vols. (New York, 1938), I, 338.

tory. He laid down stern strictures against pilfering and profiteering. Public property fairly belonged to the occupiers, but private citizens and private property should remain undisturbed. The one notable exception to this was slaves, which Lieber, going back to ancient law, did not classify as strictly property. They were to become permanently free. Commanders should protect the loyal citizens within their districts, throw the burden of the war as much as possible upon disloyal ones, and hamper these hostile ones with whatever measures seemed necessary.

Shifting his attention to the relationship of the two belligerent armies, Lieber classified the types who were eligible to treatment as prisoners of war along the general rules laid down in the paper on guerillas. Most assuredly, he emphasized, Negro soldiers should receive the same treatment as other prisoners—and neither be shot nor sold into servitude. This section was the result of ugly propaganda spreading through the North. Other stories about conditions at Libby Prison and Andersonville led Lieber to outline rules for the fair treatment of prisoners of war. Lieber's sharp strictures on exchange and paroling, already anticipated by Halleck in General Orders 49, helped end the flagrant abuses which had been so helpful to the Confederates.[46]

Finally, because it was designed for an internal conflict, the code contained a definition of insurrection, civil war, and rebellion. It stipulated that all the relations arising from application of the rules of war in a conflict with the rebels did not constitute recognition of the government, nor would it prevent the legitimate government from trying the leaders for high treason upon the end of the rebellion.

With open pride Lieber surveyed his work—the first code of laws of land warfare—and termed it "our little pamphlet . . . short but pregnant and weighty like some stumpy Dutch woman when in the family way with coming twins." Lieber might well be proud. General Orders 100 served as a basis for almost all subsequent codes. But recognition was slow, for the Union commanders and military governors seem to have attached relatively little importance to the order. A few days after its completion, Secre-

---

[46] Lieber to Sumner, November 28, 1862; Lieber to Halleck, January 7, March 4, 1863, Series 2 *Official Records*, IV, 946; VI, 32–33. Hesseltine, *Civil War Prisons*, 96.

tary of War Stanton sent instructions to Governor Andrew Johnson of Tennessee that were in keeping with the code but did not mention it by name. This was typical. Most regulations throughout the remainder of the war seem to have been in harmony with it, but did not necessarily use it as a basis.[47]

As the Confederate Secretary of War tartly suggested, the broad latitude of General Orders 100 permitted many abuses. General Butler at Norfolk functioned wholly within the letter of its provisions. Yet his enemies insisted that he inaugurated a despotic regime which drained the revenue and trade of the area into the pockets of his Boston and Lowell cohorts. This was scarcely in keeping with the spirit of the instructions.[48]

Quite possibly the order did help somewhat to standardize the basic conduct of the war. One British authority on the laws of war cited only a single major incident—Sherman's unannounced bombardment of Atlanta—as being clearly out of keeping with its provisions. At the close of the conflict, more than one Union officer who had been administering occupied territory informed Lieber how helpful the order had been. It was seldom mentioned by name, and as yet lacked the aura of authority which would come with time. Judge advocates prosecuting cases hesitated to apply those of its provisions which seemed novel until the War Department obtained ample precedents from the chief author. However, the Supreme Court utilized it almost immediately in the case of *Ex Parte Vallandigham*.[49]

The growing standardization of conduct of the armies in 1864 and 1865 was primarily due to the increased experience of some

[47] Series 3 *Official Records*, III, 122–23; Lieber to Halleck, October 3, 1863. For an excellent survey, see R. H. Gabriel, "American Experience with Military Government," *American Historical Review*, XLIX (1944), 630–43, especially 637–38.

[48] B. F. Butler, *Private and Official Correspondence* . . . , 5 vols. ([Norwood, Mass.,] 1917), vols. II, III; F. H. Peirpoint, *Letter . . . on . . . Abuse of Military Power in the Command of General Butler in Virginia and North Carolina* (Washington, 1864); *Peirpoint's Pamphlet* (Norfolk, Va., 1864); T. J. Wertenbaker, *Norfolk, Historic Southern Port* (Durham, 1931), 238–54.

[49] Lieber to Tyler, February 8, 1864; Lieber to Matilda Lieber, November 15, 1865; Halleck to Lieber, September 30, 1863; Lieber to Halleck, October 3, 10, 12, 1863, March 20, 1866. *Ex Parte Vallandigham*, 1 Wall. 243, 248–49. Justice James Moore Wayne in delivering the opinion of the court that it had no power to review by *certiorari* the proceedings of a military commission stated that Burnside had acted in conformity with General Orders 100, paragraph 13, which provided for military commissions. Spaight, *War Rights on Land*, 171.

commanders, the weeding out of others who were irresponsible, and the zealous efforts of General Halleck to bring about uniform regulations.

When the Union army communicated General Orders 100 to the Confederate officials, they immediately made propaganda use of it. The public in the North was scarcely aware of its existence. While a few of the Republican newspapers voiced mild approval, the anti-Administration press used it only as one more opportunity to lambast the policy of emancipation. Not so in the South, where high officials berated it as an additional proof of Northern perfidiousness. Confederate Secretary of War James Seddon analyzed the order in a lengthy diatribe comparing the humanity of the Southern armies with the cruelty of the Union forces. He dismissed it as "a confused, unassorted, and undiscriminating compilation from the opinion of the publicists of the last two centuries," by "a German professor" unfamiliar with American liberties. With more truth, he acidly charged that "a military commander under this code may pursue a line of conduct in accordance with principles of justice, faith, and honor, or he may justify conduct correspondent with the warfare of the barbarous hordes who overran the Roman Empire." Jefferson Davis continued the attack in his message to the Confederate Congress in December, 1863. He castigated the clause on "military necessity," then contrasted the devastation Union forces were spreading in the South with some of the more humanitarian dictates of General Orders 100.[50]

Despite the propaganda use Southerners made of the regulations, they showed vital concern over the drastic new provisions concerning paroling and prisoners of war. Moreover, they took advantage of the fact that the order bound the Union forces as completely as their own. They sought at once to apply it in a case of purported wanton violence and unauthorized destruction of property.[51]

Hostilities had scarcely come to a close before General Orders 100 began to acquire authority and the extreme veneration of army officers and experts on international law. Chief Justice Chase

[50] New York *Herald,* May 19, 20, 1863. Series 2 *Official Records,* VI, 41–46; Series 4 *ibid.,* II, 1047–48.

[51] Series 2 *ibid.,* V, 670, 689, **744, 755, 767**; VI, 18, 35–36. Hesseltine, *Civil War Prisons,* 95–96.

of the United States Supreme Court lauded it as "really a great work." The "Instructions" inspired Bluntschli, a German political theorist, to prepare a similar treatise which was in large part little more than a translation. Soon it was the basis for a code of the laws of war drawn up by a congress of scholars, and this in turn led to the Hague Conventions of 1899 and 1907. The Hague regulations, still in effect, according to Elihu Root "gave the adherence of the whole civilized world in substance and effect to those international rules which President Lincoln made binding upon the American armies." [52]

General Orders 100 remained the standard instructions for the United States Army through the Spanish-American War and the Philippine insurrection. By this time it had been drilled into so many classes of West Pointers—many of them taught by Lieber's son, Norman—that army officers looked upon it with the deepest reverence. The new manual of land warfare which supplanted it in 1914 stated in the preface that it contained everything essential from the old, and whenever practicable the original wording. As late as 1925 an instructor at the Army Service Schools, Fort Leavenworth, lauded it as "probably the most important of all documents on the subject of the rules of land warfare." [53]

Basic Field Manual 27–10, issued in 1940, was used during the Second World War. Indirectly, through the Hague rules, it per-

[52] Salmon P. Chase to Lieber, October 8, 1866. J. K. Bluntschli, *Das Moderne Kriegsrecht der civilisirten Staaten als Rechtsbuch dargestellt* (Nördlingen, 1866) ; New York *Tribune*, May 25, 1866; Ernest Nys, "Francis Lieber," *American Journal of International Law*, V (1911), 392–93; G. B. Davis, "Memorandum Showing the Relation Between General Orders No. 100 and the Hague Convention with Respect to the Laws and Customs of War on Land," *ibid.*, VII (1913), 466–70; Root, *Addresses on International Subjects* (Cambridge, Mass., 1916), 93–94. Root made a similar assertion before the Republican National Convention, June 21, 1904. Root, *The Military and Colonial Policy of the United States*, 106–107.

[53] Root, *Orders and Instructions Issued to Military Officers in the Philippines* . . . , 57 Cong., 1 Sess., House of Representatives, Document No. 596 (Washington, 1902). Colonel H. A. Smith, in charge of American occupation forces in the Rhenish city of Trier, justified the impressment of guides on the authority of "General Order 100, which has been our Bible in such matters ever since the Civil War." Smith, *Military Government* (Ft. Leavenworth, Kans., 1920), 16. "Everything vital contained in G.O. 100 . . . has been incorporated in this manual. Whenever practicable the original text has been used herein because it is believed that long familiarity with this text and its interpretation by our officers should not be interfered with if possible to avoid doing so." U.S. General Staff, *Rules of Land Warfare*, War Department Document 467 (Washington, 1914), 7. C. M. Dowell, *Military Aid to the Civil Power* (Ft. Leavenworth, Kans., 1925), 30.

petuated many of the regulations of the earlier instructions. Directly, in some of its phrases it still carried the words and spirit of Lieber and General Orders 100. In the 1940's, American armies of occupation in Japan and Germany were still bound by Lieber's solemn stipulation that: "The United States acknowledges and protects, in hostile countries occupied by them, religion and morality; the persons of inhabitants, especially those of women; and the sacredness of domestic relations. Offences to the contrary shall be rigorously punished." [54]

[54] U.S. War Department, *Field Manual 27–10, Rules of Land Warfare* (Washington, 1940), 78.

341

XV

Forging a Nationalist Victory

L
I E B E R labored in every possible way throughout the war to bring about the triumph of his nationalistic concepts. Secondary only to his achievements as a legal adviser was his indefatigable work as a publicist. He regarded Republican policies as the main hope of the Union, and, while he codified laws of war for the army, he no less zealously spread propaganda for his party in newspapers, pamphlets, and on the hustings. Throughout the war, he feared that Democratic victories at the ballot box would bring a dissolution of the Union as rapidly as Confederate victories in the field, and his ardent nationalism found forceful outlet in defense of the Republican program.

Lieber's German origin coupled with his scholarly reputation made him a valuable asset to the Republicans in New York City where the Democratic Tammany machine depended heavily upon the immigrant vote. He found ready acceptance at party councils, served in a wide variety of organizations both moderate and radical, and contributed impartially to William Cullen Bryant's militant New York *Evening Post* and Henry Raymond's temperate New York *Times*. Though he leaned toward the Radicals, he would not align himself unequivocally with any Republican faction; he feared that bickering within the party might lead to political defeat. Characteristically he exclaimed to Sumner, "God prevent foolish splitting of the *Nationals*." Like Stanton, Lieber successfully stayed on the best of terms with a wide variety of Republicans. While he remained in high favor with William Cullen Bryant, Henry Ward Beecher, and Hamilton Fish, he became increasingly influential among the more conservative merchants and capitalists of Wall Street.[1]

[1] Lieber to Sumner, January 26, 1864, Lieber papers, Henry E. Huntington Li-

342

Beginning with the day in May of 1861 when flag-raising cere-
monies at Columbia College inspired Lieber to write a patriotic
song, the aging professor participated prominently in numerous
public demonstrations. In mid-July, 1862, after the discouraging
failure of McClellan's Peninsular Campaign, he presided over one
of the stands at a mass meeting of "Loyal Citizens" in Union
Square, and boldly proposed to them the highly unpopular expedient of drafting troops. It was not necessarily despotic, he pointed
out, and would touch wealthy idlers for at least a substantial sum.
Meanwhile, at the main stand, thousands of copies of Lieber's
"Song on Our Country and Her Flag" were scattered among the
crowd which sang lustily to the accompaniment of a "Grand
Chorus" and band: [2]

> We do not hate our enemy—
> May God deal gently with us all.
> We love our Land; we fight her foe;
> We hate his cause, and that must fall.
>
> . . . .
>
> Let never Emp'ror rule this land,
> Nor fitful Crowd, nor senseless Pride.
> *Our* Master is our self-made Law;
> To *him* we bow, and none beside.[3]

A few months later Lieber was invited to speak at a Union Mass
Ratification rally, and he presided at a meeting honoring the
Radical New York politician-general, James S. Wadsworth. In
the spring of 1863 he became acting president of the Loyal League
of Union Citizens, and delivered a forceful and effective address
at the inaugural Union Square meeting of the Loyal National
League.[4]

brary. All manuscripts referred to in this chapter, unless otherwise identified, are
from this collection.

[2] J. A. Stevens (ed.), *Proceedings at the Mass Meeting of Loyal Citizens, on
Union Square, New-York, 15th Day of July, 1862* . . . (New York, 1862), 19,
26–27, 66, 69–71.

[3] Lieber, *A Song on Our Country and Her Flag* [New York, 1861], 2 pp.

[4] J. H. White to Lieber, October 6, 1862, Lieber papers; Lieber to Bancroft, October 27, 1862, Massachusetts Historical Society; note on reverse of Lieber to Sumner,
April 20, 1863; Lieber, *No Party Now But All for Our Country* . . . (Loyal Publication Society No. 16, New York, 1863), 1. Lieber also served on the National War
Committee (Stevens to Lieber, October 8, 1862), and became chairman of the New

Nevertheless, Lieber's mightiest efforts as ever were with the pen. He felt strongly the need to succor the Union cause in the winter of 1862–63. When the defeat at Fredericksburg followed the slaughter at Antietam, even the most enthusiastic supporters of the army became disgruntled and wholeheartedly sick of the war. "Times are sad—too sad," observed Lieber in Washington at Christmas time. "The tone of the milit[ary] men here is very bad; I am one of the very few among those I see who say: Do not give up." [5]

While winter stalemated the armies, the Democrats worked arduously through newspapers and pamphlets to win votes. They campaigned among the disaffected soldiers against the inept management of the war, and played upon the long-standing differences between New England and the Middle West. With alarm Lieber listened to rumors that the West might even join the Confederacy and quickly decided some drastic measure was necessary to close the widening schism. The New England-sponsored protective tariff, he decided, was the greatest cause of irritation in the Ohio Valley.

"Could but New England, in this hour of greatest peril in our momentous struggle, be induced to relax her protective acerbity, and be induced to veer around to rational trade and unshackled exchange," Lieber appealed to Sumner, "it would be a most efficacious healing salve. It would be a measure of the truest and purest statesmanship." The impressionable Senator, by no means willing to be known as an uncompromising protectionist, replied: "There is nothing which patriotism can give which we will not do," and forwarded the note to Governor John A. Andrew. The Massachusetts governor returned it with the tart comment, "the Professor seems to me to be dreaming." [6]

But already Lieber had turned in other directions. What legislation could not achieve might come about through wide distribution

York Union League publication committee in 1865. Lieber to Sumner, January 25, 1865.

[5] Lieber to Matilda Lieber, December 17, 1862.

[6] Lieber to Sumner, January 14, 1863, with appended comments by Andrew and Sumner. Andrew asked for a definite plan, and Sumner noted: "In reply, I have asked a specification. What can be done? There is nothing which patriotism can give which we will not do. But the duties now required for revenue create an ample protection."

of "an able, lofty, penetrative pamphlet, showing the baseness as well as the injustice of this attack on New England." Leaflets were being scattered broadside throughout the country and were being read as never before. Could not a well-written essay close the gap and combat the " 'Democrats' in their shameless flunkyism to the South?" Lieber appealed to the venerable Horace Binney of highly protectionist Pennsylvania to pen the magic document.[7]

Binney was too aged to undertake the tracting, and Lieber feared he himself would be suspect as a foreigner. Nevertheless the publicist turned to pamphleteering not merely as a device to foster good relations between East and West, but as a potent means to check the growing political success of the Democrats. "The cars, on my return from Washington, were full of discharged soldiers," the shocked professor reported early in February, "and such loud, nasty, infernal treason I have never believed my ears should be destined to hear. I changed cars, but it was everywhere the same." [8]

Among Lieber's friends and associates plans quickly took shape to form "a Publication Association chiefly for the army to counteract the base camarilla of 'World' renown," which was disseminating "disloyal" newspapers and pamphlets among the troops. The Democrats were even quicker with their counterplans and on February 13 met at Delmonico's to organize the "Society for the Diffusion of Political Knowledge." They elected S. F. B. Morse, inventor of the telegraph, as president, and listened to speeches by George Ticknor Curtis, the historian of the Constitution, and Samuel J. Tilden, who was to lose the presidency in the disputed election of 1876. The Society, backed by millionaires who guaranteed Morse ample funds, quickly began publication of a series of pamphlets opposing abolition and the abrogation of civil liberties.[9]

Stung to speedy action, the "Union men" met the following evening to form a "Loyal Publication Society" to distribute "journals and documents of unquestionable and unconditional loyalty"

<hr />

[7] Lieber to Binney, January 15, 1863.   [8] Lieber to Sumner, February 10, 1863.
[9] *Ibid.;* S. F. B. Morse and others, *The Constitution* . . . (Society for the Diffusion of Political Knowledge, No. 1), 9; E. L. Morse, *Samuel F. B. Morse: His Letters and Journals,* 2 vols. (Boston, 1914), II, 423–24. The New York *Evening Post* sharply attacked the organization, February 7, 9, 10, 14, 1863.

345

throughout the United States. The Society dedicated itself especially to combat among the troops the insidious "efforts now being
made by the enemies of the Government and the advocates of a
disgraceful PEACE." [10]

Lieber to his delight became chairman of the publications committee, and at once solicited manuscripts from Bancroft, Holmes,
Longfellow, and other prominent writers. Although his solicita-
tion failed, he soon filled a more pressing objective of the organization while he was in Washington revising the rules of war. He
arranged for the distribution to the Army of the Rappahannock of
thirty-six thousand copies of "loyal" newspapers.[11]

For once Lieber possessed an adequate outlet for his own facile
pen. Altogether he produced ten out of the Society's ninety pamphlets, and he saw that most of the others conformed to his own
Radical Republican ideology. This he succeeded in doing without
upsetting the membership, an interesting admixture of professors
and professional men, merchants and brokers. It was a difficult
achievement, for the cautious mercantile groups so predominated
that the Society was open to the same attack that the *Herald* made
upon the interlocking Loyal National League: "What is 'The Loyal
National League,'" the *Herald* inquired. "The *Tribune* says it is
'like the great Corn-Law League of England.' That is very far
from it—it is simply a Contractor's league." [12]

Within a couple of months Lieber struck the keynote of the
organization in a short speech at the inaugural of the Loyal National League. Although it occupied only eight of the 216 pages
of proceedings, *No Party Now But All for Our Country* attracted
preponderant attention. Numerous publication societies reprinted
it and circulated it around the country by the tens of thousands
—greatly to Lieber's surprise and gratification.

[10] J. A. Stevens, Jr., *Proceedings at the First Anniversary Meeting of the Loyal
Publication Society* . . . (Loyal Publication Society No. 44, New York, 1864), 8.
Edith E. Ware, "Committees of Public Information, 1863–1866," *Historical Outlook*,
X (1919), 65–67. Frank Freidel, "The Loyal Publication Society . . . ," *Mississippi
Valley Historical Review*, XXVI (1939), 359–76.

[11] Lieber to Bancroft, February 23, 1863, Massachusetts Historical Society;
Holmes to Lieber, March 1, 1863. Stevens, *Proceedings at the First Anniversary
Meeting* . . . , 9, 11. Lieber wrote Lincoln, June 16, 1863, "We have distributed
over the U. States not far from 150000 copies of pamphlets, broadsides [newspapers],
and wish to do a great deal more." Lincoln papers, Library of Congress.

[12] New York *Herald*, May 20, 1863.

The theme was a simple attack upon the Democrats. In time of war, party lines could no longer stand, and a man must take his choice between loyalty and disloyalty to his government. Then Lieber sketched the uncompromising Radical program to which one must adhere to be loyal: conquest of the South, compression and speedy extinction of slavery, support of conscription, and support of the government from "unfriendly and mischievous neutrality." Thus far, every Radical Republican would agree with Lieber, but next he made so intemperate a denunciation of Lord Lyons, the British minister at Washington, that even Sumner winced and administration newspapers wrote earnest rebuttals. Because Lord Lyons had conversed with Democratic leaders, Lieber cried out, "We pronounce every foreign minister accredited to our government, who tampers with our enemies, and holds intercourse with disloyal men among us, as failing in his duty toward us and toward his own people, and we await with attention the action of our government regarding the recent and surprising breach of this duty." [13]

After a few months Lieber came to realize that his attack had been unwarranted. He finally wrote Sumner in June that he was glad a convention of Loyal Leagues at Utica which endorsed his program had omitted the anti-Lyons passage. Thenceforth he assumed a rather equivocal attitude. While he indulged in repeated anti-British tirades in his private correspondence with Sumner, he counseled the militant Senator to moderation in his public utterances.[14]

Intermittently throughout the spring of 1863 and into the long, nervous summer which brought Gettysburg and the surrender of Vicksburg, the political warfare continued. Lieber channeled a

[13] Loyal National League, *The Sumter Anniversary, 1863* . . . (New York, 1863) and *Opinions of Prominent Men . . . on the Anniversary of Sumter* (New York, 1863). Lieber, *Address by Francis Lieber, Chairman of the Council's Committee on Addresses, Read at the Meeting by their Request*, broadside (New York, 1863); Lieber, *Address* . . . (New York, 1863), 12 pp.; Lieber, *No Party Now* . . . ; *ibid.* (Union League No. 19, Philadelphia, 1863), 8 pp. Sumner to Lieber, April 15, 1863, Harvard University; Washington *National Intelligencer*, April 22, 1863.

[14] Lieber to Sumner, June 8, 1863. See also Lieber to Sumner, January 26, 1864, and numerous letters in the Lieber-Sumner correspondence. Lieber denounced the insolence of the British Tories in a letter to Lincoln, October 22, 1864, Lincoln papers, Library of Congress.

large part of the Loyal Publication Society pamphlets toward the army. He and his associates were hopeful that the soldiers, if properly indoctrinated, would vote the Union ticket. Democrats feared the same thing, and with malice Governor Seymour of New York cited a passage in the *Civil Liberty* in his message vetoing a bill to give the vote to New York soldiers.[15]

Although Democrats flung Lieber's words repeatedly at the Republicans, the scholar stiffly declared his stand to be consistent. Indeed, he said that in future editions he would not modify his strong warning against allowing soldiers to vote in a unit as they did in Cromwell's army and in France. He continued to regard "deliberating and debating" armies as repugnant, but strongly favored the Civil War procedure of allowing soldiers as citizens to cast absentee ballots in their home election districts. Lieber overlooked the fact that the mode of molding the soldier-voters' opinions was little different in either situation.[16]

For the Democrats to quote this well-known Radical was nothing new. In congressional debates Representative S. S. Cox had already cited the *Civil Liberty* against conscription. Lieber had protested this as a distortion, and through a learned Republican, M. R. Thayer of Pennsylvania, carried his protest to the floor of the house. Moreover, Lieber had even supplied data to Sumner to aid Senator Henry Wilson in framing a conscription bill. Subsequently he feared that a certain declaration of his (that the French allowed the purchase of exemption for a sum equivalent to $300) had led to a similar provision that gave the well-to-do a chance to avoid military service.[17]

These Democratic attacks, far from demolishing Lieber's posi-

---

[15] Lieber to Allibone, April 28, 1863.

[16] Lieber to Sumner, March 6, October 11, 1864. Cf. *CL*, 118–19.

[17] Lieber, *CL*, 119: "as matters now stand and as our feelings now are, we should not consider it compatible with individual liberty—indeed, it would be considered as intolerable oppression—if we were forced to spend part of our lives in the standing army." Lieber's reply to Representative Cox was, of course, that he was referring to peacetime conscription. Lieber to Thayer, January 2, 14, 1864; Thayer to Lieber, January 12, 1864. Lieber to Sumner, January 28, February 10, 1863. Sumner requested the data and turned it over to Henry Wilson, chairman of the Senate military affairs committee, who was responsible for the Enrollment Act. Lieber to Halleck, January 6, 1864. Sumner sent on to Lincoln one of Lieber's letters militantly urging conscription. Lieber to Sumner, July 6, 1863, enclosed in Sumner to Lincoln, July 8, 1863, Lincoln papers, Library of Congress.

tion, were an indication of his growing prominence as a publicist. Besides his *No Party Now But All for Our Country,* he wrote during 1863 a tract on *The Arguments of Secessionists,* first read at a Union meeting in September, and an attack upon slavery bearing the self-explanatory title *Plantations for Slave Labor the Death of the Yeomanry.* The Loyal Publication Society printed both pamphlets, and in addition the Union League of Philadelphia issued the latter one. During the same year Lieber also wrote five or more letters to the press.[18]

At the beginning of 1864, the quartermaster general, Montgomery C. Meigs, asked Lieber if the army could legally employ idle prisoners of war. The scholar wrote a lengthy reply buttressed with numerous precedents strongly in the affirmative. Meigs at once sent the letter to newspapers to sway public opinion, but nevertheless the army failed to act. International law did permit prisoners to work, but fear that the Confederates would retaliate by employing Union captives in unhealthful or dangerous occupations deterred army officials from introducing Meigs's proposals.[19]

Already in January, 1864, faint preliminary rumblings of the crucial presidential election were beginning to reach Lieber's ears. In common with most Radicals, he disliked Lincoln's moderate policies, and long since had exchanged tart remarks with his friends. "We are giving our most precious blood, and yet the President hesitates to use the negro!" an admirer exclaimed to him in the fall of 1862. "How I wish we had such men as you in the Cabinet instead of vacillating know-nothings." [20]

Lieber continued to be critical of Lincoln through 1863, but when the most militant Radicals began to promote the candidacy

---

[18] Lieber, *The Arguments of Secessionists. A Letter to the Union Meeting. Held in New York, September 30, 1863* (Loyal Publication Society No. 29, New York, 1863), also published by the Loyal Publication Society under the title, *Slavery Plantations and the Yeomanry* (New York, 1863), and by the Union League as *Slavery in Point of Social Economy; Slavery, Plantations* (Philadelphia, 1863). It appeared in the New York *Evening Post,* September 19, 1863 under the title, "Slavery in point of Society [*sic*] Economy."

[19] Lieber to Sumner, February 4, 1864; Lieber to Halleck, October 15, 1864; Halleck to Lieber, October 16, 1864; Meigs to Lieber, February 1, 1864. W. B. Hesseltine, *Civil War Prisons,* 193. Series 2 *Official Records,* VI, 893–94; New York *Times,* February 3, 1864.

[20] J. P. Thompson to Lieber, September 15, 1862.

of Frémont and Chase, he viewed the potential split in the Union vote with marked trepidation. "The mind of the people is rapidly settling, or is already settled on Lincoln's re-election," he reported to Sumner in mid-January. The Radical scholar could not agree with the President, but could understand his popularity: "Presdt Lincoln has impressed the people with the conviction that they always can know where to find him, which you may recollect I dwelled upon in my Political Ethics as one of the most potent elements of power." [21]

When in February Lieber succeeded the aged Charles King as head of the Loyal Publication Society, he announced to Sumner that the organization would back "the fairly and largely nominated man on our side." He added "I wish you could say to all the world *hush* about the presidency." Firmly, Lieber held the Loyal Publications Society to that "hush" policy. While the Union League of Philadelphia had already published a pamphlet endorsing Lincoln, the New York Society remained silent. When one of the most active workers in the organization invited Lieber to become president of the New York Frémont club, or at least to preside at the first rally, he emphatically declined: "I am convinced," he warned, "that every personal election movement at this time can only tend to weaken us. . . . I believe the nomination of my friend General Frémont can have no other effect than the division of our force, but not his election." [22]

Even after Lincoln's nomination in early June, Lieber and his associates remained more anti-Democratic than pro-Lincoln. The armies still were none too successful, and the Confederate general Jubal Early created consternation by raiding the environs of Washington. Lincoln had stirred up the ire of the Radicals by pocket-vetoing the Wade-Davis reconstruction bill, and anti-Republican peace sentiment swept the country. "L[incoln] loses many friends as to the election," Lieber reported gloomily. "I mean to emigrate if McClellan be elected." [23]

[21] Lieber to Sumner, January 16, 26, 1864.

[22] Lieber to Sumner, February 14, 17, 1864; Sinclair Tousey to Lieber, March 16, 1864; Lieber to Tousey, March 17, 1864, contemporary copy. Anonymous, *Abraham Lincoln* (Union League No. 69, Philadelphia, 1863). On June 5, 1864, Lieber wrote Sumner deprecating a Grant meeting in Union Square as a fiasco.

[23] Lieber to Sumner, July 5, 1864.

By the end of August, the President despaired of re-election and showed his cabinet a sealed slip of paper upon which he had written an unfavorable prediction of the election results. The Radicals, disliking Lincoln and feeling themselves in a hopeless minority, even held a conference to consider overthrowing their nominee.[24]

"Yester-day I was called to a meeting at D. D. Field's, where many States were represented," Lieber reported to Sumner on August 31. "All agreed that Lincoln cannot be re-elected, unless great victories can be obtained soon, which is next to impossible on account of the worn-out state of the army of the Potomac. Winter Davis was there and stated that Linc. in presence of Corwin had said: I am a beaten man, unless we can have some great victory. It was agreed that a committee should call on Linc. to withdraw (which of course he will not do, or not be allowed to do by his cabinet) and that a convention at Cincinnati should be called, (whether Lincoln agree or not) to settle whether the friends of the country should nominate a new candidate (probably Grant) or continue for Lincoln."

The meeting left Lieber feeling baffled and bewildered. "What are you going to do in this chaos?" he exclaimed. "If we come triumphantly out of this war, with a presidential election in the midst of it . . . I shall call it the greatest miracle in all the historic course of events. It is a war for nationality at a period when the people were not yet fully nationalized, in a political sense." [25]

Lieber had declined to sign the request for Lincoln to withdraw as a candidate, and because many key Radicals did not support the movement it collapsed almost immediately. Most coolheaded thinkers felt like Theodore D. Woolsey, Yale's cautious president: "I care nothing for Lincoln but care immensely for the union and for rooting up slavery." With a will most of them plunged violently into the campaigning. None was more vigorous than Lieber.[26]

Under Lieber's aggressive leadership, the Loyal Publication Society, which from time to time had limped for lack of funds, became a great distributing center for campaign literature. Its

---

[24] J. G. Randall, *The Civil War and Reconstruction*, 620–21.
[25] Lieber to Sumner, August 31, 1864.   [26] *Ibid.*

presses poured forth pamphlets and broadsides by the hundreds of thousands. Between September and the election it distributed more than a half-million pieces of literature.[27]

Lieber worked hard to acquire and disseminate effective propaganda material. From Judge Advocate General Joseph Holt he obtained copies of the government-printed report on the Indiana copperhead conspiracy. Again, he gathered together a collection of pamphlets, and sent them with a note to Henry Ward Beecher, who from the pulpit of Plymouth Church was campaigning vigorously for Lincoln. "I must ask your indulgence," acknowledged Beecher, "for having used the closing part of your letter, in my discourse of last Sunday night. It was a view, itself striking, and proceeding from you, it had great effect. I judged that you would not hesitate, for the public good, to allow me such a liberty." [28]

The national sentiment changed with phenomenal rapidity. Atlanta fell, the public became disgusted with the peace plank in the Democratic platform, and Frémont's clique of Radical recalcitrants plumped for Lincoln in return for the removal of the moderate Montgomery Blair from the cabinet. Yet in New York, with its tremendous urban Democratic machine, the election remained in the balance up to the counting of the ballots. In consequence, the Loyal Publication Society concentrated its pamphlets upon the city voters rather than the soldiers, and Lieber addressed himself to the important German segment of the electorate.

At top speed he turned out an effective and widely distributed campaign pamphlet: *Lincoln or McClellan*. Lieber reminded the German workingmen of the sorrows that division into many petty states had brought to the fatherland. They had come to America to obtain the political and economic blessings of a unified nation. If they wished to avoid delivering themselves over to a "grinding tyranny far worse than any endured in the oppressed countries of Europe," they should defeat the party planning to surrender the Union to Southern landholders.

[27] Loyal Publication Society, *Final Report and Address of the President* . . . (New York, 1866). In 1864 the organization distributed 470,000 copies of its own publications and 45,000 exchanges. Of these, 120,000 were distributed in New York City and 83,000 in the remainder of the state. *Proceedings at the Second Anniversary Meeting* . . . (New York, 1865), 1, 18–19.

[28] Holt to Lieber, October 8, 1864; Beecher to Lieber, October 25, 1864.

"If you would have masters set up over you, on this principle, vote for McClellan," warned Lieber. "Would you retain your equal rights as the citizens of a free country, vote for Lincoln, who has been an honest working man like yourselves." [29]

With mixed feelings Lieber learned that the *Tribune* could not print the little address fast enough and that all day long clusters of "Dutchmen" stood at the *Tribune* bulletin board earnestly reading it. "There is this humiliating fact in it," he mused, "that throughout my life I have been forced to observe that the passages or entire writings of mine, most quoted, most popular, are the least profound, the least characteristically my inmost own. I have sometimes felt this bitterly." [30]

Any acid introspection the professor might harbor quickly dissolved in his elation over the sweeping Lincoln victory. When the ballots had been counted, he jubilantly sent Sumner a bookmark inscribed: "Two days after the Great and Good Election of '64. Behold! *For* Mac one full-grown pair of States, and also—Delaware." Noting that many of the votes had changed at the last minute, Lieber felt that the Loyal Publication Society had indeed been a potent Republican agency. In his final presidential address, he proudly proclaimed that it "did good service in times of anxiety and glory, and . . . contributed no inconsiderable share in bringing about one of the greatest national acts in all history— the re-election of Abraham Lincoln." [31]

After the election, with General William T. Sherman marching punitively across Georgia and with the North reeking from wild tales of Confederate prison atrocities, the war threatened to enter its darkest phase. Radical Western senators led by Ben Wade and Zach Chandler, through their mighty engine for propaganda and coercion, the Committee on the Conduct of the War, had issued a sensational report on the allegedly brutal treatment being meted

[29] Lieber, *Lincoln oder McClellan? Aufruf an die Deutschen in Amerika* (Loyal Publication Society No. 59, New York, 1864), 4 pp. The pamphlet also appeared in English as the Society's publication No. 67, and in Dutch as No. 71. It was widely reprinted by the Philadelphia Union League, the New York *Tribune,* and other agencies.

[30] Lieber to Sumner, October 11, 1864; Lieber to Thayer, October 14, 1864.

[31] Lieber to Sumner, November 10, 1864; Lieber, notes on back of Erastus Cornelius Benedict to Lieber, November 21, 1864. Loyal Publication Society, *Final Report* . . . , 12.

out to Union soldiers in Southern prison camps. Radical journals took up their clamor and with public opinion behind them, they tried to force President Lincoln and the army to adopt punitive measures.[32]

As the press continued to inflame public opinion with increasingly lurid stories about Libby Prison and Andersonville, the vindictive Wade introduced resolutions in the Senate to retaliate with identical treatment of Confederates in Northern stockades. Lieber was quite ready to believe the atrocity stories to the last detail; indeed he himself was busy spreading a report that the pious "Stonewall" Jackson had opposed giving quarter to Union troops because they were fighting in an unrighteous cause, but he wholeheartedly opposed descending to the same level as the wicked Confederates.[33]

Quite realistically, the professor accepted the validity of retaliation as a weapon to redress grievances (he had so written in General Orders 100). Since it could work with equal force against the North, it should consist of stern but absolutely correct punishment. He lamented the presidential order in the summer of 1863 to retaliate against Confederates who sold Negro prisoners back into slavery by imprisoning them at hard labor, because he considered execution a more fitting equivalent. At the same time he had protested to Halleck when he heard rumors that General Ambrose E. Burnside threatened to hang ten Confederate officers for every Union officer hanged by the South. In retaliating, he had warned, the army must use exact equivalents and not adopt "Ten eyes for one Eye. If one belligerent hangs ten men for one; the other will hang ten times . . . ten, and what a dread geometrical progression of skulls and cross bones we would have!" [34]

[32] Williams, *Lincoln and the Radicals*, 342–48; Hesseltine, *Civil War Prisons*, 172–209. Lieber's Loyal Publication Society issued as Pamphlet No. 76, a *Narrative of Privations and Sufferings of United States Officers and Soldiers While Prisoners of War in the Hands of Rebel Authorities. Being the Report of a Commission of Inquiry, Appointed by the United States Sanitary Commission. With an Appendix Containing Testimony* (New York, 1864).

[33] Williams, *Lincoln and the Radicals*, 352. Lieber to Sumner, December 26, 1864, January 9, 1865; Lieber to Halleck, January 9, 1865; Lieber, "Stonewall Jackson and Our Prisoners," New York *Times*, January 9, 1865.

[34] Lieber to Halleck, June 2, August 3, 1863. Halleck replied, June 3: "I do not think Genl Burnside has made any such threats. If he has, he will not be supported by me. I shall permit no such acts, if I can help it." With similar restraint, Lieber had delineated the bounds of retaliation when he heard of the Fort Pillow massacre. Lieber to Halleck, April 19, 1864.

Even before Wade, Chandler, and Jacob Howard, like three avenging prophets from the Old Testament, opened their fight in the Senate to have the government starve and freeze Southern prisoners in retaliation for alleged similar conduct in the Confederacy, Lieber had taken alarm at the House debates. In a letter to the New York *Times* he denounced senseless retaliation in kind, and in repeated letters to Sumner urged him to block the proposals when they came before the Senate.[35]

Sumner, who cherished his standing as a legal scholar and idealist, readily agreed. When debate began on the resolutions toward the end of January, to the great delight of the Democrats he charged valiantly into the path of his fellow Radicals. Armed with historical precedents, he delivered a learned address which he climaxed by reading large sections of a letter from Lieber.[36]

"The provision that the Southerners in our hands shall be watched over by national soldiers who have been in Southern pens is unworthy of any great people or high minded statesmen," Sumner quoted Lieber as saying. "I abhor this revenge on prisoners of war because we would sink thereby to the level of the enemy's shame and dishonour. . . . If we fight with Indians who slowly roast their prisoners, we cannot roast in turn the Indians whom we may capture. . . . I believe that the ineffable cruelty practiced against our men has been unequalled in the history of our race . . . but counter cruelty would not mend matters. Those who can allow such crimes would not be moved by cruelties inflicted upon their soldiers in our hands. These cruelties therefore would be simply revenge, not retaliation, for retaliation as an element of the Law of War . . . implies the idea of thereby stopping a certain evil." [37]

Wade and Chandler snarled retorts so ferocious that Sumner's Massachusetts colleague, Henry Wilson, snapped that as he listened he "thought that the old slave-masters had come back again . . . [with] all their insolence and something more than their coarseness." Several times Lieber's name incidentally came into the debates. The Radical Howard professed himself amazed at Lieber's language, as "rather ostentatiously quoted" by Sumner,

[35] Lieber to Sumner, December 21, 24, 26, 1864.
[36] *Congressional Globe*, 38 Cong., 2 Sess., 382.
[37] *Ibid.;* Lieber to Sumner, January 22, 1865.

and insinuated that it was a slur upon the Senate and pedantic rather than practical. His only reply to Lieber's logic was a long peroration more rhetorical than penetrating.[38]

While Howard attacked the "humanitarian and sentimental doctrine," of Sumner and Lieber, the Democrats ironically came to their defense. Garrett Davis of Kentucky informed Sumner that Lieber's letter was "immortal," and Reverdy Johnson of Maryland told the Senate that Lieber was "not only a jurist in the general acceptance of the term, but . . . a publicist of the highest possible reputation." [39]

Sumner stayed remarkably close to the line of argument suggested to him by Lieber. He introduced an alternate resolution very similar to one the professor outlined, and strongly defended his friend in subsequent debate. "Professor Lieber can need no praise from me as a practical writer and thinker on questions of international law," Sumner retorted to Howard. He called attention to General Orders 100: "There is no Senator, not excepting the Senator from Michigan, who might not be proud to point to such a monument of fame." Again, he cited Lieber at length, this time reading his cogent argument from the New York *Times:* The jurist favored cutting the Rebel prisoners off from the pleasant comforts of life given them by subservient Northerners; he firmly opposed revoltingly barbaric treatment which in practice Northern opinion would not tolerate.[40]

The debate ran on another three days, but Sumner and Wilson with their temporary allies, the Democrats, successfully withstood the Radical assault. Sumner succeeded in emasculating Wade's resolution with a proviso that retaliation upon prisoners should be "in conformity with the laws and usages of war among civilized nations"; several other qualifications were added, and to the intense disgust of Wade and Chandler, the subdued version of their measure passed by an overwhelming 27 to 13 vote.[41]

[38] *Congressional Globe*, 38 Cong., 2 Sess., 382–83, 431, 499. Lieber was also criticized by Senator Timothy O. Howe of Wisconsin, 517.

[39] *Ibid.*, 454, 459. Lieber to Sumner, January 28, 1865.

[40] *Congressional Globe*, 38 Cong., 2 Sess., 473–74. Lieber to Sumner, January 22, 26, 1865.

[41] *Congressional Globe*, 38 Cong., 2 Sess., 520–21. For analyses of the entire debate, see Williams, *Lincoln and the Radicals*, 352–54, and Pierce (ed.), *Memoir and Letters of Charles Sumner*, IV, 211–12.

Lieber rejoiced over the victory, then turned to Halleck, who had hailed with delight the defeat of the "barbarous resolutions," to plead for moderation among the troops laying waste the deep South. From one of Sherman's officers, Henry Hitchcock, Lieber received a long and graphic letter gloating over the treatment that South Carolina would shortly receive. Alarmed, Lieber implored General Halleck "to stay the hand of ruthless revenge." He admitted how well South Carolina deserved chastisement. "Let Sherman, if such a thing be possible, levy the heaviest contributions, let him lay the yoke of retribution heavy on the offenders of that offending State, but let there not be ruthless burning, killing, violating women by the soldiery. Besides, it demoralizes an army." General Halleck replied calmly that Sherman would act coolly and systematically, not willfully and wantonly.[42]

Events moved quickly during February and March. As the Confederacy crumbled, Lieber reiterated four conditions of peace: "No armistice, no adoption of rebel debt, no slavery, no division of the country." He presented these propositions in the form of resolutions to the Union League Club which adopted them by acclamation. Slavery already was on the way to being abolished, and when the news arrived early one morning in January that Congress had approved the thirteenth amendment, he was so excited that he could not shave.[43]

In March came Lincoln's second inaugural, and Lieber ranted over Sumner's report that Andrew Johnson had been intoxicated when he took the oath of office in the Senate chamber. Indignantly he exclaimed that the Vice-President should be "drowned in a hogshead of whiskey." [44]

[42] Lieber to Sumner, January 30, February 7, 1865; Henry Hitchcock to Lieber, January 15, 1865; Lieber to Halleck, February 11, 1865; Halleck to Lieber, February 18, 21, 1865. When Columbia burned, Halleck accepted Sherman's report that the Confederates were to blame. Halleck to Lieber, April 11, 1865.

[43] Lieber to Sumner, February 2, 10, 1865. As late as November, 1864, Lieber had feared the administration would make peace without abolishing slavery. When General Butler purportedly followed Lincoln's views in extending an olive branch to the South, the publicist passionately argued against concessions: "What have we been fighting for all this while? What have we re-elected Mr. Lincoln for?" Lieber to Sumner, November 22, 1864, enclosed in Sumner to Lincoln, November 24, 1864, Lincoln papers, Library of Congress.

[44] Lieber to Sumner, March 11, 16, 1865. Sumner's letter to Lieber describing Johnson's alleged drunkenness is not in the Sumner papers at Harvard University. Probably Sumner asked Lieber to destroy it.

A few days later Beecher called with an invitation from Stanton to make a visit of inspection to Charleston. The former South Carolinian, perhaps fearing mob attack, declined. He worried greatly about Lincoln's visit to conquered Richmond early in April and urged Sumner to induce him to return. If anything happened to the President, the country would have Johnson as chief executive, shuddered Lieber. "Imagine that calamity." [45]

Lincoln re-embarked unscathed for Washington. While he was on a steamer coming up the Potomac from City Point, Sumner put into his hands a letter from Lieber proposing a general proscription of the Rebel leaders. The publicist feared that the Republicans could not shut them out of all offices and that shortly they would again cause trouble in the Senate. He wished for the trial and execution of a dozen to twenty of the top men, or failing that, their flight to Europe. He appended two lists of potential victims: Those who must be included—Davis, Beauregard, Wilder, Stephens, and Breckenridge; those who could not be excluded—"General Lee &c.&c." The President, Sumner reported, "read it with much interest." [46]

Already Lieber's attention was turning largely to postwar problems, and on April 9, with the surrender of Lee at Appomattox, military affairs began to assume a secondary role. The aging publicist could consider his war contribution completed. Nationalism, proclaimed from the banners of the industrial North, was triumphant; Lieber had worked for its victory in every possible way. He had developed legal rationale for nationalistic policies of the President and the Radical Republicans alike; he had prepared a code of land warfare to help standardize the conduct of the national army. Through his writings and dissemination of propaganda he had minimized state, sectional, and intraparty schisms menacing the Union cause, and had consistently interpreted the war as a struggle for a strong, unified American nation. This new nation, as he demonstrated in his writings on the international law of war and neutrality, should then assume its proper role among the world community of nations. Lieber's vision was of a

[45] Lieber to Sumner, April 1, 4, 9, 1865.
[46] Lieber to Sumner, April 1, 4, 1865. See also letters of March 22, April 9, 1865, Lieber papers. Sumner to Lieber, April 17, 1865, Harvard University.

nationalism far from chauvinistic, a logical concomitant of progressive internationalism.

Lieber did not have long to rejoice over the victory of his ideals. On the morning of April 15 he arose and found black headlines: Lincoln had been assassinated. Shocked, stunned, he cried passionately for bloody revenge:

"My God! That even this should befall us! It is Slavery, Slavery. . . . The draft ought to go on again, or volunteers be called, to sweep, literally to sweep the South. No coquetting! Drive the fiends from our soil, and let Grant be a stern uncompromising man of the sword and sword alone, until the masses in the States rise against their own fiends, and hang them or drive them out, and until the masses offer themselves, re-revolutionized, back to the Union, freed from Slavery and assassins. . . .

"The murder of poor, good Lincoln is no isolated fact. The applause to Brooks, the secret Societies, the filibusters, the *murders* in our war, the raiders, the Fort Pillow men, our riots here, the drunken lawlessness all over the South, the burning of their cities, the massacre now in Washington—it is all, all one fiendish barbarism." [47]

The era of Reconstruction had arrived.

[47] Lieber to Halleck, April 15, 1865; Lieber to Sumner, April 15, 1865.

XVI

Harvest Fruits

Wprecedingcap="true"HAT is hellish treason in the mouth of a traitor, is true when it comes from loyal lips—it is well that it has happened," Lieber confessed to Sumner even before the assassinated President had reached his grave. "Lincoln could not die a more glorious death. It raises him high above others in our annals, and as for our cause—I remember your hasty lines of March 13, ending 'Alas! Alas!' We were fast drifting to namby-pambyism." With state-rights doctrine and Northern flunkeyism toward the South still rampant, Lieber reasoned that the victory of nationalism could be complete only through a new order—the complete rule of the Radical Republicans.[1]

In common with Radicals of greater prominence, Lieber piously paid public tribute to Lincoln, and aspired to use his martyrdom to force a stern peace upon the South. He drew up a set of resolutions for the faculty of Columbia College. After lauding the assassinated President as "one of the kindest-hearted, most forgiving, purest, and most magnanimous rulers recorded in history," they stated the professors' resolve increasingly "to implant in the young deeper love of country . . . and to strengthen the resolution of this people to show by condign punishment the deep conviction they have of the enormity and guiltiness of the rebellion." [2]

If Lincoln appeared as a great murdered saint, the outraged public might back the Radical demand to crush the South. Lieber,

[1] Lieber to Sumner, April 23, 1865, Lieber papers, Henry E. Huntington Library. Hereafter in this chapter all manuscripts, unless otherwise cited, are from this collection.
[2] "Proceedings at Columbia College," newspaper clipping enclosed in Lieber to Sumner, April, 1865.

as his contribution to the canonization, proposed to Levi P. Morton, the wealthy owner of the American News Company, the publication of a memorial compilation of the President's addresses. When it appeared under the title *The Martyr's Monument,* with fitting acknowledgment to Lieber, the scholar sent a copy to President Johnson. With similar assiduousness he pressed Congressional leaders to erect a suitable statue of Lincoln on a prominent site in Washington.[3]

The righteous professor had not fully forgiven Andrew Johnson for his disgraceful conduct on inauguration day, but for the moment regarded him as an excellent successor to the dangerously kindhearted Lincoln. Although he continued somewhat suspicious that "softness" might crop out, he tentatively accepted Sumner's evaluation that the new President was pliable in the hands of the Radicals, "discreet, properly reserved, but firm and determined." [4]

Lieber quickly utilized his avenue of approach through Sumner to suggest to the President his ideas upon reconstruction. He was impressed by a letter from Colonel John A. Baker of North Carolina, a former student and old Whig for whom he had obtained a pardon. Baker urged that Negroes receive "all the immunities of free white men." At once the publicist forwarded it to Sumner together with his own plan of reconstruction: Southerners should rise against the "spurious secession legislatures," reorganize, and offer themelves without slavery for readmission by Congress.[5]

Senator Sumner called on President Johnson and read the suggestions. He reported back enthusiastically that Johnson "said at once that he accepted every word of it; that colored persons are to have the right of suffrage; that no State can be precipitated into the Union; that rebel States must go through a term of probation. . . . I was charmed by his sympathy, which was entirely different from his predecessor's." [6]

[3] Anonymous, *The Martyr's Monument* . . . (New York, 1865) ; James Speed to Lieber, June 27, 1865; Lieber to Sumner, October 26, 1865; Lieber to Schuyler Colfax, November 29, 1865 (copy).

[4] Sumner to Lieber, April 17, 1865, Sumner papers, Harvard University. Lieber wished Johnson "triumphant success." Lieber to Johnson, April 23, 1865, Johnson papers, Library of Congress.

[5] Baker to Lieber, April 10, 1865; Lieber to Sumner, April 19, 1865; Lieber to Halleck, April 22, 1865.

[6] Pierce (ed.), *Memoir and Letters of Charles Sumner,* IV, 243.

Radical hopes that Johnson would co-operate in a Draconian reconstruction soon met a setback. Even before the more militant Republicans began to realize that his policies favored the small farmers of the South rather than the big businessmen and party leaders of the North, his general pardoning of prominent ex-Confederates began to mar their dreams. Lieber, in common with others, feared the government was losing its opportunity to try the Southern notables for treason or even to drive them out of the country.

Fortuitously the political theorist provided a simple formula which with foresight he had inserted into General Orders 100, the rules of land warfare. The status of a prisoner of war or paroled prisoner, he had posited, was purely military rather than criminal. Now he elaborated his view in a newspaper letter: Prisoners of war were clearly answerable for war crimes, whether poisoning, assassination, or cruelty to prisoners. A paroled soldier held the same position as one actually incarcerated, hence was still subject to trial if he had violated the rules of war. As for the civil status of the parolee, it was the same as that of any other person who had been in rebellion, since the military parole would come to an end with the conclusion of the peace. By implication, the paroled prisoners of war still stood responsible for the civil crime of treason, of waging war on the legitimate government, and might be tried for it in the civil courts.[7]

Attorney General James Speed thanked Lieber warmly for his argument, which tried so studiedly to spike the growing assumption that the capitulation brought pardon or promise of pardon. Officials subsequently found it a useful device to justify the trial and execution of Henry Wirz, the hapless commander of the notorious Andersonville prison, in the face of the fact that Wirz had been included in the surrender-on-parole of Johnston's forces.[8]

[7] Lieber, "The Status of Rebel Prisoners of War," New York *Independent*, May 10, 1865, reprinted in Lieber, *Miscellaneous Writings*, I, 293–97. Lieber clearly emphasized his preference for use of the civil courts in a seven-point memorandum to Attorney General James Speed, July 15, 1865, entitled "Reasons why Jefferson Davis ought not to be tried by Military Commission for complicity in the unlawful raiding, burning &c." Lieber papers, Library of Congress. The administration, which had inclined toward trial by military commission, later instituted proceedings in the civil courts. Gideon Welles, *Diary of Gideon Welles . . .* , 2 vols. (Boston, 1911), II, 335 *et seq.;* Randall, *The Civil War and Reconstruction*, 806–808.

[8] Speed to Lieber, May 20, 1865; Randall, *The Civil War and Reconstruction*, 803.

Lieber's dictum spread hatred and fear among the ex-Confederates. Actually the Radical political theorist wished only the military trial and punishment of war criminals and the civil trial for treason of a few leaders. While Lieber steadfastly maintained that rebellion was treason, he admitted that the lawful government for a time could not protect the citizens of the insurgent area. Consequently it could no more punish temporary obedience to the rebel government than could a government repossessing itself of a conquered district punish the people for temporary allegiance to the conqueror. Lieber expressed these views in a memorandum he never published; his public statement drew the denunciation of the Southern press: [9]

"Stanton per Lieber bases his whole superstructure upon the assumption that Gen. Grant's proposition of April 9 was but a military parole . . . of no civil function. . . . This theory . . . ignores all reference to the well known and plainly implied intentions of the high contracting parties, which are consecrated by the surrender, and so fails to touch the essential justice, humanity and dignity of the question." [10]

In a moment of pain, a distinguished Louisiana physician wrote Lieber: "I am an old and sincere admirer of your great works on Political Philosophy—especially of your treatise on *Civil Liberty and Self Government* which I have thumbed and marked all over with a truly filial affection. Voila pourquoi j'écris—

"Can you reconcile your teachings and your practice? How can *you* lend yourself to the policy of the most unscrupulous, cruel and vindictive party (the Radical wing of the Republican) that ever existed? . . .

"The South is already a wilderness, a burning hell. Instead of pacificating by a generous, Christ-like policy, the Administration with *you* for its great legal adviser, is about heaping additional sufferings on four millions of human hearts already overwhelmed with mortification and misery." [11]

To admonitions like these Lieber paid no attention. He melted,

[9] Lieber, "Two things forgotten," memorandum, September 21, 1866.

[10] Clipping from a New Orleans newspaper in W. H. Holcombe to Lieber, June 7, 1865.

[11] Holcombe to Lieber, June 7, 1865. The following day, Holcombe wrote apologizing for taking "a most unwarranted liberty with a distinguished stranger."

however, when he received a gentlemanly note from one of his former students, William L. Trenholm, son of the Confederate Secretary of the Treasury. Trenholm, who was in New York, politely asked if he might call on his former professor. The request was "embarrassing yet touching" to Lieber, who replied he would be glad to resume friendly relations with former South Carolina College students and associates, if they would respect it as "a settled point that our country's acts and sufferings shall not be mentioned." [12]

While Lieber's forthright views brought him under assault in the South, he felt they were also responsible for a bitter humiliation at Columbia College. Without warning in June, 1865, President F. A. P. Barnard of Columbia University requested the Board of Trustees to oust the professor. His official reason was the lack of necessity for a separate chair of history and political economy in the undergraduate college; his private justification was a charge that Lieber was thoroughly incompetent. Staggered by the move, the proud professor could only fall back on the explanation that Barnard was playing university politics to punish him for his Radical Republicanism.[13]

Lieber had not rejoiced at the election of Barnard to succeed his elderly friend, President Charles King, who resigned in 1864. At the outbreak of the war, Barnard had been Chancellor of the University of Mississippi. When he arrived in New York in 1862, Lieber regarded him somewhat suspiciously and cautiously inquired of A. D. Bache, head of the Coast Survey in which the ex-Chancellor had found a minor position, if Barnard had not been a rampant secessionist at the beginning of the war.[14]

Barnard had indeed equivocated. He had pledged his orthodoxy on slavery to the trustees of Mississippi, and as late as a month after the firing upon Fort Sumter had written in justification of the Confederate cause. Shortly after he reached the North, he can-

[12] William L. Trenholm to Lieber, June 16, 1865; Lieber to Trenholm, June 15, 1865, contemporary copy, Lieber papers, Huntington Library. Lieber to Ruggles, June 15, 1865, Lieber papers, Library of Congress.

[13] Lieber to King, June 9, 1865, Lieber papers, Library of Congress; Lieber to Sumner, June 25, 1865. For a careful analysis, see Dorfman and Tugwell, "Francis Lieber: German Scholar in America," *loc. cit.*, 284–88. Thompson, *Ruggles of New York*, 163–65.

[14] Lieber to Bache, May 24, 1862, Rhees collection, Huntington Library.

celed rumors of these activities by writing a violent public letter in which he described how he had witnessed the growth of a vile slaveholders' plot against the North. He became, therefore, an eligible candidate for the presidency of Columbia University.[15]

Lieber continued distinctly cool. At the inaugural he undoubtedly had listened with approval to Barnard's attack upon "the insidious doctrine of Darwin," but writhed when the president went on to label the theological seminaries of Germany "schools of irreligion." Here was a man whose views were almost as repugnant to him as Thornwell's.[16]

President Barnard more than reciprocated Lieber's animosity, and within six months of his inauguration was advocating the removal of the powerful professor. In March, 1865, he proposed to Hamilton Fish, the chairman of the Board of Trustees, that to facilitate the development of a school of mines, the Trustees should consolidate Lieber's fields of history and political economy with the chair of English and philosophy.

Lieber's courses were of "very little educational benefit," the president assured Fish. The field of history was too vast to teach undergraduates; instead the English instructor should provide them with bibliographies as a basis for independent study. Further, Lieber's lecture method of instruction was "grossly out of place." "Lectures on History may do in Universities, where the audience are graduates, and where mental discipline is not the object of the teaching," Barnard believed, but they were "singularly ill-suited to the wants of undergraduates." Much the same criticisms applied to political economy.

Later Barnard repeated these impersonal strictures in his formal report to the Trustees, but in his earlier letter to Fish he had launched an open attack upon Lieber: The instruction methods made the courses a farce. On Mondays the history professor lectured, and he was not a fast talker. On Fridays, he sat silent all hour while the students wrote and "tell him back what he told them on Monday." "The instruction is substantially thrown away," Barnard flatly charged. "The Professor continually com-

[15] Dorfman and Tugwell, "Francis Lieber: German Scholar in America," *loc. cit.*, 284–85 *et seq.*

[16] Lieber to Fish, October 9, 1870 (copy) ; Dorfman and Tugwell, "Francis Lieber: German Scholar in America," *loc. cit.*, 286.

plains of the listlessness, inattention, imperfect performance and general ill-behavior of his classes. These classes, with scarcely an exception, are attentive, diligent, orderly and apparently interested in their studies every where else." Only his own personal intervention, Barnard insinuated, had quelled an incipient student revolt, and he added ominously, "I trust the calm may last—at least through the academic year." The solution was simple: since Lieber taught only four hours a week, abolish his chair.[17]

Fish mentioned none of this to Lieber, who was flabbergasted when Barnard made his official recommendation in June. Protesting privately against the charges, the chagrined professor considered it beneath his dignity to make formal answer. He felt certain that the accusations of want of discipline in his classes were a mere afterthought. If he had told the students of the proposal, they would certainly have circulated a petition in his behalf. True enough, his chair had been a sinecure, but he pointed to his continued willingness to teach more than the allotted four hours, and inquired if his name were not worth something. "I should not wonder if the whole thing is *political*," he snorted. "Am I forsooth to be sent away from Columbia Col. because so '*Confoundedly national?*'" It would be a sorry "reward for all I have tried . . . to do for the country!"[18]

The endangered professor quickly enlisted the aid of his powerful friends, Fish, King, and Ruggles. They were not able to save his chair, but did obtain his transfer to the School of Law where under the friendly aegis of Dean Theodore Dwight he would fill the chair of constitutional history and public law. His salary would remain four thousand dollars. When the humiliation wore off, Lieber admitted to Fish that he would be happier in the Law School.[19]

During his years at Columbia College, Lieber had taught dili-

[17] F. A. P. Barnard to Fish, March 23, 1865, Columbiana Collection, Columbia University.

[18] Minutes of the Board of Trustees, Columbia College, 61:147, Columbiana Collection, Columbia University; Lieber to King and Ruggles, July 9, 1865, Lieber papers, Library of Congress; Lieber to Sumner, July, 1865.

[19] Lieber to Fish, June 23, July 1, 6, 8, 1865; Minutes of the Board of Trustees, Columbia College, 61:162–63, 165–66, 174; "Report of Committee on Salaries," 1866, Columbiana Collection, Columbia University; Lieber to King, June 9, 1865; Lieber to Ruggles, not dated, June 12, 15, 1865, Lieber papers, Library of Congress; Lieber to Sumner, June 25, July, 1865, Lieber papers, Huntington Library; William Betts to Lieber, July 6, 1865, Lieber papers, University of South Carolina.

gently and sincerely. He had endeavored unsuccessfully to bring to fruition the dream of many decades to make Columbia truly a university on a plane comparable to those in Europe. War had combined with inertia to thwart most of these plans and the enrollment in 1865 was still only 150.[20]

Doubtless the restless professor, with his incessant grumbling over petty annoyances and the wartime cut in salary, had been a source of irritation to the administration. Nor was he an ideal undergraduate instructor. He disliked immature students and as late as 1864 had again recommended that the age of entrance be raised to sixteen. By his own estimate he labored an average of three hours in the preparation of each of his lectures, and they continued to be of a quality seldom equaled in American colleges of his day. Yet by their very nature they baffled or bored the average immature boy accustomed to the simple memorization and recitation of text assignments.[21]

To his Columbia students, Lieber's character must have seemed enigmatic. Unsympathetic and a martinet toward the dullards, yet he was so sentimental that tears filled his eyes when during an examination students requested extra time for one of their number who had been wounded in the assault on Fort Fisher. He lavished attention and small awards, such as a pair of mounted portraits of Hampden and Pym, upon his favorites. In return he called upon them for numerous small favors. To these few he was a source of endless inspiration. One such student twenty-four years later recalled his "novel and interesting" methods of teaching history: [22]

"He first and to a greater degree than any other one of our professors sought to put us Collegians on a higher level than school-

[20] Minutes of the Board of Trustees, Columbia College, June 5, 1865, 61:140, Columbiana Collection, Columbia University.

[21] Lieber to King, June 9, 1865, Lieber papers, Library of Congress; Lieber, "Suggestions for President King as a basis for discussion on the distribution of instruction" [1864]. For Lieber's complaints, see numerous notes in the Columbiana Collection, Columbia University. Lieber's lecture notebooks are in the Lieber collections at the Huntington Library and Johns Hopkins University. For a printed example, see "The Rise of Our Constitution and its National Features," Lieber, *Miscellaneous Writings*, II, 17–85.

[22] Lieber to Thayer, April 23, 1867, Lieber papers. Cardboard with portraits of Hampden and Pym, inscribed to D. B. Olyphant, December, 1860, New York Historical Society.

boys, to make us take an interest in his subject for itself and for ourselves and not for marks. He was always holding high ideals up to us for emulation, stimulating us to independent and original study and trying to enlarge our horizon by the philosophic breadth of his own views. His lectures, his peculiar modes of having recitations made and his various plans and aids in memorizing and systematizing what was to be learned—all these recur to me now as very valuable, as marking an effort to introduce to us some of the best features of the German University. I fear he often overshot his mark and received but an inadequate response from the callow minds before him. But I also feel sure that his good seed was not all wasted and that some of it, though germinating late will even yet bear good fruit." [23]

It did bear much fruit. John W. Burgess labeled Lieber "a distinct failure" as a teacher, but was prevented only by illness from becoming one of Lieber's students. Burgess, who was probably the leading American political theorist in the latter half of the nineteenth century, paid testimony in his own career to the fact that "as a writer Professor Lieber instructed the United States and the world." [24]

One of the most outstanding liberals of the latter part of the century, Henry Demarest Lloyd, attended classes at Columbia Law School. Though Lloyd came to differ with the views of Lieber, he learned from the professor the theory and methodology that launched him upon a great reform career. Lieber showered Lloyd with his early pamphlets, delivered a lecture which Lloyd arranged at the Evening High School, and helped launch him as a worker for the American Free-Trade League.[25]

The students in the Law School were more mature and more appreciative of Lieber. With zest he reported in 1869 that he did not "remember having ever enjoyed the sympathetic interest of any class in a higher degree." Again, in 1871, one reason he gave

[23] J. H. Emerson to Matilda Lieber, September 3, 1881, copy.
[24] J. W. Burgess, *Reminiscences of an American Scholar* (New York, 1934), 70.
[25] Lieber to Lloyd, March 11, April 11, 12, November 18, November, 1871, Lloyd papers, Wisconsin State Historical Association. The present writer is deeply indebted to Professor Chester McA. Destler for calling his attention to these letters and supplying him with copies of them. Destler, "A 'Plebian' at Columbia 1863–1869," *New York History*, XXVII (1946), 306–23, has a keen analysis of Lieber's influence upon Lloyd.

for retracting his decision to retire was that his numerous students were urging him to stay on another year.[26]

In July, 1865, before he had become reconciled to being shifted to the Law School, and while still convinced he had been persecuted for his Radical Republican views, Lieber went to Washington. There he basked in the warmth of approbation these same views brought him there. At last, after all his years of hard work and bitter frustration, he received a full measure of respect and veneration from the cabinet leaders.

Attorney General Speed, who had succeeded Edward Bates as a correspondent and admirer, met Lieber for the first time and insisted that the scholar stay at his home. Secretary of State Seward came to call, still convalescing from the assassin's wounds he had received the night Lincoln was killed, but "smoking lustily with his piece of India rubber in his mouth."

Lieber delighted in this attention, and showed his open irritation when he called upon President Andrew Johnson and found the executive office so filled with pardon seekers that it was difficult to converse. Testily he urged the President to stop the practice of granting interviews to these people: "The nation does not set up the presidency for this abominable thing." [27]

In a much happier mood, the elderly professor called upon Secretary of War Stanton, whom he considered the greatest man the Civil War had produced. He was always ready to overlook Stanton's brusqueness and unpleasantness because he felt that the Secretary, while no Carnot, had run the department ably in the face of overwhelming difficulties, and to his great credit "kept down the arrogance of the sword." [28]

Stanton was in a singularly affable mood, and to Lieber's great delight introduced him to General Grant, whom the scholar had

[26] Lieber to Fish, April 23, 1869, December 4, 1871, Fish papers, Library of Congress. In the Law School Lieber was to deliver one lecture weekly between 1:30 and 2:30 in the afternoon, to each class. The Trustees resolved "That lectures on Constitutional History of England be delivered to the Junior Class, and on that of the United States to the Senior Class; and also a Course on Modern Political History to the Junior Class, and on Government to the Senior Class." Minutes of the Board of Trustees, Columbia College, 6:174, Columbiana Collection, Columbia University.

[27] Lieber to Sumner, July 28, 1865; Lieber to Matilda Lieber, July 13, 1865.

[28] Lieber to Horatio Woodman, January 6, 1870, Massachusetts Historical Society. Lieber to [Duyckinck or Benson J. Lossing], December 25, 1865, Lieber papers, Library of Congress.

not recognized in his civilian garb. The previous November, the Secretary had sent word indirectly that he wished to give Lieber remunerative employment as a reward for his services to the country. Now he was as good as his word. He provided a better position for Lieber's one-armed son Hamilton, a lieutenant colonel's commission for Norman—who had served capably as judge advocate on General Banks's staff at New Orleans—and appointed Lieber himself chief of a newly established bureau for the collection of rebel archives.[29]

Stanton's immediate purpose was to find incriminating evidence for the prosecution of Jefferson Davis. He assured the cabinet in mid-July that Professor Lieber with a sizable staff would be able to sift through the Confederate papers in about a fortnight. Then, presumably, the trial could procede. Compiling evidence was not to be the simple task the Secretary of War had envisaged, and the responsibilities of the Archives Office of the War Department came to be much larger than Stanton had originally conceived. It served many functions besides that of providing evidence for treason trials.

Though Lieber received his appointment as archivist as a political reward, he was in actuality filling a difficult and responsible position for which few men in the United States were as thoroughly qualified as he. The Confederate records as they came in from the field were entrusted to a historian with an eye to posterity. Soon he proposed a larger role for his office. Many of these letters and documents, he assured Stanton, must be "of the highest interest for the historian and of great importance to the Government. They are useless unless registered and deposited in regular archives—classified and indexed."[30]

[29] Lieber to Matilda Lieber, July 14, 16, 1865; E. D. Townsend to Lieber, July 25, 1865. Lieber was to receive the pay of a colonel of the cavalry, $2,532 plus an allowance of $370 for fuel and quarters. War Department, General Orders No. 127, July 21, 1865, War Archives. Unfortunately this section was completed before the writer had an opportunity to consult two comprehensive accounts of Lieber's activities as an archivist: Carl Lokke, "The Captured Confederate Records under Francis Lieber," *The American Archivist*, IX (1946), 277–319, and Dallas Irvine, "The Archive Office of the War Department Repository of Captured Confederate Archives, 1865–1881," *Military Affairs*, X (1946), 93–111.

[30] Lieber to Edwin M. Stanton, memorandum, [April? 1866], Stanton papers, Library of Congress; Welles, *Diary of Gideon Welles*, II, 355; Lieber to Halleck, September 10, 1865, Lieber papers. "Regulations for the Archive Office of the War

Though the Radical scholar hunted with zest for criminal evidence, he looked forward equally to the time when the records would be properly arranged and open to qualified historians. That, he thought, would reveal to the entire world the full enormity of the Southern perfidiousness. He chafed because Stanton would not permit him to publish immediately the more lurid documents since he was sure that before long the Democrats would come into office and destroy the records. "In less than ten years the Archives will exist no more," he would lament as he communicated juicy bits to friends, "and the liars will tell me—should I live then, that I told a lie." [31]

Before the end of August, Lieber began his duties in a rickety Washington warehouse already piled high with papers hastily gathered from all over the occupied South. He immediately assigned his son Norman, who had been detailed as his assistant, to supervise twelve clerks in the sorting and general classification. Much of these papers were in a completely chaotic state. General Halleck had gathered up quantities from the ground when he arrived in Richmond. They were intermingled with street dirt and debris, and in such an apparently hopeless disorder that Lieber, despite his lifelong love of preservation, once even declared he wished for a bonfire. Gradually the clerks brought the material into rough order. By the middle of September they had gone through 428 boxes, 71 barrels, and 120 mail sacks, and were ready for a more careful examination of the important papers.[32]

In the process, the clerks had sorted out quantities of irrelevant materials: quantities of Confederate bonds and money, naval instruments, and a box of blankets. There was even a bag of United States mail and a shipment of Christian Commission schoolbooks which somehow had strayed into the collection. Furthermore, Lieber was custodian of trunks containing the personal belongings of Jefferson Davis and P. G. T. Beauregard. The Louisiana general ultimately secured the return of his property. Davis fared less

---

Department," August 23, 1865; G. N. Lieber to E. D. Townsend, November 9, 1865, Archives Office Letterbook No. 1, p. 91, War Archives.

[31] Lieber to Halleck, May 23, 1866; Lieber to Sumner, July 2, 1866, Lieber papers. Lieber to L. H. Whitney, Archives Office Letterbook No. 1, p. 79, War Archives.

[32] Lieber to Halleck, September 10, 1865. Lieber to Stanton, September 1, 15, 1865, Archives Office Letterbook No. 1, pp. 8, 32, War Archives.

well, and some years later the Archives Office sought official permission to burn his woolens because they had become riddled with moth holes.[33] During the next two years, Lieber, in accordance with instructions from the adjutant general, E. D. Townsend, supervised a detailed examination and arrangement of the documents so that they would be in proper order for reference or publication. The Office briefed and classified according to content the more important papers, including the personal correspondence of Jefferson Davis and other Confederate leaders. Lieber turned some papers over to other departments or bureaus—the postal materials to the Post Office Department, the former United States District Court records to the attorney general's office, and archives of the medical corps to the surgeon general for the preparation of a medical history of the war. The bulk of the documents remained in the Archives Office where they were part of the basis of the 154 published volumes of official records of the Union and Confederate armies and navies. The papers of the Confederate government were to stay in the War Archives much as Lieber had arranged them.[34]

During the early months of the sorting the urgent immediate objective of compiling evidence for the trial of Jefferson Davis obscured the long-range goals. Lieber and his staff worked hectically in absolute secrecy, surrounded by soldiers on guard. No person not employed in the office could visit it or inspect any papers without the written permission of the secretary of war or his assistant. As Lieber came upon materials he thought incriminating, he excitedly sent copies to Stanton. Finally, on January 18, 1866, he transmitted a complete report.[35]

[33] Lieber to Stanton, August 28, September 1, 15, 1865; G. N. Lieber to Townsend, October 31, 1866; Lieber to Townsend, November 2, 1866, Archives Office Letterbook No. 1, pp. 4, 9, 32, 235, 237, 240; Townsend to Lieber, November 6, 1866, War Archives. Lieber to Halleck, September 10, 1865, Lieber papers.

[34] Townsend, "Instructions regarding the carrying on the work in the Archive Office," in Archives Office, Letters Received, Box 17292. See also Archives Office Letterbook No. 1 and Endorsement Book No. 1, p. 58, item 1, War Archives. U.S. War Department Archive Office. *Regulations for the Archive Office of the War Department* . . . ([Washington], 1865).

[35] *Regulations for the Archives Office of the War Department.* . . . G. N. Lieber to Townsend, January 11, February 15, 1867, Archives Office Letterbook No. 1, pp. 256, 273, War Archives. W. S. Washburn to Lieber, September 17, 1866, Lieber papers.

The zealous Radical discovered no sensational documents of a highly damaging nature. He enjoyed functioning in an air of high secrecy and often hinted about his findings to his friends. These letters to Rutherford B. Hayes, H. W. Halleck, S. B. Ruggles, and others, sometimes on paper "befouled" with the rebel letterhead, contained the admission that he had found much that made him fulminate, but little that was villainous.[36]

After the first month, he admitted knowing only that "Beauregard is the veriest coxcomb, corresponding with scores of Misses . . . Jefferson Davis quiet; once he says of Butler 'justly called the beast.'— All tenderly beloved by their wives." Lieber hooted at designs for the Confederate flag: "Such a tasteless, coarse, crude, boastful, silly people, I feel perfectly sure never existed before." [37]

By the spring of 1866 Lieber had evidence a little more concrete: a report by Governor Zebulon Vance of North Carolina, Jefferson Davis' adroit political foe, that Confederate troops had ferociously mistreated persons accused of desertion, another by a Confederate congressional committee denouncing the indescribably loathesome conditions in war prisons, and a letter from a Georgia soldier to Davis complaining that prison guards were shooting Yankees without provocation. To Lieber's great disgust, he came upon a letter from a Georgian proposing to form a corps of assassins to kill the leading men of the North, which Davis in his methodical, unimaginative way had "respectfully referred" to the Secretary of War.[38]

After sifting through 270,000 letters, all Lieber could report was much vague evidence of this sort. He had found a good bit, but not what the Radical Republicans needed to hang men. By the time the Archivist made his reports to the House Committee

[36] Lieber to Stanton, August 25, October 3, December 1, 1865, January 18, August 25, 1866, Archives Office Letterbook No. 1, pp. 2, 62–64, 106, 123, 224, War Archives. Stanton to Lieber, October 28, 1865, Lieber papers. Lieber to Hayes, June 29, 1866, Hayes Memorial Library; Lieber to Halleck, September 10, 1865, Lieber papers; Lieber to Ruggles, March 15, 1866, Lieber papers, Library of Congress.

[37] Lieber to Halleck, September 10, 1865; Lieber to Drisler, October 18, 1865, Lieber papers. Lieber to ?, October 7, 1865, Historical Society of Pennsylvania.

[38] Lieber to Halleck, March 20, May 23, 1866; J. E. Anderson to Jefferson Davis, June 23, 1864, copy, Lieber papers. Lieber to Ruggles, March 15, 1866, Lieber papers, Library of Congress. Lieber had his clerks make for him a set of copies of the Confederate cotton loan correspondence, and a few letters he considered lurid, now in the Lieber papers.

of the Judiciary late in the spring of 1866, he realized this fact and lamented, "The trial of Jeff. Davis will be a terrible thing—volumes, a library of the most infernal treason will be belched forth—Davis will not be found guilty and we shall stand there as completely beaten. The time was lost, and can never be re-covered." This was correct: Davis never stood trial.[39]

Although the Radical Republican scholar ardently desired to see a few ex-Confederates swing, ordinarily Lieber viewed proposals for trials with a hardheaded realism. He was momentarily carried away by enthusiasm in a conversation with Secretary of the Navy Gideon Welles. When Welles asked if Admiral Raphael Semmes could be prosecuted, Lieber quoted his formula on the status of prisoners of war. Consequently, the naval secretary advised his judge advocate general, John A. Bolles, to confer with Lieber. Bolles sent a copy of Semmes's parole and asked whether or not the commander of the *Alabama* could be tried on the charge of escaping in the English Channel after he had given the signal of surrender. Lieber replied soberly that Semmes's offence, even if proved, clearly had been only a violation of the laws of war and

---

[39] Lieber to Halleck, May 19, 1866, Lieber papers. Lieber reported to the Judiciary Committee on evidence: "I. Of a circumstantial character tending to confirm that adduced at the conspiracy trial in relation to the complicity of the Rebel Government in the assassination of Abraham Lincoln. II. Evidence showing that Jefferson Davis entertained propositions to assassinate Abraham Lincoln and the most prominent men of the North. III. Evidence showing that Jacob Thompson, Clement C. Clay, Beverley Tucker, George N. Sanders and W. C. Cleary were the accredited agents of the Rebel Government at the time the conspiracy to assassinate President Lincoln was formed." Subsequently he sent evidence "showing that the rebel government was cognisant of the treatment which prisoners of the Union Army had to endure in the South." Lieber to J. F. Wilson, May 18, June 23, 28, July 5, 1866; Lieber to G. S. Boutwell, undated, Archives Office Letterbook No. 1, pp. 171–72, 198, 200–201, 204, 218; Wilson to Lieber, May 4, June 22, 1866, J5, J6LRAO, War Archives.

A twenty-page copy of Lieber's first report to Wilson is item No. 55947 in the Stanton papers, Library of Congress. He was successful only in presenting evidence that Thompson and other Confederates in Canada were accredited agents of the Richmond government. The only connection he could find between the Confederate officials and the plot to assassinate Lincoln was evidence that Surratt's Tavern had been a station on one of the routes for sending communications through the Union lines. He cited the letters of a number of fanatics to Davis offering to assassinate prominent Northern leaders. The nearest approach to an atrocity was a protest from K. J. Stewart in Toronto to Davis, December 12, 1864, that some overzealous persons paid $100 of Confederate funds to a man to bring boxes of smallpox-infected clothing to Washington and sell them at auction. See *House Reports*, 39 Cong., 1 Sess., No. 104.

did not involve "deep moral turpitude." The Confederate admiral signed his parole believing he would not be tried for his *Alabama* offence; to the public the charge might appear flimsy, consequently Semmes might better be merely exiled.[40]

Except for the unfortunate commandant of Andersonville prison, none of the Confederate leaders suffered anything worse than varying periods of imprisonment. This did not mean that Lieber's work as archivist was of no value to the government. He prodded officials to locate additional papers and made recommendations for the better preservation of those in his charge. Also, the archives had an immediate, practical worth. One of Lieber's first official acts had been to send Stanton a bill presented to the Confederate Secretary of War by a secret agent who was also trying to collect from the Union officials. This was the beginning of a vast number of similar services. From the Confederate records, Lieber gathered essential evidence for numerous claims cases. After he finished his organizing work and left his office in the summer of 1867, the archives continued to be of growing use. They supplied much valuable evidence for the Claims Commission and enabled treasury officials to identify and obtain former Confederate property. From the 1870's on, they served as a check on the validity of pension claims. Many an applicant was found to have served in the Confederate ranks.[41]

Although the aging scholar held an honorable position as Chief of the Archives Bureau and enjoyed great prestige as a publicist, he felt little sense of triumph in the postwar years. The North had indeed won, and the Radicals were in a strong position, yet all seemed sordid, bewildering, and unsatisfactory. "We live at a fearful period—murder, forgery, robbery, licentiousness, rebellion of the worst and fiercest kind continued," he lamented to his wife in an all-too-characteristic refrain. "Do you not also feel like pressing to-gether as people who love one another do on deck

[40] Welles, *Diary of Gideon Welles*, II, 407. Semmes to Hartsuff, May 1, 1865, copy; Lieber to Bolles, January 24, 1866, Lieber papers. See also Archives Office Letterbook No. 1, pp. 124, 127–30, War Archives.

[41] G. N. Lieber to Philip Henry Sheridan, September 6, 1865; Lieber to Townsend, September 15, November 6, 1865; Lieber to Stanton, July 12, 1866, Archives Office Letterbook No. 1, pp. 15, 31, 33–89, 215, War Archives. Lieber to Stanton, August 26, 1865, Archives Office Letterbook No. 1, p. 2; Letterbooks Nos. 1 and 2; scrapbooks, War Archives.

a vessel which is surrounded by yawning danger which they cannot do anything to avert?" [42]

The times seemed most unsettled, and somewhat credulously the professor swallowed the infinity of rumors circulating around Washington. He heard, and believed, that President Johnson was often drunk and leaned more and more on Democratic "lackeys"; the unrepentant Rebels, having even tried to spread yellow fever in the North during the war, were now plotting to wrest back control of the government; the Southern women in Georgetown wore lockets containing portraits of John Wilkes Booth.[43]

Most of this was flimsy hearsay, but by autumn Lieber had filled in his bill of particulars with tangible evidence. He read the constitutions and black codes of the new state governments of the South, mushrooming into existence under the new President's lenient plan of reconstruction. They filled him with deep apprehension, for they seemed to modify as little as possible the previous servitude of the ex-slaves. With deep indignation he wrote Senator Sumner that the Alabama ordinance excluding Negro testimony from the courts was "literally revolting, revolting to reason, to the jurist, to decency, and to humanity." The new black codes seemed to be no more than "the old slave code minus the slave owners' responsibilities—poor as they were." "Do you recollect," he inquired, "that I always said we ought to retain 50,000 men, for five years, to keep a thumb on the South?" [44]

Charles Sumner, Thad Stevens, and their militant cohorts needed no such goading to inaugurate a Radical plan of reconstruction when Congress met in December. As early as August Sumner had outlined a clear-cut plan to Lieber: turn the whole question of reconstruction over to Congress where it belonged; inaugurate an interim military rule in the South; exclude everyone from the public service who had helped sustain the rebellion; and enforce equal rights for Negroes.[45]

[42] Lieber to Matilda Lieber, August 21, 1865.

[43] Sumner to Lieber, August 11, 1865, in Pierce (ed.), *Memoir and Letters of Charles Sumner,* IV, 250; Lieber to Sumner, August 10, October 26, December 1, 1865.

[44] Lieber to Sumner, September 30, October 1, November 17, 1865, Lieber papers. Cf. Lieber to Stanton, July 30, 1865, Stanton papers, Library of Congress.

[45] Sumner to Lieber, August 14, 1865, in Pierce (ed.), *Memoir and Letters of Charles Sumner,* IV, 256–57.

In essence, the Radical professor could subscribe to a program like this. He lamented with special bitterness the conciliatory course of the administration toward the Confederate leaders, but he viewed the problem of the Negro both more and less realistically. He was less realistic since he did not see the possibilities of universal Negro suffrage in the South as a device to maintain the Republican party in power. Or at least he was not ready to condone "Black Reconstruction" for such a party end. He was too stanch a defender of property rights to subordinate them even to the party of which he was so ardent an adherent.

Lieber was more realistic because his long years in South Carolina had given him a familiarity with the Negro and the social structure lacking to almost all his fellow Radicals. Although he intensely disliked the system of large plantations, he was no warm partisan of either the small independent farmers whom Johnson represented or the emancipated Negro. The colored people represented to Lieber an unfortunate lower class which must achieve a higher position in society, but could reach it only after much travail: he had not entirely sloughed off his schemes of a decade and a half before. Assuredly the Negroes should enjoy equality before the law, but most of them in their abysmal ignorance were far from ready for the ballot.

In the spring of 1865, the political theorist already had disagreed with his Radical acquaintances on this point. Salmon P. Chase lamented that the resolutions he drew up for the New York Union League failed to recommend universal Negro suffrage, but Lieber did not capitulate. Negroes as components of the lower class were no more fit to participate in elections than the rest of the unschooled masses. At first Lieber proposed to Sumner that Negro suffrage should be a state affair; later he proposed a literacy test. The scholarly Massachusetts senator began by thinking kindly of the requirements, then reflected that since it would also bar large numbers of whites from the polls, it would be highly unpopular.[46]

The publicist tried to circumvent Sumner's objection by proposing to give the ballot to everyone who already could vote, who had fought in the Union army, or who could read. "Remember," he

[46] Chase to Lieber, February 18, 1865; Lieber to Sumner, May 4, August 11, 1865; Pierce (ed.), *Memoir and Letters of Charles Sumner*, IV, 256.

THE LIFE OF FRANCIS LIEBER

declared subsequently, "that we have States in which the blacks outnumber the whites, and in the course of the animated politics of a free country, every distinction whatever may become party distinction. Would you side in such a case with blacks?" While later he never directly attacked the mode in which agents of his own party herded the illiterate Negroes to the polls, he never modified his old warning that universal suffrage among ignorant people would lead almost inevitably to "democratic absolutism" —rule by demagogues.[47]

On the positive side, more than a year earlier the resourceful professor had proposed safeguards for the emancipated slaves. In the spring of 1864 he had circulated through Congress a manuscript later printed in which he urged a long series of amendments to the Constitution. Notable among them were a definition of citizenship that would protect the Negro and a stipulation that states should receive representation in the House proportionate to the number of persons they admitted to the electorate. Upon this basis, Lieber would leave the question of Negro suffrage to the states. In February, 1865, Sumner formally presented to the Senate Lieber's suggestion on representation; the Washington *Chronicle* warmly commended the plan. Significantly, both this and the definition of citizenship came to be embodied in the Fourteenth Amendment, but the provision paring down representation of states not admitting Negroes to the polls was never enforced.[48]

In the fall of 1865, Lieber counseled Sumner not to raise the issue of Negro suffrage. "It would weaken you and our side altogether," he erroneously prophesied. Lieber was sure it could succeed only through a constitutional amendment, and he felt certain that President Johnson would kill that.[49]

The alert scholar worried even more about the emergent social structure of the New South. In one of the most forceful of the pam-

[47] Lieber to Sumner, October 22, 1865. See, for example, Lieber, *Miscellaneous Writings*, II, 215–16.

[48] Lieber, *A Letter to Hon. E. D. Morgan . . . on the Amendment of the Constitution Abolishing Slavery . . .* (Loyal Publication Society No. 79, New York, 1865), 4 pp.; Lieber, *Amendments of the Constitution, Submitted to the Consideration of the American People* (Loyal Publication Society No. 83, New York, 1865), 31, 33–34, 38–39, reprinted in Lieber, *Miscellaneous Writings*, II, 137–79. Chase commended Lieber's proposal to limit representation as an effective although difficult means to secure Negro suffrage. Chase to Lieber, February 14, 1865. Washington *Chronicle,* February 12, 1865.

[49] Lieber to Sumner, October 5, 1865.

378

phlets for the Loyal Publication Society, he had execrated the old plantation system as a basic evil. Now he continued the same attack. Lieber did not foresee the emergence of the share-crop and crop-lien systems which were to reduce the Southern masses, white as well as black, to a state of virtual peonage. Instead he feared the continuation of the large plantations on a labor-gang basis, which some of the new black codes seemed to make highly probable. The freedmen, he warned Sumner, "should be hired out by one, or two, or three wherever this is possible to mechanics or other people who are, or are willing to become small farmers. We must break up the latifundia holders." [50]

The program of Radical reconstruction that Sumner and Stevens rapidly developed in 1866 did not receive the professor's unqualified support. He was prepared to see the Radicals oppose the reuniting of Virginia and West Virginia and granted that in matters like this the country stood above the Constitution. He rejoiced wholeheartedly that spring when the Radicals signalized their seizure of control by repassing the Civil Rights Bill over the President's veto. Yet he gagged when they continued to block the thoroughly loyal Tennessee representatives from their seats in the House, and admonished Sumner to admit them. "People begin to think," he warned, "that keeping them out looks like a taunt to the President." [51]

Publicly Professor Lieber still subscribed unreservedly to Radical Republicanism. When Christian Detmold, a wealthy New York German, gave him $250 to spend in the congressional campaign of 1866, he utilized it to distribute a little anonymous pamphlet calling upon the electorate to support congressional reconstruction. Only Congress and the "mild and righteous" Fourteenth Amendment could save the nation from the President, the Democrats, and the South. He stooped to vilify Johnson with a fourteen-point indictment and warned the voters they must choose between the President and "Congress and the Country." [52]

Lieber used extravagant language in the campaign pamphlet,

[50] Lieber to Sumner, September, 1865. Lieber, *Slavery Plantations and the Yeomanry.*
[51] Lieber to Sumner, February 7, March 19, April 9, 1866; Lieber to Woolsey, April 12, 1866.
[52] Lieber to Sumner, October 8, 1866; [Lieber], *For Whom Will You Vote? . . .* [New York, 1866].

but when the Radicals won a huge congressional majority he remained singularly silent and unjubilant. He seldom mentioned reconstruction in his letters to Sumner, and to a new and more moderate correspondent, Representative Martin Russell Thayer of Pennsylvania, he confided his qualms. If the Radicals deemed territorialization of the South necessary, he hoped they would do it in just one or two states as an example to frighten the rest. Instead the leaders drew up plans to return the entire South to military control preparatory to establishing Republican machines greased with Negro votes. Before the pattern became apparent, Lieber queried anxiously, "What is Sumner now after?" [53]

Nor did the political theorist think better of the program as it unfolded during 1867. Once again Lieber was splitting with Sumner over reform issues. He objected most strongly to the means by which the Radicals were forcing the ballot into the hands of the Negro and gloomily accepted as inevitable the setbacks in the fall elections. The poor white, whether Northern or Southern, he observed, "wants to kick the negro, all democratic hypocrisy and cant to the contrary not withstanding." Sadly he placed the blame squarely upon his friend Charles, who had "done us great mischief." "Sumner, Stevens &c run the cart into such a mire that we shall be able to extricate it only by sacrificing a good deal of our best luggage," he lamented. "Nor do they remember that bad arguments even for the best of causes, come back like curses to roost at home." [54]

The only salvation might be the election of Grant in 1868. By the summer of 1867 Lieber had become convinced that the popular general, nominally a Democrat before the war, could be counted upon by the Republicans. Grant would stay closely under the tutelage of his wealthy and safe political mentor, Representative Elihu Washburn. Already the professor viewed him less as a great leader than as a necessary figurehead through which the Republican party could retain power. Grant in a deplorably "ugly" manner had helped pave the way for Johnson's impeachment by returning the War Department to the Radical Stanton after the President had entrusted him with it. "I dare say," Lieber specu-

[53] Lieber to Thayer, December, December 10, 1866.
[54] Lieber to Thayer, October 11, November 30, undated letter, 1867.

lated, "that stupid silence upon which Grant prides himself, misled Johnson." [55]

Nonetheless, Lieber accepted the logical consequences of Grant's betrayal, the impeachment and trial of President Johnson for violation of the Tenure of Office Act. He had long been hesitant while Radicals cried for impeachment. Sumner had queried him in January, 1867, as to whether or not Congress could pass a law suspending the President during the proceedings. Lieber opposed the measure as unconstitutional and against custom. It would enable Congress to use a protracted trial as a virtual expulsion from office, and it would be likely to strengthen Johnson because of its irregularity.[56]

Through the early months of 1867 Lieber continued to feel that impeachment would be "a severe shake," which Congress should avoid if at all possible. Gradually his animosity toward Johnson drew him away from his cool legalism. He convinced himself before long that it was highly justifiable and by no means would create a dangerous precedent. Before the end of the year he was ardently hoping the House Judiciary Committee would "find enough filth to poke a stick into it, with a card attached to it: 'Impeachment.' " [57]

During the trial in the spring of 1868, Lieber was at a fever pitch of excitement. He scoffed at Johnson's able defense that he was testing the constitutionality of the Tenure of Office Act when he ousted Stanton in defiance of Congress. Only the Supreme Court, the professor held, could decide questions of the conflict of laws. When the Senate (by a majority of one) acquitted the President, Lieber greeted the outcome with such chagrined incredulity that he even inquired darkly if those who voted for Johnson had been bribed.[58]

Through the period culminating in the impeachment trial, Lieber's head continued as ever to buzz with a multitude of reform schemes. The array of changes he had proposed for the Consti-

---

[55] Lieber to Thayer, August 31, undated letter, 1867.
[56] Lieber to Sumner, January 16, 1867; Lieber to Thayer, January 14, 1867.
[57] Lieber to Thayer, January 29, December 9, undated, 1867.
[58] Lieber to Sumner, March 28, April 24, 1868; Lieber to Thayer, March 2, April 29, May 24, 1868.

tution in 1864 included not only measures to protect the Negro but others to require plenary allegiance to the Federal government, define treason more precisely, and provide the mode for trial. Because a Federal court in 1861 had regarded the statute prohibiting the slave trade as unconstitutional, he even wished a provision to class the slave trade with piracy. Altogether, Lieber suggested seven elaborate amendments. Even these did not cover all the constitutional reforms he deemed desirable. He would have liked to limit the presidential term of office to a single six-year period; give the chief executive the authority to veto single items in the appropriation bills; prohibit Mormon polygamy; and enable cabinet members to speak on the floors of Congress.[59]

Actually the political theorist did not believe that the Constitution forbade access to the floor to the department heads. In 1865 he tried to initiate a congressional movement in favor of this change he had so long advocated. His friends in the House warned him it would be unpopular because it had been adopted by the Confederacy. Lieber accepted defeat, but could not help wondering if some of his former students at South Carolina, familiar with his ideas, might not have been responsible for the Southern innovation.[60]

When a convention met in 1867 to revise the constitution of the state of New York, Lieber took full advantage of the opportunity to advocate further reforms. Under the sponsorship of the powerful New York Union League Club he prepared a lengthy critique of the old constitution and listed many desirable changes. Many of them were minor, as for instance, a suggestion to eliminate property qualifications for Negro voters, but in the field of penology they were drastic. In 1865 Lieber had sent a questionnaire to state officials throughout the United States. He had thus gathered detailed information on the inadequacy and frequent injustice of the prevailing system of vesting full pardoning power in the hands of the governor.[61]

[59] Lieber, *Miscellaneous Writings*, II, 172–79. See also Lieber, "Notes from the People. Direct Taxation Apportioned According to Population," New York *Times*, January 28, 1866.

[60] Lieber, *Miscellaneous Writings*, II, 173. Edward McPherson to Lieber, February 6, 1865.

[61] Lieber, *Reflections on the Changes Which May Seem Necessary in the Present Constitution of New York* (New York, 1867), reprinted in Lieber, *Miscellaneous Writings*, II, 183–219. Enos Throop to Lieber, August 15, 1865, New York State

At the convention, Lieber gained widespread support for his proposal that a pardon board be created to check the governor. The state executive would not be able to free a convict without first submitting all the papers in the case to the advisers, who would prepare a written recommendation. The suggestion failed when the people of New York defeated the new constitution at the polls, but in subsequent years state after state created similar pardon boards. Ironically New York did not create one until 1918, and by then penologists had turned so completely to the newer techniques of parole and probation that they were little interested.[62]

Lawyers looked less kindly upon a memorial Lieber addressed to the convention arguing against the principle that juries must reach a unanimous opinion in penal trials. The nonagreement of jurors was one of the major causes for the frequent failure of justice, the political theorist insisted. A jury out for any length of time reached only an accommodative rather than real unanimity, and a single recalcitrant holdout on the panel could defeat the ends of justice. A "hung jury" leading to retrial, in effect subjected the accused to the double jeopardy prohibited in the Bill of Rights. While no nation outside of the United States and England prescribed unanimity, even within this country the Supreme Court based its decisions upon a majority vote. Probably with reference to the Southern obsession over minority rights, Lieber pointed out, "In legislation, in politics, in all organizations, the unanimity principle savors of barbarism, or indicates a lack of development." In its place he recommended two-thirds agreement in all civil and penal cases, excepting for a three-fourths agreement in those involving capital punishment.[63]

Library; Lieber to Emory Washburn, April 30, 1865; Washburn to Lieber, May 6, 1865.

[62] Lieber, *Miscellaneous Writings*, II, 185–91. See also Lieber to Theodore W. Dwight, June 27, 1867, which was printed for distribution. Lieber to Emory Washburn, April 30, 1865; Emory Washburn to Lieber, May 6, 1865; Lieber to Mittermaier, March 1, 1866, copy. Pennsylvania created a pardoning board in 1873, Louisiana in 1879, and Kansas in 1885. Between 1897 and 1918, 23 other states created advisory boards, and 7 others advisory officials. Wayne L. Morse and others (eds.), *The Attorney General's Survey of Release Procedures. Pardon* (Washington, 1939), III, 90–93. Here and elsewhere, the present writer is indebted to Dr. Peter Lejins for helpful suggestions on criminology.

[63] Lieber, *A Reprint, with Some Additions, of Document: State of New York, No. 26. In Convention, July 12, 1867. Memorial from Dr. Francis Lieber, Relative*

Lieber also suggested several lesser penal reforms. He denounced the lax system of allowing judges to pass suspended sentences indiscriminately. Too often they gave them for political reasons to habitual criminals. The pardon boards should exercise this authority. In addition, the board should have power to make more complete amends than a mere pardon to innocent persons wrongly convicted.[64]

Many of the recommendations reflected the wish of the well-to-do Union Leaguers to substitute more efficient, conservative government for the boss-ridden administration of New York State and City. Privately Lieber often expressed his shocked indignation over the machine misrule, which he thought comparable to the worst excesses of Imperial Rome. His twofold desire to clean up the government and improve the quality of the electorate typified the Liberal Republican approach in years to come. He demanded rather nebulously the abolition of the rotation-of-office spoils system, but suggested no more concrete remedy than appointment of more responsible state officials for perhaps a six-year period. In order to take the state courts out of politics, judges should be appointive and hold office during good behavior. He confided to Andrew Dickson White that he would have liked also to curb the power of the state supreme court, for he disliked its growing tendency to adjudge state laws unconstitutional; its decisions almost always favored state rights.[65]

More drastic schemes might break the Tweed Ring stranglehold upon the City of New York, which Lieber later lamented dishonored "Republicanism as foully as the Royal Harlots, Isabel and Christina have disgraced monarchy." He had long since theorized that urban areas were the feverish quickening agents of civilization which the placid rural districts protected from overheating. Demagogues more easily won control in cities, especially in those of America which were flooded with foreigners unfamiliar with democratic institutions but active in politics. In

to Verdicts of Jurors (New York, 1867) ; Lieber, "The Unanimity of Juries," American Law Register, October, 1867, 728–32, reprinted in Lieber, Miscellaneous Writings, II, 463–68. Lieber to J. K. Bluntschli, August 23 and October 1, 1867, copy.

[64] Lieber, Miscellaneous Writings, II, 190–93.

[65] Ibid., II, 193–98, 201–202. Lieber to Sumner, November 10, 1866; Lieber to Thayer, September 7, November 1, November 11, 1869; Lieber to White, February 24, 1868.

election years the great urban menace was "Irish wickedness and German Lagerbierophilism." [66]

As a temporary expedient, Lieber wished to create an upper house of the New York City Council for which only taxpayers could vote and to vest financial control in carefully restricted state-appointed officials. To improve the quality of the electorate, he would bar foreigners from the polls until they had become citizens, allow counties to compel school attendance, and exact a literacy requirement for voting. [67]

Even in these high-minded proposals for revising the state constitution, Lieber did not entirely forget Radical Republican politics. Theodore W. Dwight, Dean of the Columbia University Law School, warned him that the Democrats would try to push through the convention a proposal for woman suffrage as a means of bringing their party back into power. Dean Dwight even feared the ruse might succeed. [68]

The old professor was horror-stricken. He remembered the strictures in his *Political Ethics,* and added some pages to his recommendations on the divinely ordained place of woman in the home. Woman was an emotional rather than reasoning creature; "politics would undoubtedly unwoman her, and her essential character would be lost." Women were not a class apart; through their husbands they already exercised their influence at the polls. If women entered politics, then what? "How would we like to have a female president, and what would it lead to?" [69]

More frankly, the scandalized scholar lectured to his law students on the dangers of *"La revolution in permanence."* "The polls are frequently in grog shops, in this blessed city," he warned the gallant young men. "Adopt women's voting and I suppose the voting places will be, occasionally at least, in those cellars which advertise 'ready made love' by red ribbons gathering the door curtains. This is very cynical, but so is our whole city." [70]

Indeed the cynical professor did not reckon with the brash

[66] Dorfman and Tugwell, "Francis Lieber: German Scholar in America," *loc. cit.,* 282–83; Lieber to Thayer, November 11, 1869; August 15, 1868.
[67] Lieber, *Miscellaneous Writings,* II, 214–19.
[68] Lieber to Andrew Dickson White, February 28, 1867.
[69] Lieber, *Miscellaneous Writings,* II, 207–10.
[70] Lieber to White, February 28, 1867.

younger generation. One of the daughters of his friend, the solid Massachusetts Representative William Hooper, bridled at Lieber's published remarks and wrote a spirited anonymous retort for the *Nation*. She inquired, "Is a voice in the government of one's own country necessarily so undesirable a privilege that its effects can only be compared to 'those produced in women who enjoy the turf . . . ?' " With similar logic she made an absurdity of each of his arguments. She concluded tauntingly that they reminded her "so forcibly of the ineffectual clucking of a hen whose brood of ducks are just taking to the water for the first time, that I cannot but suspect that as ducks can swim, so women may be able to vote without injury." This stung the proud publicist, but because it came from a woman, he chivalrously declared only that it was "*de haut en bas* . . . and will use no other term." [71]

[71] Lieber to Sumner, undated, 1867; "A Woman in Reply to Dr. Lieber," *Nation*, V (1867), 35–36.

XVII

Nationalism and Internationalism

AMID the chaotic bickerings, sordid machine politics, and crass materialism of the Reconstruction period, the elderly Professor Lieber repeatedly proclaimed to the confused public his interpretation of the essential meaning of the new era. Though he himself was buffeted by the swirling crosscurrents, he steadfastly tried to pilot public opinion along the main channel: the victory of the North must mean the triumph of nationalism.

Long before the Civil War came to an end, Lieber drew upon and refined some of the concepts he had earlier set forth in the *Political Ethics* and the *Civil Liberty*: "The normal type of government in our period of political civilization is the national polity." The United States had been and must continue to be, not an agglomeration of sovereign states, but a nation. It must, moreover, fill its proper responsibility in a world in which no state any longer exercised hegemony over the rest. Lieber envisaged an array of coequal nations, of which the United States was one, that "like Olympic chariot-horses, draw abreast the car of civilization." [1]

Time and again in the years following Appomattox, Lieber pondered the twin concepts of nationalism and internationalism, which to him were the epitome of his political thought and the true significance of the era. He set them forth in his correspondence, deduced corollaries and courses of conduct from them, and

[1] Lieber, *Miscellaneous Writings*, II, 161–64 *et passim*. For a brilliant analysis of Lieber's nationalist thought, see Curti, "Francis Lieber and Nationalism," *loc. cit.* He expressed this concept so forcefully in one of his lectures at South Carolina College in 1846 that one of his students wrote a detailed account of it in his diary. Patterson, *Journal of a Southern Student*, 29–30.

in 1867 summarized them in one printed page which he felt epitomized his teachings of thirty years. This "Fragment" he broadcast among his eminent acquaintances as "a leaf of my testament." [2]

Lieber's avowal of nationalism drew remarkably high praise. It seemed veritably to make "the round of the whole country, like a thought or verse which everyone has long *felt,* but was unable to express." Many a newspaper, and even *Harper's Weekly,* with its huge circulation, published it and congratulations came from prominent persons of many shades of political belief. Horace Binney, the conservative octogenarian; George Bemis, the able expert on international law; Charles Eliot Norton, the young aesthete; and Wendell Phillips, the fervent reformer, all joined in praising the syllogism. [3]

On a western tour in the fall of 1867, Senator Sumner quoted an early version with approbation in a highly successful lecture which he delivered repeatedly, "Are We a Nation?" Anson Burlingame, who had just returned to the United States at the head of a Chinese mission, told the author that General Halleck had quoted it amidst much applause at a state dinner in San Francisco. General James A. Garfield, a rapidly rising congressman who was engaged in a scholarly interchange of letters with Lieber, wrote flatteringly that it was misnamed a "Fragment"; it was no less than "the Philosophy of the History of Civilization condensed into a page." [4]

Delighted by such compliments, the erudite political theorist elaborated his "Fragment" into a twenty-three-page pamphlet which he published as a rather out-of-the-ordinary contribution

[2] Lieber, *The National Polity is the Normal Type of Modern Government* (New York, 1868), Lieber to White, March 17, 1868, Lieber papers, Henry E. Huntington Library. All manuscripts referred to in this chapter, unless otherwise identified, are from this collection.

[3] Lieber to Bluntschli, May 1, 1868, copy; Binney to Lieber, December 10, 1866, copy; Bemis to Lieber, March 27, 1868; Norton to Lieber, April 13, 1868; Phillips to Lieber, December, 1868.

[4] Lieber to Sumner, September 1, 16, October 26, 1867. Sumner, *The Works of Charles Sumner,* 15 vols. (Boston, 1870–83), XII, 190, 196–97. Sumner consulted Lieber in the preparation of his oration and Lieber presided when he delivered it in New York. Lieber to Bluntschli, May 1, 1868, copy; Garfield to Lieber, December 15, 1868, Lieber papers. Garfield sent Lieber a list of congressmen who would like the "Fragment." Lieber to Garfield, [January 2, 1869], Garfield papers, Library of Congress,

to the presidential campaign of 1868. He inscribed it with a flourishing dedication to General Grant, who he felt could best carry out its principles, and prefaced it with his credo compressed into a single phenomenally polyphrase sentence: [5]

"The National Polity is the normal type of Modern Government; Civil Liberty resting on Institutional Self-Government is the high political calling of this period; Absolutism, whether Monarchical or Democratic, . . . its pervading danger; and increasing International Neighborliness with growing Agreement of National Forms and Concepts, its fairest Gage of the Spreading Progress of our Kind." [6]

What were the components of a nation? "A numerous and homogeneous population . . . permanently inhabiting and cultivating a coherent territory, with a well-defined geographic outline, and a name of its own—the inhabitants speaking their own language, having their own literature and common institutions, which distinguish them clearly from other and similar groups of people; being citizens or subjects of a unitary government, however subdivided it may be, and feeling an organic unity with one another, as well as being conscious of a common destiny." [7]

Without these factors states did not possess a national character and could not "obtain that longevity and continuity of political society which is necessary for our progress." Manifestly the United States did possess these essentials, and one of the major objectives of the Civil War was to preserve that national character. [8]

Internationalism was a requisite complement which would not result in the obliteration of nationalities. "The multiplicity of civilized nations, their distinct independence, . . . and their increasing resemblance and agreement are some of the great safe-

---

[5] Lieber, *Fragments of Political Science on Nationalism and Inter-Nationalism* (New York, 1868), reprinted in Lieber, *Miscellaneous Writings*, II, 225–43. Lieber to Thayer, September 30, 1868, Lieber papers. Lieber to Grant, June 23, 1868, Hayes Memorial. The dedication brought forth a difficult effort from the general: "Your friendship for me, shown so frequently and so flatteringly, is a source of great gratification to me, personally almost a stranger to you, and all the more so because I see in your friendship a patriotism and love of country which actuates it much more than any regard for mere person. Again allow me to thank you for many kindnesses." Grant to Lieber, October 19, 1868.

[6] Lieber, *Miscellaneous Writings*, II, 225.   [7] *Ibid.*, II, 227–28.

[8] *Ibid.*, II, 228, 231–39.

guards of our civilization." By co-operating as a commonwealth of nations, the great states through their economic and cultural interdependence could achieve for all mankind a higher and finer type of existence. To Garfield, Lieber put it more succinctly: "The Modern Law of Nations rests chiefly on the law of good neighborhood or kindly vicinage of the Common Law, applied to Nations." [9]

The dual theme of nationalism and internationalism was henceforth to dominate Lieber's thinking. In American affairs it was a rationale for his support of Grant and led him to ponder problems of sovereignty, citizenship, immigration, and expansion. Overseas it motivated him to wish with equal fervor for the unification of Germany through the iron leadership of Bismarck. To a still larger extent it turned his attention to international affairs: proposals for the establishment of a congress of jurists to codify international law, extension of the laws of neutrality, arbitration of the *Alabama* claims, free trade, international copyright and international standards of weights, measures, and money.

Matters like these so engrossed Lieber that shortly he relegated politics to a secondary role in his thinking. Though long since he had come to regard Grant merely as a necessary symbol who could lead the Republicans to victory, he explained in the fall of 1868 that three points would lead him to vote the party ticket: "Our nationality, Our Good Faith in money matters, Our Good Faith in eradicating the idea of a Man-Thing." [10]

Because the accession of Grant brought the achievement of these three objectives, Lieber was willing to close his eyes to the unparalleled corruption of the new regime. Within a month after Grant took office, the disgruntled idealist labeled his term the "Epoch of Mediocrity," and complained that the new President's phenomenally bad appointments were unique in history. Logically, Lieber moved toward the Liberal wing of the Republican party, and peppered its leaders with suggestions for reforms. Nevertheless, he continued to consider nationalism and the other objectives so paramount and was so afraid that they might fail

[9] *Ibid.*, II, 240–43. Lieber to Garfield, March 27, 1869, Garfield papers, Library of Congress. Lieber elaborated these ideas in his writings and correspondence.
[10] Lieber to Thayer, September 3, 1868.

with the defeat of the Republican party, that at the ballot box he remained one of the most regular of the Stalwarts.[11]

Lieber also remained a Stalwart upon every economic question save the tariff. Even to a greater extent than most Liberal Republicans, he failed to recognize the basic maladjustments of the new era, and seemed scarcely to realize that the mushrooming business interests had upset the delicate economic balance of *laissez faire.*

The elderly scholar only occasionally noted the change wrought by the enormous demand for supplies during the war. He had lashed corrupt contractors with his scorn, and lamented in 1863 "The commercial cancer . . . is eating faster and faster." No solution occurred to him, save, perhaps a sobering depression. "Has it ever struck you as it has me," he inquired of Charles J. Stillé, the head of the Sanitary Commission, "that, while it is true that modern Civilisation stands in need of much wealth, and of greater wealth, it is nevertheless true that almost all truly great Periods are poor ones?" [12]

Even in the lush postwar era, observations like these were almost the sum total of Lieber's thinking upon the problem. He berated the bribery of legislators and the building of large party slush funds but was blind to the new moguls of finance who made the corruption possible. Personally he was impeccably honest, and, like Sumner, amidst his worldly friends in Wall Street and Congress he retained a naïve innocence. Perplexedly he asked Representative M. R. Thayer if he should invest in Union Pacific bonds. Since they had the backing of the United States he could not understand why they sold for less than government securities. When his friend Speaker Schuyler Colfax, who was deeply enmeshed in the Credit Mobilier deal, was nominated for the vice-presidency, Lieber did not think him the best possible candidate but rejoiced because at least he was an honest man.[13]

Even had the idealistic scholar been aware of the questionable

[11] Lieber to Thayer, April 8, September 2, 1869.

[12] Lieber to Stillé, February 21, 1863, Historical Society of Pennsylvania.

[13] Lieber to Thayer, October 25, 1866, May 24, 1868. When Lieber indignantly wrote Garfield he had been offered $50 if he would recommend a stranger for a professorship, the congressman replied he had been offered $500 to secure someone a post office. Garfield to Lieber, March 19, 1869, copy, Garfield papers, Library of Congress.

dealings between some congressmen and the masters of capital, he would have accepted them as one more unpleasant price to pay for the all-important nationalism. He was well aware of the delicate interrelationship between the Federal credit and the financial interests which served as a bulwark of the government, and espoused an uncomplicated Hamiltonian view: The forces in favor of strengthening the Federal government stood for funding the debt, resumption of specie payments, and deflation. Most former Copperheads and Rebels, Democrats and State Righters favored repudiation, greenbackism, and inflation.

Though Lieber wrote a hundred-page manuscript on money in which he conventionally pointed out the moral and economic evils of inflation, his basic objection was that it would weaken the Federal structure. He enthusiastically commended the support Sumner and Garfield gave to the movement for specie resumption, and was quite oblivious to the manner in which it would unduly reward the wealthy and bring distress in the agrarian West. With equal fervor he fought against his rich fellow members of the New York Union League Club when they passed resolutions urging Congress not to renew the income tax. The legislators dropped the levy, and Lieber anxiously inquired of Garfield what they would substitute to help pay off the debt.[14]

The political theorist viewed the constitutional problems of the new period with similar consistency. Wherever necessary he sacrificed the precepts hallowed in the *Civil Liberty* on the altar of nationalism. When the question of reuniting the Virginias was being debated in 1866, he admitted to Sumner that Congress had acted unconstitutionally in establishing West Virginia. President Johnson, Lieber recalled, had told him that the Constitution provided for every exigency, even a rebellion. "He might as well," commented the professor scornfully, "in a conflagration, save a whole city from being devoured by fire, by the law of trespass or the police act." The war was fought to save the nation, not the fundamental law. "The Country stands high above the constitution."[15]

[14] Lieber, "What is Money?" *Haines Legal Adviser,* Chicago, February 1, 1868; Lieber to Sumner, February 2, 1868, Lieber papers; Lieber to Garfield, May 16, 1868, June 26, 1870, Garfield papers, Library of Congress; Lieber to Sumner, June 24, 1870, Sumner papers, Harvard University.
[15] Lieber to Sumner, February 7, 1866.

Constitutional aspects of reconstruction legislation consequently did not bother the ardent nationalist. As soon as the President appeared recalcitrant, Lieber solemnly pronounced Congress "the most important of all the branches of our government." When Chief Justice Chase showed himself unsympathetic toward some of the laws, he lamented, "What is to become of our 4 years struggle and final victory, if S[upreme] Court unravels our toilsome web?" He averred that he had always taught that the highest court was no fourth estate, but merely a body which incidental to deciding cases could handle questions in the realm of conflict of laws arising between acts of Congress and the Constitution.

Fearful of the manner in which the tribunal was "disintegrating and denationalizing us," he insisted it should not set itself above the President and Congress. He admitted to Sumner: "When, years ago, I warmly wrote in praise of the principle that the Supreme C[ourt] could settle . . . the doubtful constitutionality of a law, I did not contemplate a great rebellion—a territorial mutiny, lying beyond the scope of the constitution, being decided upon by written law and letter-lawyers." [16]

Subordination of constitutionalism to nationalism was by itself insufficient protection for America. Lieber saw another major threat to the integrity of the United States: dilution of American blood by too large an admixture of unassimilable peoples. That could come about in two ways: through unwise immigration regulations, or unfortunate annexations.

While the prosperous leaders of the West were still encouraging the importation of cheap coolie labor, the alarmed Lieber feared that the Pacific Coast would become "mongolified" by the prolific Chinese "who invade our country similar to the Norway rat." "Is the developed White Race to rule this earth and ultimately to spread over the globe," he queried, "or are other races partially to absorb it?" Subsequently he recommended to Secretary of State Fish the adoption of a constitutional amendment to bar entrance of all nonwhite peoples.[17]

The beneficent immigration of North European peoples, espe-

[16] [Lieber], *For Whom Will You Vote?* Lieber to Thayer, December, 1866; Lieber to Sumner, December 25, 1866, April 15, 1867.
[17] Lieber to Ruggles, November 12, 1868, Lieber papers, Library of Congress. Lieber to Fish, April 15, 1870, copy.

cially Germans, was, of course, an entirely different matter. It needed no especial encouragement since Lieber was sure it would be quite fast enough if not hindered from the other side. He wished to see careful regulation of the immigrant ships to protect the passengers from fraud and disease. At the port of debarkation, a central immigration bureau should keep a register of arrivals, bar criminals and the unfit, and "draw, with a wise finger, channels in which as by itself almost the immigration streamlets would flow to the west." [18]

Before the immigrants could become fully participating citizens they must achieve naturalization in an orderly manner. Countless thousands were swelling the vote of urban machines through fraudulent papers. These were difficult to detect, since state courts conducted much of the naturalization in a haphazard manner. Even before the election of 1868, rumors of impending frauds determined Lieber to take action. His worst expectations were more than fulfilled, and illegal voting in Philadelphia cost his friend Thayer a judgeship. Speedily he memorialized the House to pass legislation entrusting naturalization exclusively to the Federal judiciary. Congress did nothing, but Lieber, undaunted as always, renewed his efforts through the State Department.[19]

If the United States must carefully supervise the admission and naturalization of even those potentially the best citizens, it must exercise even greater caution against unwarranted territorial annexations through which it might swallow up undigestible masses. A quarter century before, the political theorist had justified conquest of the Mexican territory as a means of putting unused lands to a divinely sanctioned use. Now after the Civil War he frowned upon all aggrandizement which might add to the size but not the strength of the nation. He was no more ready to abandon expansion than to overturn the Constitution; he insisted only upon subordinating it to nationalism. He looked longingly toward the

[18] Lieber to Ruggles, February 23, 1867, Lieber papers, Library of Congress; Lieber to Thayer, September 29, 1869, Lieber papers; Lieber to Garfield, December 15, 1869, Garfield papers, Library of Congress. New York *Times,* September 29, 1869. Lieber had recommended the establishment of cholera police in a letter to Seward which the Secretary of State forwarded to Congress. Seward to Lieber, June 23, 1866.

[19] Lieber to Thayer, October 8, 1868; Thayer to Lieber, October 10, 31, 1868, Lieber papers. Lieber to Garfield, December 13, 1868, Garfield papers, Library of Congress.

northern territories inhabited by English-speaking white people who could easily become Americans: "The manly annexation of Nova Scotia, not by haggling, cheating or war, but by the manly action of the people and the equally manly yielding of the British Government, would . . . be one of the choicest acts or procedures in all history." [20]

To other expansionist clamor, Lieber turned a deaf ear. Most of the schemes seemed to him utterly fantastic. Facetiously he informed a friend he would like a mission abroad, "Say, to the Sultan to buy the Archipelago; or to Egypt, to purchase the pyramids; or to Italy to acquire Vesuvius." When General Halleck wrote that he had made a confidential report to the War Department urging the acquisition of British Columbia, the professor made no reply. "There was an emperor of Rome," he reminded Andrew Dickson White, "who wisely contracted the limits of the empire." [21]

The publicists' indignation over the purchase of Alaska, an unpopulated wasteland which surely American farmers could never settle, was both deep and voluble. Just before Sumner described the new possession in a glowing, scholarly speech, the publicist wrote him flatly that the acquisition was "utterly *inconceivable* or unintelligible." He granted that "organic expansion may strengthen," but warned the Senator that "mere extension weakens." Among friends, Lieber spouted that this "Charlotte Russe" was a senseless, low political trick which added to the United States no more than "a useless yet costly piece of map." [22]

Unhesitatingly Lieber heaped even more thorough maledictions upon schemes for Caribbean expansion. He was rather resigned to the expectation that Spain's two remaining colonies, Cuba and Puerto Rico would gravitate into the American orbit, but was ready to fight stanchly elsewhere. In 1868 his hope that the House would refuse to vote Seward funds to annex the Virgin Islands was fulfilled. Two years later he again took alarm when President Grant enthusiastically fostered a scheme for the annexation of

---

[20] Lieber to Bluntschli, October 11, 1869, copy. Cf. Lieber, *Miscellaneous Writings*, II, 412–13.

[21] Lieber to Thayer, January 22, 1868; Halleck to Lieber, January 28, 1868; Lieber to White, April 2, 1867.

[22] Lieber to Sumner, April 9, 1867; Lieber to Thayer, April 13, 1867.

Santo Domingo. He regarded it as a measure for the sole purpose of enriching a handful of speculators which would add still
more Negroes and Catholics to America's overabundance.

"Alaska was merely puerile," the publicist confided to Garfield,
"but Domingo is rascally on the part of . . . moral slovens near"
the President. Gladly he filled the Representative's request for
erudite arguments against annexation, but warned against the use
of this specific one. It might have a detrimental effect upon Grant's
forthcoming campaign for re-election, and obviously Lieber felt
even corruption in high places was secondary to the national disaster of letting the Democrats return to power.[23]

Although Sumner had favored the purchase of Alaska, he led
the Senate bloc opposed to Santo Domingo and crushed both of
Grant's attempts to push through the project. For the time being
expansionism seemed dead. When Lieber came upon a document
that seemed to indicate that in 1868 Seward had even toyed with
the idea of buying Greenland and Iceland, he regarded it as a
"grimly ludicrous" curiosity rather than a menace. He cited it to
Garfield as the most startling illustration of American greed for
land, and added, "Happily things have taken a different turn. The
Icelanders come to us and settle in Minnesota instead of Americans spending money for the icy isle." [24]

The outcome of the fight over expansion had not been so happy
for Sumner. Combined with contentions over the *Alabama* claims,
it led to an open rupture with Grant. The President, who was now
learning the tactics of political warfare, prepared a maneuver to
crush his foe. In March, 1871, the Senate dropped Sumner as
Chairman of the Committee on Foreign Relations. Lieber deplored the move as an unwise step toward a Republican debacle.[25]

Sumner's enemies asserted that the ouster served an essential

[23] Lieber to Fish, March 17, 1870, Fish papers, Library of Congress; Lieber to
Bluntschli, October 11, 1869, copy; Lieber to Thayer, January 8, 1868, December 24,
January 3, 1871, Lieber papers; Lieber to Garfield, December 24, February 2, 6, 24,
1871, Garfield papers, Library of Congress; Garfield to Lieber, February 25, 1871,
Lieber papers.

[24] Lieber to Garfield, [July 13, 1872], Garfield papers, Library of Congress; Lieber
to Fish, April 7, 1871; Fish to Lieber, April 10, 1871, Fish papers, Library of Congress; Lieber to Thayer, March 26, 1871. Brainerd Dyer, "Robert J. Walker on
Acquiring Greenland and Iceland," *Mississippi Valley Historical Review*, XXVII
(1940), 263–66.

[25] Lieber to Garfield, March 10, 1871; Garfield to Lieber, copy, March 11, 1871,
Garfield papers, Library of Congress.

purpose. They hinted that the Senator's extreme demands for damages had blocked the way to a peaceable settlement of the *Alabama* claims. These claims, which had embroiled the United States and Great Britain ever since the Civil War, grew out of the contention that the British had violated the international law of neutrality by allowing Confederate raiders to be constructed in their ports. Therefore they must reimburse the United States for the destruction of American shipping.[26]

The collection of large damages interested Lieber less than the establishment of essential principles to strengthen the law of nations. He looked to the future of the world community of nations, and here as elsewhere displayed the reverse side of the nationalist medal: constructive internationalism.

In the fall of 1865 he stated publicly his belief that the quarreling nations should seek a solution through international arbitration. Resort to war to collect damages was analogous to frightening a fly away from a costly piece of china by throwing a stone at it. Submission of the problem to arbitration by no means would indicate a relinquishment of national honor: "International arbitration, freely resorted to by powerful governments, conscious of their complete independence and self-sustaining sovereignty, is one of the foremost characteristics of advancing civilization—of the substitution of reason, fairness, and submission to justice, for defying power or revengeful irritation." [27]

Shortly after President Grant took office, Lieber gained a new and influential ear into which to pour his arbitration schemes. Suddenly his old friend Hamilton Fish became Secretary of State. Office seekers at once swamped Fish, who sighed to Lieber, "I wish my Dear Doctor, that this business of comfortably seating one hundred men at a time on five small chairs, was over." Nevertheless, he found time to consult the publicist most flatteringly on the *Alabama* negotiations.[28]

When abruptly the problem took a most alarming turn, Lieber

---

[26] For an exposition of this view and a refutation of it, see Charles Francis Adams, *Before and after the Treaty of Washington* . . . (New York, 1902) and D. H. Chamberlain, *Charles Sumner and the Treaty of Washington* (Cambridge, Mass., 1902).

[27] Lieber, "International Arbitration," New York *Times,* September 22, 1865, reprinted in Lieber, *Miscellaneous Writings,* II, 322–29.

[28] Lieber to Fish, March 12, 1869, Fish papers, Library of Congress; Fish to Lieber, March 24, 1869.

acceded wholeheartedly to Fish's moderate views. In April, 1869, the Senate rejected the unfavorable Johnson-Clarendon Convention negotiated while Seward had headed the State Department, by a smashing 54 to 1 vote. It then made public a highly sensational address in which Sumner calculated the indirect damages inflicted by the *Alabama* as being so high that by implication Great Britain could best liquidate them by ceding Canada.

Sumner received thunderous acclaim from the press and public. Gloomily Fish wrote that if the Senator's position prevailed, pacific settlement would be impossible. The professor agreed that war with Great Britain would lead only to infinite injury or even disaster. "Whether the acquisition of Canada be desirable or not," he emphasized, "it cannot be acquired by conquest; nor can, nor ought the American people ever assimilate a whole people by conquest. Nor could the acquisition of Canada by a ruinous war pay for that war." [29]

Within a few days Lieber assured Fish that few people desired war or even expected a "Sumner-sum" from England. However the Senator's speech had accentuated existing widespread ill feeling against the British. Perhaps after a period of quiet waiting, if the United States hinted to the British to send a titled commissioner, the public, "our Sovereign Master," might be placated. This in the end was to be Fish's policy. [30]

Already, Lieber had moved at Fish's suggestion to align the weight of international scholarship against Sumner. The Secretary of State had outlined his moderate position to S. B. Ruggles and sent a verbal request that Lieber employ his pen and enlist that of Professor J. K. Bluntschli of Heidelberg. With a will, the publicist prepared a communication for the *Evening Post* under his favorite nom de plume, "Americus."

Unless the *Alabama* claims were honorably settled, Americus warned, privateers could be outfitted in neutral ports to prey upon belligerent shipping. Both Englishmen and Americans should ponder well the consequences. If Great Britain became involved in a war, the United States would abandon its traditional neutral policy and breed *Alabamas* like wasps to sting British shipping.

---

[29] Fish to Lieber, June 10, 1869, Lieber papers; Lieber to Fish, June 8, 1869, Fish papers, Library of Congress.
[30] Lieber to Fish, May 31, June 20, 1869, Fish papers, Library of Congress.

Although some in the United States would favor such a personally profitable policy, the nation as a whole would suffer from this seriously retrogressive step.

The honor and financial welfare of this nation dictated a fair settlement. Would Americans care to see their coast assume the notorious character of the former Barbary states? "However rich it might make a few persons to prey on commerce," Lieber pointed out, "and there is no war, no political wrong on a large scale, no sinister tariff, which does not necessarily make a few persons rich—yet abstaining from this international iniquity, and being the carriers for two or three belligerents would infinitely more, and would justly increase our wealth." [31]

In addition to his own contribution, the publicist sent his Heidelberg correspondent a copy of Sumner's inflammatory remarks and asked for comments. Bluntschli surpassed even Lieber's expectations and drew up a strong indictment of Sumner for the *Revue de Droit International*. Fish waded with difficulty through the Teutonic abstractions but came out well pleased since the general conclusions met his views almost exactly.[32]

Through 1870, the Secretary of State continued to inform Lieber of the details of the *Alabama* negotiations. At one time he even toyed with the political theorist's "admirable" proposal to utilize a law faculty as arbiter. The London *Standard* took it seriously enough to denounce it in an editorial which a correspondent cabled to New York. The Treaty of Washington did not incorporate the innovation but did provide for an arbitral commission and strengthened the laws of neutrality. Lieber sent Fish his hearty congratulations.[33]

The aging professor's keen interest in the *Alabama* controversy

[31] [Lieber], "The Alabama or Laird Principle," New York *Evening Post,* May 29, 1869. The *Post* garbled Lieber's pseudonym into "Americanas."

[32] Lieber to Bluntschli, May 29, 1869, copy, Lieber papers; Lieber to Fish, September 15, 1870, Fish papers, Library of Congress; Fish to Lieber, September 12, October 4, 1870, Lieber papers. Allan Nevins, *Hamilton Fish* . . . (New York, 1937), 171–72. J. K. Bluntschli, "Opinione Impartiale sur la Question de l'Alabama et sur la Manière de la Résoudre," *Revue de Droit International* . . . , II (1870), 452–79. Rolin-Jaequemyns published Lieber's letter as an appendix, *ibid.*, 480–85. For Bluntschli's subsequent opinion, see "A German View of the Indirect Claims," New York *Times,* May 3, 1872.

[33] Fish to Lieber, September 12, 18, October 4, 1870, Lieber papers; Lieber to Fish, December 30, 1870, May 25, 1871, Fish papers, Library of Congress. New York *Journal of Commerce,* December 28, 1870. Nevins, *Hamilton Fish,* 155 *et passim.*

was symptomatic of his growing internationalism. Ever since he had codified the laws of war on land he had pressed a host of projects upon his influential acquaintances. He had been disappointed when he failed to persuade Secretary of the Navy Gideon Welles to authorize a code of naval warfare, and when he was unable to deliver lectures on the international law of war before the West Point cadets. However, in 1864 he hailed with enthusiasm the foundation of the International Red Cross which he considered a continuation and fortification of his instructions on care of the wounded in General Orders 100.[34]

Lieber's mind spouted forth a ceaseless and variegated deluge of international ideas. To Cyrus W. Field, who had finally succeeded in laying a successful transatlantic cable, he suggested details of international treaties to protect it; to Sumner he proposed neutralization of the projected Panama Canal; to Fish he recommended the abolition of the privilege of allowing diplomats to import goods for their own consumption duty-free. He felt that a scandal involving the American minister to Spain gave the United States a good opportunity to initiate this last practice. Again, during the Franco-Prussian War, he proposed granting freedom of the seas to explorers.[35]

When a group of authors and publishers renewed agitation for an international copyright, Lieber exhumed his arguments of many years earlier and repeated them with emphasis both in public speeches and private letters.[36]

With equal zest Lieber resumed the battle for economic internationalism. As in the past, he based his stand almost completely upon his unalterable faith in *laissez-faire* economics. He would accept only those changes which fostered efficiency without menacing the classical doctrines. Since he favored safe progress, he

[34] Lieber to Fish, May 26, 1866, copy, Lieber papers; Lieber to William Cullen Bryant, July 26, 1864, Harvard University.

[35] Lieber to Field, December 5, 1871, New York Public Library; Lieber to Fish, April 15, 1869, Fish papers, Library of Congress; Lieber to Sumner, March 16, 25, 1870, Lieber papers. Lieber, "Diplomatic Law," New York *Evening Post*, April 14, 1869; Lieber, "Freedom of the Sea for Explorers," *ibid.*, August 29, 1870.

[36] Lieber to Sumner, January, March 3, 8, 1866; March 19, 1868; Bryant to Lieber, March 13, 1868. Pierce (ed.), *Memoir and Letters of Charles Sumner*, IV, 294. *International Copyright. Meeting of Authors and Publishers, at the Rooms of the New York Historical Society, April 9, 1868, and Organization of the International Copyright Association*, 20–24.

signed a call for a "Conference on Reform in Taxation," and endorsed a proposal for international currency stabilization which would peg the relative value of the dollar, franc, and pound sterling. Yet, though even Sumner endorsed an eight-hour day for government laborers, the elderly professor sternly denounced this as a dangerous tampering with immutable natural laws.[37]

Lieber's faith in *laissez faire* together with his fervid internationalism combined to outweigh the nationalistic demand of the Republican party for higher and still higher tariff walls to protect the profits of Northern industrialists. He would go along with the Republicans in their demands for resumption of specie payment with its consequent deflation, but no further. He was an interesting anomaly, a free-trade Republican.

The free-trade heresy won quite a few converts among otherwise orthodox Republicans. Some were from the agricultural hinterland, others were merchants, importers, or manufacturers who would benefit directly from tariff reduction. Still others were scholars and economists with no axes to grind. In the late sixties, New York free-trade Republicans banded together with their nominal political foes, Democrats and radical reformers, to form the American Free Trade League. One of its principal writers was Lieber.[38]

Lieber prepared in 1869 a pamphlet entitled *Notes on the Fallacies of American Protectionists* which possessed all the flavor of his essays of three decades earlier. It was erudite, filled with striking examples, and organized in a manner little short of anarchic. Once more Lieber outlined his social theories and linked them with *laissez-faire* economic doctrine. He demonstrated nothing quite so well as the fullness and finality of the system he had developed during his long years at South Carolina College.[39]

Free-trade advocates warmly applauded Lieber's pamphlet. George William Curtis considered it "the most concise & luminous & practical of manuals," while Amasa Walker congratulated him

[37] Lieber to Sumner, September 13, 1867, May 2, 1868, Lieber papers; Lieber to Ruggles, December 2, 1869, Lieber papers, Library of Congress. Sumner, *Works*, XV, 79.

[38] Lieber, *Notes on Fallacies*. See review by Gustave Rolin-Jaequemyns, *Revue de Droit International* . . . , II (1870), 354–56.

[39] Lieber, *Notes on Fallacies*, 5th ed., reprinted in Lieber, *Miscellaneous Writings*, II, 390–459.

upon having performed "a great service to the country." The *Fallacies* went through edition after edition, and Lieber amplified its comments in public meetings and private correspondence. Secretary of State Fish attended a gathering at which the professor presided and admitted several years later that he was becoming less in favor of a protective tariff.[40]

Lieber's arguments for economic internationalism were cogent but warmed over; he made a far more significant contribution in the field of international law. In the postwar years he developed a fruitful three-way correspondence with Bluntschli at Heidelberg and Edward Laboulaye, a distinguished French authority. Soon the relationship bore fruit. To Lieber's delight, General Orders 100 inspired Bluntschli to prepare a full-length code of all phases of international law. The sections on land warfare closely followed the American code, as Bluntschli flatteringly acknowledged in his preface. In turn, Laboulaye translated Bluntschli's work into French, completing what Lieber liked to refer to as a clover leaf of international law.[41]

When a Belgian scholar and jurist, Gustave Rolin-Jaequemyns, founded the *Revue de Droit International et de legislation comparée,* he invited Lieber to become one of the American contributors. The elderly publicist responded with quantities of notes which Rolin-Jaequemyns translated or reviewed in issue after issue. Most of them were not new: his American writings on nationalism and internationalism, the diatribe on protection, a correspondence with a professor at the Imperial College in Peking, and much more of the same. But more significantly, he sent the *Revue* a letter repeating his frequent suggestion that a private congress of authorities on international law meet to draw up codes and conventions.[42]

[40] Walker to Lieber, December 5, 1869; Curtis to Lieber, August 31, 1870; Fish to Lieber, September 12, 1870.

[41] Bluntschli to Lieber, May 25, 1866; Lieber to Bluntschli, December 8, 1867, copy; Lieber to Drisler, October 22, 1869, Lieber papers; Lieber to Garfield, March 6, 1869, Garfield papers, Library of Congress. Bluntschli, *Das moderne kriegsrecht der civilisirten staaten als rechtsbuch dargestellt;* Bluntschli, *Das moderne völkerrecht der civilisirten staaten als rechtsbuch dargestellt* (Nördlingen, 1868); Bluntschli, *Le droit international codifié . . . et précédé d'une préface par Édouard Laboulaye* (Paris, 1870).

[42] Rolin-Jaequemyns to Lieber, December 22, 1868, August 26, November 30, 1869. *Revue de Droit International,* III (1871), IV (1872).

"A curious thing!" Rolin-Jaequemyns replied. "At the same time that you wrote me about an international juridical congress . . . Gustave Moynier of Geneva sent me the same idea." It now gained impetus and began to grow. So, under the aegis of Lieber and of the president of the conference which founded the International Red Cross, the first conferences on international law came into being in the 1870's. These were the direct forerunners of the Hague Conferences of 1899 and 1907. Although neither Astor nor Peabody provided funds for these gatherings, as Lieber had so long suggested, Andrew Carnegie was to donate huge endowments for the furtherance of international peace.[43]

While Lieber did not live to participate in these early forerunners of international organization, he carefully sketched their agenda and limitations. He wished them to lay down postulates in unsettled fields of international law. These should gain acceptance through the sheer authority of the distinguished jurists who drafted them. "I am unqualifiedly averse to [David Dudley] Field's idea of having a code of the Law of Nations drawn up and then try[ing] to make governments adopt it," he insisted. "The strength, authority and grandeur of the Law of Nations rests on, and consists in the very fact that Reason, Justice, Equity speak through men, 'greater than he who takes the city.' "[44]

When General Dufour asked Lieber's opinion on the proposal to establish an international court to prevent and repress infractions of the Red Cross regulations, he replied with an equally emphatic negative. Democratic nations would be at a disadvantage before the court, "for Governments more or less despotic can easier combine and plot." The United States would not consent to bind itself to such a court's decisions: "These permanent High Courts savour of Universal empire. . . . It is not puerile jealousy, but the necessity of autonomy which would prevent a free nation of any magnitude [from joining] a permanent international High Court."

Lieber foresaw difficulties in haling delinquent nations before the bar and in enforcing decisions and inquired pragmatically, "Who should be the sheriff of a High Court of Nations? And what

[43] Rolin-Jaequemyns to Lieber, October 26, 1871, July 10, 1872.
[44] Lieber to Thayer, May 7, 1869.

common court even, would have any impressive authority . . . [if] it were not known that its decrees would be carried out by public power?" [45]

After the election of Grant, Lieber had hoped to promote a conference on international law from the vantage point of a diplomatic position overseas. A month after the General took office, Ruggles presented Lieber with a petition to Grant signed by leading New York Republicans. It urged the President to reward the scholar for his conspicuous services by granting him a position "abroad in a representative capacity or *in international arbitrations.*" Lieber forwarded the letter to Senator Sumner to present to the President, not realizing that his old friend was hardly in a position to gain favors. In addition he sent a copy to Secretary of State Fish and waited hopefully for it to bear fruit. That it did, but the professor regarded the harvest wryly. Before a year had elapsed, Fish obtained for him the umpireship of the United States and Mexican Claims Commission.[46]

A treaty between Mexico and the United States in 1868 had established a commission to settle claims arising from the Mexican War. The American and Mexican commissioners had difficulty in selecting an umpire to settle the cases in dispute between them. Finally they nominated the prominent Republican editor, William Cullen Bryant, but he declined. Then Fish, who had previously urged Lieber's name, succeeded in convincing the commissioners of his suitability. Ambitious as always, Lieber disliked relinquishing his dream of retiring to Europe as a diplomat and was piqued at being offered an umpireship Bryant had already refused. At first he declined the position, then reconsidered, and after much prodding accepted.[47]

[45] Lieber to G. H. Dufour, April 10, 1872, draft. This was printed in the *Revue de Droit International,* IV (1872), 330–32.

[46] Ruggles and others to the President of the United States, April 8, 1869, copy. The signators were J. A. Roosevelt, Wm. T. Blodgett, Francis C. Barlow, George Cabot Ward, C. E. Detmold, J. S. Schultz, Joseph H. Choate, Theodore W. Dwight, Wm. C. Bryant, Henry W. Bellows, and LeGr. B. Cannon. Lieber to Thayer, February 12, 1868, May 7, 1869; Lieber to Sumner, April 16, December 11, 1869, Lieber papers; Lieber to Fish, April 23, 1869, Fish papers, Library of Congress.

[47] Lieber to Fish, February 2, 6, 1870, Fish papers, Library of Congress; Lieber to Fish, April 15, 1870, copy; Fish to Lieber, February 1, March 3, April 1, 1870; William Henry Wadsworth and Francisco Gomez del Palacio to Lieber, January 31, 1870; Wadsworth to Lieber, February 21, June 22, 1870; Ignacio Mariscal to Lieber, February 27, 1870; Wadsworth to Fish, June 20, 1870, contemporary copy; Binney to Lieber, February 4, 1870, Lieber papers. The position paid $6,000 per year.

Although Lieber had regarded the umpireship as distasteful, he made it no sinecure. When he began examining cases, he delved vigorously into the masses of documents which the commissioners sent him from Washington, examined precedents, and from them distilled profound and substantial decisions. Enormous quantities of claims for fantastically large sums came before the Commission. Altogether they represented more than five hundred million dollars. The commissioners scaled down a large amount of this sum, granted awards, and sent on to Lieber as umpire only those cases in which they could not agree. He continued the paring-down process, and, in keeping with the terms of the Claims Commission Convention of 1868, applied equity wherever he felt it would result in greater justice.[48]

The umpire tried to be wholly impartial, and refused to pay any attention to the numerous visits or letters of claimants. He reported proudly in the summer of 1872 that the Mexicans considered him "sternly just." "Yet I have wiped some millions from their lips," he pointed out. He showed the same zeal in reducing the claims of Americans, and confessed the "painful psychological itching . . . an umpire feels when he does not see a loophole through which he can escape assigning a monstrously large sum to a vile widow of a swindler who cheated every creditor of his." [49]

Applying the principles of equity Lieber limited greedy litigants to no more than their deserts. He well illustrated this in the Manasse decision. A Mexican general had promised to pay the

[48] Correspondence between Lieber and the commissioners is in the Lieber papers, Huntington Library; Lieber's draft decisions, numbering nearly forty in all, together with more perfunctory letters and numerous documents relating to the cases are in the Lieber papers, Johns Hopkins University. Both Palacio and Wadsworth were very friendly toward Lieber. Palacio and the Mexican minister, Mariscal, highly flattered him by translating and publishing some of his minor writings in Spanish.

Altogether 873 claims aggregating $470,126,613.40 and 144 not stating the amount were brought before the commission. Of these 580 were decided by the commissioners; 418 by the umpires, Lieber and his successor Sir Edward Thornton. Nineteen were either withdrawn or consolidated. The commissioners made 43 money awards; the umpires, 143, and the remaining 812 claims were dismissed. The awards totaled $4,125,622.20, or less than one per cent of the amount claimed. The three most notable cases, the Weil and La Abra Silver Mining Company claims, ultimately adjudged fraudulent, and the Pious Fund claim, came before Thornton after Lieber's death. Republic of Mexico, *Case of Mexico upon the Newly Discovered Evidence of Fraud and Perjury in the Claims of Benjamin Weil and La Abra Silver Mining Company* (Washington, 1878), iii. See also J. M. Callahan, *American Foreign Policy in Mexican Relations* (New York, 1932), 366.

[49] Lieber to Thomas C. Reynolds, June 15, 1872, Lieber papers, Library of Congress; Lieber to Thayer, September 19, 1871.

claimants the balance due on an account for military stores. Meanwhile he agreed to pay interest on the balance at the rate of 5 per cent per month, compounded every four months. When the case came before Lieber, he decided that the claim for the balance was valid and must be paid. However he scaled down the interest to 6 per cent per year and vented his wrath upon the claimants by omitting to grant them the customary allowance for costs.[50]

The *American Law Review* in an article on "Private International Courts" applauded Lieber's conduct of the case: "This decision well illustrates the operation of these private international courts. . . . Here was an eminently usurious contract; but there was a kernel of wheat in the midst of the bushel of chaff. What other court could so easily and simply administer perfect justice in such cases?"[51]

A decade later a graduate student at Johns Hopkins University, Woodrow Wilson, surveyed Lieber's decisions and analyzed them at a convocation in the scholar's memory. President Daniel Coit Gilman reported that Wilson emphasized "the contrast existing between the voluminous arguments upon the various claims and the clear, concise, and altogether admirable decisions of the umpire, who . . . went with few words direct to the core of each case, clearing the way with rapid argument and reaching his conclusions with unhesitating judgment."[52]

Some of the cases forced Lieber to explore indistinct realms of citizenship not previously charted in treatises on international law. One of his decisions set down the dictum, since followed, that a country cannot bestow citizenship upon a foreign-born alien against his will. In this he was overruled by the commissioners who had already agreed to regard such persons as citizens.[53]

These problems stimulated Lieber again to press for a clari-

---

[50] United States and Mexican Claims Commission, Case No. 432, *J. S. Manasse & Co. v. Mexico.*

[51] "Private International Courts," *American Law Review,* VI (1872), 410–11.

[52] [Daniel Coit Gilman], *Bluntschli, Lieber and Laboulaye* . . . (Baltimore, 1884), 20–21.

[53] United States and Mexican Claims Commission, Case No. 333, *Fayette Anderson et al. v. Mexico;* No. 460, *Benjamin Elliott v. Mexico;* No. 391, *Peter Jarr v. Mexico.* Palacio to Lieber, January 11, 16, 1871; Wadsworth to Lieber, February 28, 1871; Wadsworth and Palacio to Lieber, March 29, 1871, Lieber papers; Lieber to Fish, February 7, 1872, Fish papers, Library of Congress.

fication of naturalization laws. He recommended strongly to Fish that an applicant who declared on oath his intention of becoming a citizen should receive the protection of the United States except against his native land. In return he should become liable to military service. Further, so many cases arose in which the claimants had difficulty proving naturalization that he urged establishment in the State Department of a register of declarations of intention and naturalization. Secretary Fish agreed that the naturalization laws needed revision, and consulted the scholar upon proposed treaties on naturalization and emigration. Representative Garfield introduced in the House a bill providing for a register of naturalization, but it died in committee.[54]

Not all of Lieber's attitudes toward international and national issues were so scholarly and dispassionate. Toward two topics he reacted with the most effervescent emotionality: the Catholic Church and his native Germany. He spared no phase of Catholicism in his attacks, from raking up the massacre of French Huguenots through publishing a diatribe against the bull on papal infallibility.[55]

To his friends the elderly publicist wrote frenzied warnings: "The Roman Church is a transfer of the Roman Caesarism—stringent despotism—to an empire of religious name of fictitious origin. It is the worst of Absolutisms, incompatible with Liberty —an abject Monarchy, and we Americans will have our sanguinary contest for religious liberty here in our very bowels." [56]

Lieber's Republican correspondents responded sympathetically to his fulminations. Perhaps it was because the Catholic Irish were Democrats and an attack upon the Church was one more way to smear one's political enemies. The professor's reasons for anti-Catholicism were manifest: He had come to identify all that was fine and good and pure in government with the Anglo-American system, and into that system he would crowd a unified Germany.

[54] Lieber to Fish, March 2, 1871, copy; Fish to Lieber, April 1, June 22, 1871, August 7, 1872; Lieber to Thayer, March 6, 1872, Lieber papers; Lieber to Garfield, January 31, February 7, 1872, Garfield papers, Library of Congress. House Resolution 1701, reprinted in Perry (ed.), *Lieber*, 418–19.

[55] Lieber, "Infallibility," New York *Evening Post*, August 15, 1870; *The Protestant Churchman*, May 11, 1871.

[56] Lieber to Garfield, May 24, 1870. Lieber's anti-Catholic letters during this period were innumerable.

All that was bad, absolutist, and centralist was typified by Catholic France. Furthermore, Bismarck's difficulties in unifying Germany under Prussian leadership were arising from Catholic France, Catholic Austria, and the Catholic German principalities along the Rhine and in Southern Germany. Certainly Lieber's anti-Catholicism was largely an outgrowth of his ardent nationalism.[57]

Lieber watched with alarm what he considered the efforts of Napoleon III to force war upon a weaker, inferior Prussia. Through the late sixties he had observed with great interest, but slight understanding, Bismarck's skillful maneuvers which were to lead to unification. He looked with great favor upon consolidation under Prussian militaristic leadership, and claimed that as a youth he had always maintained against his republican friends that unity was the paramount necessity for Germany and could come only through a revolutionary king or emperor.[58]

Even when Prussia invaded Austria in 1866, the elderly veteran of Waterloo cynically complained that William I was no revolutionary king and that the conflict would be futile. "I donot believe," he predicted, "that Germany will go forth freed of a single one of her royal vermin." Temporarily the smashing victory over the Austrians at Sadowa raised his enthusiasm and he jubilantly reminded a friend that "Prussia fights for and conquers that for which Prussia put me in Prison 50 years ago or so." However, the ensuing annexation of Hanover and formation of a North German Confederation seemed a limited outcome. He sighed, "Alas! that Prussia and Germany are again accomplishing so little." [59]

When war with France suddenly broke out in the summer of 1870, Lieber shuddered with apprehension. The flow of blood would be "wide like a lake, and very deep." Fearing a bitter struggle on the Rhine while the French landed invasion forces at Hamburg or Bremen, he grieved, "my very soul is filled with that one word, one idea, one feeling: Germany." [60]

Instead the Prussians won victory after victory, and as their

[57] Lieber to Garfield, March 1, 6, 1869, Garfield papers, Library of Congress; Lieber, "Will There be War in Europe?" New York *Evening Post,* March 4, 1869.
[58] Lieber to Thayer, January 8, 1868.
[59] Lieber to Emory Washburn, July 21, 1866; Lieber to Drisler, August 16, 1866; Lieber to Sumner, July 22, 23, 1866; Lieber to Bluntschli, December 3, 1866; February 12, 1867.
[60] Lieber to Thayer, July 22, 1870.

arms triumphed, Lieber's spirits soared. He rejoiced at the prospect that the liberal and popular crown prince, "Unser Fritz," someday would become the German emperor. A strong, united Germany, gradually moving toward liberalism would counteract the malaise of French hegemony from which Europe had so long suffered. Consequently he hoped for the destruction once and for all of the repulsive and erroneous notion that the French were of a superior "Latin Race," and to Sumner suggested stern peace terms to prevent the resurgence of Gallic absolutism. Prussia should receive the best twenty ships in the French navy, two and a half billion francs indemnity, all of Alsace, part of Lorraine, and the right to attach Holland to the North German Confederation.[61]

The peace-minded Senator thought Lieber's position immoderate, but if anything the ardent nationalist was ready to stiffen his suggestions. Through the first phase of the war which saw the Germans sweep to the outskirts of Paris, the tide of American opinion surged behind him in his hatred of the burned-out despot, Napoleon III. So few dissented that Lieber expressed outraged surprise when one lone bookdealer refused to donate for a fair on behalf of Prussian war widows. Liberals sympathetically read Lieber's lavish praise of the manner in which William I ameliorated suffering through protecting private property, and Secretary of State Fish typically congratulated Lieber upon the victories of Prussia: "The victim of an unprovoked & unjustifiable war, she has wholly vindicated herself." [62]

When the besieging Germans arrayed themselves around the magnificent city of Paris and began to demand peace terms almost as stringent as Lieber's, the tide turned. The French established a republic, and American opinion, sympathetic toward the underdog, ran strongly against the stand of the bewildered Lieber. When Secretary Fish had expressed his pleasure over the Prus-

[61] Lieber to Bluntschli, August 4, 1870, copy; Lieber to Sumner, August 15, 1870. [Lieber], "The Latin Race," New York *Evening Post,* August 30, 1870, reprinted in Lieber, *Miscellaneous Writings,* II, 306–10, and *Revue de Droit International,* III (1871), 458–63. [Lieber], "What Peace Ought Germany to Make?" New York *Evening Post,* September 14, 1870.

[62] [Lieber], "King William's Proclamation," New York *Evening Post,* August 15, 1870; G. W. Curtis to Lieber, August 31, 1870; Fish to Lieber, September 12, 1870; Lieber to Thayer, September 17, 1870.

sian triumph, he had also voiced the widespread fear that the Germans might destroy Paris or exact unreasonable peace terms.[63]

To the public at large, the annexation of Alsace-Lorraine seemed far from fair. Lieber defended it vehemently as being comparable to the acquisition of Louisiana, justifiable on the grounds of necessity. When liberals proposed a plebiscite, he countered with the specious argument that citizens of Maryland and Virginia had not been asked if they wished to become part of the District of Columbia. Bryant published these opinions in the *Evening Post*, but tried to counter them in the editorial columns. The scholar privately admitted that necessity as a rationale for annexation was "a dangerous theory, but danger is not a test of truth." [64]

The nationalistic zeal which colored Lieber's attitude toward German unification led him in 1872 to espouse once more Grant's tawdry cause. He revived the same arguments he had used four years earlier, and abandoned his professorial dignity to flap the bloody shirt with unseemly vehemence. Many liberals could no longer support the graft-riddled Republican machine. They called a convention to meet at Cincinnati, and logically expected Lieber to join them, for he warmly advocated almost every reform for which they stood and withal was a free trader. His young disciple, Henry Demarest Lloyd, especially urged him to attend to lend support to David A. Wells and battle against the protectionist Horace Greeley.[65]

The elderly publicist firmly refused, and lamented that the convention would be "highly injurious to the Republican cause." He reported scornfully to Secretary Fish that he had received repeated invitations to go to Cincinnati, but that he was following the policy he had pursued ever since he first arrived in America of champion-

[63] Fish to Lieber, September 12, 1870; Lieber to Bluntschli, October 1, 1870, copy; Lieber to Thayer, October 18, 1870.

[64] Lieber to Thayer, October 28, November 2, 1870, January 26, 1871; Thayer to Lieber, February 2, 1871; Lieber to Bluntschli, March 24, 1872, copy, Lieber papers. Lieber to Garfield, January 30, 1871, Garfield papers, Library of Congress. [Lieber], "The Plebiscitum," New York *Evening Post*, October 19, 1870; [Lieber], "The Reasons of the Present Attachments of the Alsacians to France," New York *Tribune*, December 20, 1870; Lieber, "De la Valeur des Plebiscites dans le Droit International," *Revue de Droit International*, III (1871), 139–45.

[65] Lieber to Lloyd, April 23, 1872, Lloyd papers, Wisconsin State Historical Society.

ing "essential Liberty and National Unity" from the insidious onslaught of Gallican democracy.[66]

When Greeley received the Liberal Republican nomination, the professor exclaimed, "Long live presumptuous mediocrity and inanity fringed with petty talents!" The Democrats could do little but second the nomination, and Lieber returned to his old cry, "If Greeley is elected we shall have the rebels again to a certainty—and blood too." [67]

The Stalwart Republicans were seriously worried, and with good reason. Many of their most potent campaigners, including the orators Sumner and Schurz, backed the Greeley ticket. The worried Grant managers feared that the persuasive Schurz, who had long claimed credit for luring the German vote into the Republican camp, would lead it back out again. Consequently they seized with enthusiasm upon a private letter in which Lieber frothed and raged against Greeley:

"I have always taught it as a maxim of fundamental importance that he who has a right to vote is, in duty, bound to vote," the professor posited. "We come down then to this: We must vote, and can vote only either for General Grant or Mr. Greeley." Greeley's double nomination signified "concubinage between Republicanism and Democracy," and in effect, "Mr. Greeley and his followers surrender to the Democracy." If they won, the state-rights doctrine would triumph over nationalism and bring disloyal disorder, probably sanguinary confusion, financial ruin, the pensioning of Rebel soldiers, and perhaps even the assumption of the Rebel debt. Should Greeley be elected, an ironical situation would face Lieber's internationally famous friend, Sumner, who would have "not indeed to shake those hands which foully brought him to the verge of death, for they are bones in the grave, but to shake hands with those who warmly applauded, and doubtless still applaud, the cowardly and savage act." [68]

[66] Lieber to Fish, April 28, 1872, Fish papers, Library of Congress.
[67] Lieber to Thayer, May 17, 1872, Lieber papers; Lieber to Fish, July 17, 1872, Fish papers, Library of Congress.
[68] Washington *Daily Morning Chronicle,* August 6, 1872. For an explanation of how Lieber came to write the letter, see Lieber to Garfield, August 10, 1872, Garfield papers, Library of Congress. In a careful editorial, Bryant answered Lieber's argument that every citizen was duty-bound to vote. New York *Evening Post,* August

"I shall vote for Grant," the publicist concluded. Instantly the Washington *Chronicle*, with Lieber's permission, published the letter and editorially echoed his theme, "A sentiment of nationality is what we want to cultivate." [69]

The New York *Times* correspondent grasped the true significance of the letter as a lure for the German vote, and commented: "Dr. Lieber, being a German by birth, may well reply to another German. . . . He is Mr. Schurz's inferior in nothing unless the power of elocution. In learning and ability he is Schurz's equal; in character he is as stable and unswerving as Schurz is fickle and treacherous." [70]

Throughout the German-speaking areas of America, the Grant press prominently published Lieber's arguments and the *Times* commentary. Thomas C. Reynolds, a former lieutenant governor of Missouri, reported that Joseph Pulitzer, the strongest of Schurz's St. Louis supporters, "pronounced it the ablest and most 'dangerous' letter which had yet appeared for Grant." [71]

The letter so upset the New York *World* that it poured out two columns of editorial billingsgate against the author, whom it termed "a Philosopher, Blatant and Rampant." The *World* compared his attack upon Greeley with Swinburne's upon Harriet Beecher Stowe and urged the Columbia trustees to protect their students from "the weak and washy flood of such a political vituperator, the tempests of whose teapot imitate the vivacity of a small mud volcano." Terming Lieber's statement "the very *sauerkraut* of political composition," the Democratic paper asserted, "It is difficult to account for such a violent eructation of political flatulence from the mouth of a 'professor . . .' except on the suspicion that he has swallowed the wind-bags of Aeolus along with a whole cyclopaedia of political jargon." [72]

10, 1872. Lieber in his private correspondence deplored Sumner's political apostasy: "He stands on a bridge and has set fire to both ends. Even for his own sake I hope Greeley will not be elected, for Sumner would be trampled upon by the democrats like a beetle. I am grieved." Lieber to Longfellow, September 5, 1872, Longfellow House. See also Lieber to Fish, August 16, 1872, Fish papers, Library of Congress.

[69] Washington *Daily Morning Chronicle*, August 6, 1872.

[70] New York *Times*, August 6, 1872.

[71] See, for example, the Waupun (Wis.) *Leader*, August 23, 1872. Reynolds to Lieber, August 12, 1872.

[72] New York *World*, August 9, 1872. Lieber would not read the editorial. Lieber to Garfield, August 10, 1872, Garfield papers, Library of Congress. Nevertheless an

The *World*'s angry retort had one significance. It went far toward proving the assertion of the New York *Evening Post* two months later that Lieber "as a publicist was of more authority than any other man in this country." [73]

During these years Lieber indeed delighted in his recognized position as a publicist. He still sat in his multivolumed library, surrounded by busts, mottoes, and mementos, writing letters, memorials, and articles to launch as many schemes as fifty years before. He urged General Halleck to build a great public library in California, little guessing that his own books would soon go to the University of California. When he heard of a new Wisconsin library law, he sent a lengthy discussion of library systems to Lyman Cope Draper, head of the State Historical Society.[74]

Academic matters interested him as much as ever. He pressed suggestions upon his friend Andrew Dickson White, the new president of Cornell University, and urged Benson Lossing to persuade the Vassar College trustees to establish social-science courses. To Daniel Coit Gilman, geographer and librarian of the Sheffield Scientific School at Yale, he expounded his theories on geography. He urged Sumner to obtain an appropriation for a polar expedition.[75]

Lieber diligently continued his own researches. While he delved into the background of the seal of the United States Treasury, he obtained from Governor Rutherford B. Hayes of Ohio information on the origin of the name "copperhead," and from James Parton, the biographer, conjectures as to the beginnings of the phrase "pilgrim father." He himself wrote an article for the *American Historical Record* on the background of the name "America," and complied willingly when Sumner asked for material for a lecture on caste. "You are always full," the Senator flatteringly remarked. "I bring my pitcher to you." [76]

---

answer, "Politics and Palates," which sounded as though inspired if not written by Lieber, appeared in the New York *Times*. Clipping in Lieber papers.

[73] New York *Evening Post*, October 3, 1872.

[74] Lieber to Halleck, November 16, 1865, Lieber papers; Lieber to Draper, April 6, 8, 1872, Wisconsin State Historical Society.

[75] Lieber to White, November 28, 1866; April 8, 14, 1867; Lossing to Lieber, August 28, 1869; Lieber to Gilman, August 28, 1863, Lieber papers.

[76] Lieber to Chase, October 6, 1866, Chase papers, Library of Congress; Hayes to Lieber, May 1, 1867; Parton to Lieber, June, 1871; Sumner to Lieber, September

Through Representative Garfield the professor consummated one of his old ambitions and took a hand in planning the census of 1870. With less success he tried to modify the coinage legislation. He argued against the new small copper cent with its portrait of an Indian. The continent was becoming dis-Indianized, he pointed out, and anyway the coins should be large enough and have a big enough numeral to be distinguishable by gentlemen past fifty on omnibuses at night. He also proposed to Garfield that the post office print correspondence cards, and sent a sample of a type he thought would be of "infinite use." The legislator was "greatly interested," and shortly the post office began printing postal cards.[77]

Lieber encouraged Garfield to fight for civil service reform and sent the Representative a copy of his article of thirty years before demanding that the post office be taken out of politics. Garfield replied that it would "be a good thing to quote as showing how early your mind was turned to this subject." Fear of corruption led Lieber to oppose proposals for a national university in Washington. "The large appropriation it will have, if it is to exist at all," he sadly pointed out, "will make it soon, as things go now, more like a stilton cheese alive with rottenness."[78]

In New York City Lieber fostered one successful movement. He headed a committee of the Union League which lobbied in the state legislature to block the granting of large city funds to parochial schools.[79]

Even in the literary field Lieber remained active. An old acquaintance, Reynolds, asked permission to publish some of his German poems, and the elderly scholar was delighted to grant it. He headed the collection with a tribute to Washington's everyday sword. When he sent a copy of the pamphlet to Longfellow, his kindly old friend replied, "Held aloft by the right hand of Gov-

27, 1869; Lieber to Sumner, December 11, 1869. Lieber, "America—Origin of This Name," *American Historical Record,* I (1872), 253.

[77] Lieber to Garfield, December 15, 1868, January 2, February 26, March 13, 1869; March 15, and undated, 1872; Garfield to Lieber, January 23, February 25, 27, November 24, 1869; March 16, 1872, copies, Garfield papers, Library of Congress.

[78] Garfield to Lieber, May 27, 1872, copy; Lieber to Garfield, April 9, 1872, Garfield papers, Library of Congress.

[79] Lieber to Sumner, May 1, 1870. Lieber, *Abstraction of Moneys from the Public Treasury for Sectarian Uses. Over $500,000 from the City of New York alone, in 1869!* (New York, 1870).

ernor Reynolds 'Excalibur' flashes again above the waters, and I rejoice greatly." Lieber beamed, exhumed his lengthy ode on the ship canal, revised it somewhat, and sent it off for the patient Longfellow to try to insert in the *Atlantic Monthly.*[80]

Around New York the old professor was a familiar sight. Now since the Franco-Prussian War, he was especially proud of his origin, and he assumed more and more the role of an elderly German. In 1869, for the first time in years, he delivered a speech in his native tongue at the dedication of a Humboldt monument in Central Park. He spent more time associating with prominent Germans—though he still did not feel any too friendly toward the Liberal Republican Schurz—and almost daily stopped by Westermann's Bookstore and various little German shops. There as elsewhere he would hold forth to his acquaintances on his rebellious youth and his experiences at Waterloo. His audiences regarded him with great respect, but sometimes smiled a bit at his extreme self-assurance.

"I remember his coming into the office one morning with a question on his lips," George Haven Putnam, the publisher, reminisced many years later. " 'Now, friend Putnam, and you Putnam, Jr., who in your opinion is the most conceited man at this time in our country?' I saw by the expression of my father's face that the impression in his mind was the same as that in mine, but, under the circumstances, we could hardly speak out our thoughts." [81]

Lieber had lost none of his prejudices and launched as venomous attacks as ever against Jeffersonianism, Darwinism, Gallicism, and feminism. "Jefferson, the founder of the Union!" he exclaimed to Garfield. "He was the very underminer of the Union—a most mischievous ferret." As for Darwin and his cohorts, he informed another correspondent they "not only prove to you that your grand-mother was a hideous gorilla, but they do it with enthusiasm and treat you almost like a heretic if you will not agree." Lieber

[80] Lieber to Reynolds, September 7, 1871, July 21, 1872, Lieber papers, Library of Congress; Reynolds to Lieber, August 3, 1872; Longfellow to Lieber, May 30, September 9, 1872, Lieber papers; Lieber to Garfield, August 10, 1872, Garfield papers, Library of Congress. Lieber, *Ein Erguss* (St. Louis, 1872), 3 pp. Cf. Lieber, "Washington's Arbeitschwert," St. Louis *Mississippi Blatter,* October 1, 1871.

[81] G. H. Putnam, *Memories of a Publisher, 1865–1915* (New York, 1915), 9.

wondered from what animal Darwin derived the French: "Perhaps from an ancient self-cohabiting peacock." Feminists were no better. When the flamboyant Victoria Woodhull announced her candidacy for President in 1872 Lieber immediately thought the worst. A "manifest vein of lechery in the advanced women's rights women," he confided to a friend, would lead inevitably to "promiscuous intercourse of the sexes" and communism of goods.[82]

The hale old man also retained his pungent and earthy sense of humor. He refused to translate Bluntschli's code of international law into English with the remark that such a profound volume would not sell unless profusely illustrated with female nudes. Again he recounted: "I walked yesterday with a friend who said: To judge by the immense arrangements behind, of that lady before us, she cannot be above a certain low standard of virtue. I said, that would be an *argumentation a posteriori* and wrong." [83]

The fall of 1872 was the autumn of the old professor's life too. He was trying to wind up his work as umpire on the Mexican Claims Commission so that he could retire from the Columbia Law School and go to Europe. There he would attend the Brussels conference of experts on international law and would see for himself the new united Germany. He had already come to realize that he was of a passing era and confessed to Thayer, "Your letters begin to read to me, as the opinion of the next generation would sound to me could I hear it. Long forgotten things my dear friend are spoken of by you, and with freshness and kindness too." [84]

This should have been a pleasant, mellow harvest time for Lieber. He was firmly established as an elder scholar and could see aggressive younger men carrying into execution the nationalism which he had preached so long. Across the seas, the Germany for which he had shed blood as a youth had at last achieved unity. The ideas he had redundantly promoted were at last triumphant. But bleak winds of discontent still swept through the ambitious scholar's soul. Even in these days of triumph he could sense the sordid mediocrity marring the political party to which he belonged.

[82] Lieber to Garfield, July 4, 1870, Garfield papers, Library of Congress; Lieber to Thayer, March, 1871; undated, 1872.

[83] Lieber to Thayer, February 5, 1868, January 17, 1871.

[84] Lieber to Ruggles, October 6, 8, December 3, 1871, Lieber papers, Library of Congress. Lieber to Thayer, January 31, 1871.

Behind the united, powerful Germany of his dreams was the mailed fist of Prussian militarism. These were sad, drab, dull, uninspired days, the aged publicist repeatedly wrote his younger admirers. Triumph had come, but triumph mixed with the ashes of dead hopes.

Restless, querulous, Professor Lieber entered the autumn months of 1872. He hoped for the election of Grant, and penned a sturdy defense of Bismarck's anti-Catholic measures. Time had slowed him down, and he was unwell through September. One October day, as he sat listening to Matilda read, his heart suddenly failed. Ruggles was so upset that he stayed home from the opera, and a few weeks later suffered a stroke which his son-in-law ascribed in part to "intense excitement" over Lieber's death. Shocked, Longfellow wrote the sad news to Sumner in Paris. The Senator, himself ailing, was to survive Lieber for only two years.[85]

Francis Lieber died firmly convinced of his own greatness. He had indeed achieved the prominence of an eminent public figure; an Episcopal bishop delivered his funeral sermon; Columbia University years later created a Lieber professorship. For a time in the classrooms of Theodore Dwight Woolsey, John Burgess, and the new nationalist political philosophers, *Political Ethics* and *Civil Liberty and Self-Government* enjoyed a renaissance.

By the turn of the century these redundant tomes, which their author had placed in merit beside Grotius, Montesquieu, and Tocqueville, gave way to newer and more scientific texts. But the theories Lieber introduced, the words and technical terms with which he had enriched the language, remained part of the warp and woof of American culture. Though he was not, as he had supposed, a great and original thinker, Lieber had transported to the new world a rich cargo of alien concepts. Strange and difficult at first, these ideas lost their exotic flavor and became by the time of his death an integral part of the American tradition. More significant than Lieber himself, these concepts remained common coin while their innovator's name disappeared. As a conveyer and synthesizer, if not as an originator, Lieber was indeed great.

[85] Longfellow to Sumner, October 4, 1872, Sumner papers, Harvard University. Lieber, "Religion and the Law," New York *Evening Post*, September 24, 1872; New York *Evening Post*, October 3, 7, 1872. Thompson, *Ruggles of New York*, 166, 189–91.

Bibliographical Note

The standard biography of Lieber is Thomas Sergeant Perry (ed.), *The Life and Letters of Francis Lieber* (Boston, 1882), which is a compilation of excerpts from Lieber's letters and journals, prepared under the close scrutiny of his widow. Perry, later to become a distinguished Boston man of letters, was at the time young and inexperienced. He hastily cut Matilda Lieber's compilation from two volumes to one, and in so doing excluded all mention of some phases of Lieber's career and rendered others unintelligible. Perry made use of only a small part of the letters written by Lieber, and printed only six of those received by him. In the approved fashion of the time, Perry polished his subject's Germanisms, telescoped and garbled materials, linked together letters of several dates to form new ones, and failed to supply adequate or accurate editorial explanations. Nevertheless, the biography contains a few letters not elsewhere available, and a number of unique excerpts from Lieber's journals.

Some years later, Lewis R. Harley made use of Perry's compilation and the limited materials at Columbia University to prepare *Francis Lieber: His Life and Political Philosophy* (New York, 1899), a smoother, but quite thin account of Lieber's life and influence. Chester Squire Phinney, *Francis Lieber's Influence on American Thought and Some of His Unpublished Letters* (Philadelphia, 1918), is a dilution of Harley's account to which Phinney added some letters from the Library of Congress.

Early phases of Lieber's career received new and perceptive interpretation in Ernest Bruncken, "Francis Lieber, a Study of a Man and an Ideal," *Deutsch-Amerikanische Geschichtsblätter Jahrbuch der Deutsch-Amerikanischen Historischen Gesellschaft von Illinois* (Chicago, 1915), XV, 26, 35–37. The most significant study of Lieber is Joseph Dorfman and Rexford Guy Tugwell, "Francis Lieber: German Scholar in America," *Columbia University Quarterly*, XXX (1938), 159–90, 267–93. This is a brilliant, highly critical interpretation, which is of greatest value for its discussion of Lieber's relationship with Columbia University and his economic ideas. Various other publications, both in Eng-

418

lish and German, discuss Lieber. A number of important scholarly articles have been evaluated in the footnotes.

The most important single body of Lieber manuscripts is at the Henry E. Huntington Library, which obtained them from the Lieber family. The collection contains tens of thousands of items: letters from almost all of Lieber's many correspondents, and letters to some of Lieber's closest associates—Sumner, Halleck, Hillard, Allibone, Thayer, and others. Those to Sumner alone number nearly 750. In addition to letters, the collection contains vast quantities of notes, lectures, memoranda, manuscript articles and drafts, poetry, clippings, scrapbooks, annotated pamphlets and articles, and interleaved annotated copies of some of Lieber's own works. The collection contains the greater part of his personal papers, excepting his journals. Several of the period before Lieber came to America are included; at the Columbia University library are the diaries of the Waterloo campaign and the Greek interlude; the remainder were destroyed by the Lieber family. For a detailed evaluation of the Huntington Library collection, see Charles B. Robson, "Papers of Francis Lieber," *Huntington Library Bulletin,* February, 1933, No. 3, pp. 135–55.

A second indispensable Lieber collection is at the Johns Hopkins University. It includes interleaved copies of most of his important books and papers. These contain significant notations and in some instances letters of comment from important personages. In addition there are drafts of Lieber's decisions as umpire of the Mexican Claims Commission, and letters and documents from Joseph Bonaparte to Lieber.

Official records relating to Lieber's professional career, together with a few letters and some mementos, are at the University of South Carolina. Some of the faculty minute books are in his hand. Corresponding materials are in the Columbiana Room, Columbia University. The latter collection includes Lieber-Fish correspondence concerning university affairs. Lieber's correspondence as chief of the Archives Office of the War Department is in a letter book in the War Archives section of the National Archives.

The Lieber collection in the Library of Congress contains scattered correspondence and a notable group of letters to S. B. Ruggles. Many of these have been published in entirety or part in Phinney's biography and in L. M. Sears, "The Human Side of Francis Lieber," *South Atlantic Quarterly,* XXVII (1928), 42–61. Quantities of Lieber letters are in the Garfield, Fish, and Schoolcraft papers, and there is a scattering through many other collections, including the Lincoln papers opened in July, 1947.

Numerous letters between the Lieber and Longfellow families are at the Longfellow House, Cambridge, Massachusetts. The Harvard College Library possesses 175 Sumner to Lieber letters, and Lieber's letters to Sparks and Dorothea Dix.

Other notable groups of letters are in various collections at the Hayes Memorial, the Historical Society of Pennsylvania, Massachusetts Historical Society, New York Historical Society, New York Public Library, Public Library of the City of Boston, State Historical Society of Wisconsin, and State of Alabama Department of Archives and History.

Collections in the following libraries contain at least one Lieber letter: Bard College, Brown University, Duke University, Boston Athenaeum, Louisiana State University, New York State Library, University of California, University of North Carolina, University of Wisconsin, William L. Clements Library, and Yale University.

A manuscript ascribed to Lieber which is of considerable interest is an essay on "The metaphysical religion of Hegel," with an accompanying letter from Lieber to Hiram Crafts, which is now in the possession of the Reverend Walter M. Haushalter. It forms the basis for Haushalter's book, *Mrs. Eddy Purloins from Hegel: Newly Discovered Source Reveals Amazing Plagiarisms in Science and Health* (Boston, 1936), in which the author seeks to prove that Mrs. Eddy utilized Lieber's manuscript as the basis for significant passages in *Science and Health*.

The present writer has examined photostats of the manuscript at Johns Hopkins University. In many essential ways the handwriting seems to differ from that of Lieber. The hand of the manuscript, and of the alleged endorsement by Mary Baker Eddy, bear a marked resemblance. Among the many thousands of Lieber letters examined by the present writer, not one was to or from, or mentioned, Hiram Crafts. The phrasing and concepts of the letter and essay are not characteristic of Lieber. Further, at the time Lieber supposedly wrote the letter and copied the accompanying essay he was, the letter states, aboard a boat. Letters in other collections written to friends at this time are dated from New York, and make no mention of a journey by boat. Consequently, the authenticity of the document seems open to serious doubt, and it has not been used in this account of Lieber.

Shortly after Lieber's death, the University of California acquired the bulk of his library, which contained about three thousand books and pamphlets. It included a few scrapbooks, some books with annotations, and several with letters pasted in. Lieber's books are scattered through the university's libraries, but can be located through use of a manuscript catalogue which accompanied them.

BIBLIOGRAPHICAL NOTE

Much relevant material on Lieber exists in contemporary books, magazines, and newspapers, and in secondary works. Reference to these, and bibliographical information on his principal publications, has been included in the footnotes.

Index

INDEX

Bancroft, George, 50, 56, 64, 346; visits Columbia, S.C., 283

Bank of the United States, 177

Banks, Nathaniel P., Lieber visits, 308

Barnard, F. A. P., Lieber's dislike for, 364-65; tries to oust Lieber from Columbia College, 364-66

Barnwell, Robert W., 198, 285

Bastiat, Frédéric, *Sophisms of the Protective Policy,* Lieber writes introduction to, 225-26

Bates, Edward, 317, 318, 320, 369; Lieber advises on constitutional problems, 309-14

Beaumont, Gustave de, 97-103; Lieber meets, 89; Lieber visits in Paris, 215

Beauregard, P. G. T., 358, 371

Beccaria, Cesare, 102

Beck, Charles, 50, 56

Beck, T. Romeyn, writes for *Americana,* 78

Becker, Major, teacher of Lieber's, 29

Beecher, Henry Ward, 342, 358; Lieber dislikes oratorical technique, 297

Belgium, Lieber asks to be appointed minister to, 92

Bemis, George, 388

Bennett, James Gordon, 319

Bentham, Jeremy, 49, 105, 144; *see also,* Utilitarianism

Bentinck, Lord William, 176

Bentley, Richard, 111-12, 124

Benton, Thomas Hart, 237, 251

Berlichingen, Götz von, 243

Berlin, University of, 7, 26, 108

Bernard, Montague, 333 n.

Bernstorff, Christian G., Count von, 45

Betsy, Lieber slave, 236

Biddle, Nicholas, 105-106, 111, 112, 118

Binney, Horace, 345, 388; on suspension of habeas corpus, 311-12

Bismarck, Prince Otto von, 390, 408-409

Black codes, Lieber's dislike of, 376

Blackstone, Sir William, 145, 158, 315

Blair, Montgomery, 352

Blas, Gil, 243

Blockade, 314

Blücher, Prince Gebhard von, 12, 14, 15, 114, 216

Bluntschli, Johann K., 161, 162 n., 333 n., 340; Lieber persuades to write on *Alabama* claims, 398-99; writes a code of international law, 402

Boccacio, Giovanni, 43

Bolles, John A., 374

Bonaparte, Joseph, Lieber meets, 65; entertains Lieber, 72; and Napoleonic legend in *Americana,* 78

Bonaparte, Louis Napoleon, 257, 268, 277, 408-409; Lieber claims election statistics are false, 263-64; as an absolutist, 263-64

Bonaparte, Napoleon, 1, 4-5, 10, 11, 65, 231, 302, 322; Lieber's early hatred of, 3, 9; Napoleonic legend in *Americana,* 78

Bond, George, agent of Boston gymnasium, 50-51

Bonn, University of, 41, 42

Booth, John Wilkes, 376

Bopp, F. B., 178

Boston, Lieber arrives in, 53; described, 53-55

Boston gymnasium, 69; hires Lieber, 51; Lieber operates, 57-59; obtains leave of absence from, 64; Lieber continues as director of while editing *Americana,* 69; *see also,* Physical education

Boston *Post,* 304; lauds Lieber's poem on Panama Canal, 229

Boston Prison Discipline Society, 97, 186-87; Howe tries to get Lieber secretaryship, 208-10

Boston Quarterly Review, attacks *Political Ethics,* 166

Boston Society of Useful Knowledge, Lieber lectures before, 84

Boston swimming school, 20, 51, 60 n., 69; Lieber operates, 57-58

Bowen, Francis, 149 n.; attacks *Political Ethics,* 166

Bradford, Alexander W., *American Antiquities,* Lieber lauds, 182

Bradford, Thomas Gamaliel, assists Lieber, 72

Breckenridge, John C., 358

Bridgman, Laura, 182, 183, 207, 221

Bright, John, 315

Brisbane, Albert, 191

Brockhaus, Frederick A. B., publishes *Tagebuch,* 38; *Conversations-Lexikon,* 63-64

Brook Farm, 191

Brooks, Fanny, 202-203, 205

Brooks, Lee M., on relationship between W. G. Sumner and Lieber, 169

Brooks, Preston, attacks Sumner, 289

Brougham, Henry, 48, 106; acts strangely toward Lieber, 214

Brown, John, Lieber lauds, 298

INDEX

INDEX

426

INDEX

INDEX

Halsey, John J., studies *Americana*, 80

Hamarchy, 161-62

Hamilton, Alexander, 232, 268, 392

Hamilton, James, 120, 131; supports Lieber for South Carolina College chair, 121

Hammond, James H., 132; keeps pistol in Senate desk, 299

Hampden, John, 367

Hampton family, 129, 132

Hampton, Wade, 136 n., 306

Handel and Haydn Society of Boston, 54

Harlez, Herr, 17

Harper and Brothers, take over *Great Events*, 185; Lieber criticizes protectionism of, 191; publish *Property and Labour*, 191, 196

Harper's monthly, 229, 275 n.

Harper's Weekly, 388

Harrison, William Henry, 205

Hartsuff, George L., 332 n.

Harvard University, 113, 296; Lieber aspires to history professorship at, 110; Lieber seeks law professorship at, 209, 212

Hayes, Dr., Lieber promotes arctic expedition of, 297

Hayes, Rutherford B., 413; Lieber corresponds with, 373

Hayne, Robert Y., 130, 131, 132; shows Lieber the South Carolina arsenal, 120

Heckscher, Johann G. W. M., 247

Hedrick, B. S., 286

Heffter, August W., 333 n.

Hegel, George W. F., 154-55 n.; Lieber's essay on, in *Americana*, 79; does damage to science, 112

Heidelberg, University of, 27

Heinzen, Karl, dislikes Lieber's views, 233 n.

Henry, Joseph, 174

Hermeneutics, see *Legal and Political Hermeneutics*

Herodotus, 137

Herz, Henrietta, 44, 47 n., 56, 155 n.; Lieber attends salon of, 41

Hildreth, Richard, denounced, 272

Hill, Rowland, 175

Hillard, George Stillman, 166, 200, 215, 219, 221, 234, 238, 243, 249, 265, 275, 276, 286, 288, 305, 317; corresponds with Lieber, 141-42; edits *Political Ethics*, 164, 165 n.; uses *Hermeneutics*, 178; on *Dictionary of Latin Syno-*

nymes, 181; differs with Lieber over slavery, 290

History, 86, 294, 388; Niebuhr's studies, 37-38; Lieber considers study of, 88; seeks Harvard professorship in, 110; elected to chair of, at South Carolina College, 122; interpretation in inaugural, 130-31; Lieber's teaching of, 137-39; Sparks on need for texts in, 183-84; *Great Events*, 184-85; institutional energy and, 278; Columbia inaugural address on, 295-96; Lieber's Columbia courses in, 295 n.; role of war in, 305; Barnard opposes teaching to undergraduates, 364, 365; Lieber wishes Confederate records arranged for historians, 370; Lieber arranges Confederate records, 371-72; Lieber on origin of name "America," 413

History and Political Science Necessary Studies in Free Countries, 294-96

Hitchcock, Ethan Allen, and General Orders 100, 332-34

Hitzig, Julius Eduard, 41, 44, 246

Hobbes, Thomas, 165

Hoffmann, E. T. A., 41

Holcombe, Professor, uses *Civil Liberty*, 279

Holcombe, W. H., 363

Holley, Horace, 113

Holmes, Oliver Wendell, 346

Holt, Joseph, 352

Homer, 137

Hone, Philip, 209

Hooper, William, 386

Hopkins, Edward A., imports *Civil Liberty* and *Political Ethics* into Argentina, 267 n.

Howard, Jacob, 355, 356

Howard, John, 97

Howe, Julia Ward, 211; Lieber on, 203-204

Howe, Samuel Gridley, 30, 211, 219, 238, 260, 265; on *Political Ethics*, 167-68; teaches Laura Bridgman, 182; tries to obtain position for Lieber, 207-10; reports Story's death, 220; chides Lieber for abuse of Sumner, 221

Howe, Timothy O., criticizes Lieber on retaliation, 356 n.

Hubbard, Elbert, 196

Humboldt, Alexander von, 5, 7, 41, 43, 56, 246, 415; Lieber meets, 39; suggests that Lieber write on penology,

430

INDEX

Lieber, Francis (*Continued*)

why South Carolina is apathetic toward reform, 259-60; report on South Carolina prison system, 260; aids Dorothea Dix, 260-61; proposes pardoning reform, 261; begins to oppose most reforms, 261-62; attacks Massachusetts prohibition, 262; castigates Mormons and Oneidans, 262; proves falsity of French election statistics, 263-64; contrasts Anglican and Gallican liberty, 263-64; writes *Civil Liberty*, 264-66; cuts off relations with Sumner, 265-66; *Civil Liberty*, 266-79; personal appearance in 1850's, 280; considers retiring to North, 280; begins one-volume encyclopedia, 280-81; proposes schemes to aid Southern economy, 281; aspires to presidency of South Carolina College, 281-85; opposed by Thornwell, 284-85; defeated in election, 285; resigns from South Carolina College, 286; seeks Northern position, 286-87; reluctant to leave South, 287; flattered by Frémont, 289; prefers disunion to slave extension, 290-91; moves to New York, 292; advises on reorganization of Columbia College, 292-93; elected to chair at Columbia College, 293; purchases home, 293; has title changed to "Professor of History and Political Science," 293-94; relations with Columbia, 294; inaugural address, 294-96; lecture courses, 296-97; shifts to Republican viewpoint, 298; satirizes Dred Scott decision, 298-99; thinks war might bring national regeneration, 299; helps Republicans get German vote, 299-300; censured by South Carolina College, 300; explains sectional cleavage to son, 301; expounds nationalism during secession crisis, 301-304; organic theories lauded, 304-305; long opposition to pacifism, 305; sons join armies, 305-306; anguish over Oscar's adherence to Confederacy, 306; reconciliation with Sumner, 306-307; confers Columbia honorary degree upon Lincoln, 307; on Lincoln's War Message, 308; meets war leaders, 308-309; on suspension of habeas corpus, 309-13; advises Bates, 309-14; advocates slavery suppression, 314; proposes arbitration of *Trent* affair,

314-15; wants congress on international law, 315, 402-403; hopes Civil War will end state rights and slavery, 317-18; in right wing of Radical Republicans, 318-19; wishes vigorous prosecution of war, 319-20; writes on international law of war, 320-41; on guerilla warfare, 328-30; writes General Orders 100, 331-41; opposes Republican factionalism, 342; participates in public demonstrations, 343; fears New England's tariff will alienate West, 344; work in Loyal Publication Society, 344-53; writes *No Party Now*, 346-47; outlines war program, 347; anti-British tirade, 347; advocates soldier vote, 347-48; favors employment of prisoners of war, 349; feels Radicals must back Lincoln, 349-50; elected head of Loyal Publication Society, 350; attends Radical conference on Lincoln, 351; against inhumane retaliation, 353-57; fears Sherman will be wantonly destructive in South, 357; proposes peace terms, 357; recommends trial or banishment of Confederate leaders, 358; Civil War contributions, 358-59; on Lincoln's assassination, 359-61; recommends reconstruction program to Johnson, 361; declares paroled prisoners answerable for war crimes, 362-63; Southern protest against, 363; movement to oust from Columbia College, 364-66; transferred to School of Law, 366; visits government officials, 369; Stanton appoints archivist of Confederate records, 370; seeks evidence for trial of Davis, 370-73; thinks Davis will not be convicted, 374; on Raphael Semmes, 374-75; upset over sordidness of postwar period, 375-76; favors Military Reconstruction, 376; takes moderate view of Negro voting, 377-78; proposes amendments to Constitution, 378, 382; effect on Fourteenth Amendment, 378; wishes to break up plantation system, 379; begins to object to Radical program, 379-80; advocates election of Grant in 1868, 380, 390; suggests changes in New York constitution, 382; advocates pardon board, 382-84; against unanimity of juries, 383; attacks misrule of New York City, 384-85; outlines conserva-

INDEX

INDEX

INDEX